Beyond Bylines

Film and Media Studies Series

Film studies is the critical exploration of cinematic texts as art and entertainment, as well as the industries that produce them and the audiences that consume them. Although a medium barely one hundred years old, film is already transformed through the emergence of new media forms. Media studies is an interdisciplinary field that considers the nature and effects of mass media upon individuals and society and analyzes media content and representations. Despite changing modes of consumption—especially the proliferation of individuated viewing technologies—film has retained its cultural dominance into the 21st century, and it is this transformative moment that the WLU Press Film and Media Studies series addresses.

Our Film and Media Studies series includes topics such as identity, gender, sexuality, class, race, visuality, space, music, new media, aesthetics, genre, youth culture, popular culture, consumer culture, regional/national cinemas, film policy, film theory, and film history.

Wilfrid Laurier University Press invites submissions. For further information, please contact the Series editors, all of whom are in the Department of English and Film Studies at Wilfrid Laurier University:

Dr. Philippa Gates, Email: pgates@wlu.ca
Dr. Russell Kilbourn, Email: rkilbourn@wlu.ca
Dr. Ute Lischke, Email: ulischke@wlu.ca

75 University Avenue West
Waterloo, ON N2L 3C5
Canada
Phone: 519-884-0710
Fax: 519-884-8307

Beyond Bylines

Media Workers and Women's
Rights in Canada

BARBARA M. FREEMAN

WILFRID LAURIER UNIVERSITY PRESS

This book has been published with the help of a grant from the Canadian Federation for the Humanities and Social Sciences, through the Aid to Scholarly Publications Programme, using funds provided by the Social Sciences and Humanities Research Council of Canada. We acknowledge the financial support of the Government of Canada through the Canada Book Fund for our publishing activities.

Library and Archives Canada Cataloguing in Publication

Freeman, Barbara M., 1947–
  Beyond bylines : media workers and women's rights in Canada / Barbara M. Freeman.

(Film and media studies series)
Includes bibliographical references and index.
Issued also in electronic format.
ISBN 978-1-55458-269-3

  . 1. Women in the mass media industry—Canada—History. 2. Feminism and mass media—Canada—History. 3. Women journalists—Canada—History—19th century. 4. Women journalists—Canada—History—20th century. 5. Women's rights—Canada— History—19th century. 6. Women's rights—Canada—History—20th century. I. Title. II. Series: Film and media studies series

P94.5.W652C32 2011   302.23082'0971   C2011-902747-X

Electronic monograph.
Issued also in print format.
ISBN 978-1-55458-313-3

  1. Women in the mass media industry—Canada—History. 2. Feminism and mass media—Canada—History. 3. Women journalists—Canada—History—19th century. 4. Women journalists—Canada—History—20th century. 5. Women's rights—Canada— History—19th century. 6. Women's rights—Canada—History—20th century. I. Title. II. Series: Film and media studies series (Online)

P94.5.W652C32 2011a   302.23082'0971   2011-902748-8

Cover design by Sandra Friesen. Cover photo shows Margaret Colpitts as "Joan Marshall" of CBC Halifax, on the air with announcer Carl McCaull and technician Ross McNaughton. Photographer unknown. Library and Archives Canada 1996–200, CBC Fonds, item #14343. Published with the permission of the Canadian Broadcasting Corporation. Text design by Catharine Bonas-Taylor.

© 2011 Wilfrid Laurier University Press
Waterloo, Ontario, Canada
www.wlupress.wlu.ca

Chapter 2, "Laced In and Let Down," was first published in Alexandra Palmer, ed., *Fashion: A Canadian Perspective* (2004). It was revised and included in this volume with the permission of the University of Toronto Press.

This book is printed on FSC recycled paper and is certified Ecologo. It is made from 100% post-consumer fibre, processed chlorine free, and manufactured using biogas energy.

Printed in Canada

RECYCLED
Paper made from
recycled material
FSC
www.fsc.org   FSC® C103567

To the next generation

CONTENTS

ACKNOWLEDGEMENTS

As the writer of this collection of essays, I gratefully acknowledge the assistance and encouragement of many people. First of all, my heartfelt thanks to my graduate research assistants in the School of Journalism and Communication at Carleton University over the life of this project: Andrea Hunter, Stephanie Dunn, Susan Krashinsky, Claire Brownell, Ameera Javeria, Chloé Fedio and Will Stos. Among them, they did some or all of the following demanding tasks: examined and analyzed years' worth of feminist publications, transcribed the oral history interviews and immersed themselves in other archival, media and bibliographical records. In addition, none of the research that went into this book could have been done without the knowledgeable and cordial assistance of the consulting librarians, archivists and other staff at the many educational, government and media libraries and archives across Canada who helped me and my research assistants with documents, recordings, illustrations, books and other material.

Special thanks to the women who generously gave of their time and memories in oral history interviews with me, along with follow-up phone calls and emails: Kathryn-Jane Hazel, Anne Roberts, Emma Kivisild, Esther Shannon, Nancy Pollak, Fatima Jaffer, Philinda Masters, Bethan Lloyd, Debbie Mathers and Alanis Obomsawin. Mark Valcour, the radio studio technologist at Carleton's School of Journalism and Communication, helped with technical questions and kindly made me digital copies of the recorded interviews.

I am also very grateful to Jean Bruce of Ottawa for generously allowing me to cite her invaluable archived interviews with several former CBC staff members. Further thanks go to Julie Ireton of CBC Ottawa for open-heartedly sharing her radio documentary and other material on her grandmother-in-law, the CBC's Margaret Colpitts ("Joan Marshall"), and to Peggy Wightman, daughter of Margaret Colpitts, who allowed me access, via Ms. Ireton, to documents kept by the family.

Photographers Errol Young, Lori J. Meserve and André Pichette have been very generous in allowing me the use of their work to illustrate this book, as has David Milne in granting permission to reproduce the photo his father, Gilbert Milne, took of Elizabeth Long. I am also grateful to Anne Roberts and Marsha Arbour for offering me photographs from their private collections, to Nancy Pollak of *Kinesis* for granting me access to background documents in her possession, and to Philinda Masters of *Broadside* and Debbie Mathers of *Pandora*, who allowed me to reproduce cover pages from those periodicals.

Constructive feedback has always been very important to me. The anonymous readers who reviewed the original manuscript for Wilfrid Laurier University Press provided encouraging and useful suggestions. The esteemed historians of the Clio Club in Victoria, British Columbia, listened with interest to my draft conference papers based on these essays and sharpened my ideas with their very helpful comments. They are Diana Chown, Patricia Dirks, Diana Pedersen, Alison Prentice, Patricia Roy, Gillian Thompson, Sylvia van Kirk, Jean Wilson and the late Marianne Gosztonyi Ainley, who is very much missed. In addition, the students in my upper-level classes at Carleton helpfully critiqued some of these papers, asking apt questions about historical context from their youthful perspectives.

During strolls along the Rideau River near my home, my friend and former fellow grad student, Leona Crabb, talked me through the mental process of just getting started on this book. Carleton colleagues Catherine McKercher, Kirsten Kozolanka, Carman Cumming and Michéle Martin have offered further encouragement over tea, coffee, lunch and dinner. Constance Backhouse, the legal historian from the University of Ottawa, supportively brainstormed with me during our shared rides to and from regular meetings of the National Capital Committee on the Scholarship, Preservation and Dissemination of Women's History, an oasis of collegial feminist support, intense book discussions, great food and much laughter.

The staff at Wilfrid Laurier University Press, including acquisitions editor Lisa Quinn, managing editor Rob Kohlmeier, and website and marketing coordinator Leslie Macredie, have been invariably helpful in sorting out the processes and practices of book publishing. My copy editor, Marcia Gallego, was also a great help during the final crunch stage. Earlier, as my first manuscript submission deadline approached, Mary-Ev Anderson of Persuasive Proposals in Vancouver generously spent long hours reformatting "the devil" of the technical tangle of the Machar essay, which wanted to express itself in different versions of at least two well-known word processing programs, when, really, only one was necessary, especially at the same time.

As always, my deepest thanks to my life partner, Gabriella Goliger, for her fine editing, astute comments, endless patience and enduring love; and to our families and close friends for their support and encouragement. And finally, a pat on the head for Sheba, whose little black doggy paws always appeared on my keyboard just when we both needed a walk.

INTRODUCTION

This collection of essays considers the ways in which several of Canada's women journalists, broadcasters and other media workers reached beyond the glory of their personal bylines to advocate for some of the most controversial women's goals of their eras. To do so, they had to negotiate the media's institutional boundaries with their gender stereotypes and expectations of them as women who worked in the field. Here I use the term *byline* in its broadest sense, as a marker of a woman's media identity, whether she was using a pen name, an on-air alias, or her real name. Some of my subjects adopted feminized pen names and broadcast identities that appealed to their editors, advertisers and conventional audiences. While a few of those same journalists could write about bettering women's lives only in limited ways, others were more adept at subversively using their media work to further the feminist cause. There were also those women who, proudly claiming their own names, refused to conform altogether, openly and defiantly challenging the gender expectations of their day and presenting alternative ways of being female.

These essays comprise a series of snapshots, or case studies. Each of the women profiled had to have the courage to express her own convictions, given that there was some force at work, and sometimes several, to keep her silent: the laws of church and state, political backlash, patriotism, peer pressure and, always, gender and racial prejudice and the social niceties that were designed to keep rebellious females in check. These were all women one could label variously as a "heroine," a "role-model," a "character," "eccentric," "driven," "difficult," or "outrageous," all the words we ascribe to women who dare to fight for change. Any one of them might be conservative or liberal or radical; charming or reserved or cantankerous;

self-reflective or stubborn or arrogant; generous or cautious or nasty. Often it was their anger at the ways in which women's lives and work were devalued that prompted them to speak out. Sometimes their courage failed them and they bowed to editorial, advertising or other institutional influences, and at other times they swallowed their fears and sprang free of these constraints regardless of the consequences. What is important to this study is not their lapses or successes as much as their struggles to use the media to persuade women that a better day should come, if not for them, at least for their daughters, granddaughters and nieces. For these women in the media, women's rights talk went beyond legislative amendments to include more equitable institutional policies and practices as well as fundamental changes in social and cultural attitudes.

Media historian Hanno Hardt has coined the very useful term *media worker*,[1] which applies to my subjects because they performed different functions related to news of women and their concerns at different times. Each of them was engaged, to varying degrees, in those lively tensions among political activism, freedom of expression and the demands of the commercial or government-sponsored media work of her time and place. Some of the essays in this book are revisionist in nature, re-examining the journalism of women who were well known. The other chapters cover new ground with studies of media workers who have not yet found a place in the canon of journalism studies or women's history but whose contributions to the advancement of women have been pivotal.

My perspective on them is "bio-critical" and interdisciplinary, combining biography, discourse analysis of their work, the journalism studies tradition within media history and women's history. Biographical information allows us, in the words of Canadian historians Magda Fahrni, Suzanne Morton and Joan Sangster, to "secure a window into a certain historical era, understand unusual or distinctive women who stood apart in their time or explore key themes in feminist history."[2] Discourse analysis interrogates their words so that their intentions can be understood but also investigates the gendered media language and images of their social milieus, such as photographs and cartoons, as Dutch communications scholar Liesbet van Zoonen has explained.[3] The cultures of the specific print, audio and visual media in which they worked circumscribed their efforts and necessarily had an impact on how much they were able to reveal of themselves and how hard they were able to fight for social change. For that reason, my analysis considers the "journalisms" of different institutions, with their own gender dynamics, political agendas and means of financial survival in particular eras.

This approach reflects current discussions about the importance of interdisciplinary approaches to the scholarly study of journalism in general, and women in the media in particular. Barbie Zelizer, a leading

American analyst of journalism studies, believes that there should be more cross-fertilization between that field and other academic disciplines, the better to appreciate how important journalism has been to communication within society. In *Taking Journalism Seriously*, she notes that scholars have studied it mainly as a profession, an institution and a set of practices; as textual expression; and in reference to the people who produce it—all useful approaches, but none of them definitive. When any one of them is married with another discipline—for example, sociology, history, language studies, political science or cultural studies—our understanding of the terms *journalism* and *journalists* becomes all the more complex.[4]

In Canada, media history has expanded in the last decade, in line with increasing interest the field, taking a broader view of the connections between journalism and the economy, politics, technology and culture. In the 1990s, most of the literature on print media fell into several fairly distinct categories, which William J. Buxton and Catherine McKercher defined as "historical overviews, first-person accounts, biographies, accounts of particular newspapers or institutions, and focused thematic studies."[5] We are short of new historical overviews, but perhaps that is because we are still recovering much of the detail. The current list includes autobiographies from veteran journalists such as Anthony Westell and biographies of prominent media icons, such as A.B. McKillop's well-received study of Pierre Berton, the late journalist, broadcaster and popular historian.[6] Communication scholars Florian Sauvageau and David Pritchard have produced a French-language demographic overview of Canadian newsrooms at the turn of the 21st century, while Catherine McKercher has opened up new ground with her study of unions, past and present, in *Newsworkers Unite*.[7] Media historians have produced important new historical research on media institutions as well—Gene Allen on the Canadian Press news agency,[8] Marc Edge on the Pacific Press newspaper company and the media conglomerate CanWest Global,[9] and Mary Vipond on the Canadian Broadcasting Corporation during the 1930s and 1940s.[10] Recent thematic overviews include Russell Johnston's study of advertising and the media in Canada;[11] Cecil Rosner's history of a specific journalism practice, investigative reporting, in print and on the air;[12] and Dwayne Winseck's analysis of the effects of technological change on the international business of media well before the term *globalization* was coined.[13] Historian Ross Eaman has recently published his *Historical Dictionary of Journalism*, a useful tool for researchers in the field.[14]

While they provide important background on the history of the media, these books and articles do not extensively address women or gender issues, or discuss their place in the journalism studies canon. In her overview of the American scholarship on women in the media, historian Maurine Beasley called for a new interdisciplinary synthesis of women's history in the media that is not limited to the professional norms expected of male journalists in newsrooms, with their attendant emphasis on "journalistic objectivity." Beasley's model takes into account the interrelated "complexities of women's social roles" in their personal lives, their activism and their media work. In order to accomplish this new synthesis, she advocated better use of auto-biography and biography, oral history, archival research, studies of the organizations and feminist networks in which the journalists were involved, and social histories of women and the family. Those contextual considerations would lead to a deeper understanding of journalism that would be "more appropriate to women's experience" and would encompass their efforts to convey to their audiences "informative material that has wide popular appeal" using different journalistic forms.[15] She argues, "All women who have made use of journalistic techniques—gathering new information of current value and presenting it in various popular formats—have a claim to be studied as journalists, regardless of whether their primary mission has been to advocate, report, comment or entertain."[16]

The work of my subjects reflected the real-life political, economic and social conditions that most women of their time and place experienced, as amply demonstrated by a number of Canadian historians of women and the family. They have studied women of different classes, ethnic and racial backgrounds, family relationships, working conditions and political perspectives.[17] One of the key themes that tie this literature together is their insistence on women's self-determination in the face of prejudices of all kinds,[18] perspectives that apply to the media workers investigated here, as each chapter will reveal. Women's history is also becoming more interdisciplinary, embracing the contributions of scholars from other fields, including sociology, political economy, the law and cultural studies.[19]

The ongoing historical research on women in the workforce is particularly germane to my study, but mainly in the context of middle-class or "white-collar" opportunities, which is where most media workers found their niche. As Joan Sangster observes in her recent scholarship on women working for wages, class formation is an integral factor in all their experiences, one that some historians either sideline or misunderstand, however, especially when intent on exploring other intersecting factors such as gender and race.[20] Most of the media workers in this study not only identified as middle class but assumed their audiences did as well, or were at least aspiring to a more comfortable material life. The more radical ones questioned standard liberal feminism assumptions, challenging capitalism and patriarchy and striving to bring to public attention the systemic social factors, such as sexism, homophobia and racism, that limited many women's chances in life.

Whether they worked outside or inside the home, Canadian women engaged in a broad range of pro-woman activism in different eras, which historians initially described as "waves" that peaked during certain time periods and around set goals. They recognize, however, that women still occupied themselves politically in a variety of ways in the lulls between the suffragist first wave, the "women's liberation" second wave of the mid- to late 20th century,[21] and a third, more diversity-conscious wave that has yet to coalesce politically behind specific goals or agendas. Furthermore, there have been overlaps in the activism and goals of each generation.[22] As Cheryl Gosselin notes in her summary of the relevant academic studies, feminism is an "evolving intellectual tradition"[23] beyond a specific social movement, has embraced a broad range of political ideas and associations, and should take into account the contributions of women of different cultural and racial backgrounds who may not consider themselves "feminists" as such but are clearly committed to bettering women's rights. The media workers in this study all held strong and very individual perspectives on the pressing issues of their day.

Much of the existing Canadian historical literature on women in the media is centred on the early women print journalists, and comprises books and articles that are important contributions to our understanding of their work. Because there are scholarly gaps in the literature, I will provide here a brief overview of the history of Canadian women in the media, with reference to the published studies that do exist. In her foundational history, *Women Who Made the News*, Marjory Lang considered the women journalists of the 1880s–1940s as gendered subjects who were usually given assignments deemed appropriate to their female roles. They gratefully regarded their admittance to the field as a new opportunity, even though their male colleagues did not consider their social columns and women's pages real journalism and did not take them seriously.[24] In recent studies of some of these pioneers, literary and communication scholars in particular have become engaged in rhetorical analyses of their writing on a number of topics, not just women's rights, in order to connect them to their broader cultural milieus. Literary scholar Janice Fiamengo, for example, deconstructs the rhetoric used by six early female journalists when they were writing or engaged in public speaking about topics that had political and cultural currency within and beyond the women's pages. Sandra Gabriele, who interrogates the concepts of modernity and nationalism in the newspapers of the same era, explores the "gendered mobility" of two prominent women's page editors, who publicly ventured beyond their domestic spheres into the cities and the countryside, figuratively bringing their readers with them. Biographer Peggy Martin has tracked down an elusive subject in her study of Lily Lewis, who did not succeed as a writer because of her tragic circumstances, a situation that tells us a lot about the demanding field of journalism for women in her day.[25] To date, historical research on media workers who were women of colour is limited. The best work includes Jane Rhodes's biography of Mary Ann Shadd Cary, who was the editor of a newspaper for the Black community in southern Ontario in the 1850s.[26]

Other researchers are building on the strong connections between some of the journalists' work and their feminist activism in women's associations. The founding of the National Council of Women of Canada in 1893 and its local councils across the country organized mainly urban, middle-class representatives of various women's reform organizations under one umbrella.[27] The NCWC also embraced a number of women's business and professional groups, including, for a time, the members of the Canadian Women's Press Club. In those early years, a journalist's coverage of women's club activities was regarded as central to her training and career, not in conflict with it. She could simultaneously engage in and report on current debates about women's roles in society.[28] Although the CWPC was founded in 1904 as a national journalism craft association, the members of the Winnipeg branch, for example, were key promoters of women's provincial suffrage in Manitoba and later became engaged in the campaign for the federal vote as activists and journalists.[29] The journalists who produced the early women's magazines in central Canada were also taken by the suffrage campaign, as media historian Anne-Marie Kinahan reveals in her ongoing research into periodicals such as *Everywoman's World*.[30] Her findings support Maria Dicenzo's spirited argument for including early women's publications as part and parcel of the journalism history canon,[31] a perspective amply demonstrated by recent studies in Britain and the United States.[32]

After the suffrage campaigns were over, women journalists became more intent on professional advancement and less interested in combining their writing with advocacy work, adopting the stance of "journalistic objectivity," even when reporting on women's associations such as the NCWC.[33] There is still much work to be done on the generations between the wars, but Lang's overview suggests that only about a dozen or so women journalists were able to extend their reach outside of the women's pages to cover general news, business, politics and, occasionally, foreign affairs. Several of them were feminist in that they believed in women's right to equal opportunity, but their views were not always reflected in the articles they wrote.[34] A number of others have always been difficult to track because they made their living as freelancers.[35] The women who worked in the new media of radio and later, television largely replicated their past experiences in print, most of them producing, hosting or reporting for programs aimed at women in the home.[36]

Similarly, the editors of the few general circulation magazines for women in Canada generally stuck to conventional fare, reflecting women's traditional roles. In her study of *Chatelaine*, historian Valerie Korinek focused on the 1950s–1960s and the relationship the magazine cultivated with its female readers, many of whom were busy raising children in the suburbs.

During that period, a liberal feminist, Doris Anderson, became the editor, and used its pages to actively encourage Canadian women to become more involved in their own political, economic and social progress. Under Anderson's direction, *Chatelaine* began to tackle issues then considered highly controversial, such as abortion[37] and lesbianism,[38] and was a strong supporter of the Royal Commission on the Status of Women (1967–1970), which produced a resounding, if somewhat flawed,[39] report recommending changes in the laws that discriminated against women at work and in the home. In *The Satellite Sex*, I recounted some of the struggles of the women's page and feature writers who were assigned to cover that federal inquiry, a national public airing of women's grievances that resonated with them personally and professionally, confined, as most of them still were, to the women's pages.[40]

By then, another major political and professional shift was beginning for women in the media. Their determined attempts to join their male colleagues in taking on general news assignments became the subject of heated discussion among editors and reporters, but slowly and surely the women began to make progress.[41] Most first-person accounts, such as that of veteran journalist Simma Holt, mention, to varying degrees, the sex discrimination female reporters and broadcasters suffered during those years, and biographers have noted the determination of talented writers such as Christina McCall to tackle broader political subjects as well as women's issues.[42] After 1970, the CWPC saw its younger members and potential recruits flock toward the previously all-male journalists' associations, which were just beginning to open their doors to women.[43] At the same time, female media workers were expected to reject or abandon any connection in their personal lives with feminist advocacy groups, especially the new and radical "women's liberation" collectives that had begun to spring up across the country.[44] The most politically committed women had few choices other than to become involved with feminist media for little or no pay[45] or, alternatively, to undertake documentary filmmaking. The women of Studio D, the feminist branch of the National Film Board of Canada, spent many years producing documentaries for and about women and their rights, but they were not the only ones making films.[46]

By the mid-1990s, as Gertrude J. Robinson documented, women made up larger minorities than they used to in Canada's newspaper and television newsrooms—28 and 37 percent respectively—but the "glass ceiling," inflexible work hours and other systemic barriers remained impediments.[47] As Robinson noted, there is an abiding scholarly interest in women journalists' progress toward professional equality with men because, as she succinctly put it, "gender matters."[48]

In this series of case studies, I expand beyond the newsroom to consider the contributions various kinds of female media workers have made to communications in Canada, and to the advancement of women's rights over a number of time periods. In the current affairs magazines of the late 19th century, Agnes Maule Machar of Kingston, seemingly a model of Presbyterian spinsterhood, sharpened her pen and her voice as "Fidelis" to espouse her belief in higher education for women and better conditions for female workers, bringing these matters to the attention of politicians, businessmen and her sister members of the NCWC. She was a leader among the handful of known female journalists whose work was accepted for publication at a time when men dominated intellectual and political debates in Canada's newspapers and magazines. Several authors who have written about Machar have been most interested in the nature of her religious values, specifically the ways in which she expressed her piety and social gospel beliefs as part of her intellectual perspective on social reform.[49] As a media historian I am more intrigued by Machar's outlook on women's rights and how she was able to express it in the leading current affairs periodicals, which she daringly used to persuade others, chiefly men, of the value of change.

The newly established women's pages of the Toronto daily newspapers presented another, potentially feminist platform—potentially because women's rights advocates were not always able to exploit these pages as well as they might have, although some of the issues they tackled as journalists may well have had more resonance for their readers than more overtly political concerns. In their Saturday pages, Kathleen Blake Coleman as "Kit," Alice Fenton Freeman as "Faith Fenton," Emily Cummings as "Sama" and Elmira Elliott Atkinson as "Madge Merton" all debated the constrictions, dangers and potential of women's fashions, a more saleable issue for them than suffrage in the 1890s, despite their individual views on women's rights. Freeman and Cummings were both known NCWC activists,[50] while Coleman was the CWPC's first national president. In *Kit's Kingdom*, I discussed her inconsistent views on the feminism of her time, given the circumstances of her personal and working life. How could a well-schooled journalist like her, who believed in higher education and equal pay for women, dismiss their right to vote so readily for so long, I wondered, given that early in her career she had expressed some support. I felt at the time, and still do, that it had much to do with the conservative editorial position of her newspaper; in fact, she said as much herself.[51] In her analysis of "Kit's" advice columns, Janice Fiamengo mistakenly concluded that I was judging Coleman's subjectivity through a late 20th-century feminist lens.[52] On the contrary, I was very careful not to do so, and was intent on examining the intricate overlaps between women's "private" and "public" spheres in the late 19th century, as historians were debating them in 1980s, when the book was written.[53]

Since then, communications scholar Nancy Fraser has challenged the ideas of Jürgen Habermas, who originally envisioned the historical "public sphere" of political communication as comprising well-educated men. In response, Fraser raised important questions about the ways in which women as citizens have used their own "counter-sphere" of media communication to influence public life.[54] Accordingly, my original perception of women's "political" issues in Coleman's day has broadened to include the impact of fashionable dress standards on their health and well-being, which, because of editorial priorities, advertising pressures and reader interest, sparked more tendentious discussion in the women's pages than the vote did. I first explored this tension between consumerism and women's health in an essay in Alexandra Palmer's edited anthology on Canadian fashion;[55] I have updated the piece for this book, adding context from more recent scholarship.

Continuing in this revisionist vein, I next examine Francis Marion Beynon's "Country Homemakers" column in the *Grain Growers' Guide*, a Prairie weekly, where she railed against limits on the federal female franchise during the First World War. Prime Minister Robert Borden was trying to win Canadians' approval of compulsory military conscription by extending suffrage only to women of "British" descent who had menfolk fighting in the trenches, while disenfranchising German-born or other "enemy alien" men. In this chapter, I challenge the accepted narratives about Beynon, whose biographers believed that a falling out with her editor and wartime censorship resulted in her being forced to leave Winnipeg in 1917. Perhaps in search of a pacifist feminist icon, they jumped to this conclusion without comparing her columns to those of the *Guide*'s editorialists. If they had, they would have realized that her views on conscription and the franchise were not entirely purist, and that she had editorial support for them until after she left Canada. Further, her reasons for going to New York had more to do with her sense of personal and political isolation and her professional ambitions as a writer than it did with wartime censorship, although she likely sensed the coming shift in the *Guide*'s politics as well. These factors do not detract from her courage in facing down jingoists and anti-feminists in the Winnipeg of her day, but do add deeper context to her brand of political journalism, which differed radically from the more "patriotic" sentiments expressed by most other members of the CWPC and the NCWC.

The next set of essays brings us into a more modern era, and is less revisionist than exploratory. The subsequent generation of female media workers were apt to find themselves working in radio as well as print, but again, segregated into domesticated areas deemed appropriate for women on programs primarily designed for homemakers. Just as they had in the newspapers, they used the medium subversively in the cause of women's rights, if and when they could get away with it. That is certainly true of the "Women's Interest" radio programming transmitted by the Canadian Broadcasting Corporation and its affiliated stations across the country from the late 1930s through the 1950s. The CBC's first supervisor of "Women's Interest" programming, Elizabeth Long, an ardent NCWC member and a former newspaperwoman, was an important link between the feminist generations and the print and broadcast media. Born and raised in Winnipeg, she was a protégé of E. Cora Hind, the Prairie suffragist and agricultural affairs journalist, who taught her how to work in a man's world to her own advantage and that of other women. Long, using her female radio commentators, subversively introduced "equal rights" talks along with the household hints offered to the female listeners of CBC national radio from 1938 to 1956. At a time when a growing minority of married women worked for pay,[56] her listeners were invited to consider the merits of allowing wives and mothers to take jobs outside the home with the same opportunities for the salaries, promotions and benefits that their male counterparts received as a matter of course.

Long mentored a number of female broadcasters, including Florence Bird, who later chaired the Royal Commission on the Status of Women (1967–1970), the federal government inquiry that recommended a number of changes in the law, many of which feminists eventually won. One of the most controversial topics the commission dealt with was abortion, which, as of 1970, was illegal unless the woman could demonstrate to a hospital medical committee that her life or health was at stake.[57] Two reporters-in-training, Anne Roberts and Kathryn Keate (Kathryn-Jane Hazel today), were both committed socialist feminists determined to see abortion decriminalized altogether, arguing that women should have the right to choose whether and when to bear a child. They promoted the pro-choice stance on reproductive rights in their activism and their media work at a time when being an advocate of any kind was considered unprofessional.[58] Nevertheless, there was still enough flexibility in the system to allow Roberts and Keate to work around the rules, at least for a while, leading to their involvement in an attention-grabbing, nationwide media campaign for abortion "on demand." In late April 1970, the Abortion Caravan, a motor procession of women, left Vancouver and drove to Ottawa, provocatively arriving just before Mother's Day. This chapter examines Roberts's and Keate's publicity strategies in light of the resulting media coverage of the Caravanners' cross-country trek, their demonstrations along the way, and their climactic protest on Parliament Hill that forced the House of Commons to a halt. While Roberts and Keate were not the only ones involved in courting the news media's attention for the Caravan, they took leading roles in that public relations campaign and went on to lengthy careers in the mainstream media, carefully balancing their politics with their journalism and public relations work.

Other young women of their generation decided to break with conventional news media, which they considered the enemies of feminism, and devote their energies to producing their own publications instead. *Kinesis* in Vancouver, *Broadside* in Toronto and *Pandora* in Halifax were among the longest-running of the estimated 40–50 feminist publications in Canada in the 1980s–1990s.[59] The radical feminists who ran them covered a myriad of women's issues, from equal pay to lesbian identity and sexuality. They believed they had to tread carefully with same-sex love, however, constantly reminding themselves that it was only one of many feminist debates regarding freedom of choice that had to be explored with their readers. That is why their coverage of it—as frank as it often was—never dominated their editorial agendas. But it caught the attention of Canada's conservative forces anyway, who were already using this thorny issue to scapegoat feminist services of all kinds. The challenges of producing feminist newspapers with broad appeal made these publishing ventures risky in the first place, but even more so once they were accused of adopting a "lesbian agenda." Here I approach the editors and coordinators as equal members of editorial collectives, in the original spirit of their enterprises, and examine what freedom of the press—and women's right to love other women—meant to them and to feminist publishing.

Another method of exploring women's issues is documentary filmmaking, an accepted form of journalistic work, whether within mainstream convention or as an alternative genre. Alanis Obomsawin, who does not identify as a "feminist," decided not to join the National Film Board's Studio D, mainly because she wanted to produce films about Aboriginal men, women and children and their concerns. Yet, since 1975, Obomsawin, an Abenaki woman, has jettisoned the age-old stereotypes of the "Indian princess" and the hapless "squaw" in groundbreaking documentaries that depict the traditions and courage of Aboriginal women in Quebec and elsewhere and their struggles to overcome personal and political obstacles. Whether she focused on women as her primary subjects, or placed them alongside the men and children of their communities during times of crisis, Obomsawin produced films that explained their traditional roles; encouraged respect for them as mothers, warriors, leaders and teachers; and advocated for their naming, marriage and succession rights. She has long been considered a pioneering Aboriginal filmmaker in Canada, but scholars have largely overlooked her ways of depicting strong women and their aspirations, aspects of her documentary films that are well worth exploring.

Illustrating each chapter in this book are media images of women that best demonstrate the iconic femininity of their respective eras, and my subjects' acceptance, manipulation or rejection of it. As an American media historian, Carolyn Kitch, has noted, academic trends in pictorial analysis have shifted from empirical assumptions about stereotypes to searches for alternative images, to reading female representations as ideology, to deconstructing their "polysemic," or multiple, meanings. Rather than regard these theoretical shifts as progressive, Kitch asks if there isn't room for various combinations, or analytical overlaps, in these same methods, in order to best elucidate the historical context of the image at hand.[60] No matter how one "reads" them, or in which medium they appear, idealized female images have always had more credence than others, regardless of the era.

Archival research is not unlike investigative reporting, in that one simply has to dive into whatever evidence exists in order to come up with the information that leads to a better understanding of the life and work of one's subjects. A few of these media workers left some archival records at least, or if they did not, one or more of their contemporaries did. With rare exceptions, the print media are not particularly conscious of the importance of leaving their administrative documents behind, beyond copies of the newspapers and magazines they published, which are generally quite accessible. Although the CBC has kept its very useful management records, it did not do the same for much of its broadcast material, especially early radio, which was often aired live and not recorded. Fortunately, several CBC managers, program producers and broadcasters kept enough scripts and memos to provide insight into the kind of programs aired for women, starting from the late 1930s. A few oral historians and broadcasters provided other key material by interviewing Elizabeth Long and several of her colleagues and depositing those recordings in the archives.

I was able to record oral history interviews of my own with Anne Roberts and Kathryn-Jane Hazel about their involvement with the Abortion Caravan, as well as with several editor-coordinators who produced the feminist periodicals *Kinesis*, *Broadside* and *Pandora* over the years. This technique of evidence gathering was crucial to my understanding of how they functioned collectively as media workers and as activists in the feminist cause. As Sherna Berger Gluck points out, a feminist perspective is important in determining the value of women's oral history, being one "that not only understands how women's experience is gendered, but that also understands the tension between women's oppression and resistance." For academics, there are also questions of power, responsibility and cooperation in relationships with interviewees. In most cases, the subjects are not prominent people and are not used to public exposure, and it is the feminist historian's ethical duty to safeguard their vulnerabilities and personal agency, without abandoning her own critical faculties.[61] In contrast, all the interviewees in this book understand media, having worked in it, and were willing to use their full names and openly discuss their past activities in the interests of the historical record. I wanted them to speak for themselves as much as possible, and have tried to interpret all their contributions fairly and accurately, in the political context of the years during which they were activists. These years, rather than their life stories, were the focus of my inquiries, and I am fully aware that our interviews were mediated by me as the historian and by them as my subjects through that narrative, conversational prism. We are, in that sense, "negotiating and creating a text"[62] based on the experiences they relate, one that is meant to augment the journalistic record and other documents, and is influenced by my own experiences as a liberal-left feminist who did not share their political activism but usually covered the women's movement from within the mainstream media.[63]

In the case of lesbian history, one must balance the empirical need to gather evidence from a group that has been consistently marginalized with the need to come to an understanding of the value of their subjective memories.[64] The focus of the next chapter is on several lesbian-identified feminists who produced *Kinesis, Broadside* and *Pandora* from the 1980s to the mid-1990s, with the interviews providing the context for their political commitments. These particular individuals were not working alone, but benefited from the input and support of other collective members who met with them on a regular basis. I chose to focus on these editor-coordinators because of their strong, day-to-day influence over editorial and production decisions during a politically challenging time for feminists. The articles they published that centred on sexual identity politics provide further insights into their editorial choices, as well as the concerns of their contributing writers and some of their readers.

Pro-woman advocacy of a very different kind highlights the essay on Alanis Obomsawin, who recently retired from the NFB but is very busy acting as adviser, making more films of her own, and collecting well-earned awards.[65] In order to interpret her meanings of Aboriginal womanhood as best I can, I have relied mainly on my own and others' interviews with her, her own spoken narration for her films, and the ways in which she used the voices and images of the women in them. Inevitably, my interpretations of her work are mediated through my non-Aboriginal lens, but they are informed by the more knowledgeable understandings of Native women's cultures offered by Obomsawin herself and others who have lived it first-hand, such as the late Gail Guthrie Valaskakis. As a media worker, Obomsawin has produced her films in order to bring attention to the many injustices Aboriginal people have suffered, as well as to highlight their courage and strength. Her documentaries are available online through the NFB, and have been aired on speciality channels such as CBC News Network (formerly Newsworld) and the Aboriginal Peoples Television Network. They are consequently in the public domain and therefore open to the different interpretations of audiences of many backgrounds, the better to continue the ongoing dialogue about Aboriginal rights and responsibilities and, in the case of this chapter, her portrayal of the women and their concerns.

Certainly, as postmodernists argue, all this evidence taken together cannot represent a strictly "truthful" historical account, but rather one that is mediated through these women's own agendas and their subjective interpretations of their own experiences and concerns. Yet, as Valerie Raleigh Yow contends, in her assessment of oral history as a research method, postmodern fluidity has its limits, in that "each biographer must strive to get as close as possible to the lived experience. This means that we do not invent evidence, that we look at what evidence we have critically, and that we seek to discern our own biases in selecting and interpreting it," including the empathy we might have with our subjects.[66]

As someone who values clear narrative and compelling stories, I feel it is important to put these women's political experiences as they expressed them, ahead of certain theoretical considerations, especially those that have become academically fashionable in the years since most of these media workers were active. I would argue, for example, that simply subsuming all their political efforts within a postmodern analysis of the "performativity"[67] of their gender roles in the media would diminish rather than elucidate their struggles as activists. The women of the earlier generations certainly behaved, consciously and deliberately, according to contemporary norms of femininity, maternalism and domesticity, mainly as a way to attract readers and listeners. In reality, they embraced certain aspects of these roles in their personal lives but also skirted around them in order to free themselves to work outside the home and engage in discussions about women's rights in the first place. The later generations were far more defiantly in rebellion against the old gender maxims, overtly challenged male authority and tried on what were considered radically new roles for women, politically and culturally. Whether they subversively disguised themselves as perfect young ladies or "performed" their radical politics with raised voices, clenched fists or blistering newspaper columns, they deeply felt their anger at sexism. Similarly, Obomsawin and the women she filmed and videotaped also, inevitably, "performed" before the camera, both upholding and subverting traditional understandings of Aboriginal gender roles. It was one way of asserting their rights and fighting back against the historical injustices they have suffered because of sexism and racism. The point here is not their "performance" but their determination to bring about change.

Obomsawin's first non-Native language was French, her second one, English, and her films have been released in both languages. I viewed the English versions. I have not included francophone media workers and their journalism in this book, not out of lack of interest, but because I don't know their language and milieus well enough to do them justice. Thankfully, my colleague at Université Laval, Josette Brun, and several other scholars have produced new research on the history of francophone women and the media.[68] She and I have collaborated on a brief contemporary study,[69] which is one way for academics to do research that could potentially be translated into both languages. Translations of single-authored work are still too rarely done, and they are badly needed.

As the communications scholar Lana Rakow has observed, "Recovering women's means of communicating (including histories of women's media, histories of women journalists and writers, the role of technologies in women's lives, and in the construction of gender, and analysis of women's talk and gendered discourse) is critical and far from complete."[70] This book is not meant to be a chronological history of women media workers, but a glimpse into the motives of a few of them, as a way of opening up more research in the field and encouraging others to do the same. There is a lot to learn about the roles they have played in the development and expansion of women's equality rights in Canada, how much they were able to achieve or not, and why. But first we have to broaden our conceptions of the terms *journalist* and *byline* to include women who were not news reporters or who worked outside the mainstream media.

CHAPTER 1

"A More Beautiful, More Perfect Lily"

Agnes Maule Machar, Women's Sphere and Canada's Magazines, 1870s–1890s

gnes Maule Machar of Kingston, Ontario (1837–1927), was a tiny woman with an eclectic mind. In one of the only pictures of her that survive, she is dressed modestly in a dark, fitted day dress, hands demurely holding flowers, while her terrier rests contentedly at her feet. The garden and sky around her look perfect enough to furnish the backdrop for a studio portrait of the kind then just coming into fashion among the middle class. She does not look into the camera directly but gazes off to the side, with a gentle, self-effacing smile. Described by contemporaries as "elfin-faced" with "bird-like" eyes, she would never have served as a model of perfect womanhood so commonly depicted in the illustrated magazines. She looks like the "spinster" daughter of the Presbyterian manse that she was, perhaps just returned home from church.[1] There is nothing in the portrait—no books, no pen—that suggests that she was a well-known journalist, historian, poet, novelist, Christian social reformer and women's rights advocate. But once she was out of the camera's eye, it was likely that she planned to spend the rest of the day at her desk, writing about the issues that most concerned her.

Whether she was writing a magazine article, a novel or a poem, Machar brought to bear a concern for social justice based on her deeply felt Christian beliefs. She was an ardent Canadian nationalist and British imperialist, a social reformer who took Christ's directive to comfort the afflicted literally, and an early women's movement activist who believed education was the key to greater opportunities for women. To her mind, it was the well-educated, morally upright, financially secure woman, busy working at home and in the world, who could best use the talents and fulfill the destiny bestowed upon her by God, and strengthen her family, her community and the young Canada as a nation.

Agnes Maule Machar, V23-P-3,
Queen's University Archives.

Her ideas found their way into a handful of Canadian periodicals, which, in the 19th century, were essentially platforms for masculine intellectual inquiry. In the 1870s, Machar was likely the only known female writer contributing articles to these magazines,[2] despite the precedents set some decades earlier by pioneers such as Susanna Moodie, Louisa Murray and a few of their contemporaries.[3] A decade after she began publishing, her few female peers, notably her contemporary, Sarah Anne Curzon,[4] and the much younger Sara Jeannette Duncan,[5] shared her commitment to nurturing good Canadian writing, but had different political perspectives on female equality. Machar produced more than two dozen magazine articles, half of them concerning women's rights, between the 1870s and the 1890s. Her arguments were shaped by her Christian social reform agenda; the attitudes of the male editors, writers and illustrators who were her contemporaries; the shifting commercial priorities of the magazine industry; and the prevailing cultural discourse about "the woman question."

Historians Ruth Compton Brouwer[6] and Dianne Hallman[7] and other scholars have made significant contributions to our understanding of

Machar's outlook on Canadian life and society from different perspectives—religion and social justice, nationalism and imperialism, women's education and work, and her own place in literature and local public history.[8] But she is still not very well known as a leading intellectual journalist, nor has her nonfiction writing on women's rights been specifically presented as fulfilling the educative, as opposed to the entertaining function of the craft. Although she seemed to draw the line at immediate women's suffrage, Machar was still keen to persuade her readers of the value of higher education, expanded work opportunities and better pay for women, as well as various aspects of her Christian, social reform agenda, including protective legislation for working-class women. Her overt commitment to these goals was quite acceptable in a journalistic milieu in which the term *impartial* did not mean "objective," but independent of political party politics at a time when most newspapers and magazines aligned themselves with either conservative or liberal forces.[9] Her Christian faith, her belief in education and her enthusiastic involvement in various women's social reform organizations fuelled her writing. As Brouwer rightly points out, it is important to stress the crucial role that religion played in the lives of many early women's rights advocates who, like Machar, did not differentiate between their politics and their faith.[10]

Hallman and others have described Machar as essentially a maternal or social feminist, meaning that she saw women's work in the world, the "public sphere," as an extension of the moral guidance they were expected to exercise as wives and mothers in the home, or the "private sphere." A number of historians have questioned the rigidity of those definitive "spheres," arguing for more connection and fluidity between them, but Cecilia Morgan takes a pragmatic view of the public discourse in newspapers and other material records in Upper Canada in the first half of the 19th century. "There is plenty of evidence that, for men and women of particular socioeconomic, religious, racial and ethnic backgrounds in this period, the division of society along the lines of public and private was an important conceptual framework; it was used in attempts to organize that society, and it also played a critical role in shaping white, middle-class identities and subjectivities."[11] Machar, who had grown up in the latter part of this era, used the expression "women's sphere" several times in her articles to denote the particular work that she believed God had assigned women to do. While she valued their roles as wives and mothers, she believed this "sphere" intersected with that of males and should be much broader in cultural circumference, as a matter of "justice," which denoted her liberal leanings toward "equality" rights, at least on some issues.[12] She wanted women to expand their influence—as mothers, charity workers, teachers, doctors, writers, in fact, as anything God had given them the talent to be—and be paid equally with men who did the same work.[13] Her outlook reflected the importance most Protestant churches placed on women's domestic roles, while at the same time allowing women much more leeway for self-development than they would have found in the proscriptive church periodicals of the day.[14]

The key, she felt, was an education that would best prepare women for their particular roles in life, whether they were scientists, wives or domestic servants. At a time when universities were closed to women, she advocated that those who were intellectually exceptional should be able to pursue higher education, work hard at their studies and bring the best of their nurturing female "nature" to their professions. To make one's mark in the world was not "unwomanly" or masculine, or dangerous to a woman's moral or physical health as some women's rights opponents argued. It was part of God's plan. "Give a lily the richest soil, the most generous culture you like, and you will never transform it into a rose, far less into an oak. It will only become a more beautiful, more perfect lily," she argued in the elegantly formal style of her time.[15]

She wrote for periodicals that had begun publishing with nationalistic fervour shortly after Confederation to promote Canadian writers and artists and their ideas. *The Canadian Monthly and National Review* (1872–1878), for example, was inspired by the Canada First movement, an ardent, if short-lived, group of nationalists.[16] It was followed by *Rose-Belford's Canadian Monthly and National Review* (1878–1882), and then *The Week* (1883–1896). They were all meant to be both educational and entertaining to audiences schooled enough in religion, history, geography, politics, the arts, science and theatre to appreciate their sophisticated contents. Despite ongoing financial difficulties, their publishers doggedly continued to offer the educated elite a forum through which to discuss, debate and dissect questions about nationalism, education, religion and science, social and women's issues, the French question, Aboriginal concerns and other pressing matters. The Canadian content, sparse at first, was augmented by reproduced articles from British and American competitors, such as *The Spectator*, *Blackwood's Magazine*, *Harper's Weekly* and *Punch*. In a bid to appeal to readers, the editors experimented with a limited number of drawings, expensive to reproduce, to illustrate their cover pages, fiction, travel features and advertising.

Innovative technologies for publishing text and pictures, rising literacy and higher education among the working and middle classes, increasing immigration and expanding businesses all came to bear on the fortunes of Canada's magazines, as did the ubiquity of rival foreign publications, and the reluctance of the Canadian government to wholeheartedly support the young country's cultural industries. Even publishers, editors and writers who were devoted to intellectual journalism as a public service were increasingly tempted to offset their considerable expenses through advertising, rather than the traditional subscriptions.[17] The lengthy, well-researched articles of several pages that Machar wrote in the 1870s and early 1880s had dwindled to just a page or two by the mid-1890s, while the advertising content increased. Machar did not publish much journalism after *The Week* died in 1896, as her didactic style and her spiritual interests were fast becoming passé in a magazine industry that was progressively becoming less intellectual and more commercial, and shifting from overt piety to secularism. By then, *The Week*, dogged by financial difficulties, was advertising itself as a journal for both men and women, and flagged Machar's articles on the front pages, which suggests that the editors were mindful of their mixed readership and her reputation as a writer.[18]

Two other magazines of the era, *Canadian Illustrated News* (1869–1883) and *Grip* (1873–1894) also found their way into the homes of the intelligentsia. Illustrated periodicals were commercial in intent and featured predominantly graphic material, as well as articles, that appealed to as many readers as possible, including women. The images in these two magazines tell us much about the visual artillery used in the battles over "the woman question" and the cultural discourse of gender that Machar was trying to address in her writing—who was the ideal woman, who was not, and what the term *woman* should mean in the life of the nation. Because photographs could not yet be transferred directly to the printed page, the magazines copied and reproduced the images using photolithography, or stone, steel, zinc or wood engraving. *Canadian Illustrated News*, founded by George Desbarats, a bilingual, Catholic printer from Quebec City, offered informative articles with eye-catching pictures about life in Canada and abroad,[19] taking a conservative, stereotyped and commercial view of women's place in the world. Romantic portraits of beautiful and motherly women and jaunty drawings of smug society matrons and befuddled maidservants, usually Irish, were standard fare.

These publications, as well as the newspapers' women's pages and, later, women's magazines, all tended to project attractive and idealized images of women, unless they were being lampooned in cartoons.[20] We know little about most of the artists, especially in relation to their attitudes toward women, but it is clear that they invoked gender stereotypes as a way of signalling their conservative tendencies or the prejudices of their audiences, or both. To be able to sell one's work to magazines was as important to an artist as selling articles was to a journalist, and each had to pay some attention to producing work with both political relevance and popular appeal, as media historian David Spencer has demonstrated.[21] The few academic studies that analyze pictorial representations of gender in Canadian publications of the 19th century focus on John Wilson Bengough, the founder and chief illustrator of *Grip*, which specialized in satiric verse, commentary and political cartoons. In his study of Bengough, Carman Cumming discussed the politics of the artist, who was a nationalist, a committed evangelical Christian and a temperance advocate. In the 1870s he was hostile to women's rights, but by the 1880s had changed his mind and supported co-education and suffrage.[22] Intent on teaching as well as entertaining, he provided explanatory labels for his cartoons and wrote editorials about them to ensure that their humorous, if somewhat didactic, messages were not lost on *Grip*'s less knowledgeable readers.[23] He often used the female figure in various guises as symbols for the nation, the motherland and party politics, and to comment on social reforms, including women's issues, as historian Christina Burr has demonstrated.[24]

Like many other authors, Machar often culled facts and arguments from her broad reading of these domestic and foreign magazines, arming herself to participate with male intellectuals in civil but firm published exchanges about the place of Christian dogma and good works in an increasingly secular and scientific culture, and certainly the ever-vexing "woman question" and its implications for education, conditions of work, temperance and suffrage. She avidly followed this international conversation to underscore her own position on the issues, or to point out to her readers where the arguments of other writers were deficient.[25]

There are no figures available on how much she was paid for her work, but it was probably very little. The editors of *Canadian Monthly* and *Rose-Belford's* did not pay their contributors, unless they submitted fiction, and remuneration from *The Week* was paltry. It appears that Machar made money primarily from the sale of her books, especially those published overseas, and the few articles she submitted to foreign magazines.[26] We also do not know how difficult it was for her to persuade editors to take her work and how often it was rejected, but, judging from her comments to her readers, it must have been often enough. Writing in 1882, when she was 45 years old, Machar told them that she believed female authors, including those who wrote for periodicals, were better accepted than they used to be, but as writing was badly paid, she recommended it as a career choice only for women who were determined to put in the time to become very skilled. She counselled: "Tyros or dilettantes 'need not apply,' and should well count the cost of a thorough preparation for literary work before they commit themselves to what is at best an ill-paid profession as a means of subsistence. Unless they are prepared to submit to years of apprenticeship, with little or no remuneration, and to persevere in an uphill work in spite of repeated disappointments that sadly clip the wings of young enthusiasm, they had better content themselves with less ambitious aims."[27]

Through her own determination and skill, Machar was able to attract public attention as an intellectual journalist as early as the 1870s, which demonstrates that she had an unusual upbringing and thorough education for a woman of her time.[28] Because she left little behind but her work, a few letters, and the reminiscences of her literary friends, we cannot fully ascertain the impact various life events may have had on her development as a writer.[29] What is evident from these sources is that she was as much influenced by her experiences as a single, Christian, middle-class woman, educated well beyond the level of most women of her day, as she was by the social values with which she was raised, and the debates about Canada's destiny, and that of its female citizens, that absorbed her in her adult life.

Born in 1837 in Kingston, Ontario, she was the daughter of a founder and the second principal of Queen's College, the Reverend John Machar, a Scottish immigrant and Presbyterian minister, and his wife, Margaret, who was known in the community for her charitable work. Because females were not then considered suited to the professions, girls of her generation had to fight to get into grammar school and middle-class young women were not allowed to attend college.[30] When Machar was a child, there was a great deal of discussion about what kind of education would be suitable for girls, aside from basic literacy and math. Upper- and middle-class young women were expected to acquire the skills that would make them efficient household managers and hostesses, capable of promoting Christian values at home and in the community.[31] These expectations would have been reason enough for Machar's parents to want their gifted daughter to have an education that went well beyond the minimum. She attended a reputable boarding school in Montreal for a year, returning to her father's academic supervision and the extensive holdings in his library in Kingston.[32] Her studies absorbed her and gave her confidence in her intellectual abilities, preparing her to champion the cause of higher education for women in the universities that had denied her generation this privilege.

Machar, like most daughters, had to learn domestic management as well, especially as the family household was a centre of church, educational and intellectual activity. According to historian Jane Errington, the Kingston of Machar's childhood and young womanhood already had its own "rigid set of social conventions that confirmed the community's hierarchical structure and symbolically illustrated the relative ranking of its members."[33] The socially prominent women in the colony were expected to entertain business or other associates of their husbands during an era when the division between home and work was still not that strongly delineated.[34] Some sources suggest that the Machars were "well-to-do," which appears to be overstating the case.[35] But even if a minister's family was not considered "top drawer" in the economic sense, he would have been considered a community leader in the social and moral sense, and the Machar home accommodated many visitors. One of them was Oliver Mowat, a future Liberal premier of Ontario, whose father was an elder in Machar's church, and whose brother later taught at Queen's.[36] As an adult, Agnes Machar would pressure his government over higher education and the municipal franchise for women. She continued the family practice of hosting gatherings for intellectual, political and literary friends, and was certainly known to other writers who published in the same periodicals as she did.

It was her mother who taught her what women could accomplish as philanthropic community leaders.[37] Kingston and other towns in Upper Canada had a well-established social safety net of sorts, which relied on local church and other charity groups. Wives of prominent men, such as Margaret Machar, worked through benevolent, missionary and Bible societies and similar organizations. By mid-century, these women, rather than their husbands, had assumed leading roles in these endeavours, especially as the colony grew, and as the popular evangelical and secular crusades for social reform in the Anglo-American world took hold. Prominent Christian women were expected to transfer their moral leadership and responsibilities in the home to the community at large, especially to help the ill and the destitute.[38] These influences and the example her mother set were reflected in Agnes Maule Machar's journalism about the need for social reforms, including fair wages and healthy working conditions for working-class women, and her early involvement in a number of philanthropic groups and mission societies.

She also championed the right of the slowly growing numbers of professional women to work outside the home. In an era when most women grew up to be wives and mothers, Machar was neither, and she was acutely aware that there were many women like herself who would remain single or, for various reasons, have to make their own way in the world. A stigma was still attached to being unmarried, even though it was not unusual. Most girls in the Upper Canada of her generation had grown up hearing bachelors and "spinsters" being criticized from the pulpit and ridiculed in the press. Both men and women were expected to marry in order to contribute to the economic and moral stability of family, home and society; for a woman to choose not to do so was considered "unwomanly," regardless of the reasons. Nevertheless, many women married later than their mid-20s, and some not at all,[39] so while Machar's single state might have seemed regrettable to her peers, she was far from unique.

As an adult, she lived with her parents, and, when they died, with her brother John, a lawyer, social reform activist and member of the Knights of Labour. Her living arrangements were typical for a single, middle-class female of her day as women had no property rights and had to submit to the authority of father, brother or husband.[40] For single, perhaps financially dependent women such as herself, daughterly or sisterly duties, especially the major domestic responsibilities of running a household, or helping care for children, would have taken priority, for some of each day at least, over writing journalism, poetry, history or fiction.[41] It is also possible that she taught Sunday school, a common duty among educated church women.[42] For some years, probably later in life, she enjoyed the companionship of Matilda

Speers (d. 1950), her younger "faithful friend and helper," who figured in her will and whose grave in Kingston's Cataraqui Cemetery is adjacent to her own.[43] Tilly, as she was known, likely helped relieve Machar of some of her domestic burdens, allowing her more time and energy to read the historical and religious studies that so influenced her, and to put her own ideas into writing. Other friends, both female and male, valued her personally and professionally as well, including the writer and poet Ethelwyn Wetherald, who admired and encouraged her, and George Monro Grant, later a principal of Queen's University, who agreed with her on the value of higher education for women, but not on the importance of prohibition.[44]

Undoubtedly, Machar needed their support. It was still considered questionable for a woman to write learned tracts, especially in her own name. According to Wetherald, Machar had been writing under several pseudonyms from a young age, and went through the usual anguish of all beginners. Her mother tried to discourage her at first, fearing the "notoriety" that published writing might bring her. Possibly she simply did not want her daughter to be hurt by sneering public critiques of her hard work, and felt that it would be more modest and seemly for her to focus on doing good for other people, as she did herself with the Female Benevolent Society. The young Agnes Machar tended to shrink from publicity, but she seemed to be more willing to take on the challenge of being something of a public figure as she matured, even though she rarely wrote as a journalist under her own name.[45]

Perhaps in deference to her mother's wishes, she wrote anonymously until she was in her mid-30s, when she adopted Fidelis, meaning "faithful," the pen name with which she was most closely associated. According to Wetherald, she chose it for spiritual reasons, explaining, "Faithfulness is the quality I must value and care most to possess."[46] It was a common practice among both male and female writers to adopt a pen name, one that would establish a specific public persona, allow the writer the freedom to write in several, sometimes competing publications, and provide at least some privacy and protection from malevolent critics. Male magazine publishers of that period were already embroiled in discussions about whether or not articles and editorials should be signed or remain anonymous, mainly as a measure of their growing independence from party politics.[47] For a woman daring to venture into what was still considered the male literary sphere, the name she chose to use could take on a freighted meaning. The brave insisted on using their real names because they clearly wanted to make the point that women writers had something to contribute and should be respected. More often, they chose masculine or androgynous *noms de plume*, or just their initials with or without their family names, to hide their gender and give them "male" authority as writers and commentators. Others chose pen names to identify the writer with a dearly felt sentiment, such as the importance of spiritual faith in the case of Machar, who did not hide the fact that she was a woman, even though there were readers who simply assumed she was male.[48] By the 1890s, when female writers began writing regularly for women's pages in the daily newspapers and more commercial magazines, they generally adopted suitably feminine monikers to signal to their readers that they were "womanly" women with domestic acumen and motherly instincts (see Chapter 2 in this volume).

Their choice of pen name, the self-effacing language many women used in their writing, and their habit of quoting prominent authorities, especially male experts but also prominent female ones, all contributed to a literary culture in which they often denied or minimized their own authority.[49] Machar often cited male expertise on women's rights, suggesting that her confidence sometimes wavered, but her voice, perhaps strengthened by her religious convictions, could be firm as well, especially when she invoked lists of historical and contemporary female icons to bolster her arguments. She could also be sharply critical of smug Christian dogmatists who spurned the poor, businessmen who oppressed their workers, society mothers who encouraged their daughters to waste their days on trifles, and die-hard conservatives who continued to oppose women's right to an education and fair wages years after they began attending university and had proved their mettle there and in new occupations.[50]

Scholars have found it a challenge to pin a label on Machar's politics. Their various perspectives on her feminism and social activism have reflected the expanding literature and shifting feminist analyses in the fields of women's, social and labour history over the last 30 years. At different times, and by different writers, Machar has been referred to as conventional, conservative, moderate and liberal but never as radical. Several feminist scholars, especially those writing in the 1970s and 1980s, found Machar's outlook disappointingly restrained.[51] But, as Hallman has argued, most female activists at the time combined a plea for equal justice as a matter of human rights with maternal feminist arguments. She believes that, seen in the context of her male colleagues' more deeply entrenched attitudes, Machar was not as much of a conservative as other writers have suggested.[52]

Influenced, perhaps, by some of the more progressive men around her, like George Monro Grant, Machar believed in the liberal principles of individual equality in a utilitarian society, that is, one in which one strives to do the most good for the most citizens. She was fond of quoting the British writer John Stuart Mill, whose democratic model of freedom of the press appealed to her, as did the ideas of Mill and his partner, Harriet Taylor Mill, on women's equality.[53]

This liberal outlook, combined with her maternal feminism and her Christian social reform beliefs, formed the core of Machar's analysis on education, equal pay, temperance and suffrage. Her approach was not to demand rights for herself or anyone else, but to rationally lay out the facts of the matter under discussion as she saw them, debate others with respect and strive with a Christian spirit for conciliation and consensus. No matter which topic she tackled, her rhetoric, as Janice Fiamengo has noted, was "impassioned, rigorously logical, full of moral conviction and designed to change minds."[54]

She could be inconsistent on some issues, however, especially when it came to the questions of class and female labourers. Machar did not believe in a socialist or feminist revolution, but rather wanted change to come from within capitalism and patriarchy. She was uneasy with both communism, which she saw as the antithesis of Christianity,[55] and outspoken demands for women's rights. She did not discuss women of other races in her journalism, except as icons of other religions or cultures, such as Hinduism, a knowledge that reflected her interest in Christian missions overseas.[56]

Machar's intelligence, her religious outlook, her measured reasoning and her maternal feminism might have made it difficult for male intellectuals to dismiss her easily. In Christian circles, women were responsible for the "moral housekeeping" of their home, and were expected to guide and comfort male and female family members.[57] Machar took on this role publicly, which was consistent with her oft-stated position that educated women must work to improve the world. She was using her intellect and her writing, as well as her reform activities, to do so. In general, Machar appears to have earned a fair amount of respect in the tightly knit intellectual journalism circle of her day. She took her place among the men, debated with them frankly, corrected them when they patronized or misquoted her, and advocated ideas about Christianity, Canadian nationalism, social justice and the role of women that more conservative commentators viewed as contentious. Later, she also publicly debated prominent women over the issue of protective labour legislation for working-class women, repeating her arguments in her journalism as well as in her fiction.[58]

The views of women's rights activists like her were, however, criticized by some prominent editors and writers such as Goldwin Smith, who was for a time quite influential in journalistic circles in Toronto. Smith moved to Canada in 1871 after achieving prominence as a writer and professor in Britain and the United States. It was Smith, working with Graeme Mercer Adam, who helped manage *Canadian Monthly* and was the editor "in everything but name" for its first few years, before leaving to start his own publication, *The Bystander*.[59] Adam, who was more supportive of women than Smith, continued to labour at *Canadian Monthly* and edited its successor, *Rose-Belford's Review*, for most of its short life until it died in 1882. But Adam, too, did publish writers who could be quite "vicious" about women's rights, as well as the opinions of those who supported expanded public roles for the female sex.[60] The next year, Smith, who had temporarily abandoned *The Bystander*, replaced Charles G.D. Roberts as editor of *The Week*. In a letter to her older friend and, possibly, mentor, Louisa Murray, Machar confided that she found Smith controlling as an editor, allowing only "the appearance of papers ... which echo his own opinions or else have no opinions at all." She believed Roberts, the magazine's first editor, left because of Smith's interference.[61] For Smith's part, he often praised female writers and supported higher education for women, but through the 1870s to the 1890s, presented a consistent argument: that women properly belonged in their own sphere of home and social life, separate from men, not with them in political or business life.[62]

Other writers, British, American and Canadian, some of them anonymous, used sarcasm to attack women's rights supporters.[63] Machar took umbrage at magazine material that denigrated any woman "who desires to cultivate the powers God has given her." As an example, she criticized an article that appeared in *Blackwood's Magazine*, which made fun of the efforts of women in English provincial society who were trying to improve themselves by going to lectures and other cultural functions, the author insinuating that they were merely trying to be fashionable. "Few of them can shine by good looks, and they are bound to cultivate a habit of babbling." Machar abandoned her usual conciliatory approach in her response: "That remarks so flippant and vulgar in tone should appear in a first-class magazine is only an illustration of the essentially low ideal of womanhood which still clings to many conservative minds.... But whatever chaff may mingle with the grain of genuine self-culture in English women, there can hardly be two opinions as to the arrogance, the unchivalrous and unmanly spirit of the man who goes out of his way to bespatter with what mockery he may any attempt—however rudimentary—of women to rise to some higher objects of interest."[64]

The approved cultural image of perfect womanhood still centred on women's activities in the home, not what they were trying to learn outside of it.[65] Machar was on a mission to have women rethink this idealized role, at least up to a point. She had already seen changes in expectations of women over the previous generation, she wrote, which could only help them improve further. The idea that they were primarily wives and mothers had not altered much; it was just that now they were expected to do more to be companions and helpmeets to their husbands, an attitude that had taken on some social currency by the 1870s and one that she shared. Their efforts to become better educated and more skilled could only benefit themselves, their marriages, their children and Canadian society, in her view.[66]

Machar's essential ideas about the value of education did not change through the 1870s to the 1890s, but reflected the ongoing struggles women were having in their attempts to gain entrance to institutions such as Queen's and the University of Toronto. Her first journalism in *Canadian Monthly* on this issue was written in 1875 when universities in Canada were still reserved for privileged young men who were going on to a career in the professions. Those who opposed the presence of women in institutions of higher learning argued that women lacked the reasoning powers of men. Machar did not disagree but declared that it was not the fault of the women but of the education most of them had received. "Had boys been, for generations past, educated on the same miserably superficial system which has been the rule with girls, filling their minds with an undigested chaos of heterogeneous facts, and expanding their energies on a number of so-called accomplishments, all imperfectly acquired, it is probable that their minds would have exhibited much of the superficiality and inaccuracy which have so long been held to demonstrate the great mental inferiority of women." Anyway, she went on, not all women, given the law of averages and their higher proportion in the population, will marry and have children, although, she hastened to add, "this is her happiest destiny" when the marriage is "a good heart union." There would be many women who would have to earn their own bread, and for that, they needed more than basic knowledge.[67]

By the late 1870s, the question of higher education for women, and co-education, had become highly politicized. In 1877 Canada's first female doctor, Emily Stowe, who earned her medical degree in the United States,[68] founded the Toronto Women's Literary Club. It provided a forum where women presented and discussed papers on history, literature and politics, and debated topics such as higher education and professions for women, their working conditions, the municipal franchise and other aspects of women's rights. These meetings, essentially educational in nature, helped prepare the members for more involvement in public life and, eventually, the fight for suffrage. Machar, who still resided in Kingston, was an honorary member of the TWLC and had her papers and poetry read there. The club was part of a web of women activists. Many of the members, including Machar and Sarah Curzon, also belonged to the Women's Christian Temperance Union and other reform groups. While the club's activities were regularly reported in the *Toronto Globe*, possibly by one of its own members, newspaper writers in general tended to joke about such organizations, sneering at the very idea that women should read, discuss or lecture on complex intellectual topics, let alone entertain papers from their sister members about women's place or women's work. Historian Heather Murray writes that they were treated with more suspicion than were philanthropic women's clubs, partly because their activities were out of the public eye.[69]

Machar's articles on higher education and other matters echoed the aims of the women's groups, like the TWLC, in which she was involved. By 1878, shortly after George Monro Grant became principal, Queen's allowed women into its arts programs.[70] It took another six years for women to be admitted to the University of Toronto, where the issue was especially controversial. When the TWLC met with Principal Daniel Wilson in February 1882, he rejected its request that women be allowed to attend class because he believed that women should be educated separately from men. Commenting in *Rose-Belford's* a month later on the "crab-like" nature of women's progress, and his "hard and unjust" decision, Machar noted that Queen's had already successfully set the precedent. Why then, she asked, should there be "a serious question in the minds of many as to the propriety of admitting them as pupils to university classrooms ... lest such a step should prove subversive to 'due order and discipline.'" That rationale not only underestimated students of both sexes, she wrote, but was a moot point, as decorum at Queen's had actually improved after women were admitted. To the objections of some provincial politicians that women had their own sphere in life and were not suited to a university education, Machar responded that "neither all men nor all women are formed in one unvarying mold" and that some women did have intellectual interests and abilities that should be nurtured through a university education. "Where such exceptional talent exists, should not a wise State make provisions for its proper training and development? Or is it to be suppressed and wasted because it happens to exist in the brain of a woman?"[71]

The TWLC succeeded through a public petition in persuading the provincial legislature to approve co-education at the University of Toronto, but the stubborn Wilson resisted until he was finally forced to comply with a government order in council in 1884. By that time the TWLC had become the Canadian Woman's Suffrage Association, with a Toronto branch.[72]

Bengough, who actually supported co-education, lampooned Wilson, the Suffrage Association and college girls in a cartoon he published in *Grip* in October 1884, when women were first admitted to the University of Toronto. He depicted Wilson as a stern professor, holding a switch, addressing the female students. Behind him a frumpy and witch-like representative of the Suffrage Association supervised his reluctant welcome of her charges, who ranged in appearance from conventionally pretty to junior intellectual. A notice on the lectern forbidding "flirting" and "mashing" was a reference to fears that the female students would become morally loose. They might also join their male classmates in striking and boycotting classes, a form of rebellion then common on campuses. Furthermore, there was the subversive implication that a university education would turn these young women into crone-like suffragists themselves.[73] While this cartoon can be read as critique of exaggerated masculine fears of female intellectual aspirations, it made fun as well of the women who had them.

Caricatures of the "College Girl" were common in late 19th-century publications on both sides of the Atlantic. She was most often depicted as

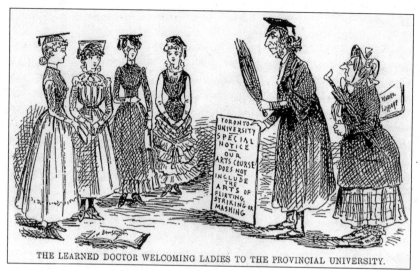

THE LEARNED DOCTOR WELCOMING LADIES TO THE PROVINCIAL UNIVERSITY.

J.W. Bengough cartoon from *Grip*, 11 October 1884.

someone who had intellectual pretensions, or simply could never have the brain of a man. Her older mentor figure, the single, educated spinster, was often satirized in the press as a "bluestocking," a dismissive expression suggesting that women who competed intellectually with men, especially in the public sphere, were ridiculous, selfish and beyond male control. Because many women who lobbied for higher education also favoured some form of the franchise for women, bluestockings and suffragists could be one and the same in the public mind.[74]

Machar recognized that social conservatives like Goldwin Smith and Daniel Wilson were just upset over major changes in what they saw as the right order of things, especially regarding relations between the sexes. Writing in September 1878, she noted that an "able and respected" writer in *Rose-Belford's*, whom she did not name, had earlier asked of its readers: "Strike man's work out of the world and what remains? From all the benefits that women enjoy, strike off those for which they are indebted to man, and what remains?" To which she replied, one might ask the same thing if the sex roles were reversed. The writer, D. Fowler, had argued that men did more work in the world than women as a rule, and "repayments" for these "obligations" must precede "rights." Fowler further argued that only a woman with the late writer Harriet Martineau's "power," intelligence and competence could succeed at her chosen career, and Martineau was only a "very moderate" believer in women's rights because she recognized her exceptional status.[75] His remarks about Martineau likely struck a chord with Machar, as both writers supported higher education for women and were well-known "female authors," a label that tended to attract critical scrutiny, especially from male peers.[76]

Rather than argue that skill has no sex, Machar wrote that education could only enhance the skills women already had; for example, a woman could become a doctor "and at the same time, be none the less, a true, high-minded, *womanly* woman."[77] Medicine was a natural profession for women with their nurturing instincts, she argued, and women doctors were better suited to shy children and modest female patients who felt intimidated by male physicians. Machar used her studies in the classics to good account, educating her readers by reciting the long history of women healers, concluding it was simple prejudice that kept 19th-century women out of medicine.[78]

Her line of argument was often used by other supporters of women going into the profession. The resistance of most male doctors was due not only to conservative attitudes toward women, but to their feeling that women were associated with healing cults, which would be detrimental to the establishment of medicine as a respected profession. Above all, they were afraid of competition in a field that many of them already saw as overcrowded.[79] Machar felt that the fact that women were drawn to medicine despite the barriers and the prejudice against them was a point in their favour, and that once women had won their battle and the medical men started treating them as respected equals, "things will fall to their natural level; when it will probably be found that there is work enough for even exceptional women without interfering with the interests of 'the more worthy gender.'"[80] She was, however, quite aware of contemporary attitudes against the mixing of the sexes when sensitive topics such as the human body were discussed. She assured her readers that female medical students could be taught in separate colleges from the men and could learn to tend to the needs of other women and of children, or they could become medical missionaries, another one of her ideal professions for women. In this and other ways, she did not support full co-education.[81] Missionary work was one of the few roles for women outside the home that her own church officially sanctioned, but she clearly took a more liberal view of what they might accomplish, perhaps because she was very active in her own church's missionary society and knew what the overseas work would entail.[82]

There were few other professions women could enter in those days other than teaching and nursing and the allied occupations of librarian and social worker. Women had taught, nursed and cared for their family members and neighbours for years in the colonies before schools and hospitals were established, so the idea that they should do it more formally was not radical in itself. These were seen to be nurturing, care-giving occupations that suited women's nature, while allowing work outside the home for middle-class women, and some social mobility to those from the working class.[83]

Machar approved of these opportunities for much the same reasons but felt women should have more occupations to choose from, fair treatment on the job and equal pay for equal work when warranted.[84] Their numbers had increased in more areas of the workforce by that time, not just in the professions but in shops, offices and the telephone exchanges as well. Women were still paid less than men, however.[85] It was assumed that a single woman who was not financially supported by a male relative needed only a living wage until she married and her husband could take care of her. Her husband, on the other hand, would be supporting her and their children and needed a "family wage." This was, of course, a very narrow view that culturally reinforced notions of "separate spheres" and ignored the economic reality that both middle-class women who had no male support, and most working-class women whose husbands received little pay, had to work to help support their families.[86]

When Machar tackled the subject of equal pay, she was very direct. In 1879 she told her *Rose-Belford's Review* readers that male chivalry toward women was no excuse or substitute for paying them poorly, and was simply a charade that masked mercenary motives. "The principle of paying women less than men for the same work is one so essentially unjust that only a thoughtless and blind conventionality could so long have perpetuated it.... The moment that the principle of self-interest comes into play, the average man is more ready to grind down, to over-reach, to underpay, to cheat outright a woman than a man, just because he thinks he can do it with more impunity. It is small wonder if women feel that the compensation of a thin veneer of social courtesy for the ability to earn an honest independence is very like offering a stone for bread."[87]

As a strong advocate of education, she felt that female teachers, for example, should be trained and paid as well as their male colleagues.[88] Teaching was the second-largest occupation for women, after domestic service, but the school boards were among the worst offenders when it came to unequal pay scales. The prevalent maternal ethic meant that females were confined to teaching the youngest children while men taught the more senior students, which meant that women teachers earned half as much as the men.[89]

In December 1875, the *Canadian Illustrated News* had published a magazine cover that acknowledged the growing but still limited number of occupations for women, "at work" in their various tasks, such as teaching children, serving customers and caring for the sick. Most of these women appeared contented, a romanticized notion at a time when women of different ages and backgrounds in all occupations were poorly paid. There were no exhausted factory girls, or overworked domestic servants, in this montage. All the women seemed happily engaged in their activities, suggesting that their work was really no threat to the status quo. The artist, Vincenz

Katzler, was Viennese, so on the face of it, the illustration had nothing to do with women's occupations in Canada. The fact that the magazine chose to publish it, however, suggests it would have resonated for Canadian readers, who had very limited ideas, in the 1870s, as to what women could accomplish, assuming that they were cut out only for certain kinds of care-giving occupations, while men were suited to many more.[90]

In reality, nothing could compare with the sheer physical drudgery endured by many working-class women, who badly needed better wages. By 1871, 34 percent of the women in the paid labour force in Toronto were working in factories, including the textile industry.[91] From its beginnings in 1877, the Toronto Women's Literary Club had lobbied for civic reforms such as regulated hours and rest breaks, and separate toilets for factory workers and shop clerks.[92] Much of Machar's concern centred on these women, their husbands and their families. She deplored the awful conditions under which they worked in factories and shops, the "wretched, rickety board hovels"[93] in which they lived, and their paltry wages. She upheld all workers' rights to organize,[94] and believed that businessmen should pay their workers fairly and provide decent housing for them, that municipal institutions should provide make-work projects in the winter when jobs were scarce, and that churches and social reformers should encourage temperance and support prohibition. She felt that it was impoverishment and despair more than anything else that led working-class men to drink, and sometimes their wives as well, but alcohol addiction only brought more poverty and physical abuse, from which the mothers and children should be protected.[95]

Machar did not confine her efforts to writing about the problems of poverty, poor wages and harsh working and living conditions for women, but was an activist in the cause through her membership in a number of evolving social reform groups. They included the Women's Christian Temperance Union, which, by 1891, had 9000 members across Canada, 4000 of them in Ontario. The WCTU was initially concerned with prohibition, but broadened its agenda to include other issues.[96] Machar also became a leading member of the fast-growing National Council of Women of Canada, founded in 1893 as an umbrella group for a number of middle-class women's organizations across the country, including the WCTU. By 1900, the NCWC linked 7 national women's organizations and 21 of its own Local Councils of Women from Prince Edward Island to Vancouver Island, each one consisting of representatives of different local women's societies and institutions. The Toronto local council, for example, quickly became established with 23 affiliated women's groups in that city alone, most of them representing various women's benevolent and social reform organizations. The many social reform goals of the NCWC and its member groups included better education and professional training for middle-class women and improved working conditions for women working in factories and shops,[97] who found it almost impossible to make ends meet.[98] Machar was an executive member of the national group and president and founder of the Local Council of Women in Kingston, which she represented at the National Council meetings. When she wrote in *The Week* about the continuing exploitation of working-class woman in the 1890s, it was in the context of what the NCWC was or was not doing about improving workplace conditions for them, not so much for their own good but to protect their health as the future mothers of strong Canadian children. Factories, which could be particularly dangerous, were often noisy, filthy and badly ventilated. Women who worked in the "sweating system," often sewing at home at piece rates, were often exhausted. Shop girls were kept on their feet all day, a requirement that was commonly thought to be dangerous to their reproductive organs. Women without children barely scraped by, and those with dependents actually fell short of the cost of living, which, in 1889 in Toronto, was four dollars a week.[99]

In 1895 and 1896, Machar and her Kingston Council of Women tried to get the National Council to adopt a resolution supporting a nine-hour day for female factory workers, many of whom worked longer hours in order to be allowed Saturday afternoon as well as Sunday off.[100] She reported on the proceedings, carrying the debate to the pages of *The Week*. Shorter hours should not mean less pay, she argued, because the workers would be more efficient and would produce just as much.[101] Machar also recommended shorter hours for shop workers, inspections of establishments with as few as one or two workers—an acknowledgment of the poor conditions of the "sweating system"—and a Dominion Factory Act to standardize regulations across the country. She concluded by appealing to the economic interests of her middle-class readers, who likely included council members, as well as to their maternalism, patriotism and Christian spirit. "It is impossible, apart from higher considerations, that the real prosperity of the country at large could ever be promoted by the physical, mental or moral degradation of those on whose efficient and healthy lives, the well-being of a future generation must to a great extent depend."[102]

Many of the National Council members were philanthropists and wives of business leaders, and should have known about these unhealthy working conditions, but they hesitated to pressure for improvements immediately. Machar told her readers that following "an earnest discussion," they had unanimously decided to have their local councils gather as much information as possible on working conditions for female factories workers so they could consider the matter again at their next annual meeting.[103] Three months later, Machar found herself defending that resolution in print against the sneers of another periodical, *Saturday Night*, and the Trades and Labour Council, which had concluded that the NCWC had simply shelved a resolution asking for a reduction in working hours for factory women. Some members at the meeting, she explained, were afraid that such protective legislation would result in making employers less inclined to hire females, that "the alternative seemed to lie between starvation and a strain of overwork which enfeebles the constitutions of many of our future wives and mothers, and so must have its natural results on the enfeebled constitution of another generation." Other council women, felt, on the contrary, that the labour market would eventually adjust itself to new regulations, as it had in the past, and all would be well. But the basic problem was that the members did not initially feel qualified to take a strong stand in either direction, and would have been criticized if they had. She ended with an invitation to the Trades and Labour Council and other informed parties to send in their suggestions to the NCWC.[104]

When the women's council met again the following year, Machar wrote that its members would again consider the issue of shorter working hours for factory women, despite some of their apprehensions, for "even those who engage actively in philanthropic work sometimes seem to work under a dread of in some way overstepping the limits of a woman's sphere." It was their duty, however, to consider these things, as every good mother wants the community to be a livable place for future generations. The avowed philosophy of the NCWC—"the application of the Golden Rule to law, custom and society"—was one that strongly appealed to Machar. She felt that this principle, properly utilized, "would soon solve all our social problems and restore the social health of the community."[105] But other influential members still felt that women would not be able to compete for jobs if they were singled out for protective legislation. At no time during these gatherings did the NCWC recommend that equal pay become law as well.[106]

After the 1895 general meeting, some journalists in the popular press accused the council members of being more interested in helping factory women than improving the conditions under which they kept the domestics they hired to help them run their homes.[107] Servants, especially the Irish, and their Canadian mistresses were often the butt of cartoons and jokes in magazines such as *Canadian Illustrated News*, no matter how seriously each woman might take her own working or supervisory role in real life.[108] The NCWC members and women like them were concerned with how to best manage their household help when the two class cultures were essentially foreign to each other, while the servants wanted better working conditions and more respect.

In 1891 domestic servants made up 41 percent of the women in the labour force, the largest single group. Many of them were immigrants, mainly from the British Isles, who had come from poor or unhappy circumstances, and were easy targets for suspicious legal authorities. They seldom stayed in one place long and, when they could, took jobs in factories and shops, because they disliked the low social status, poor pay and little personal freedom of domestic service.[109] Their employers were still constantly complaining that it was hard to get good help. In writing about the domestic issue in *The Week*, Machar acknowledged that council members might feel conflicted about the discussion, but insisted that women like themselves were the ones who must tend to grievances such as long hours of work. She took care, however, to criticize both servant and mistress. "No doubt the hours during which domestic servants are required to be on duty are often far too long, even to an inhuman extent, and the monotony of the ever-recurring round of household tasks, with little outside interests to relieve it, is often very trying, especially to undisciplined natures with few resources within themselves. On the other hand, the natural incapacity and almost total lack of preliminary training for their work is one cause of the unduly long hours of work, which with greater skill and method on the part of the worker, might be greatly shortened."

Another problem was the living conditions in many of the homes. Better hygiene and "a higher development of conscience" among employers were Machar's somewhat mild suggestions for improvements to servants' sleeping quarters in damp basements or cramped attics. She and the NCWC also advocated the age-old remedy of domestic training schools for young women in a bid to standardize domestic service and remove some of the social stigma attached to it.[110]

Her next article on the council's discussion of the matter was partly prompted by an unnamed male correspondent who claimed to have done an extensive survey of the conditions of domestic help and found them wanting. She took him at his word and reminded mistresses of their duties to their servants, appealing to their Christian consciences and maternal attitudes. They should, she wrote, at the very least, have Sunday off as their day of rest, "to which, in the very terms of the commandment, they are entitled. "May we not hope that the day will come when every such mistress will regard herself as much responsible for the comfort and welfare of a young female domestic in her house as she would for that of a young guest, and will devote to her a portion of the same motherly care?"[111]

Despite her attempts to be even-handed in her coverage of the NCWC's debates, and the frustration she might have felt at its members' lengthy attempts to reach consensus, Machar clearly was more impatient than most of them to see changes in the conditions of women's work. The council, however, was slow to respond with substantial recommendations to improve factory and shop conditions.[112] As domestic servants were not covered under legislation, little was done officially to improve their circumstances.[113] The NCWC did, with some ambivalence, foster the professionalization of nursing and the founding of the Victorian Order of Nurses for Canada.[114]

Mindful of the importance of the council's reputation as a women's group, Machar was always very careful in the way she wrote about its deliberations and its leaders,[115] perhaps because some of its discussions were contentious, particularly regarding full women's suffrage, which it was slow to endorse. While she defended the right of women to become lawyers, and did not question their intellectual grasp of the law or their ability to speak well in public,[116] she seemed to draw the line there and did not suggest it could be a stepping stone for women who wanted to enter politics, as it already was for men. There was a general prejudice against outspoken "platform women," even social reformers,[117] one that Machar seemed to share, at least earlier in her career. Writing in 1875, she declared: "It is only a half culture that makes 'masculine' women—the shallow and noisy pretenders who have dragged the 'Rights of Woman' in the mire till they have made the very term a by-word!"[118] It seems that the same prejudice that kept women out of law and politics also discouraged many of them from demanding the vote, as even the most progressive women demurred at the idea that the verbal rough and tumble of public debate suited their nature.[119] Unsigned doggerel in *Grip*, published in May 1878, underscored those assumptions, and made fun of women who did dare to demand their rights. "The Female Righter" read in part:

> I want the right to make a speech,
> Before a yelling crowd,
> And high upon a platform screech,
> And objurgate out loud.
> I want the franchise of the land
> Which now the men have got,
> To vote on all I understand
> And all that I do not.[120]

In Canada, suffrage supporters timorously started showing their colours, however. In May 1879, someone writing as "M" on "The Woman Question" declared in *Rose-Belford's Review* that it was time women were granted the full franchise, for "she can never shape her own career, never be the arbiter of her own destiny, so long as she has no voice in framing the laws under which she lives, and to which she is amenable." M's readers were further reminded that twenty-five years earlier, "how few—and those counted as womanish men, mannish women, fanatics, or lunatics—were willing to confess any leaning toward, or friendship for, the so-called 'Woman Movement?' Today, how many of the keenest politicians, quick to scent the coming breeze, are avowing themselves in its favour!"[121]

The fact that this writer presented these opinions anonymously demonstrates that they were still quite unpopular. Perhaps in response to this article, Machar tackled the subject the following month. Taking her cue from the British social historian Charles Kingsley, one of her heroes, she coun-selled women to be patient and not too noisy in their demands. But, in this case, she was referring to extending the municipal franchise to women who had property, a reform the TWLC backed for tactical reasons, which they later regretted because of its limited application.[122] Machar wrote that with-holding the vote from female property holders would one day be seen as "an antiquated survival of semi-cultivation. But this result will never come by empty agitation." Noting that an anti-suffrage member of the Ontario Leg-islature once claimed that women were not "clamouring" for the franchise, she remarked: "The women of Ontario might well have replied that to their minds, 'clamour' was no special gratification for this or any other privilege, and that they were quite content to wait with patience and dignity till a growing common sense should gracefully yield that which they do not crave as a personal boon, and would seek and use only for the public good."[123]

The importance of the franchise had not initially been a major issue for the TWLC. According to Murray, "The TWLC's goals remind us that, for many late nineteenth century women, it was a desire for education, rather than a more abstractly envisaged 'vote' that moved them to action and organ-ization." Nevertheless, as Murray also suggests, the club's broader agenda, including its desire for municipal reforms, likely sparked the realization that the full franchise would be necessary to bring them about, leading to the TWLC's subsequent reconstitution as the Canadian Woman's Suffrage Association in March 1883.[124] The previous year, a limited municipal fran-chise had been given to spinsters or widows who owned property, but the new association clearly felt that was not enough.[125]

Cartoons that appeared in *Grip* at the time seemed to be supportive of the women lobbying the attorney-general of Ontario, Oliver Mowat, who wanted neither prohibition nor suffrage, but seemed to pretend otherwise. Bengough depicted him as being disingenuous and indecisive in his pur-ported support. This was brave of the cartoonist, as his brother Thomas and sister Mary both worked for Mowat's Liberal administration and the Grip Printing and Publishing Company was its major printer for some years.[126] In this cartoon, Mowat is receiving a petition for suffrage in the fall of 1883, some months after the TWLC was reconstituted as the Suffrage Association. Mowat is depicted as being deceitful, clearly assuring the women that he would take their request seriously, while quietly discarding it behind his back, and by implication, behind theirs. The women are set types—over-weight matrons are usually perceived to be overbearing as well; the bespec-tacled older bluestockings are clearly not really "womanly women"; while the younger one and the girl signify political naïveté, too young and unso-phisticated to understand the issues, misled by the older women in one way and by Mowat in another. The setting suggests that his office is as shabby as his treatment of these women.[127] Although the artist was committed to

GRAND TRIUMPH" FOR THE WOMAN SUFFRAGISTS.
MR. MOWAT TAKES THEIR PETITION INTO HIS CONSIDERATION !!

J.W. Bengough cartoon from *Grip*, 24 October 1883.

suffrage because he saw it as a way to bring about prohibition, and also delighted in making fun of the anti-suffragist Goldwin Smith, he was actually ambivalent about gender roles and women activists himself. As Cumming has noted of Bengough's work, "There is no vision of women actually taking part in the raw life of politics. The idea seems to have been that women would vote for righteous causes and then withdraw into their homes."[128]

Machar did eventually join a NCWC committee studying the extension of the franchise, but the articles she wrote for *The Week* in 1895 and 1896 were focused mainly on the issues the women discussed at annual meetings. Because the council's member groups were divided over the franchise, the organization did not endorse it until 1910. The Ontario WCTU, of which she was also a member, was slow to support full suffrage as well. In fact, Machar did not write in support of the vote for women until the campaign came to a head during the First World War (see Chapter 3 of this volume.)[129] Given her commitment to other reforms, and her impatience with social injustice, it seems inconsistent of her to counsel patience on the issue of the vote for women. But because she left little in the way of personal papers, we are not likely to ever learn why she held back. It is possible that the brooding editorial presence of Goldwin Smith at *The Week* discouraged her in some way, or that she saw the council as too divided for her to take a public stand as one of its leaders and spokeswomen, or perhaps she never did change her initial stance that women should wait quietly and patiently for the inevitable to happen. After *The Week* folded in 1896, Machar wrote less journalism, and turned her attention mostly to history and fiction for both adults and children.[130]

Agnes Maule Machar had come of age in Upper Canada in the mid-19th century, when middle-class women were barely educated, and were expected to remain in the home as daughters, wives and mothers and engage only in womanly duties, such as charity, in the outside world. She never fit this proscribed role for a number of reasons. She was well educated, she never married, and she chose to follow a varied literary and journalistic career in the public eye, as well as become engaged as a social reform activist. She couched her writing and her activism for women's rights in the light of her Christian faith, her liberal philosophical beliefs, her maternal feminism and her patriotic fervour for her young country. Even though her approach was welcome in some circles, her life choices and advocacy on behalf of women made her, and women like her, vulnerable to criticism and resistance from male editors such as Goldwin Smith and the butt of cartoons and doggerel, even from reform-minded men such as J.W. Bengough. Eventually, expanding commercialism in the periodical industry robbed her of her platform as an advocacy journalist, but she was able to use other literary genres to continue her social reform mission through her writing.

Rather than being pilloried for her less radical views, Machar should be understood in the context of the entrenched, if shifting, Christian values that permeated Canadian society in the 19th century, as well as the ongoing media debates about the quality and future of the young country and the expanding "separate sphere" of its female citizens. These factors influenced both the ways in which "exceptional" women like her could demand changes that would benefit Canadian women, but ones that would allow them only limited progress. Her position as an educated, middle-class, Christian woman guaranteed her a leading advocacy role as a journalist and activist on behalf of women who wanted a university education and professional training, as long as she made sure to emphasize how these new opportunities would transform them into more "womanly women" and better mothers for God and the new nation. Her approach to protective legislation for working-class women incorporated essentially the same ideals and mission.

Her position in the NCWC made her an apologist for its less progressive and outspoken members, who offered any number of excuses for not demanding immediate, forceful reforms, such as better conditions for their own domestic servants, equal pay and the vote. Their timidity, gender biases and class interests, and the more conservative tenets of their faiths shored up her own biases and stifled her better reformist instincts as effectively as would an editor's blue pencil or a derogatory cartoon. There were few prominent women journalists in that era, and in the eyes of her contemporaries, she was respected enough to be read, and even debated, which was seen as accomplishment enough. Her impressive grasp of history and philosophy, her colourful, didactic style, and her best intentions, combined with a true educator's drive, allowed her to teach her readers what she thought they needed to know to bring about change.

CHAPTER 2

Laced In and Let Down

*Toronto Journalists Write about Fashion
and Health in the Daily Press, 1890–1900*

*Will the millennium ever arrive, I wonder, when we women can wear
easy shoes, larger gowns, less back hair piled up on our craniums, travel
about in fact as though we had lungs and hearts and livers, and not do
as we now do, push these organs out of place with whalebone and steel
and buttons and tight sleeves and neckbands?*
—Kit of the *Daily Mail*[1]

D uring the late 19th century, women were not only taking on new roles
in society, but they were also deciding how to dress for them. Many
turned for guidance to the daily newspapers, where a new professional,
the woman journalist, was offering news and commentary about the world
of fashion and advice for women on how to dress and present themselves.
That advice often included encouraging their readers to adopt dress that was
healthy, becoming and comfortable, and warning them about the dangers
of tight-lacing corsets, or other dubious practices. Still, the economics of
the newspaper business, which depended more and more on advertising,
ensured that the journalists did not encourage an outright revolution in
women's attire.

This chapter focuses on the specific functions of the fashion features
in Canada's daily newspapers, institutions with their own political and
economic priorities during the late 19th century. Contemporary cultural
attitudes about consumerism, gender and their work as women in the male-
dominated media all shaped the messages that the Toronto writers discussed in this chapter relayed to their readers about fashion and women's
place in the world. As journalists writing material for female readers, they

were intellectually "laced in," separated from the exciting male world of "hard news" journalism, and confined to a constraining corset of the mind that was designed to enhance their feminine sensibilities rather than their eclectic curiosity. Their editors and their readers also expected them to be upright, matronly and moralistic advice givers to the hundreds of people who wrote in seeking guidance.[2] These journalists traversed this narrow world of women's furbelows and fripperies carefully, however, aware that loosening their intellectual stays or letting down their hair might be interpreted as a serious threat to the commercial interests of the newspapers for which they toiled.

Despite any frustration they felt about this state of affairs, the journalists did enjoy, at least with their eyes, the dresses, hats, mantles and coats that were the mainstay of their fashion features. They were consumers, too. But they also knew that too much intellectual or moral rebellion might cost them paid work, public recognition and even the modest freedoms that their journeys into the everyday work world afforded them. Consequently, their columns about fashion were multi-textured and often contradictory, reflecting their conflicting feelings of resentment, frustration, concern and enthusiasm. Although they encouraged their readers to experiment with healthy dress reform, a movement that advocated more hygienic and less restrictive clothing for women,[3] they also tended to draw the line at any perceived masculinity in women's dress, especially anything resembling trousers.

Women's fashion features of all kinds were an expression of the growing consumerism of the late 19th century, spurred on by the growth of department stores, and fostered in turn by the advertising that financed the newspapers. The advertising industry was still young, and most newspaper editors were not fully aware of the advantages of what we would identify today as niche marketing—in this case, a ready-made female audience.[4] Consequently, their approach to having a women's page, with its own woman editor, could be inconsistent. Sometimes, newspapers would carry plenty of advertising but no women's page as such, or would publish occasional articles from anonymous writers using feminine pen names. In 1893, for example, the Toronto *Evening News* published only a regular fashion illustration called "Our Daily Fashion Plate."[5] Finally, in 1899, the *News* introduced "The Woman's Page," edited by "Donna" and featuring contributions from "Ikabel," "Irene," "Gretchen," "Cleo" and, finally, "Isadore,"[6] who went on to become the editor of the same page, while most of the other writers disappeared.[7] The use of pen names came from an earlier literary tradition and served several functions. It allowed a writer to be anonymous, to freelance for competing publications, and to create an attractive public persona with whom readers could identity.[8]

The fashion features that appeared in Canadian newspapers included a broad range of articles, from lavishly illustrated fashion spreads from the

American syndicates to brief paragraphs on the latest in spring hats, hurriedly written by the local women's page editor or a freelance journalist. Some newspapers had women's pages, which usually appeared on Saturdays, and consisted of an eclectic mix of articles on many issues of interest to women, both social and political, which testified to the energy, interests and imaginations of the journalists who wrote them. A typical page might begin with a discussion of the latest fashions available at a local department store, or a serious essay about the writer's recent visit to a street shelter for women, or a debate about suffrage, or, perhaps, a light-hearted and flowery description of a spring walk. This main feature might be followed by a description of a local society ball, gossip about royalty or famous entertainers gleaned from American or overseas newspapers, recipes, sewing tips, a poem or two and some book reviews. Some journalists also ran an advice column, a popular innovation of the time.[9]

Scholars have written many articles and books on the gendering of consumerism and the vexing question of what constitutes and influences fashion, work that is only just beginning to develop in Canada.[10] In recent years, they have been shifting their focus from sociological analysis toward cultural analysis and postmodern perspectives.[11] The influence of gender, ethnicity and class on consumerism as it has been expressed in the media constitutes overlapping areas of that debate. In her work on two American magazines, the *Ladies' Home Journal* and the *Saturday Evening Post*, Helen Damon-Moore argues that these publications, which were founded in the late 1800s, "aided in the creating, development and sustaining of the commercialization of gender, and the gendering of commerce." She also points out that the interplay among editors, advertisers and readers must be understood in historical and cultural context.[12]

In recent years, a number of authors have shifted the theoretical emphasis away from the idea that these magazines essentially oppressed women to discussions of the writers' and readers' free will or "agency" in their ways of presenting and deciphering content about women's proper roles and dress.[13] The latest research explores the connections between advertising, consumerism and modernism in the press as scholars from different fields ponder the imagined functions of women in a world still ruled by men.[14] Historian Marjory Lang has aptly described the women's section of the Canadian daily newspaper as "a halfway house between consumer advocacy and advertiser" in which the journalists saw themselves as household guides who were providing an important service to their readers.[15] More recently, Sandra Gabriele has demonstrated that women's page journalists conveyed the importance of modernity, newspaper consumerism and nationalism in their writing, even as they took purported breaks from their "domestic" realms in order to explore the Canadian city and countryside.[16]

An American media historian, Susan Henry, has urged researchers to consider women media workers as producers of women's culture, and to explore their everyday tasks as journalists and their relationships with their readers.[17] Such analysis, I believe, should include the work of women journalists who wrote about fashion and were consumers themselves, but also saw female dress as a health concern. This article addresses the ways in which four women's page writers, competing with each other on the Toronto dailies, juggled these different aspects of the dress question.

They were all prominent women whose real identities and personal politics were generally known, and who worked on various daily newspapers for several years. They were Kathleen Blake Coleman, writing as "Kit" of the Toronto *Daily Mail*; Alice Fenton Freeman, writing as "Faith Fenton" of the Toronto *Empire*; Emily McCausland Cummings, writing as "Sama" of the Toronto *Globe*; and Elmina Elliott Atkinson, who wrote under her own name, and as "Madge Merton" or "Ella S. Atkinson" for the Toronto *Globe*, the *Montreal Herald*, and the *Toronto Daily Star*, among other publications. These women were all middle class and well educated, the norm for women working on the daily newspapers at the time.[18]

Kathleen Blake Coleman was the editor of "Woman's Kingdom" for the *Mail* from October 1889 to February 1911, staying on after the *Mail* merged with the *Empire* in 1895 and became a Conservative Party organ. An Irish immigrant, she became a journalist in Canada in order to support herself and her two children. She was a loner by nature, and, although she believed in higher education and equal pay for women and was a late suffrage supporter, she was not a women's rights activist. She did, however, help to establish the Canadian Women's Press Club to advance the professional status of women journalists and writers.[19]

Toronto-born Alice Fenton Freeman produced "Women's Empire" in the *Empire* every Saturday from 1888 to 1895, losing her job to Kit when their two papers merged. Freeman, who was also a schoolteacher, used her journalism as Faith Fenton to supplement her regular salary. She had a reputation as a "graceful" and "thoroughly womanly"[20] woman, given to philosophizing about nature and life in general. Best known for her later travels in the Yukon, she sent the first press dispatch from Dawson in 1901. A member of the National Council of Women of Canada, she was a suffrage activist and probably the most outspoken feminist of the four journalists, despite the fact that she worked for a Conservative newspaper.[21]

Emily McCausland Cummings was from Port Hope, Ontario. During 1893 and 1894, the widowed Cummings earned her own living writing and editing "From a Woman's Standpoint" in the Saturday *Globe*, a newspaper generally associated with the Liberal Party. Later, she became the newspaper's Ottawa correspondent. The daughter of an Anglican rector, she was active in church

Kathleen Blake Coleman ("Kit"), Library and Archives Canada, PA-164721.

Alice Fenton Freeman ("Faith Fenton"), photo by J. Fraser Bryce, Library and Archives Canada, PA-212241.

Emily McCausland
Cummings ("Sama"), Library
and Archives Canada,
PA-57336.

missionary societies and, like Faith, was a leading member of the National
Council of Women of Canada. Her pen name was Sama, which Cummings
claimed was Japanese for "lady," suggesting that she wanted to project a conventionally feminine image that was also exotic and alluring.[22]

Elmina Elliott (Atkinson), born in Oakville, Ontario, wrote "Women's
Work and Ways" for the *Globe* in 1891, and subsequently contributed freelance articles to the same newspaper, which also used American syndicated
writers. She married her newspaper editor at the *Globe*, Joseph E. Atkinson, in 1892, moved with him to the *Montreal Herald* in 1896, and back to
Toronto three years later, when he became the publisher of the local *Evening
Star* (later the *Toronto Daily Star*), a newspaper aligned with Liberal and
progressive causes. Once married, she did not have the same financial struggles as did Coleman, Freeman and Cummings, and it appears that her husband was happy to publish her maternal feminist writing, usually under
her Madge Merton byline. Her articles indicate that she was a strong supporter of temperance and female suffrage, but did not approve of women
running for public office or becoming directly involved in politics. While
these might well have been her true sentiments, it is also possible that she
felt protective of both her own and her husband's morally upright reputa-
tions, and of his newspapers' economic interests.[23]

Elmina S. Atkinson ("Madge Merton"), Archive of the *Toronto Star*, with the permission of the Atkinson Foundation.

These writers, like many other middle-class women, were taking on new challenges in the work world outside the home. While Kit, Faith, Sama, and Madge generally supported the advancement of women, one of their primary duties as women's page editors and writers was to explore the world of fashion and encourage their readers to become enthusiastic consumers of various modes of dress. Fashions reflected changing roles for women and measured the cautious one-step-forward, two-steps-back rhythm of public acceptance. Thus, the extravagant bodice of the 1890s, for example, could signal either businesslike efficiency with stiff, high collars and ties or feminine charm, with ruffles and lace.

It was the journalist's job to guide her readers on the importance of taste and personal style, and to interpret and comment on the latest trends. She was supported in this endeavour by the advertising copy and the syndicated articles that helped fill the space on her pages.

Almost 50 of Canada's 119 newspapers subscribed to American wire services and also bought American features and advertising as pre-set type forms called boilerplate.[24] Canadians avidly read American newspapers and magazines, and much of the fashion material the journalists ran on their pages focused on the latest trends from New York and other international fashion centres. Canadian dailies regularly carried features accredited to

Day and night wear, Toronto *Globe*, 6 May 1893.

Harper's Bazaar, other fashion magazines and various U.S. newspapers, including fashion letters describing the latest attire worn by society leaders in London, Paris, Vienna and even Dublin.[25] In addition, the Toronto woman journalist was clearly expected to originate some fashion material of her own by investigating what was available to local consumers in their own stores, and keeping up to date by making the occasional trip to New York.

The journalists actively spread fashion's influence in these ways partly because this industry was closely linked with the advertising that financed the newspapers. By the 1890s, most Canadian dailies were still aligned with the major political parties but were relying less on those allegiances and government printing contracts for their survival and more on business practices. Advertising, subscriptions and newsstand sales financed most of the newspapers, which were quickly adopting newer and faster presses and other technologies. By 1900 the newspapers consisted of over two-thirds advertising, and could no longer survive without it. In the early 1890s there were seven dailies in Toronto—including the *Mail*, the *Empire*, the *Globe* and the *Star*—that were in constant competition for both readers and advertisers. Their readers came from all classes. By the 1890s most men and women in Toronto had at least basic literacy skills, and many more middle-class boys and girls had been to high school, owing to the education reform movement of that era. How many readers there were for each newspaper is impossible to gauge for that time period, although many Toronto families took two papers every day. Circulation figures for the dailies began appearing on some of their mastheads in the 1890s but were not at all reliable because they were used to attract advertisers and were therefore often inflated. By 1900 the Saturday women's pages of the two leading papers, the *Globe* and the *Mail and Empire*, might have had at least an estimated forty thousand readers, with the *Star* trailing well behind.[26]

During this same period, publishers began consolidating their press holdings into chains, increasing display (pictorial) advertising and lavish illustrations, and dividing their newspapers into sections that would appeal to different kinds of readers, including the women's pages. They were aided in this by the establishment of advertising agencies that worked as go-betweens for the newspaper and their business advertisers.[27] Historian Mary Vipond notes that the advertising dollar was the "principle motive for the stylistic changes that popularized and diversified the contents of Canadian newspapers in the late 19th century."[28] On the women's pages, there were small ads from local or national companies touting items that ranged from riding habits to patent medicines and useful items for the home sewing market. Many women still made their clothes at home, so boilerplate ads for sewing machines and for dry goods such as fabrics, threads, linings, skirt bindings and fasteners were common.[29]

The content of these advertisements reinforced what newspaper editors and advertisers assumed were the typical female reader's primary interests as a consumer: her personal appearance and conduct, her family's health and the upkeep of her home. Similarly, the woman journalist was expected to appeal to these same consumer interests in the articles she wrote, the fashion notes she ran, and even the advice she gave to the readers who wrote to her. It was her duty to do so.[30]

The journalists must be understood in the context of the professional expectations placed on them in their workplace as much as for the contents of the articles that they wrote. As women writing primarily for women, they were metaphorically assigned to the private or domestic sphere reserved for middle-class females in late Victorian culture, much like the dressmakers and milliners who produced the fashions about which they wrote.[31] This gendered separation between public and private was arguably more myth than fact, however, as these journalists ventured into the world at large every day, as did most other women.[32] Nevertheless, they worked from home or in the women's department, a physically separate area of the newspaper building from the newsroom where the male journalists and editors produced news stories that were considered vastly superior and far more weighty than the "gossip and chit-chat" that belonged to the women's realm.[33] In keeping with the value placed on their work, the women were paid less than the men,[34] and they were not encouraged to aspire to anything more challenging. Contemporary advice books counselled fledgling women journalists to write "light" articles about feminine beauty and domestic concerns, rather than substantial work on business or politics, because that was what the public expected of them.[35] As women's page writers or editors, they were supposed to please their readers, thereby satisfying their publishers and advertisers. Their work, then, reflected a distinct female culture that was less valued than the male business of hard news, but was designed to contribute to the overall financial health of the newspaper concerned.

A journalist's relationship with her female readers, especially their responses to her, was one measure of her popularity, and an important factor in attracting lucrative advertisements. But the related discussion among scholars about whether audiences play an important role in influencing cultural production, that is, the contents of these pages,[36] is a difficult one to assess in historical context, especially more than a century after the fact. While fashion features, like other news copy, tended to stress the exotic or sensational, this emphasis may have been quite out of proportion with the public's actual acceptance of those trends.[37] It does appear from the journalists' own advice columns that readers did influence the content of the women's pages to some degree, although we cannot know for certain who these readers were, how they chose their favourite newspaper, or how much attention they really paid to the articles they read. The journalists may actually have made up some letters themselves, again to attract readers, or reused them from time to time to make their workloads lighter.[38]

The advice columns gave readers some opportunity to make a direct connection with the journalists, who answered their queries about a wide range of topics, including "politics, polemics, physiology and pimples," as Kit of the *Mail* once put it.[39] Few of these letters were actually published. The journalists chose only the ones they wanted to use, identified the readers by their pen names, quoted excerpts or gave the gist of their questions or comments, and selectively answered them. Occasionally, however, the women's page writer posed a specific question with the intention of running some of the letters she received in return. When Madge asked her *Globe* readers to define the well-dressed woman, "A.J.W." replied with both a common-sense approach and a degree of impatience at social expectations. "The sphere in life in which a woman moves and her means should determine to a great extent her style in dress; so also should her age, her figure and complexion. A woman who can please her critics in her dress will need more wisdom than King Solomon possessed."[40]

Because the journalists understood this kind of frustration, much of the practical advice they offered their readers had to do with the affordable ways in which women could improve their appearance.[41] But they also understood their readers' and advertisers demands for news of the latest fashions, whether they were affordable or not. The newspaper editors insisted that their women's page writers "write up" these trends as full-length articles outside of their advice columns, and accommodate matching advertisements on their pages as well. The editors seemed to feel that such material was a given for a women's page, but that directive frustrated some of the journalists who wanted to write about issues other than women's dress. They were not alone. In 1891 there was a debate on the subject in both the United States and Canada—prompted by a series of articles in the *New York Herald* on what women readers wanted on their pages: news of women's rights and other serious matters, or fads and fashions?[42] Faith Fenton of the *Empire*, who was challenged by her readers to prove her womanhood by writing about dress,[43] told them, "I have never tried to pose as a man, although I do not care about fashions. I am most keenly interested in national affairs."[44] She would prefer her page to consist of "just a sprinkle of fads and fashions," mixed in with more substantial issues, such as news of women's work. She tended to blame women journalists and their female audiences for the editors' emphasis on lighter matter. "The difficulty with the daily papers is that follies and fashions have filled the woman's columns to the exclusion of more sober matter. And as editors are quick to perceive and supply the public demand, I presume we have only ourselves to blame."[45]

However, several of her readers made it clear to her that they, too, preferred more intellectual fare, rather than what one of them referred to as the "intentionally trashy" material they were given. When another reader demanded no restrictions at all on the women's page, Faith signalled her editor's inability to cope with such a revolutionary change. "Visions of woman suffrage, communism, libel suits and general anarchy would flit before him in quick succession," she wrote.[46] In another column, she mentioned wrangling with the foreman of the composing room, where the galley of her page was set, over ad space. She wanted to keep as much of her five-and-a-half-column page as possible for her own writing and resisted his attempts to insert a big ad, which, she wrote, "must go on our page by promise to the advertiser."[47]

In addition to having to give up their editorial space, the journalists were also expected to act as uncritical agents for Toronto businesses, endorsing new fashions or products available to local consumers. Faith, for example, went to Murray's department store, a prominent Toronto establishment, two or three times a year to learn about the latest fashion trends. In January 1894, the store's various department heads gave her a list of tips, including the following, which she passed on to the *Empire*'s readers:

–Dress skirts are of walking length and full.
–Pearl lace is expensive, but is extensively used for evening gowns.
–Sleeves are much puffed.[48]

The connection between the women's page editor's role and the advertiser's product was not lost on readers. When "A Business Woman" wrote Faith an unpublished letter that was no doubt critical, the journalist replied in print that she was "not under orders. This is not an advertising page." She explained that she was simply acknowledging the courtesy of the people at Murray's who helped her write about fashions. In fact, department stores were avid advertisers as well, often taking out full-page display ads in the newspapers. The more they advertised, the more the newspapers concerned favoured them with reduced business rates.[49]

Similarly, Kit regularly discussed consumer products or services in her columns, but insisted that she did not get paid for her endorsements.[50] One of her toughest and most exhausting assignments was to judge fifteen hundred entries to an ad-writing contest, sponsored by the *Mail* and local businesses that were anxious to understand what kind of ad copy appealed to women. She praised her contestants for their creative work, gave her readers a lesson on writing ad copy, and sent the twenty best entries to the sponsors, who chose the top three winners and awarded them with generous prizes: a fashionable mantle worth $45, an ostrich feather fan worth $25, and a folding bamboo silk screen worth $20.[51]

Advertising copy, direct or disguised, was not the only material that superseded the features about other matters that the women wanted to write. Drawings were a common component of the 19th-century newspaper, and were often used to illustrate the topics explored in the accompanying article, for example, Kit's investigation of "Charles Dickens' London" and its still apparent social ills.[52] Believing, with reason, that fashion-conscious women felt obliged to measure up to a certain image of natural beauty,[53] the newspaper editors increasingly replaced the more sober drawings with lavish pen-and-ink illustrations depicting the latest modes. Faith used more and more fashion features and illustrations, which took up half her page in the *Empire*.[54] The *Toronto Globe*, which carried columns by Sama and Madge, often featured drawings with brief descriptions, such as the various styles of ball gowns for 1893.[55] The *Empire* and the *Globe* were competing with each other and with Kit of the *Mail*'s "Woman's Kingdom," which also carried prominent fashion plates.[56]

Kit seemed the most unhappy about having to run so much fashion material, especially after Faith left the scene following the merger of the *Mail* with the *Empire* in 1895. Kit had always preferred more intellectual topics,[57] arguing that imported women's fashion magazines already provided readers with ample coverage of the subject.[58] She complained that she was being pressured by her "man-editors" at the *Mail and Empire* to do more fashion articles than she had before, and she asked her readers what they wanted.[59] One respondent, Mary E. Duncan, felt that a women's page without fashions was like a farmer's page with nothing about farming. But a reader who called herself "Another Kit" argued against too many fashion features, observing that editors did not understand the women's market and were not very successful with it. The reader complained: "I suppose men editors, as a rule, consider that women are not capable of appreciating much else than fashion and receipts [recipes], and no doubt that is why a woman's page edited solely by men seems so flat to the average woman. I have heard men say that a woman's paper cannot, as a general thing, be made to pay, and no wonder, if that is the way men editors seek to please us."[60]

That same day, Kit claimed that most readers who wrote in response to her appeal did not want "Woman's Kingdom" turned into a fashion page and gleefully ended the debate. "Well, I think that's enough girls. We have worsted the editor, and the next time he approaches me with 'What about a fashion page now, for the ladies?' I shall trot him off to the file and make him read every one of these letters over again and defy him with a triumphant 'Now!'"[61]

Her victory was short-lived, however. Her editor had no doubt noticed that her advice column had always been peppered with her responses to readers' questions about fashions, so much so that Kit had sometimes complained about the tediousness of repeating the same advice about skirt lengths, the latest colours for spring or fall, and homemade remedies for freckles "every Saturday."[62] Despite her protests that women were interested in the affairs of the world, too, "Woman's Kingdom" continued to feature its staple of fashion illustrations and notes. Assigned to go to New York to cover a high-society wedding, Kit grumbled, "I am upon fashions, which I cordially detest but are supposed to be necessary to a Woman's Page."[63]

Of the four journalists, only Sama complained that she would like to write more about fashions, as many of her readers requested. But, she wrote, "even if it were possible ... I am afraid there would arise a perfect howl throughout the office concerning 'want of space.'"[64] She seemed to be saying that the requested fashion features would have to be added to her other material and the advertisements, not replace them, and her editors at the *Globe* already begrudged the space given over to women's interests.

Aside from news of fashion, the journalists were also expected to supply flattering write-ups of the expensive apparel that the mothers, wives, sisters and daughters of prominent government leaders, professionals and businessmen wore to exclusive social events. Descriptive accounts of what these women wore to high-society weddings, the Governor General's Ball and other fancy-dress venues appealed to class snobbery and public curiosity, but the fashions of the wealthy could also attract opprobrium from press commentators and readers when judged to be too extravagant.[65] These events did give the women's page editors an opportunity to educate their readers about upper-class dress codes and etiquette, thus presenting the elite as role models for all their readers.[66] The Toronto journalists promoted the belief, as did most of their contemporaries, that style and cultural behaviour "trickled down" from the upper classes, regardless of the fact that they could also originate with working-class women.[67]

Many historians believe that shop girls and factory workers copied fashionable dress as a sign of independence, as did secretaries, saleswomen and telephone operators.[68] Women professionals, such as teachers, welcomed their expanded horizons, but many of them were aware of being on public display and were uncertain how to maintain their femininity in their new roles, since there were few role models for them to emulate.[69] The Toronto journalists addressed their questions, providing the answers these new working women sought while invoking the lessons of household thrift in fashion as well as in other domestic matters. Generally, the journalists agreed that a woman should do her best with what she could afford, and not dress above her social station in life. As Madge succinctly put it, if a woman was not dressed "in accordance with her means, we cannot call her well-dressed."[70]

The class-conscious journalists strongly cautioned against putting on airs, or straying too far over the class line. Domestic servants, Kit wrote, should not try, on their days off, to emulate their mistresses because they just looked silly in "those terrible splashes of ribbons, those hideous chains and lockets and bangles which appear every Sunday afternoon."[71] She was annoyed by the Irish domestic servant, or barefoot "Bridget," a stereotype, for abandoning the peasant dress of her homeland for the corsets, over-embroidered white skirts and supercilious air of the new world. Kit commented to another "Bridget," who wrote to her, "'Liberty' had come to the Irish country girl. She could 'spake her moind' and was going to, now she was in a free land—and I don't want any of her, Bridget."[72] Her sentiments said as much about the prejudices commonly held against the Irish working class as they did about fashion.[73]

Despite the sometimes patronizing attitudes of the journalists who wrote the women's pages, women of all classes looked to them for sophisticated guidance and leadership on the variety of styles and choices they could wear. The journalists demurred from setting themselves up as paragons of fashion, however. When a reader apparently asked, "Do you believe in fashion, Madge Merton?" the journalist replied rather ambivalently that she believed in fashionable clothing, but only up to a point. She didn't want to have to live up to the latest trends, mainly because women who did were often stared at, and "women resent the gaze which measures, dissects and forms opinions about their garments."[74]

The role of the women's page writer was to translate for her readers, sometimes literally, the finer points of high style, making it accessible, affordable and locally available. In one of her columns, for example, Faith explained a number of fashion terms, most of them French, for the benefit of her less worldly readers, who were no doubt grateful to learn that a *filet* was not fish or steak, but a waistcoat or vest, and that *suivez-moi* was not an enticing invitation but the falling ends of ribbons.[75] While the newspapers all ran illustrations of the latest seasonal apparel, including sumptuous spring hats, the women's page writers did not always take them seriously, and suggested alternatives.

"THE PICTURE HAT."
By Kindness of Wm. Stitt & Co., King street West, Toronto.

A fashionable woman's crowning glory, Toronto *Globe*, 25 March 1893.

Sometimes Kit used subversive humour when giving advice, especially when she did not approve of some new trend. The best way to make a fashionable hat, she once wrote, was to take a hat shape, beat it up thoroughly and then trim it with "four rows of lace, a bunch of ribbon, some lilac or yellow tulips all bunched up at the back, several yards of jet lace, two rows of withered cornflowers, a snake's head, a bunch of grass, a bare twig and a bird's head stuck on the crown."[76] She was ridiculing the latest fad in millinery for the spring of 1891, stuffed snakes and birds, which she regarded as both foolish and cruel.[77]

As well as acting as fashion barometers for their readers, the journalists provided advice on how women could dress themselves well at the least expense, or sew their own versions of the latest fashions. Sama explained how, by saving feathers and other material from her old hats, a woman could duplicate, for two dollars, a fashionable chapeau that would ordinarily cost her twenty-five dollars in the shops.[78] Madge also gave advice to her readers. A "plain skirt with a long, double-breasted coat-bodice will look well in tweed" with large buttons or feather trim, she told "Little Dorrit."[79]

Regardless of their attempts to be helpful, most of the time the journalists promoted fashions that were well beyond most women's financial reach, including their own. The need to foster consumer consciousness in their readers to please advertisers and local merchants likely had much to do with this anomaly, regardless of the average woman's limited budget. More than one reader complained about the extravagant fashions that Kit chose to highlight on her pages. But the journalist, who was not a fashion plate herself,[80] argued that even she liked to read about what she could never afford. Essentially, she was inviting her readers to share a fantasy that took them beyond the mundane, toned-down versions of the leading French styles that were available to them locally: "Dear sisters, nobody ever did write practicable fashions—at least, I never read a fashion letter yet that didn't revel in passementerie and diaphanous draperies, jewelled ceintures, and loves of bonnets that only cost $25 or so. Labourers' wives, or merchants' wives for that matter, can hardly afford the wonderful garments that are written up by fashion writers, but even newspaper people ... like to write about these lovely things which they never can hope to have themselves."[81]

On other occasions, she became reverential and wrote up fashions in the same breathless prose other journalists used. She appreciatively compared a gorgeous lace and satin nightgown she saw in the trousseau of a "young American Belle" to a "moonlight sonata," adding "the thought of anyone going to bed in it made me shudder."[82] Similarly, Madge could be downright syrupy in her role as a chronicler of fashion, once describing feather boas as "fluffy bits of vanity. They embrace the rosiness and whiteness and smoothness of complexions by their lustre and depth of color.

They flutter in the wind and they cling with bewitching tenderness to pretty white necks and even flirt a little with stray locks from my lady's coiffure."[83]

Sexual appeal was important to women's culture throughout the 19th century,[84] but personal deportment and healthy living were also valued in this era of rapid change in gender roles. Social reformers encouraged women to strengthen both their political and their physical muscles. A number of middle-class women joined various organizations to increase their impact on social policy and conditions in the workplace, and participated in healthy leisure activities such as tennis, bicycling and archery.[85] There were limits to the journalists' enthusiasm for healthy living, however, especially when it came to encouraging physical strength in women. Gentle exercise was acceptable, as long as the beauty of a physically active woman predominated over her athletic abilities. Kit naughtily made this point clear in a column about the benefits of archery to a well-rounded figure. "A woman looks ten times more graceful and is a better target for Cupid any day while she is 'loosing the string' than at any other kind of outdoor amusement I can think of. Archery is better for 'salt cellars' than either singing or tennis."[86]

While changing fashion and other cultural trends reflected women's more active lives, there was no immediate revolution in what they wore and how they behaved. According to fashion historian Lois Banner, the two feminine icons touted in the 1890s were "the voluptuous woman," modelled after stage performers such as Lillian Russell, and the tall, athletic and patrician Gibson girl, who was slowly replacing her. The Gibson girl was created by an illustrator for *Life* magazine, Charles Dana Gibson,[87] and was depicted as middle class, although she sometimes belonged to high society. She was the American "new woman" who wore skirts, blouses and suits for street wear, played sports, and pursued a career. She was not a radical, however, for motherhood was still her ultimate goal. Faith used a picture captioned "C.D. Gibson's Typical American Woman," on her page in the *Empire* in December 1893.[88]

The Toronto journalists did not always take these icons seriously, and, despite their media roles as fashion boosters, could be quite critical of the kinds of images that ordinary women were expected to live up to. According to Faith, the "new woman" was not real, but was a "mythical creature of the syndicate letter or magazine article who serves well enough as a dummy for needy writers to trick out in feminine apparel."[89] The middle-aged Kit bemoaned the lack of fashion plates representing women who were older, or not perfectly shaped. She said fashionable women were always depicted as young, slim and beautiful, when most women were nothing of the kind.[90]

There was, indeed, some tension between the cultural images promoting the ideal or "new" woman, and the social reformism that suggested that women had more important matters to think about than fashion accessories. Faith saw it as a woman's right to pursue beauty aids of different kinds,[91] but, as a feminist, believed that women's movement leaders should dress and conduct themselves in both a modern and a ladylike fashion if they wanted their ideas to be accepted. Of the political meetings held in the Women's Building at the 1893 Chicago World's Fair, which she attended, she wrote, somewhat defensively: "It was a wonderful week of womanly intellectuality and pretty gowns. For be it known unto the cynical men of Canada that the day of strong-minded frump has passed, and the day of the clever, deep, broad-thinking, daintily-gowned woman has arrived." She was drawn enough to their activities to become a member of the newly established National Council of Women of Canada, while Emily McCausland Cummings—or Sama to her readers—took on an executive role in the same organization after she, too, attended the Chicago meetings.[92]

Banner has suggested that, in the United States, there was a split among women over fashions, or, as she puts it, "feminism opposed fashion and ... the 'fashionable' woman opposed the 'natural woman,'"[93] but others such as Wright have argued for more complexity in that analysis.[94] When the Toronto journalists criticized fashions, it was not because they thought a woman's appearance did not matter, but because they believed that her apparel should not restrict her movements or otherwise jeopardize her well-being, especially in an era when all women needed dress that could better accommodate their increasingly active lives. At the time, more middle-class women were becoming teachers, nurses or office workers, while working-class women struggled on in factories and at home, often to produce the cumbersome outfits the more privileged women wore.[95]

Perhaps because it was a novelty, healthy dress reforms designed to modify women's fashions became a hot topic for the journalists, who believed that tightly laced corsets, restrictive bodices and sleeves, heavy layers of petticoats, and long hems that trailed in the mud were both uncomfortable and dangerous to a woman's health. The dress reform movement originated in the United States in the 1850s, and introduced ladies' bloomers, which were wide leggings that gathered at the ankles and were worn under knee-length tunics. As historian Barbara Kelcey explains, the reformers argued that the outfit, also referred to as Turkish trousers, was not only clean and modest but would help women work more comfortably and efficiently. The fashion never became generally popular, however, because most critics regarded the mode as masculine and immodest, especially in comparison to the heavy layers of petticoats under long skirts that typically covered the entire lower half of the female body. Twenty years later, the next generation of reformers also tried to persuade women of the value of less cumbersome clothing to their health, but first emphasized the dangers of rigid, tight corsets. They were particularly concerned about the practice of tight-lacing that restricted the wearer's ability to breathe properly, and put too much pressure on her internal organs. Women wore corsets because the truly fashionable female was expected to have an hourglass figure with a tiny waist and attractive bosom. Kelcey has observed that women's dress reform was an issue that attracted little activist support from Toronto's organized feminists, who seemed at the time to be reluctant to disrupt the gender and class status quo in that regard. She also raises the possibility that it was men, both family members and employers, who discouraged women from adopting any fashion that threatened their masculinity.[96] Nevertheless, there was still enough interest in dress reform in the 1890s to spur some newspaper discussion of the pros and cons of corsets and healthier attire in general.

By that time, there were two different but overlapping international branches of dress reform, one seen as more feminist and practical and the other as more "aesthetic" or "artistic." While feminist dress tended to be loose but plain, sensible and bordering on the "masculine," "aesthetic" dress was flowing and graceful, often featuring Liberty prints and inset yokes of white muslin, or lace frills at the neck. Another version of this style, Greek dress, with its empire line, was also popular.[97] Fashion scholars believe that feminists saw reform dress in terms of physical, psychological and economic freedom, while anti-feminists saw the style in terms of healthy, natural motherhood.[98] But the issue was not that clear-cut. By the 1890s, both reform camps had been taken over by club women, who mostly advocated simple "alterations of currently fashionable dress."[99]

Historians and other scholars have made much of the role that corsets played in women's fashions and still debate the extent of tight-lacing among Victorian women. Barbara Ehrenreich and Deirdre English have provided a grim description of its effects, combined with the heavy clothing that most women wore:

> A fashionable woman's corsets exerted, on the average, twenty-one pounds of pressure on her internal organs, and extremes of up to eighty-eight pounds had been measured. (Add to this fact that a well-dressed woman wore an average of thirty-seven pounds of street clothing in the winter months, of which nineteen pounds were suspended from her tortured waist.) Some of the short-term results of tight-lacing were shortness of breath, constipation, weakness and a tendency to violent indigestion. Among the long-term effects were bent or fractured ribs, displacement of the liver and uterine prolapse (in some cases, the uterus would be gradually forced by the pressure of the corset out through the vagina).[100]

The Toronto journalists' occasional railings against tight-lacing were *de rigueur*, given the current debate in which critics blamed corsets for a number of perceived threats to a woman's health and morals, including endangering her reproductive organs and arousing her sexually.[101] The journalists may also have been overreacting. Valerie Steele argues that the evidence that suggested that this practice was actually common in Victorian society is questionable, as most corset waist measurements were actually between 20 and 28 inches with the average size being about 22 inches. She believes that the medical profession in particular exaggerated the extent of tight-lacing; what was at stake was the role of women as healthy wives and mothers, especially as corsets were also associated with sexual intimacy and fetishism.[102]

It is apparent that the Toronto journalists were not necessarily opposed to women wearing corsets, which would have been a radical position at the time, but were concerned about the tight-lacing made possible by steel-reinforced eyelets. Sama of the *Globe* wrote that the practice was worse than Chinese foot binding. "One can live without walking," she said, "but it is still necessary and fashionable to breathe."[103]

In 1893 Madge conducted a useful survey of ten Toronto doctors, including the feminist leader Dr. Augusta Stowe-Gullen, to obtain their opinions on corsets. The reactions varied, but some echoed the belief of the segment of their profession that advocated moderate tight-lacing as a necessary support and a general benefit, claiming that it helped blood flow to the brain rather than to the nether regions.[104] Dr. Stowe-Gullen was among those surveyed who felt the corset should be worn loosely or not at all. Madge let her readers know that she herself disapproved of tight-lacing, which she believed weakened the muscles and could result in ill health in one's offspring.[105] Six years later, little seemed to have changed. In 1899 Madge wrote an angry column about what she called the "habit of tight-lacing in women," adding that many of them were quite convinced that they were doing no such thing. Blaming the practice for the common health complaints among women, she suggested they ask their doctors—and particularly a woman doctor—for guidance. "No normal woman should suffer from the ills that women bear, and no quack medicine will cure them and keep them cured while they bind their bodies and force the whole physical machinery out of place, reducing its supply of blood, inviting inflammations, indigestion, abnormal growths, wasting lungs, purple noses, red hands, those hot flashes, shortness of breath, dizziness, weak backs and all the rest of it that we hear so much about in these days."[106] There was nothing wrong with being stout, she assured them in a subsequent column, but "a contorted waist and swelling figure above and below is hideous in its deformity.... A corset does not reduce corpulency. It only moves it."[107]

The other journalists revealed their own personal preferences, letting their readers know that they had rebelled against corsets for themselves, at least the tighter ones. The more radical Faith told her *Empire* readers that she had abandoned her own corset altogether in favour of a short-sleeved, ribbed cotton shirt, similar to the Health Brand vest manufactured in Montreal, "and now a corset seems to me the cruellest and hardest thing woman ever invented—if she did invent it."[108] In 1891 Kit of the *Mail* wrote, discouraged, about a renewed fashion in London for "19 and 20-inch corsets," noting that dress reformers did not seem to be making their influence felt after all. "I was goose enough to get a tailor-made gown from London recently. A friend brought it out, and now I can't get into it under a 22-inch corset, and *as I won't wear one*, I have the delightful pleasure of looking at my gown."[109]

Dress reform promised more than just freedom from tight corsets, however. Shorter and looser skirts were seen as more hygienic than longer ones, especially in rainy and muddy weather, even by male editorial writers.[110] Heavy skirts that brushed the ground, still common in the 1890s, were very uncomfortable to wear once they got wet and dirty.[111] Sama of the *Globe* described just what the ordinary women went through on a wet day in Toronto in 1894:

> Each (woman) was holding an umbrella in her right hand, and with her left was grabbing her skirts behind in the vain endeavor to keep them off the wet pavement. As she did so, she usually showed, quite unconsciously, less or more of her underskirts and stockings, and by degrees those willful skirts slipped from her hold and touched or trailed in the water, to the ruination of their after appearance, not to speak of consequent cold or sore throat ... and I thought to myself, "If a man were forced to endure what those women are enduring for one day only, he would raise such a riot that it would be the talk of the town." Why do we not adopt a suitable costume then? Simply because we lack the courage.[112]

It is likely that this journalist had already been personally influenced by the dress reform movement. Two years earlier, Sama had covered one of Elizabeth Jenness Miller's first visits to Toronto. Mrs. Miller had her own dress reform company, which sold patterns and sewing materials and also published a magazine. According to Sama's approving account, this "womanly woman" modelled a "rainy-day outfit" for her Toronto audience, which consisted of a dress that ended just below her knees and gaiters that extended to just above them. Sama observed that one day she just might adopt the style herself, but only "when public opinion has cut its eye-teeth and learned wisdom."[113]

The debates about dress reform and the benefits of exercise were really thinly disguised concerns about gender identification and sexual liberty. It was the advent of the bicycle that brought arguments about femininity in dress to a head in the 1890s.[114] Apparel such as divided skirts, wide "oriental" trousers, and bloomers allowed more freedom of movement, but conservative critics saw them as a threat to a woman's essential femininity, and perhaps her chastity as well. Much of this apparel, and the criticism of it, was not really new, as the bloomers used as gymnasium dress were the descendants of those worn by some suffragists and other dress reformers in the 1850s. So were the knickerbockers and divided skirts some women wore two or three inches off the ground while they were bicycling,[115] which raised fears among conservatives in Toronto in the 1890s that women were becoming masculine.[116] "Rex," who read Madge's page, made it clear in a letter to her that women should not transgress gender lines: "A woman is well-dressed when she wears womanly garb, and not well-dressed when she affects the garments and manners of a man," he declared.[117]

In her response to another complaint from a critical male reader, Faith displayed an understanding of the cultural nature of social gender divisions that bordered on the radical. When "An Old Bachelor of Three-Score-Years-and-More" complained to her about bloomers, she replied, "The 'womanliness' of any costume is not inherent, but a matter of custom. Had you never seen women in other dress than trousers and coat, while men wore skirts, you would have deemed it an equal sacrifice of 'womanliness' had a transposition of garments been proposed."[118] Faith well understood that dress reform could herald new freedoms for women. As her younger "sister" put it in one of her columns, "Why, every woman will be a girl, and every girl a child again when we get our oriental trousers. Oh those blessed bicycles!"[119]

While the sport of cycling caught on, the "masculine" garb did not, at least not in Toronto. The "new freedom" inevitably inspired a mix of the old and the new in fashions. In Canada and the United States, most women chose not to rebel too strenuously against social mores and their own fashion sense, and compromised with shorter or divided skirts rather than adopt undisguised bloomers or trousers.[120] In 1891, according to Faith, there were two bicycling clubs in the city, with about twenty women members. Her description of one of their outfits indicates that they retained their conservative fashion sense, and were not ready to make a stand for real physical freedom.

> One handsome costume consisted of a plain skirt of fine dark blue cloth, with a few pleats at the back. The skirt is lined throughout with glazed lining, to ensure freedom from friction. The bodice is a close-fitting basque, with high collar and sleeves, finished with black silk cord and buttons, the front of the bodice being trimmed with military braid and frogs. The whole effect is stylish and rich, and the costume clearly resembles a riding habit. Underskirts may be dispensed with and riding trousers or bloomers worn with the skirt.... None of the ladies wear the much talked-of divided skirts, nor see any necessity for it.[121]

In contrast, women riding bicycles in Chicago were outfitted in short divided skirts worn above gaiters that covered the lower legs, according to Kit, who found them far more sensible than the "too long" skirts worn by women who rode in Toronto. She once claimed to enjoy wearing divided skirts herself,[122] but usually she advocated both comfort and femininity. "There is more deadly mischief in half an inch of lace petticoat than in forty pairs of knickers," she once wrote.[123]

New fashions above the waist also presented a challenge to observers who were anxious about gender identity. Especially problematic were the plain shirt fronts, ties and vests that were coming into vogue along with empire lines and shorter hems. Madge didn't like the style and blamed her own "unfashionable" taste,[124] believing ruffles were "ten times" more becoming on women than the "stiff shirt front and orthodox tie."[125] Of one new style, she wrote, "And now you must have a waistcoat back to your blouse. The belt is found to be unworthy of the confidence placed in it, and some girl with a brother decided that straps and a buckle keep the gathers in order and blouses are to be so fashioned for future use."[126]

Kit declared that the "masculine girl is depressing" and that her shirt front was "a vast blunder.... The female form divine will not accommodate itself to [it]."[127] She also believed that if there was to be dress reform, it should be brought about carefully. "No woman, or committee of dress reform women, should try this sort of thing in an obstinate, overbearing way; the consent of those who change must be gained very slowly."[128] Perhaps this caution on the part of the journalists contributed to the lack of enthusiasm about dress reform. As a movement, it had more intellectual than physical impact in Canada, as it did elsewhere. Part of the problem may have been the fear of changes in the social order that new fashion freedoms would have signalled.[129]

The fashion articles, illustrations and advice columns that appeared in Toronto's daily newspapers in the last decade of the 19th century certainly underscored the gendered nature of consumerism, as well as its complexity. As journalists who individually supported some women's causes, Kit, Faith, Sama and Madge were not always champions of fashion, but they were not indifferent to its charms either. They were inconsistent in their approach to writing fashion news and commentary, partly because of the professional and social pressures on them as women journalists who were expected to respond to the multiple and conflicting demands of readers, editors and advertisers. Although they occasionally railed against fashion's most repressive and unhealthy aspects, ridiculed its excesses, and supported moderate changes in women's dress and deportment, they played, by and large, a promotional role where the latest trends were concerned. It was a role very much in keeping with the business direction of Canada's newspapers at the time, and one that prevented the journalists from writing about many of the issues they cared about, such as gender politics. Their proscribed role likely offset the effects of any column they did manage to write that might have truly challenged the established gender divisions between women and men, and class divisions among women readers.

CHAPTER 3

Suffragist and Peace Advocate

Francis Marion Beynon, the Grain Growers'
Guide *and the Politics of the First World War*

A n iconic photograph of Francis Marion Beynon has her wearing a softly feminine pastel dress, smiling but facing away from the camera, an image almost ghostly in its lack of definition, belying her straightforward, passionate writing about women's rights. The snapshot, apparently taken on a summer day, seems to catch her in the act of disappearing—which, in fact, she did, at least from Canada, during the First World War.

Beynon was a leading social reformer and the women's page editor of the *Grain Growers' Guide,* the weekly voice of the Prairie farmers' co-operative movement, based in Winnipeg, Manitoba. Canadian historians have generally cast Beynon as a feminist pacifist heroine because of her opposition to a federal women's franchise based on ethnicity, and her related, controversial stance on military conscription during the First World War. The success of the Canadian government's plan to implement compulsory recruitment of soldiers hinged partly on extending the federal vote only to women considered British subjects who had menfolk serving overseas, and denying it to "enemy alien" immigrants of both sexes whose homelands were at war with the "mother country." At the time, western Canada had been experiencing a dramatic influx of Eastern European immigrants, which made many of Winnipeg's civic leaders, who were mainly of British descent, uneasy.[1] But Beynon resisted conscription without a public referendum, championed the voting rights of immigrants of both sexes, and supported freedom of speech and of the press on both issues.

According to various versions of her story to date, Beynon's "radical" politics sparked serious disagreements with George F. Chipman, her editor at the *Guide,* likely over wartime censorship restrictions. These accounts claim that she either resigned from her job or was "forced" to do so, "due

Francis Marion Beynon, Archives of Manitoba N-13687.

to her public opposition to male conscription." There was also an "angry" exchange with her close suffrage colleague, Nellie McClung, and it was said that her sister members of the women's press club may have black-balled her. In late June 1917, she left for, or "fled" to, New York City, where she joined two other pacifists in her family: her sister Lillian Beynon Thomas and brother-in-law Vernon Thomas. They had both written for the *Manitoba Free Press*, whose editor, John W. Dafoe, fired Vernon Thomas early in 1917, underlining the animosity between "militarists" and "pacifists."[2]

This chapter reconsiders Beynon's position on the war and the women's vote in the light of a deeper reading of the archival records and within the broader context of the journalism of the period, the findings demonstrating that her beliefs, motivations and actions were more ambiguous and complex than previously recorded. While she was clearly a feminist and a peace advocate, her decision to leave Canada had little to do with wartime censorship. It was much more likely due to her own creative ambitions, the pro-military climate in Winnipeg and, especially, the shifting federal loyalties of her employers at the *Guide*, who were deeply involved in agrarian politics and, in the end, willing to compromise on the women's suffrage question. This evidence comes from her columns; the *Guide*'s editorials and other features; the records of its parent companies; and the papers of Beynon's family members, her associates and the social reform groups they joined.[3]

Specifically, my detailed comparative analysis of her columns with the *Guide*'s editorials, which no other researcher has carried out, raises questions about the timeline and extent of her conflict with her editor, George F. Chipman, over conscription and the limited federal franchise.[4] Outside of francophone Quebec, most Canadian churches, labour unions, farming groups and women's associations supported the war effort. But their western leaders initially questioned conscription, or how it was to be enacted, and their reasons had as much to do with protecting farmers' and labourers' rights as they did with the cause of peace.[5] Despite the advances of commercialism in the press, publishers and editors still took political positions on major public issues[6] and were now divided over wartime concerns. Because of those loyalties, and the slowly tightening censorship regulations imposed by the state, most journalists also found it necessary to compromise their personal convictions and rights to freedom of expression. But there was still a fair amount of leeway for Beynon to express her views while she remained in Winnipeg, with the support of Chipman and her newspaper. The authorities did not really clamp down until well after she had left.[7] Once the *Guide* dropped its own insistence on the necessity of a public referendum on military service, it still published Beynon's opposing comments, with one possible exception, for some weeks after she left Winnipeg in June 1917. It was only later that the *Guide* officially changed its

stance altogether, supporting conscription and condoning the limited federal franchise for women, leaving her to protest in other Winnipeg publications from her new home in New York.

The "woman movement," as it was referred to then, sought the right to
vote on several interrelated grounds. Not only would it give women the
clout they needed to help bring about the political and economic reforms
they felt would improve Canadian society as a whole, but it would also
grant them equal rights as citizens.[8] The federal female franchise was seen,
on the Prairies at least, as the next political step after women there won
the right to vote provincially during 1916–1917 under the leadership of
Beynon, Lillian Thomas and Nellie McClung, among others. As far as the
federal franchise was concerned, the newspaper records and personal correspondence show that both Beynon and Thomas disagreed with McClung
over how, not whether, it should be limited during the war. This was a public rift among comrades that was neither angry nor prolonged, and had as
much to do with suffrage politics as with peace activism. Further, while
there was definitely animosity between "patriot" and the few "pacifist"
members of the women's press club branches,[9] the minutes from the Winnipeg club meetings clearly demonstrate that the blackball debate had nothing to do with Beynon or the war. Nevertheless, given the contentiousness
of the wartime atmosphere in Canada, she can still be safely counted among
the more radical of social gospel reformers when it came to pacifism,[10] the
women's franchise and freedom of the press.

One cannot really appreciate Beynon's position as a writer, feminist
reformer and peace advocate without some insights into her background and
views and the kind of journalism the First World War produced, in this case,
in a farming newspaper with a left-liberal political agenda. Francis Marion
Beynon (1884–1951) was already a well-known journalist and social activist
before the war started, as was her older sister, Lillian Beynon Thomas
(1874–1961). They were born in Streetsville, Ontario, and raised, with their
four brothers and a sister, in a strict Methodist family who moved to a hard-
scrabble homestead in Hartney, Manitoba, when the children were still
young. As adults, Francis, Lillian and at least three of their four surviving
siblings lived together in Winnipeg, sharing a housekeeper who cleaned
and cooked for them, leaving them free to work full time.[11] By 1906 Lillian,
who had spent a few years teaching, was writing for the *Free Press* under
the pen name "Lillian Laurie."[12] In 1911 she married her progressive-minded
colleague, Vernon Thomas, a British immigrant, but continued her agrarian
social reform work and her journalism. They had no children.[13]

Francis Beynon, who apparently never married, also taught school for
awhile and then became one of the first women to work in advertising, for
Eaton's department store in Winnipeg, before she was appointed the *Guide*'s
women's page editor in 1912 and became actively involved in the agrarian

women's movement.[14] The sisters, who were raised as temperance adherents, had become social gospel advocates, joining the generation of feminist Christians that succeeded Agnes Maule Machar and her contemporaries (Chapter 1). In Winnipeg they counted among their friends J.S. Woodsworth, a Methodist minister who held similar views to their own. His church and its All People's Forum, which the Thomases and Beynon actively supported, ministered mainly to the poor, the labourers and the immigrants of the city.[15] Other friends included John W. Dafoe, the Liberal editor of the *Manitoba Free Press*, and his family,[16] and George Chipman, the left-leaning editor of the *Guide*.[17]

As women's rights activists and journalists, the two sisters helped weave a web of interrelated and mutually sustaining social reform groups across the Prairies. They were key initial organizers of the women's sections of the grain growers' associations, Women's Institutes and Homemakers' Clubs, all intent on helping farm women cope with their difficult lives.[18] While Beynon's page, the Country Homemakers, commercially resembled standardized women's pages with its ads for fashions and household goods,[19] unlike her Toronto antecedents (Chapter 2), she was able to devote her editorials to the causes close to her heart, which she usually introduced in short essays. Beynon advocated an end to laws that discriminated against women with regard to marital property, homesteading and other rights, and she promoted the female franchise as key to those reforms. Her sister Lillian wrote similar material in the *Free Press* and its weekend publication, the *Weekly Free Press and Prairie Farmer*.[20] Behind the scenes, they encouraged rural women such as Violet McNaughton and Gertrude Richardson to take leadership roles in the agrarian women's movement, believing that it should be run by farm women, not city-based journalists such as themselves.[21] They also established the Political Equality League (PEL), aligning it with several reform groups that successfully campaigned for the provincial female franchise in Manitoba, Saskatchewan and Alberta between 1912 and 1916, a story that has been well documented elsewhere.[22] Aside from Vernon Thomas and George Chipman, the male members of the Winnipeg PEL included Fred J. Dixon, an independent, left-leaning member of the Manitoba legislature. Of its female members, at least ten, including Beynon, Lillian Thomas, E. Cora Hind and Nellie McClung, were also active in the Canadian Women's Press Club (CWPC) and used their journalism to support the feminist cause. The press club, in turn, was affiliated with the National Council of Women of Canada (NCWC), whose politically diverse members represented several women's groups across the country, but whose official publication, *Woman's Century*, supported the war.[23] The issue of mandatory military conscription and its connection with the federal women's franchise would do much to test such personal, professional and organizational ties.

The *Grain Growers' Guide* gave Beynon the feminist platform she needed, and she, in turn, was loyal to the newspaper's broader goals. The *Guide* was the tightly controlled and well-financed weekly publication of the grain growers' and farmers' associations and their companies. It supported the economic and political goals of the agrarian co-operative movement, and was similar in content to other farm publications in Canada and the midwestern United States.[24] The *Guide* represented the interests of three Prairie farmers' groups: the Manitoba Grain Growers' Association (MGGA), the Saskatchewan Grain Growers' Association (SGGA) and the United Farmers of Alberta (UFA). These associations had been formed in the early years of the 20th century to help farmers fight for more equitable treatment from government and the privately owned grain companies.[25] The founders of their Grain Growers' Grain Company, a farmers' co-operative, saw themselves as both farm workers and capitalists,[26] and sold equal numbers of shares to all their farmer stockholders, including the directors, while trading on the Winnipeg Grain Exchange.[27] But the company was dogged by an adversarial mainstream press and rumours that it was not dealing fairly with the farmers.[28] It needed a way to fight back and make its intentions understood, mainly by persuading farmers and their families of the value of an equitable, "sane and **Christian**" cooperative movement.[29] The answer was its own newspaper, the *Guide*, first published as a monthly, then as a weekly through its subsidiary, Public Press Limited.

The parent company and the grain growers' associations kept as much control as possible over the Public Press through stock options; shared board directorships; sustaining grants to supplement subscriptions and advertising; and annual funding for an educational campaign, to be conducted through the *Guide*, about the benefits of the co-operative movement, free trade, direct legislation and other government reforms, including the female franchise.[30] The newspaper insisted on its mission as the independent voice of grain growers and farmers, and denied any political party loyalties,[31] but, regardless of their claim that the *Guide* was "designed to state the truth and nothing but the truth," the directors could be quite cautious about the company information that appeared in it.[32] They were also determined that the *Guide* not be considered a socialist publication, an ideological position it considered too rigid.[33] Despite the war, the Grain Growers grew, their companies were successful and the newspaper became self-sustaining, boasting the largest circulation of any farm publication on the Prairies by 1918.[34]

George F. Chipman took "complete charge" as editor-in-chief in 1911, but it was already an established practice at the *Guide* to confer over contentious editorials as well as management matters with other company executives. They included Thomas Alexander Crerar, who, at different periods, was head of the Manitoba Grain Growers' Association, president of the

Grain Growers' Grain Company, a director of Public Press Limited and a member of the management committee of the *Guide* with Chipman for a number of years.[35] Later, Crerar would become the federal Minister of Agriculture in the Union government of Sir Robert Borden, a passionate advocate of military conscription.

Up until late 1917, however, the *Guide* resisted conscription and the limited federal franchise for women, and was free to do so. Beynon's departure for New York had nothing to do with military censorship, although, as with other newspapers, the *Guide*'s wartime content was influenced to some degree by the federal government's pro-British policies. As historian Jeffrey Keshen has explained, most English-language newspapers, even some labour ones, favoured the war, willingly published propaganda produced by the British or Canadian authorities and acquiesced to the slowly evolving censorship regulations. After the Office of the Chief Censor, Ernest Chambers, was established in June 1915, most editors heeded his rules and warnings, especially where troop movements and other sensitive information were concerned, but the strictest regulations were not enforced until 1918,[36] well after Beynon had left Canada.

Each government legislation aimed at mobilizing the war effort was usually followed several months later by new censorship regulations, few of which were strongly enforced. For example, national registration, which provided a list of manpower and other assets, was introduced in 1916 in anticipation of military conscription, and in January 1917 the government introduced censorship regulations that barred any material that might prejudice "the operation or administration of any act or Order in Council concerning national service." A new Military Service Act that provided for conscription was proposed in June 1917, after Beynon had already decided to leave for New York, and became law two months later, after she arrived. It still allowed objections to conscription in principle, but forbade influencing anyone to disobey orders to enlist.[37] Even so, the new Union government did not act on that legislation until after the December 1917 election was over; in essence, the election itself came to be seen as a public referendum on the issue.[38] In the meantime, the labour publication *The Voice* and a socialist paper, the *Western Clarion*, published anti-conscription views without censure.[39]

This timeline means that both Chipman and Beynon had been relatively free the year before the December 1917 election to use the *Guide* to challenge how conscription should be brought about and any suggestion that enemy alien men and women should be barred from voting. While they may have been concerned about the possibility of censorship, they need not have worried too much. Chambers reluctantly left farm publications and most labour and left-wing ones in Canada alone for most of the war because Prime Minister Robert Borden's government did not want to stir up antagonism among such relatively strong interest groups, especially when an election was due. It was politically safer for the government to target enemy alien foreign-language papers from both sides of the Canadian–U.S. border, American pacifist publications, or others that were critical of Britain.[40]

Although we know little of her private character, Beynon's public persona was straightforward, open-minded and occasionally acerbic. She began her tenure as the editor of the Country Homemakers columns by dispensing with the "fussy little curly wurlies"—the effeminate designs that usually graced women's pages—and paying homage to the "staunch homemakers" of the Prairies, who, she wrote, gleaned much of their knowledge through "Nature and Necessity."[41] The *Guide* boosted women's suffrage and other social reforms mainly because the farmers needed a broad base of political support, but Beynon insisted on her editorial autonomy from the start. She wrote: "In supporting the woman's cause I am only expressing one of the deepest convictions of my own mind. If it were not so, I would find another position, for I am afraid I have not much patience with those people who cut their opinions to suit their occupations."[42] While this chapter focuses mostly on her editorials, rather than correspondence with her readers, it is important to note that she did not hesitate to engage them in debates about conscription and the women's vote, and some of her most pertinent views were expressed in those exchanges. Many readers supported her position, while other disagreed, but, in line with *Guide* policy and her own views, she published their positions regardless of where they stood.[43]

Beynon initially based her pro-suffrage and anti-war arguments on a book by the feminist writer Olive Schreiner, *Woman and Labor*, which was advertised in the *Guide* and distributed to readers for $1.25 though Public Press.[44] She echoed Schreiner's contention that if women could vote, they would put an end to war, even though they had the strength and endurance to bear arms if necessary. Women, she explained, particularly hated war because of the pain, effort and grief they experienced giving birth to their sons and raising them, only to see them die young on the battlefield.[45] The reality of a world conflict and how ordinary women responded to it would soon test her views.

In August 1914 Britain declared war on Germany, sweeping up its various dominions as allies. In joining the fight, Canada wanted to establish its own maturity as a nation, while the majority of its citizens of Anglo-Saxon descent were still very loyal to the "mother country."[46] As early confidence that the war would be short-lived[47] quickly dissolved into stiff-lipped acceptance that it would not,[48] the *Guide* published as much news and commentary as it could. It ran numerous photographs and stories, at least some from the government's Press Office, that both glorified battle and mourned its destruction, features that included news of British and Germany victories in various battles and skirmishes.[49] It also published editorial cartoons condemning war,[50] including some representing Germany as a cruel, tyrannical invader.[51]

Beynon was shocked when war was announced, blaming it on "the old barbarous assumption that might makes right. How unutterably stupid!" Women had no say in the matter, she pointed out, angered to the point of incoherence. "And it is this infamous thing that men say we women must not be given the right to decide upon that it is because it is men who fight it must be men who legislate about wars. Do these people ever ask themselves who it is that suffers the long years of privation that follow the war, who it is that supplies the men for the battlefield, who it is that stays at home and agonizes for husband, or son or brother out at the front?" War benefited only the armaments industry that fostered it; in reality, it spawned economic depression, killed young men, dispirited their families, wrecked their homes, and destroyed art treasures, libraries and other cultural sites.[52] She ran several anti-war illustrations, some expressing her view, common among social gospel advocates, that war simply went against the teachings of Christ, whom she called "The Prince of Peace." One drawing depicted a mammoth soldier as "War" holding a bloodstained sword over a large pile of slaughtered people. The caption read, "Nineteen Centuries After Christ."[53] In another drawing, Famine, Death and Destruction made up a fearsome trio presiding over a ruined landscape.[54]

Beynon was still prepared to accept, however, that it was necessary to join "democratic" Britain against "autocratic" and "militaristic" Germany, a position supported by the *Guide*[55] and most of the country's newspapers throughout the war, and by the male and female leaders of the grain growers' associations.[56] These sentiments were not just in line with official Canadian government propaganda, but may also have reflected her true feelings. As historian Terry Copps has pointed out, most Canadians acted on what they knew at the time.[57] Beynon even defended the fact that there was no official Canadian representative sent to a women's peace conference in Washington, D.C., organized in March 1915 by suffragists who wanted to form a women's peace party. At the time, the United States was neutral and was staying out of the war. She praised the women's efforts, but explained that Canadian women, while they did want peace, did not send an official delegate "because they realize that a peace concluded now would be interpreted by Germany as a triumph for their militaristic party, and the women of this Dominion are not willing that a peace shall be made until Germany has been made to realize that the age of autocracy is past."[58]

In other ways, she was likely influenced by the outcome of the International Congress of Women, which met at the Hague the same year. According to a pamphlet circulated among feminist groups, the delegates demanded immediate negotiations for a permanent peace led by neutral nations, universal disarmament, and an international body to broker future conflicts so that war would not break out again. The delegates also demanded that no territory should be exchanged in a peace settlement without the permission of its residents; that trade among nations should not be restricted; and that women should be given equal political rights with men, including the franchise, so they could use their influence to maintain peace.[59] Although Canada did not send an official delegate to this meeting, and ignored its suggestions, Beynon supported these ideals in a number of her columns, as did other pacifists.[60]

The war was not going well for the Allies, and by the spring of 1916, Beynon had given up on the popular idea, which justified Canada's involvement in many minds, that they were fighting a war that would end all wars.[61] Over the next year, she emphasized the need for an early peace and a fair settlement, in order to avoid war in the future. She pointed out that socialists and suffragists in Germany shared these views, and, after the United States joined the war in the spring of 1917, she questioned whether the Allies might be interested in acquiring territory, which she felt was wrong.[62] Her position on military recruitment was consistent with these sentiments, particularly her insistence on a public referendum first, the conscription of wealth to pay for the war, and the rights of enemy aliens of both sexes to vote.

Perhaps, like many of her pacifist contemporaries, she was torn between her opposition to war and her sympathy for the soldiers and their families. She did not demand that men refuse military service, or scorn the men who had enlisted, but insisted, out of fairness, that married and single men should be recruited at the same time, rather than bachelors first, a stance that annoyed several of her readers.[63] Mainly, she questioned how money was being raised to help the wives and families of dead and wounded soldiers. Charitable donations, she wrote, would only go to "repair work, in mending bullet holes in men who, until a day or two ago, were absolutely sound in health. Is that an ugly way to put it? It is not nearly so ugly as the reality over there in the European trenches."[64] She increasingly argued that the federal government, through its voluntary Patriotic Fund, was relying on public generosity to raise money when it should be helping the soldiers by levying income taxes on all citizens, especially war profiteers, instead.[65] The financial burden of war, she maintained, should be equally borne by everyone, and soldiers and their families should not have to rely on "occasional and spasmodic charity."[66] She tartly dismissed most of the fundraising undertaken by well-meaning volunteers as inefficient, which likely did not endear her to her various women's group colleagues who were busy donating their time and energy to the home-front war effort.[67] At one press club meeting, she objected to a Local Council of Women proposal supporting a Tag Day to raise money.[68] She would rather see public donations used for education for peace after the war was over.[69]

According to Roberts, Beynon's column was "a useful, consistently anti-war information source" on peace activism, along with the labour publication *The Voice* and a socialist paper the *Canadian Forward*.[70] But, in expressing these views, Beynon was not out of step with her newspaper's editorial position, either. The *Guide* did not abandon its own stance that world conflicts should be prevented or, failing that, settled through peaceful arbitration.[71] The newspaper joined the Methodist Church in emphasizing the need for an international peace court.[72] It declared that neither side would win the war as far as its economic impact was concerned, and also mourned the destruction of several European cities on both sides of the conflict because of the heavy fighting.[73]

While the grain growers' associations supported the Patriotic Fund, the *Guide* also came to insist that the government should be doing more to help Canada's soldiers through taxes, even after the federal Pension Committee suggested a substantial raise in war benefits. The newspaper challenged the government to impose taxes on land to raise the necessary funds, which would be more equitable, it said, than charity. It would also discourage land speculation, which the *Grain Growers'* strongly opposed.[74] The *Guide* also advocated public ownership of the railways and other utilities for the public good during the war.[75] On the conscription issue, it, too, demanded a public referendum first, the conscription of wealth as well, and the right to vote for enemy aliens.[76]

These were not popular positions to take. Talk of peace in some quarters did not cancel out the fervently patriotic, often jingoistic public agitation in favour of the war, among both men and women, and in a number of Canadian newspapers, making the atmosphere toxic for peace activists. During the 1915 Christmas season, pro-war supporters had placarded Winnipeg with signs that read, "He who talks peace is a traitor."[77] Some publications cheered on the military officers who publicly and loudly challenged fit men who were still in civilian clothes to join up. They were supported by aggressively patriotic women who, not satisfied with collecting funds and creature comforts for soldiers, tried to pin white feathers, signifying cowardice, on the lapels of men who were not in uniform.[78] By mid-1915 Beynon's position on women and war had shifted, becoming less idealistic. In her review of Nellie McClung's new book, *In Times like These*, she praised the author and fellow press club member for her "bright and fearless handing of the issues" but cordially disagreed that women were less militaristic than men. Wrote Beynon: "I have been reluctantly compelled to change my mind. Never have I heard even a soldier say the cruel things about the non-enlistment of our young men that have come from the lips of women, tho' it's true they were most of them women who had no one very near to them to go."[79] But even these two long-time suffrage allies would soon find themselves on opposite sides of the conscription issue.

While some Canadian suffragists held similar views to Beynon, they were decidedly in the minority.[80] In Canada, there was a great deal of debate among the various women's groups about the federal franchise, not just because they saw it as a tool in the fight for women's rights, but because they also knew it would give them a say in Canada's military contribution to the Allied war effort, especially whether or not there should be conscription. By late 1916 the women of British Columbia, the Prairies and the Yukon had all won the right to vote in provincial or territorial elections, but Canadian women living farther east had not. Two main questions were at issue: whether the federal vote should be limited only to women who had already won it provincially, and whether it should exclude women who were enemy alien settlers in Canada. These debates, which overlapped, came to a head in 1917 in the months before Beynon left for New York.

Since the Prairie franchises had been won for women, the Political Equality League had changed its name to the Political Education League, devoted to teaching women about the responsibilities of citizenship.[81] But it also took up the cause of the federal franchise. Its leaders, including Lillian Beynon Thomas in Manitoba, were trying to respond to the confusing differences in the Canadian electoral law regarding the status of women in each province and territory, and whether or not they all could be regarded as "persons" entitled to vote federally and sit as members of Parliament. It did not help that they were getting mixed messages on this complex issue from federal politicians.[82] Publicly, Thomas stated that despite the slowness of women in the east to win the provincial franchise, she still felt confident that the suffrage groundswell was growing and soon every Canadian woman, regardless of ethnic background, would be able to vote at both government levels. In the meantime, given the failure of MPs from the east to support a federal suffrage bill, "if the full federal franchise (for all Canadian women) cannot be obtained, then let the women be satisfied with the federal franchise on winning the provincial franchise, [but] … a limiting of the franchise that would take it from women who already have it, is out of the question."[83] In other words, while the PEL could support giving the federal franchise only to women who had already won the right to vote in provincial or territorial elections, it would not countenance any attempt to withhold it from a woman solely on the grounds of her enemy alien status.

The PEL's stance was not only pragmatic, but it appears to have been born of a certain political resentment in western feminist circles. In privately relaying her position to Violet McNaughton, her Saskatchewan suffrage ally, Thomas wrote, "I am not prepared to speak officially," but she felt that women who had not fought first for the franchise in their own provinces should do so before being allowed to vote federally because they needed the education in citizenship a suffrage campaign would give them. Without that, they had "no vision." She was especially annoyed at women who had never fought for the vote in Manitoba in the first place and were now anxious to limit it. "Some women are such toadies."[84]

During the summer of 1916, Thomas's public views had also appeared on her sister's page in the *Guide*. Beynon was away, taking a creative writing course at Columbia University in New York, and "L.B.T." (Lillian Beynon Thomas) was sitting in as editor of the Country Homemakers page.[85] When Beynon returned to Winnipeg, she advocated the same views, saying she, too, believed all women who had the provincial vote should also have the right to vote federally and become MPs, as did the *Guide*. To further challenge generally conservative views about women's proper sphere, she enlisted the *Guide*'s artist to create cartoons demonstrating that women had already shown themselves perfectly capable of overcoming domestic challenges to exercising the provincial franchise. Some walked long distances to the polling booth, others brought their babies along, and one group even served lunch to neighbours there. Certainly, she strongly opposed any attempt to keep enemy alien women in those provinces from voting federally as well.[86]

Among the grain growers there had already been some debate about disenfranchising "foreign-born" men and denying the vote to their women on the grounds that they were not literate or knowledgeable enough about Canadian affairs to vote, a view not all the suffrage leaders shared.[87] Racial animosity, Beynon noted, was rooted in "the demand for uniformity," which led to distrust of foreigners. It was the same spirit, she said, that would crucify Christ again were he to reappear and preach peace, and she hoped that well in the future people would come to realize there was no crime in being different, and those who were would be valued because "they have a new way of looking at things."[88] This was not a new position for her to take. While she had long advocated a strong education to better assimilate foreigners, especially the children,[89] she generally respected immigrants' rights, and once defended Black women against racial and sexist slurs.[90] The debate over the enemy alien vote not only stirred up animosity against immigrants, however, but also threatened to split the agrarian suffrage movement, which was already trying to negotiate a women's franchise with a federal government that was making its own demand for compromise.

At the end of December 1916, Nellie McClung, whose son had enlisted in the military, had suggested to Prime Minister Borden that he give the vote only to women who were "British" or Canadian born and had male relatives fighting for the Allies. But Beynon objected in her *Guide* column, writing that McClung was speaking for herself and should have sought the endorsement of women's leaders "in the suffrage provinces," meaning those that already had the provincial female franchise. Beynon, while acknowledging that some of those leaders might agree with McClung, pointed out that democracy should apply to all women. Immigrant women, she wrote,

had come to Canada in the first place at the invitation of the federal government and should have the same rights as other women. No one should
be excluded from the franchise because of an accident of birth. She was
sorry to "unalterably" disagree with McClung, but "if a serious attempt is
made to exclude these new women citizens from the franchise, my tongue
and pen will do their little best by way of protest."[91]

Three weeks later, Beynon published a response from McClung, who
chided her gently for not first allowing her to explain herself. She saw the
partial franchise as a "war measure" only, she wrote, justifying it on the
grounds that it was mainly "British" women whose men were fighting in the
war, not often the foreign-born ones. She also said, perhaps disingenuously,
that she had merely given the prime minister her personal opinion and it
was not meant to represent the policy of any women's organization; nor
was she trying to publicize the idea. "A partial franchise seems to me better than none and opens the way for the full measure," she explained. But,
reluctant to cause a rift in the suffrage moment, she ended her letter by
withdrawing her suggestion. Beynon responded warmly, relieved that there
would be no break between them. She also said that she felt McClung had
not given sufficient thought to the difficulty newly disenfranchised women
would have winning the vote back later. If she had, she would have insisted
that all women fight for it together, for "Mrs. McClung is a generous
woman."[92]

McClung had written publicly as well to Lillian Thomas in her role as
"Lillian Laurie" of the *Free Press*, explaining that she did not think Canadian women were yet united enough to fight for a federal franchise, but
that they would support her proposal. Thomas, who did not agree with her
either,[93] charitably, but privately, distinguished between the woman and
her beliefs. She wrote to McNaughton in confidence, "It is not Mrs. McClung
that we are opposing, but her ideas. We all realize the splendid work she has
done and is doing, but this is too fundamental a matter to be passed over."[94]
McClung, pressured to back down, soon signed a PEL franchise committee
letter officially supporting a legislative bill that would, had it passed, given
the federal vote not to all Canadian women, but to "all women who have the
Provincial vote."[95] The *Guide* and the *Free Press* publications ran editorials
that took the same approach as the PEL.[96]

In the spring of 1917, Prime Minister Borden finally moved an amendment to the Dominion Elections Act that would give the federal vote to all
women across Canada before the next election, but did not mention if it
would allow them to be elected themselves. He also indicated that the legislation would not be dealt with in the current Parliamentary session.[97] The
issue of whether enemy alien women should vote, however, was not dead, and
was connected to the next phase of his plans concerning military recruitment:
finding a way to make sure that Canadians voted for conscription.

In the meantime, there had been ongoing public debate in Canada on mandatory conscription, not just of men, but of wealth as well. Fundamental to those discussions was the question of freedom of speech and the press at a time when wartime censorship regulations were tightening. Most English-language newspapers supported conscription of all manpower because it supposedly did not distinguish among classes, and would force reluctant francophone Quebecers to support the war equally with the rest of the country's citizens. The *Manitoba Free Press*, for example, was anxious that more men join up in support of Britain, and criticized the federal government for not doing more about recruitment, which was lagging.[98] It opposed the idea of the conscription of wealth first and accused trade unions, who supported it, of "hiding behind bleeding France, martyred Belgium, valorous Britain and their allies."[99] The editor, John Dafoe, had two soldier sons and did not have much patience with pacifists. Early in 1917 he fired Vernon Thomas because he publicly shook Fred Dixon's hand after the politician stood in the Manitoba legislature and defended the rights of conscientious objectors. At the time, Beynon wrote to Violet McNaughton, "That's how much freedom there is left in this country."[100] As Vernon Thomas, a progressively minded man, later wrote to J.S. Woodsworth about his years at the *Free Press*, "I was, I think, all the time writing up to the limit for which the paper and its readers would stand."[101] It is also telling that while Lillian Thomas advocated strongly for women's rights, regardless of ethnic background, in her columns, she rarely discussed peace issues of any kind in the *Free Press* or *Prairie Farmer*, although she apparently supported pacifism privately.[102]

In late April 1917 the women's press club gave Thomas a farewell party, and presented her with a brooch. She had also received an affectionate note from McClung, emphasizing their long-time friendship, and a certificate of appreciation from the PEL. After scrawling "this is not good-bye" in the press club's guest book,[103] Thomas left Winnipeg and, apparently with some difficulty, joined her husband in New York, where he had found a job on a financial journal.[104] On the way there, she found that America's recent decision to join Britain and its allies in the war meant suspicion and tighter security at the border. Beynon told her readers that in late April she had accompanied an unnamed "lady of excellent repute," mostly likely Lillian Thomas, as far as the American immigration point, an experience they both found somewhat daunting. The "scandalized" immigration officer almost refused the woman entry when he heard that she was paying her own way, even though her husband already had a job in the United States. Beynon commented to her readers, "Apparently a woman capable of supporting herself was not nearly so desirable a citizen as one who had to depend upon some man for support." The woman was eventually passed on to a physician, who asked her "such intimate personal questions as one might expect from one's own family doctor," information she would share only with a close female relative such as her sister. Beynon declared to her readers that the U.S. authorities should assign a woman physician to female immigrants. The border once was touted as an "imaginary line" between Canada and the United States, she added, but "with the increase of national feeling is daily growing more tangible."[105]

Despite the involvement of the United States in the war, and the militaristic pressure on Canadians to help the Allies defeat Germany through conscription, Beynon and the *Guide* continued to question the federal government's policy and championed the rights of anyone else to do so as well. The conscription issue had already been thoroughly aired at the Manitoba Grain Growers' annual meeting in January 1917. There, Chipman had insisted that if there were to be mandatory enlistment, then wealth should be conscripted first, a stance that labour activists had already taken, and with which Beynon had also agreed, even publishing an unattributed statement on her page that everyone should be earning the same annual salary and taxed at the same rate.[106] The *Guide* noted that the issue was a divisive one for the farmers, with some members of the MGGA ready to endorse conscription on the spot. After "heated discussion," however, they supported the current government census of national manpower, but demanded that a census of wealth be taken "immediately" as well. They also supported their own National Political Platform. It demanded free trade rather than protectionism that would favour Britain and its allies first, neutral countries next, and enemies last.[107]

During the debate on trade, some individuals at the convention tried to block Fred Dixon from addressing them on this issue because he was also known to support the rights of conscientious objectors. It was Chipman who came to his aid, helping persuade the delegates that freedom of speech should prevail, as long as it was understood that every speaker there differed "radically" from Dixon's position on military enlistment.[108] Chipman, while supporting Dixon's rights on principle, also seemed to be cautiously distancing himself and the MGGA from the same stance. Without mentioning the incident specifically, Beynon pointed out to her readers that every individual's convictions were the products of their experiences in life and not easily changed. "To question the sincerity of advocates of an opposing belief is bigotry."[109] But, with the war continuing, and the decision of the United States to become involved as well, the militaristic atmosphere only intensified, with mandatory recruitment becoming more likely every day.

Finally, in May 1917 Prime Minister Borden returned from visiting soldiers at the front and meetings with Allied leaders in Britain to announce that Canada would introduce selective conscription immediately, meaning that single or widowed men would be drafted first, and, if necessary, married men next.[110] Even this decision did not cause a split between Beynon and the *Guide*. The current censorship regulations barred any material that might prejudice the administration or operation of national service,[111] so Chipman might not have wanted anyone on the *Guide* to come out against conscription in principle, even though they could technically still do so. But, given the position taken recently by the MGGA, which was otherwise divided on the issue, the newspaper and Beynon appeared to feel safe enough to still insist that there should be conscription of wealth first, and that the conscription of men should not be enforced without a public referendum. The *Guide* and Beynon both pointed out that wealth was being conscripted in Britain and the United States through taxes as part of the war effort, whereas in Canada there was no such policy. They argued that the omission left armaments manufacturers and others profiting from the war, and even urging compulsory recruitment of young men to face death, injury and, possibly, venereal disease. This situation led Beynon to condemn as "hypocrites" businessmen who profited from the war and opposed the conscription of wealth while they criticized as "unpatriotic" the underpaid working men who did not want to join the military.[112] For its part, the *Guide* editorialized, "No sacrifice of wealth can ever equal a sacrifice of life. But let the sacrifice of wealth be made in some measure approaching the sacrifice of our soldiers, and then, and only then, is it just to demand conscription of men." The *Guide* also argued that conscription should not be necessary in the first place because there were potentially more volunteers willing to enlist, especially if the government imposed taxes to raise money for better weaponry, munitions and other supplies to support them. This was the same position the Manitoba Grain Growers took some months earlier. They, too, felt that those who did not serve should be obliged to materially support the war, especially rich political and business leaders who would never be sent to the front themselves.[113] According to Crerar, it was "the most important question there is before us today, outside of the Trade question."[114]

The *Guide* continued to make the same arguments about conscription of wealth as well as men, but did not mention a referendum, one way or the other, after early June 1917.[115] It argued, not for the first time, that the government had the right to conscript both wealth and men, for, "in such a crisis, the conscription of money and the conscription of wealth in all forms is not out of harmony with the true principles of democracy,"[116] a sentiment that was still well within the censorship restrictions imposed by the government. Beynon, however, continued to insist on a referendum, a view that her newspaper continued to publish.[117]

There were several skirmishes over conscription and enemy aliens' rights in Winnipeg that spring. Beynon publicly scolded the National Council of Women of Canada, meeting that year in Winnipeg, for supporting both conscription and military training in schools for the duration of the war, saying their position would only encourage more militarism.[118] Moreover, she still found it necessary to defend the right of enemy alien women to vote in the next federal election, asking her readers to put themselves in the place of immigrant women suddenly denied their rights of citizenship.[119]

But, without the supportive presence of her sister and brother-in-law, Beynon found the city "trying," with more wounded soldiers in the streets, and a heightening pro-war atmosphere.[120] Even before her sister left, Beynon seemed discouraged at the political turmoil at home and abroad. "Evidences of social corruption, of political manoeuvring, of national bigotry, and of private greed and vindictiveness happened along altogether, until one felt that it was hardly worthwhile keeping up the struggle for justice and kindness in our dealings with our fellow-man. One was inclined to ask why anyone should risk position and friendships and comfort for a people so filled with hate and suspicion and corruption."[121] At one anti-conscription rally in June, Fred Dixon was attacked, but not too seriously injured, by returning soldiers.[122] Then the authorities declared that they would not be responsible for any harm done to anyone who attended a pro-conscription meeting to raise objections to the government's policy; neither would they allow protestors to meet on their own. Beynon tartly commented in her column that the declaration "gives the lie to the theory that the Union Jack stands for personal liberty and freedom of speech, as opposed to the Prussian ideal of the subjection of the rights of the individual to those of the state."[123]

It is easy to conclude that the political situation deeply discouraged her. That was partly true, no doubt. It is more difficult to confirm, without solid evidence, that she might have been targeted by either the authorities or pro-war thugs, as suggested by other historians.[124] Nor is there evidence that unhappy advertisers and readers had ganged up on her.[125] What is clear is that she had already been considering other reasons for leaving Winnipeg. After her experience in New York the previous summer, taking the writing course at Columbia University,[126] she had decided that she needed more creative stimuli. She told her readers that she wanted to "Follow the Gleam," in other words, explore other possibilities in her life, in this case, fiction writing. At the beginning of May 1917, just after her sister left, she led her page with the last verse of Alfred Lord Tennyson's poem "Merlin and the Gleam," explaining that "The Gleam ... may be a new business undertaking, a change of occupation, a pleasure trip or a migration in a new country." She also referred her readers to a popular romantic novel that explored life's possibilities and would not fail, Beynon said, to stir "half-dead dreams."[127]

In her last column, published after she left Winnipeg near the end of June, she told her readers of her decision. She did not cite any personal, political or professional difficulties or the recent debates over the female franchise and conscription as her reasons, but suggested that she simply wanted a creative change. She wrote that she was heading for "the Mecca of all writers on this continent, the city of New York." She added that her "relations with the editor, the staff and the readers have been so exceedingly pleasant that it is a real wrench for me to break off and enter upon what may or may not prove to be a wider field of usefulness. One can only hope that what appears to be 'The Gleam' may not prove to be a will-o-the-wisp." She pointedly told her readers that she appreciated hearing from all of them, regardless of ethnic background or their facility with the English language. Together they had explored tolerance of each other's views, and when that failed, it was only because of "a very human inability to see four square where our emotions were too deeply touched." She also took the opportunity of putting to rest a romantic rumour or two, saying her long-time insistence that single and married men should serve in the military together had nothing to do with her personal circumstances, on which she did not elaborate. She was aware, too, that some people had scoffed at her demanding the conscription of wealth because, after all, she was leaving the country and would not be affected. But she hastened to assure her readers that the little money she had laid away was invested in Canada until after the war was over, which suggests that she originally intended to return then.[128] She left behind some written material, but, for the next six weeks, also contributed new articles for the Country Homemakers page from New York, some of it dealing with politics back in Canada.[129]

After she had arrived in the United States, on June 30, her brother-in-law intimated in a letter to J.S. Woodsworth that Beynon foresaw that the once radical Chipman would bow to pressure over the necessity for a referendum on conscription, not that he blatantly had done so up to that point. Chipman seemed no longer anxious that it was necessary to test public support in that way. Vernon Thomas wrote: "Francis is well satisfied at having left the *Guide*, for its editor, G.F. Chipman, is standing for conscription without a referendum. At least that is what it looks like when a lot of fine phrases are eliminated.... It would seem that he has not strength enough to swim upstream."[130] Indeed, the *Guide* had stopped insisting on a referendum by early June just as Beynon was about to leave for New York, but still demanded conscription of wealth as well as men, and defended enemy aliens' rights well into the election campaign in the autumn.[131] But Beynon held firm. In one of her last columns in the *Guide*, she discussed the approaching federal election and the split in the opposition Liberal Party over the conscription issue with Sir Wilfrid Laurier's supporters opposing it, and other Liberals, and the Conservatives, wanting "compulsion." She noted that if a majority of Canadians voted in a referendum for conscription, Laurier, were he to be elected prime minister, would have to enforce it. "The real truth of the matter is that these people are afraid to trust democracy. They know that if the question of conscription were put to a vote of the people of Canada it is very doubtful whether it would carry."[132] But it was also true that other people, including some western politicians, argued for a referendum because they thought it would prove that the public would support conscription.[133] In her final column in the *Guide*, Beynon was still castigating war profiteers and supporting freedom of speech on both sides of the border.[134]

In the months after she left Winnipeg, the *Guide* slowly changed its stance on both conscription and the enemy alien vote. Over the summer and fall, Dafoe managed to persuade Crerar, Chipman and the members of the Grain Growers' Grain Company that the political position of the grain growers and the potential of their Farmer's Platform would best be served by joining forces with a united government under Robert Borden rather than aligning themselves with the Liberals, whose main anti-conscription sentiment came from francophone Quebecers. The Farmers' Platform included full women's suffrage and a system of personal and corporate income taxes that would, among other things, distribute the country's wealth more equitably in support of the war effort.[135] He also persuaded them, however, that they would have to compromise on military recruitment if Canada was to help Britain win the war against Germany.[136] Initially, the *Guide* castigated the Borden government over the Military Services Act and the Wartime Elections Act, introduced in September 1917, which made no mention of the conscription of wealth and disenfranchised enemy aliens while giving the vote to soldiers at the front and to women with menfolk fighting overseas.[137] Then, a month later, Crerar, with the approval of the board of directors of the Grain Growers' Grain Company, accepted Borden's request that he become his Minister of Agriculture, a decision he had been mulling over for some weeks. Although Crerar and Chipman apparently did not consult with the board of the Public Press,[138] the *Guide*'s tone immediately changed.[139] Editorially, it emphasized the importance of compromise if the farmers were ever to gain power in Ottawa. "The union government is framed on the basis of a political truce and the organized farmers, we believe, are willing to hold firmly to that truce until the end of the war."[140] Borden was dead set against a referendum to decide conscription, but also promised what later turned out to be a short-lived exemption for farmers' sons needed at home for food production.[141] The newspaper also reassured the women of Canada that after this election, they would finally have the full franchise in time for the next one.[142] At that point, the head of the Local Council of Women had already pledged her support, at least, to Crerar and the Union government.[143]

It was this "truce" and not wartime censorship that Beynon referred to when she wrote to Violet McNaughton early in October, just before Crerar was sworn in. Still, she seemed a little puzzled over reasons for the shift in the *Guide*'s political allegiances. "I tried to tell Mr. Chipman before I left that I thought that *The Guide* was making a mistake in following the lead of the *Free Press*, but there may have been outside pressure brought to bear on him. Anyway, they ommitted [*sic*] all the last copy I sent in because I said there would, and could, be only one issue in the coming election—the question of conscription. At least I assume that was the reason." It appears that she either was not aware that Chipman had published her August article, cited above, on conscription, or, perhaps, she had sent in another one that he did not publish. She wondered if both he and Crerar had been "bought over to the side of the enemy" with political appointments. She also said she had heard that the Grain Growers wanted to start a new, independent newspaper in Winnipeg, which suggests they were not all happy with the *Guide*.[144] In truth, Chipman heard a number of complaints from farmers that the *Guide* had "sold out," especially on conscription.[145]

Although she was in New York, Beynon was still unwilling to give up the fight, but she was torn over how much she could, or even wanted, to do for the cause. In November, a month before the election, she revealed to McNaughton that an associate editor of the *Guide*, a Mr. Weir, had just written to her saying that if she were to return to Winnipeg, she would be "a great power" in the anti-conscription campaign in the west. By this time, the local Anti-Conscription League had become a Workers' Council and insisted, among other demands, on freedom of speech. But she felt it was "too late and that my pacifist opinions would interfere with my usefulness, but his letter quite upset me nonetheless for I don't want my disinclination to break off the work I am engaged in at present to hinder me from rendering any possible service to the radicals of my own country." At the time, she was apparently beginning to "hear more often from editors," likely a reference to her fiction writing, but she could not financially afford a trip back home. Clearly, she was torn between her creative efforts and her duty as an activist journalist. She said that she had replied to Weir that she was "willing to do my best even though I can express myself much more effectively through the medium of writing than speaking."[146] Her contribution to the anti-conscription campaign was most likely an article she produced that appeared in the Winnipeg labour newspaper, *The Voice*. She wrote: "This election is the fight of democracy against Canadian militarism, Canadian capitalism and the Canadian press." She argued that the franchise regulations removing the right to vote from enemy alien citizens set "a dangerous precedent," betraying both the immigrants who had come to Canada in good faith and the Canadian soldiers who had died in the war fighting for "a free and honorable" country. She urged Canadians to restore "the tarnished honor of Canada" by voting against Borden and his Unionist candidates. The heading over the article, "A Message of the Women Grain Growers of Western Canada," suggested that it was written on behalf of the organization, which raises the question of how much support her views might have had among her old Prairie suffrage and grain grower comrades, such as McNaughton.[147] She later wrote to McNaughton again, telling her how disappointed she was in the outcome of the federal election. "It seems there was such a spirit of terrorism abroad that everybody was afraid to come straight out and say where they stood. On the other hand, if there had been more unselfish spiritual devotion on our side, it might have been responded to by the best elements among the people.... However, that is easy enough to say at this distance. The fact remains that the worse possible blot has been put upon the page of Canada's history by the endorsation of the franchise act."[148]

The *Guide*, however, was delighted at the outcome of the election, pointing out that there were now 43 MPs from the west in the House of Commons, as opposed to the previous 27, and that leading members of the grain growers on the Prairies had been elected. It acknowledged that its critics had been accusing the *Guide* of selling out, but it believed the Union government would be "honest, efficient and progressive," and that the farmers would be in a much stronger position to influence Canadian politics, especially when the war was over.[149]

While political compromise was not easy for some agrarian reformers, it is difficult to assess how much damage the conscription and franchise issues did to the cohesiveness of the women's suffrage movement. There were certainly some personal attempts to forgive and forget. Just as the election campaign was ending, Nellie McClung visited New York on her way to Washington, D.C., where she was to address American suffragists. She stayed with the Thomases and Beynon, who was living with them then. We don't know whether Beynon was still angry with their visitor because of her initial support of the ethnically limited women's franchise, and her ongoing opposition to Laurier's Liberals, but the atmosphere in the house appears to have been forgiving. In a letter to J.S. Woodsworth, Vernon Thomas indicated how difficult the debate over conscription had become, especially when social reformers like McClung had sons or other male relatives fighting in the war. "I believe she is a good woman, earnestly anxious to do good. She has her eldest boy at the front, in the trenches, a mere boy, and so there you are. It is difficult for her to think it is all wrong. Yet in her heart she hates war and well knows that it is wrong." His letter, coincidentally, was written on the day of the Canadian federal election, when women who were "British subjects" voted for the first time, and many foreign-born men and women could not.[150] In later years, McClung hosted Lillian Thomas during a visit to Calgary, championed her as a fiction writer, and wrote her a warm letter of condolence and advice when her husband died, closing with, "I'll love you forever. You have always been my dearest friend."[151] It was, perhaps, in character for these Christian-minded reformers and suffragists, who advocated reconciliation of nations and international sisterhood, to practise the same generosity of spirit with each other for friendship's sake and in the best interests of the women's movement.[152]

Had she stayed in Winnipeg, Beynon might well have found it hard to forgive many of her other suffrage and press club colleagues who supported conscription,[153] as well as her former colleagues at the *Guide*. Several women who wrote for Dafoe's *Free Press*, including E. Cora Hind, its agricultural editor, had wholeheartedly volunteered to produce election pamphlets and other material on behalf of the Unionist candidates, even though the federal government had just passed the bill disenfranchising enemy aliens.[154] But they had not tried to blackball Beynon. The women's press club did not meet in late spring or summer, so if they did give her a farewell party and a gift, as they had her sister, it was not recorded in the minutes.[155] When they reconvened in September 1917, one of the most outspoken members, Genevieve Lipsett Skinner, did suggest that they "blackball" women they considered "persona non grata,"[156] but further entries in the club's records on this matter demonstrate that she wanted members to have to pay dues to their local press club branches before they could enjoy the perks of belonging to the national club, perks such as reduced railway fares for travel to their conventions. Skinner and her supporters were targeting members the Winnipeg branch considered "deadwood" for their purposes, not someone whose political views they opposed.[157] After Lillian Thomas returned to Canada, she was welcomed back into the press club, whose members supported her in her new career as a fiction writer and playwright. It is unlikely that she would have rejoined her former colleagues and sat on the club executive if her sister had been a victim of their collective animosity.[158]

Francis Beynon never returned to the club but remained in the United States until near the end of her life. Aside from her journalism, family letters and some sleuthing by Anne Hicks, we know little about the rest of her career. Family members of the next generation believe that she had a fiancé who had died in 1916 while fighting at the front, although this event is never specifically mentioned in her columns or any other archived documents. Her one novel, *Aleta Dey*, written in New York, is a didactic treatise on war, peace and reconciliation, essentially reflecting views she had earlier espoused in her columns. While the heroine of the title was also a suffragist and pacifist journalist, and the novel is autobiographical in several other details, it is mainly a work of fiction and does not, to my mind, provide resounding detailed evidence concerning her working or personal life in Winnipeg.[159] We do know that, having saved a little money, Beynon planned to stay in New York "indefinitely," take more courses at Columbia and, if she could not find success as a short story writer, look for another job in advertising.[160] After she published her novel, she took a job with an ad agency in Providence, Rhode Island, but, although she found like-minded "radical" friends there,[161] she did eventually return to New York. There, for a few years she took over writing the newsletter at the local Seaman's Mission from her sister after Lillian Thomas returned to Winnipeg. Beynon freelanced under different names, which has made her career hard to track, but she appears to have stayed in New York, living at one point in Greenwich Village. She found the city stimulating politically and culturally, even though the humid summer weather gave her severe headaches.[162] She did not return to Winnipeg until shortly after Vernon Thomas died in 1950, and, ill with cancer, passed away within a year. Lillian Thomas died in 1961.[163]

Beynon's story demonstrates the complex wartime connections among Prairie feminism, social gospel reformism, agrarian politics and newspaper culture. We can't really appreciate her contributions, and contradictions, without positioning her within the milieu of the *Grain Grower's Guide* and its political, social and economic goals, as well as within the Prairie suffrage and pacifist movements. Otherwise, her story becomes only a half-told paean to feminist pacifist heroics that does not really acknowledge the combined impact on her and her associates of wartime anxieties, divided editorial loyalties, shifting Prairie politics and suffrage campaign compromises.

The historian Barbara Roberts once defined peace activists as those who support peace mainly during peacetime, and pacifists as those who continue to strive for peace even during wartime, a position, she added, that was usually considered radical, sometimes even treasonous, and certainly challenged patriarchy.[164] My own view of Beynon was that she was not a strict pacifist because she did not demand an immediate end to Canada's involvement in the war; in fact, she defended the fight against Germany's militancy, especially at first. She also demanded a referendum before conscription was enacted, leaving the impression that she would have agreed with forced military recruitment if the public did. Still, there is no doubting her essential commitment to peace and reconciliation, given her response to the results of the 1917 election. As it turned out, she was angry when she was proven wrong—the Canadian public did support conscription, no matter how much she might suspect, with reason, that the government, through propaganda, censorship and manipulating the franchise, frightened people into silence and engineered its own victory.

Referring to Nellie McClung's changing perspectives on conscription, especially after her son enlisted, Randi Warne observed that "a plurality of positions on pacifism may be morally defensible from a feminist perspective." Although it is a forgiving explanation that does not satisfy more critical historians,[165] perhaps it was this understanding that enabled Beynon and her sister to reconcile their differences with McClung. Certainly, neither of them was targeted by their colleagues in the women's press club who actively campaigned for Borden's Union candidates.

Beynon had her own inconsistencies, not unlike many suffragist feminists in Canada and elsewhere.[166] Her position on the democratic right of all women to vote federally matched that of the PEL and her own newspaper, but she nevertheless agreed that it should be limited only to women who already had the provincial vote, even if she insisted that enemy alien women should be included in their number. This was a compromise born of feminist pragmatism, given the confusing state of Canadian law at the time. It was also a reflection of western women's impatience with their eastern sisters' inability or lack of will to catch up with them.

Given the political and social divisions over the issue in Canada at the time, Beynon's was a complex outlook, which was not unusual among her associates at the *Guide*, who found their own political ideals compromised over the course of the war. It is useful to keep in mind as well that government censorship and propaganda may also have affected, to some degree, what was said in the pages of the *Guide*, as did agrarian politics, making it difficult to read her with confidence. Nevertheless, none of her published views could have been considered "treasonous" by the authorities under the censorship restrictions then in force. With the exception of the referendum question, her positions on conscription, the franchise and peace advocacy were still in editorial line with her own newspaper and its editor, George Chipman, for several weeks after she had left for New York. There is no evidence to suggest that she was fired or forced to resign from the *Guide*; if anything, she saw the writing on the wall and made the decision to leave for her own reasons, some of which were no doubt political and spiritual, but others definitely creative and personal, especially her desire to be a fiction writer. Beynon undoubtedly did feel betrayed once Crerar, Chipman and the Grain Growers' Grain Company board of directors eventually decided to openly support the Union government, a feeling she alluded to when she castigated the Canadian press in her article in *The Voice*, objecting to conscription and discrimination against enemy alien voters. It was only after the Military Services Act was enacted by the new government, in 1918, that Chipman philosophically accepted the stricter censorship regulations that came with it, mainly because he had come to share Crerar's fears that the Germans were winning the war.[167]

For as long as she had the full editorial support of her newspaper, Francis Marion Beynon could express her strong beliefs in an early peace; reconciliation with one's enemies; the rights of all women, enemy aliens and conscientious objectors; and freedom of expression and of the press. Among her sister members of the Canadian Women's Press Club in Winnipeg, however, she was virtually alone in her defence of a democratic vision that would not allow discrimination on the grounds of gender, one's country of origin or political views. Her position—and theirs—raises important questions about the influence of editorial and peer control on women journalists who wish to advocate for their own rights and those of others, especially in times of war. In this case, patriotism and agrarian politics eventually took precedence over the right of all women to vote, not just those who had men close to them fighting at the front. So it was that Beynon, who had once been one of the strongest media voices and political organizers in the fight for the rights of women, left Canada, deeply disappointed in the press and harbouring great fears for the country she left behind.

CHAPTER 4

"We Were ONLY WOMEN"

Elizabeth Long, Equality Feminism and CBC Radio, 1938–1956

In October 1961, Elizabeth Long received a letter asking her to recall her experiences as the pioneer supervisor of Women's Interest programs for the 25th anniversary of the Canadian Broadcasting Corporation. The interview would run on one of the radio magazine programs she originated, *Trans-Canada Matinee*. Long, who had retired to her hometown of Winnipeg, responded that she had little in the way of surviving records to account for her 18 years of CBC network service in Toronto. She fully understood the historic significance of women's programming; it was just that other people didn't. The scripts she had carefully filed on a storeroom shelf had been thrown out, without her permission, and even keeping her archive close to her desk did not prevent its destruction. As her term as supervisor ended and she was vacating her office, Long left behind broadcast documents she had been collecting for years, intending to pick them up later. "I was *not told* the weekend on which I was to be moved and arrived Monday morning to find all my precious historical material dumped into a carton with the contents of two ink wells dripping all over it."[1]

As most early CBC programs were aired live, rather than recorded, program scripts were among the few records of their contents. They were written, edited and followed carefully, partly to guarantee broadcast quality and concise studio timing, and, during the war years, as a bow to censorship regulations and as a defence against criticism from politicians.[2] Yet the CBC's own historians had not thought to take responsibility for archiving much everyday, on-air material, beyond a few scripts and some "soft cut" discs that were recorded for rebroadcasting in different time zones, but not for preservation.[3] As Long commented to her former colleague Marjorie McEnaney, "And as we both know ... who would think it worthwhile to save anything related to talks by women?"[4]

This chapter reconstructs from various sources Elizabeth Long's story, mainly from her own sometimes acerbic perspective and the recollections of her colleagues. It provides a detailed profile of Long, her feminist intentions, her pragmatic methods, the impact she had on her female commentators, and the content of their broadcasts. As a senior programmer, Long fostered female on-air talent, hiring, training and nurturing most of the Women's Interest commentators at the CBC at the time. While supporting daytime audiences in their home duties, Long and her commentators introduced them as well to information about their lack of rights that linked back to the suffrage era and preceded the feminist struggles of the late 1960s onward. Long's mandate not only included local, regional and national programs, but she also informed Canadian women about their counterparts around the world through a system of exchange broadcasts with other countries. It was her way of trying to foster international human rights, including women's rights, as well as peace and understanding during and after the war. In order to carry out her mandate, she actively enlisted the help of various women's groups and became active in them herself, as did several of her protégés.

In recent years, there has been a renewed scholarly interest in the CBC regarding its origins, public service mission and audiences,[5] as well as in commercial radio programming for women and the role of early female broadcasters.[6] This chapter supports Michele Hilmes's contention that gender played a pivotal role in the cultural structuring of radio as a medium,[7] although, in the case of the CBC, this was not so much for commercial reasons. The CBC's information programs, including talks for women, were government subsized[8] and designed to inculcate a sense of citizenship that was already laced through with increasingly flexible gender expectations. Like the women's pages in the newspapers, on which it was modelled, Long's Women's Interest niche reinforced women's domestic roles while allowing her programmers, broadcasters and listeners to explore more educative, feminist perspectives on their place in Canadian society. Her story is an instructive chapter on the links between the broadcast media and the women's movement in Canada, further illustrating the contention of Joan Sangster and other historians that feminism continued to have a life of its own between the "first" and "second" waves.[9]

Historical sources on Elizabeth Long are relatively rare and scattered among various collections, but it has been possible to reconstruct her efforts using recorded interviews and archived documents, including her own brief memoir of her years in broadcasting.[10] The conversations colleagues taped with her during and after her time at the CBC centred on her personal perspectives and feminist activities more than her career;[11] however, a former CBC producer, Jean Bruce, later recorded invaluable discussions with several of Long's colleagues about her approach to broadcasting for women,

Elizabeth Long on the occasion of her retirement, *CBC Radio Magazine*, April 1956. Photo by Gilbert Milne. Published with the permission of David Milne and the Canadian Broadcasting Corporation.

and her ways of supervising her commentators, as part of an oral history project. Those interviews were supplemented by others conducted and recorded by Long's contemporary, Elspeth Chisholm, and by Alison Taylor, then a graduate student, who wrote a detailed thesis on the early history of women in the CBC.[12] While the recordings bring these colourful individuals to life and are valuable in themselves, they should be understood as reflections of their subjective memories that must be considered against other evidence, including the papers in various archives.[13]

Filed along with Long's 50-page memoir in the CBC's records is an unsigned note, possibly from the corporation's archivist, stating that the 12 short chapters were the only historical record of Women's Interest programming. They were edited for "superfluous" detail and retyped, but the originals are still there, along with Long's photo and an article about her retirement in *CBC Radio Magazine*.[14]

Long's own fonds are not personally revealing but do give some insights into her career and feminist activities. They contain publicity articles, copies of radio commentaries on women's issues, letters from former colleagues and documents regarding her women's club activities. The richest source on her life and career is her correspondence with McEnaney, which her friend kept in her own collection. Long wrote to her regularly after she retired, her letters filling in some of the scarce details about her personal life, her early career, her CBC experiences, their ongoing strategies for winning more status and recognition for their female colleagues, and their volunteer activities with women's clubs and peace groups.[15] Other useful sources include the papers of CBC commentators Florence Bird of Ottawa, who wrote and broadcast as "Anne Francis," Mattie Rotenberg of Toronto, Ellen Harris of Vancouver, and Margaret Colpitts of Moncton and Halifax, who was known on the air as "Joan Marshall."[16] There are other references to Long in the papers of a few CBC managers,[17] and in the records of the Canadian Women's Press Club.[18]

Elizabeth Dundas Long (1891–1978) was born, raised and schooled in Winnipeg, the third child of Alfred J. and Margaret Mackay Long. She had a younger sister, Janet, who became a social worker,[19] and two brothers, Alfred Jr.,[20] who had infantile paralysis, and T. Mackay Long, who later became a lawyer.[21] It seems that they were brought up in comfortable, middle-class circumstances, as the family home was decorated with oriental rugs and mahogany furniture.[22] Her outgoing, popular mother entertained modestly, however, and instilled humanitarian values in her children, who were taken to services at the United church. "I don't know when I started to feel responsibility to communicate my ideas—the real Prometheus urge to change things for the better," Long wrote to McEnaney. "No doubt it stemmed directly from mother always using me to carry food to old people, and also to help my crippled brother." The highlights of her childhood included taking young Alfred to the theatre, where they were both seated in the front row and invited backstage after the performances. She also remembered adventurous canoe trips in the beautiful local countryside that she loved to explore. Long was shy and socially awkward,[23] but a very bright, intellectually curious youngster, who loved history and literature, but was otherwise easily bored at school.[24] Nevertheless, she graduated from Wesley College with a bachelor of arts degree when she was only 18 years old.[25]

Long started to become politically aware during the provincial suffrage campaign, although she was still somewhat naive and not quite prepared for the cut and thrust of political debate, or rural humour, especially from a female leader. She recalled once hearing Nellie McClung suggest that, like the stubborn old grey horse on the family farm, the premier, Sir Rodmond Roblin, might need a sharp prod on the hindquarters to make him move forward on the vote for women. "I was rather shocked that a nice looking woman would talk that way about a nice looking man, who, after all, was head of our government." Long also recalled that on her first election day, her family members effectively cancelled out each other's votes. A Conservative scrutineer smugly assumed that because her father was going to vote for the party, the entire family would do the same. When they arrived at the polling station, Long's mother and two brothers voted for the pro-suffrage Liberals, while she and her sister voted with their father for the anti-suffrage Conservatives, mainly because they felt sorry for him. Clearly, at that point in her young life Long did not fully appreciate the choice the ballot bestowed on her.[26]

The First World War was the other major event of her young womanhood, one she found quite difficult. She felt so much sympathy for the young men who went off to the front that she impetuously became engaged to several in succession, "so I could kiss them, according to the custom of that day. And of course they were getting killed as fast as new ones appeared. No wonder I was upset." She also worried, given the generosity of her affections, about having to face the ones who did return.[27] In the meantime, she knitted socks for the soldiers and worked at a boring bank job until the end of the war when she began her newspaper career. She had realized, with the help of a psychology counsellor, that she needed challenging work to keep her emotional equilibrium. "I never did get engaged much after that," she said, because if she married, "I was afraid I'd have to stay at home."[28]

Long wrote for the social and women's departments of the *Winnipeg Tribune*, the *Winnipeg Free Press*, and later as associate editor and columnist "Jane Allen" on the *Free Press* weekly magazine, the *Prairie Farmer*. She also freelanced articles to Canadian and overseas publications.[29] She joined the local branch of the Canadian Women's Press Club (CWPC) after she and her sister attended a Christmas party there in 1921.[30] Long was elected its president in 1925 and later ran unsuccessfully for other executive positions, losing another presidential bid to Lillian Beynon Thomas, who renewed her membership in 1928, several years after returning from her wartime exile in New York. By that time, peace had been restored among the pro- and anti-conscription factions within the club (see Chapter 3). During the 1930s, Long served with Thomas on the executive, and because she loved a good party, also helped plan the annual Christmas dinners and took part in skits lampooning the newspaper business.[31]

The person who had the strongest influence on her was E. Cora Hind, the agriculture editor of the *Winnipeg Free Press*.[32] During the 1920s and 1930s, they worked together on the press club's constitution, membership and other committees.[33] Hind, one of the original press club suffragists, was a feminist mentor to Long, who had a hard time with a difficult editor at the *Prairie Farmer*. She often found herself "defending my space in the paper and my rights to keep my own copy on my own page with no snatching at the last minute behind my back. But I had Cora Hind as my pattern, complete with staging a mad [a tantrum] about once a year!"[34] In 1936, when the aging Hind was about to embark on a long journey, Long told her that if she fell ill and needed help she would go to her and bring her home. Grateful for the friendship of her younger press colleagues, whom she liked to encourage, and touched by her offer, Hind wrote her words of comfort on the recent death of her mother. Knowing that Long was frustrated with her newspaper job, she also counselled her to spread her professional wings, writing, "You have time now and the ability to do work with a wider scope and you owe it to yourself and the opportunities which your goodly upbringing have given you to get busy."[35]

In August 1938, after weeks of negotiations, Long left Winnipeg for Toronto to take up her new position as assistant supervisor of Talks in charge of Women's Interest programs, becoming the first female executive at the CBC. According to Long's CBC memoir, it was Charlotte Whitton, a conservative feminist, renowned social welfare expert and writer, who had suggested she apply for a job there.[36] Long was a cousin of the general manager, Gladstone Murray,[37] and her contemporaries assumed that she got the position through him, likely because family, social and professional connections were common among CBC employees.[38] A few months earlier, Murray had addressed the CWPC's national meeting in Winnipeg, encouraging the members to write for radio. As Long was in charge of hosting delegates and guests, he likely saw her there, although it's not certain exactly who offered her the new position.[39]

Whether or not she took advantage of her relationship with Murray, Long understood that to use the airwaves for the advancement of women, individually and collectively, she must never forget that men were in charge.[40] That may be why the programming she promoted rarely if ever contravened social expectations of homemakers, even while she tried to bring the wider world to them and supported female colleagues who sometimes presented a more radical vision to listeners and to management. Long was an ardent monarchist, as well as a feminist, an internationalist and a peace advocate, not an unusual combination among the well-educated women of her generation and class. All these perspectives were present in the broadcasting she supervised over the years.[41]

The CBC was still young and in transition in 1938. The federal government had established its predecessor, the Canadian Radio Broadcasting Commission, in 1932 as a way of strengthening nationhood and citizen engagement, especially against strong cultural incursions from the United States over its more powerful airwaves. Originally conceived as a publicly owned, cross-Canada network as well as a broadcasting regulator of all radio stations, the CRBC actually consisted of a hodgepodge of newer public stations and established private radio affiliates linked in an uneasy political and economic alliance under its stewardship. Media historian Mary

Vipond notes that the CRBC helped reinforce a national consensus around small-l liberalism, which was an identifying, "common sense" marker of the cultural elite in this country, as it was in Britain and the United States. But the CRBC, which could not overcome management problems, lack of funds and accusations of partisanship, was reorganized into the Canadian Broadcasting Corporation in 1936. Like the CRBC, the CBC projected a generally liberal outlook while striving to establish its authority as a public broadcaster of general interest, educative and entertaining programming that would attract many different kinds of listeners across the country—listeners from all classes, not just the well educated and well off. The competition for audiences was stiff, however. Canadians living near the U.S. border could tune in directly to the more powerful signals from American stations as well as to their own local commercial ones, which also carried some popular, pre-recorded American shows as well as Canadian content.[42] As very few wives—only 4 percent—worked for pay outside the home at the time,[43] women's programming filled airtime during the day, when they were going about their daily routines, their husbands were at work and the children were in school. Radio signals from afar were best heard at night, however, which meant it was difficult for Canadian homemakers to listen to American daytime shows, such as the *Martha Deane* program from New York, during the Depression. Instead, independent, local Canadian stations provided them with shows featuring household hints, fashion news and child-rearing tips;[44] for example, CFRB broadcasters Kate Aitken and Claire Wallace had their own loyal audiences in Toronto,[45] and there were like programs in other cities from Halifax to Vancouver.[46] When the CRBC became the CBC in 1936, it did not have network programs for women, a situation Long was hired to rectify. Under the direction of the CBC's Talks supervisor, she was responsible for organizing local, regional and national female commentators for her Women's Interest broadcasts,[47] sharing the production staff with other programs.[48]

While the CBC might have been generally liberal in its broadcast outlook, that perspective did not extend to inclusion of female staff on an equal basis with men. Many of her male colleagues were kind to her when she first arrived, Long recalled, "but a bit puzzled about what I was going to do as they had the firm conviction that there was little place for women in broadcasting."[49] As a newspaper veteran, she was overwhelmed by the radio medium at first, because there seemed to be "no rules" and experimenting with new ideas for a fickle audience was the norm.[50] She likened her busy schedule to "getting out an extra edition of the newspaper all the time,"[51] but soon learned that the key to success in network broadcasting was "planning."[52] It was harder for her to learn to cooperate with everyone else around her.

Her CBC colleagues remembered her with that ambivalent mixture of fondness, grudging respect and condescension often reserved for older, strong-minded women. Long was short in stature and slightly plump, with attractive, aquiline features, bright blue-grey eyes, a quick wit and a ready laugh, but was rather abrupt in her manner. By the time she arrived at the CBC, she was in her mid-40s, with greying dark hair. Colleagues who knew her well understood that she had a very sharp mind but it often raced ahead of her ability to articulate her ideas, so that anyone conversing with her had to pay a great deal of attention in order to follow what appeared to be her erratic train of thought. McEnaney explained, "Elizabeth was a great puzzle to the men in the department. I think they thought she was half witted. And it was so far from the truth. She had an extremely high IQ.... I got to know her so well and knew how this brain worked so that I would, quite often when the meeting was over ... have to go and interpret to the rest of them what Elizabeth had been trying to say." Long's relations with her male colleagues were always uneasy. "I wouldn't say that she could work *with* men. She thought she could but the men knew she couldn't. But she survived."[53] Elspeth Chisholm, a Talks programmer, recalled another co-worker likening Long to a "grasshopper" whom her male colleagues sometimes thought was "dotty. But she always had a reason for everything."[54]

She also liked to run her programs her way, brooking little interference. "Well, of course I'm awfully surprised if ... any person doesn't agree with me or even opposes a plan I have, especially when I've set my heart on it," she admitted to McEnaney. Usually, she would sleep on a problem, which would help her come up with "the smoothest set of words" to help her break any impasse.[55] Her newspaper experience and Cora Hind's example "had made me so tough they could not undermine my confidence, but I had the advantage of working in a field in which I had no rivalry ... from the men." She had also learned to keep her ear to the ground, making it "a practice to be especially considerate of the men the others did not regard (as) tops. Time and again one of these would give me a tip on what the boys were saying." She made sure to get to know the wives of her colleagues, as well.[56]

Sometimes the senior men were simply dismissive of her efforts, especially in the beginning. The first time she went to Montreal to interview women for jobs in her unit, the supervisor in charge of the office "could not think of any space he could give me to see interviewees but the ante-room to the ladies' toilet. I thanked him enthusiastically, of course." A few days later, as he was about to leave for a trip, he asked courteously if he could do anything to help her, and she promptly responded by requesting the use of his office while he was gone. "He was hooked and from then on I took over his status in (his employees') eyes. A strange psychology."[57]

In 1943 the Talks department was reorganized into Talks and Public Affairs, and Neil Morrison, a CBC programmer in his late 20s, became Long's immediate supervisor. Morrison's eye problems prevented him from joining the military, and, because of the war, there were few men with more experience around. Under his supervision, the unit expanded into a network of national and regional producers responsible for getting all public information programs on the air locally, and contributing to the national programs, regardless of genre or audience interest. By this time, the CBC was picking up more listeners as Canadians were interested in hearing the war news from a national perspective.[58] Morrison, who considered himself a liberal, recalled that most of the older male supervisors at the CBC were "male chauvinists" and technical experts, who tended to be very conservative where women were concerned. "Elizabeth put up vigorous fights for women's interests and for her programs and a lot of the men were really kind of afraid of Elizabeth. It didn't pay to get into a fight with Elizabeth. She didn't give in very easily."[59]

He never managed to endear himself to Long, however, who confessed to McEnaney that she never trusted him, because he tried to interfere with her programming, including her choice of on-air experts on women's concerns. "That's why I kept my experts to myself. Also why get things more mixed up than they were anyway? I really disliked Neil very much.... So I unconsciously forgot everything he might have challenged."[60] Although she later claimed to have had a fair amount of autonomy,[61] she still had to consult with him when she would rather have run her own independent unit.[62] From his perspective as supervisor, he had to referee staff disputes, which sometimes included conflicts between Long and other personnel, regardless of gender. "Miss Long sometimes has a tendency to stand upon her rights more firmly than she needs to," he once explained to a senior manager in Vancouver regarding her difficulties with the uncooperative female producer in charge of Women's Interest programs there.[63] He did not always go to bat for Long, however; he once told a Montreal producer to make up her own mind about keeping an upper-middle-class female commentator on the air despite Long's criticism that her "upper-crust" style of radio delivery was not suited to her generally middle-class audience.[64]

Morrison also knew that Long preferred female to male producers for her programs, but he felt that there was less conflict in a mixed-gender unit than in a predominantly female one, and saw no reason why production staff should be assigned according to their sex. She, on the other hand, believed that a male producer was "no help or critic" of homemaking as a technical field when it came to putting the programs on the air. Also, a male manager pointed out to him that a female producer would be better able to negotiate her way through the various women's clubs that supported the Women's Interest broadcasts.[65]

Morrison saw Long's brand of feminism as being rooted in an earlier time, suggesting that she was somewhat old fashioned in her convictions. "Elizabeth really almost belonged to the suffragette generation, you know," compared to her successor, Helen James, who, he felt, tended to take women's rights more for granted.[66] Although late in her career James came to the public defence of CBC women, she nevertheless agreed with that comparative assessment. "She was a very strong feminist. Yes. And I wasn't. And I'm not.... She had the courage of her convictions." James recalled that she was relieved to know, when she was hired in 1945, that she would be producing different news and current affairs programs and would not be entirely "relegated" to women's broadcasts, mainly because the male CBC programmers had a limited idea of what they should entail. "They thought that women's interests were cooking, childcare, household management.... Many of them didn't seem to realize that women were persons and had as broad interests as men. And so there was this kind of dead hand that one felt on top of everything, keeping, restricting the program material." She recalled that Long had to fight hard to broaden this limited perspective.[67] Although it was possible that women made up the majority of the listening audiences throughout the programming schedule,[68] men's voices dominated the "masculine" Talks and Current Affairs programs in the evenings,[69] while women's voices broadcast domestic content during the daytime under Long's watchful eye.

This gender stratification on air, which Hilmes refers to as the "devalued feminine,"[70] was reflected in the pay, benefits and promotions that were high on the list of inequities all women suffered within the CBC, systemic prejudice that was common in other workplaces during the middle years of the 20th century.[71] Long, who at one point made $3000 a year—over $1400 a year less than Morrison did[72]—always felt that the corporation never really valued the women programmers and broadcasters whom she taught, counselled and encouraged. Even though she would tell them that the real kudos they earned would not be money but attracting an audience,[73] and some of them were content just to be working in radio,[74] she was well aware that their pay should be higher, especially as most of them broadcast five times a week. "Year in and year out, I worked on that, but when an increase was forthcoming it always just preceded a jump in the cost of living. That battle I never won."[75] Her commentators were mostly married women, working as freelancers on yearly contracts, making anywhere from $25 to $50 a week, which was less, Helen James recalled, than their male counterparts working on prime-time evening programs. It was also less than women's programming in the private sector that was supported by advertising.[76] Acquiring a better-paid, permanent job at CBC radio was not really an option, however. Staff positions with benefits and pensions were open only to men and single women who were supervisors, programmers, producers, news reporters, announcers or support staff. Under federal civil service regulations, married women did not qualify for any of these permanent positions because, it was argued, their husbands would take care of them. This assumption belied the fact that after the war, a number of married women still wanted to work, either to help support their families or because they had "personal reasons" for doing so, even though they were under considerable political and social pressure to return to domesticity.[77] The pension regulations reflected an underlying resentment from both women and men against middle-class wives who worked for pay, especially if they were prominent in the community.[78] Long, who as a single woman did not suffer the same disadvantage, quietly plotted behind the scenes with McEnaney, who was married and led the struggle for women's rights within the CBC.[79]

Long devoted most of her attention to bringing issues of concern to women through her programming rather than overt activism on the job. Her immediate and pragmatic goal was to use the radio to woo and inform housewives, much as she had during her extensive newspaper career. "My experience led me to the firm conviction that women would find listening entertaining if you could offer them information that was of practical use to them at the moment," she told one interviewer.[80] As a feminist, she also felt that the average housewife's intelligence should not be underestimated, and that they wanted to know about the wider political, economic and social issues that affected them and their families. According to McEnaney, Long "was a champion of women's rights and this was always evident in the programming."[81] She took advantage of every opportunity to further the cause, which took its place among the recipes, sewing tips and child-rearing advice. Long and her commentators, her friend explained, "were trying to widen the horizons but they weren't trying to push women out of the home, particularly if they had small children,"[82] but that did not stop her from advocating equality rights. In September of 1953, for example, she sent her commentators across the country a long memo, meant as broadcast material for their use, outlining the main arguments of Simone de Beauvoir's book *The Second Sex*, just published in English from the original French. De Beauvoir stressed the importance of economic independence for women if they were to make other gains in society. Long told her commentators that there was no evidence in the book regarding media rumours that de Beauvoir was a Communist, which would have made the author persona non grata at the time. "I would suggest that you look over the book if you find the opportunity, as the approach is different from that of other recent books on 'the woman problem.'"[83]

One of the other lessons Long had learned from Hind was to cultivate the interest and support of different women's groups in her work. She forged strong relationships with several of them, including the Canadian affiliate of the International Council of Women (ICW), the National Council of Women of Canada (NCWC); the Consumers Association of Canada (CAC);[84] and the Canadian Women's Press Club (CWPC),[85] telling them about her programs and consulting them about women's issues.[86] This practice was in line with the CBC's policy of liaising with various citizen groups in order to gather advice, information, participation and feedback on its programming.[87] Helen James recalled an example of what she considered one of Long's "excellent" ideas. "Mr. [Louis] St. Laurent made a speech one time saying he wanted to hear from the women of Canada. So Elizabeth Long got in touch with the national organizations and set up a series, 'Dear Mr. Prime Minister.' And so spokesmen for those organizations wrote, as it were, a radio letter to the Prime Minister about their concerns."[88] Probably the most influential of these women's groups was the NCWC, which was an umbrella organization of national women's clubs, many of which had a number of local affiliates, as did the NCWC itself. Its national membership statistics have always been difficult to pinpoint accurately, but historian Naomi Griffiths believes that its official documents reached an estimated audience of three-quarters of a million women in 1943, its 50th anniversary year. Long and several of her protégés served on its executive, as well as holding positions with the ICW, a worldwide organization.[89]

During the war, much of the CBC programming for women focused on their best home-front efforts,[90] and occasionally, Long and her staff earned media kudos for their informative broadcasts.[91] Essentially, much of the CBC's Talks and Current Affairs programming was designed to educate listeners for citizenship in a more peaceful, secure and democratic world.[92] The 1944–1945 "Talks for Women" reflected the interest among Canada's intellectual and political leaders in planning postwar reconstruction with daily women's programming that often dealt with domestic concerns as well as weightier matters, such as women's work and the status of women.[93] Long explained in her CBC memoir, "During the anxious years women workers had learned how many women mastered new crafts right here in Canada, and now earned better income in the employment field. Broadcasts on women's wartime jobs met with continuing enthusiasm, and workers who could get a chance to listen, made copious notes to share with others in the same frame of mind."[94] On regional CBC stations and affiliates, there were 10- to 15-minute broadcasts three to five days a week, featuring regulars such as Margaret Colpitts ("Joan Marshall") in the Maritimes, Mary David on the Prairies and Ellen Harris in British Columbia. Listeners across the country could also hear special network series on housing needs, rural affairs, child guidance, women and work and "the postwar woman." They could tune in to *How Freedom Works* on women's political responsibilities as citizens and *Are You a Leader?* designed to train club women and other interested listeners in group organization. For several of these series, the CBC provided a suggested reading list of academic and general interest books and other material. The radio schedule pamphlet advised female listeners to "time your rest period for this hour, or keep your mending basket at hand.... Invite friends or neighbours to form a listening circle to hear one special series weekly, while you knit or sew." It also suggested that women's clubs build these series into their regular meetings, or form a radio committee and recommend them to their members.[95] The pamphlets, Long recalled in her CBC memoir, were sent out to women's groups and other organizations twice a year to inform their current listeners, to attract new ones to Women's Interest programming, and to cement her own connections to these various women's groups.[96]

For the broadcasts to be successful, Long had to make sure the local commentators and the national ones, as well as the program planners and producers, were all working together. She wanted her commentators "to report on local happenings, or interview women leaders who had a special story to tell," and she gave them as much support as she could.[97] She held their hands when they ran into problems with their local producers,[98] sent them background material on prominent or interesting individuals in their areas, and forwarded government press releases to give them more story ideas to help them fill their daily time slots. Starting in 1944, she also organized program meetings by mail so they could give each other encouragement and tips. She urged them to swap their radio scripts, sent them the CBC's on-air regulations, and even told them to pre-record two or three programs in case of illness.[99] She urged them to take on as much work as they could handle, persuading a reluctant Ellen Harris, for example, to broadcast from Vancouver five days a week instead of three, despite the fact that she was married and had a family.[100] Harris and Colpitts, who both had young children, were able to manage their broadcasts and domestic duties only with household help.[101]

According to one of Long's protégés, Shirley Brett Foley of CBC Montreal, Long wanted her commentators to be "the eyes and the ears and feet of the housewife."[102] She clearly did not want a women's page of the air, the usual fare on daytime information radio, which Colpitts described as "a bit of music and a household hint and a bit more music and something off the wire about fashion or you know, something very … well very light, interesting, but not the sort of thing that Elizabeth Long had in mind. She wanted us to deal with the people in our community and the situation in our community and the news events," and do it accurately. Colpitts discussed various topics, from "Democracy in the Home" to the mining disaster in Springhill, Nova Scotia in 1956.[103] On the other side of the country, Harris, who strongly believed in equality of the sexes, used the Vancouver night school schedule to encourage women to learn all kinds of skills, including nontraditional ones, such as cabinet making and basic plumbing repairs. "It just shows what you can do when you try."[104] She also explained the political issues involved in the 1948 municipal election campaign, urging her women listeners to get out and vote,[105] a message in line with Long's own convictions.

Margaret Howes, a CBC producer in Montreal, recalled that Long "really was a feminist" because she valued women's domestic role, felt they should be informed about the world, and insisted on their "status and worth." She applied strict professional standards, no matter what material her commentators used. "She was concerned about women getting the right information and lots of information and she set up her programs I think with that in mind.... It was definitely broadcasts aimed at the person who was busy doing things around the house, or at home for other reasons, but it was really—it was to meet her interests as a woman part of the time, but also meet her interests as a person and a functioning citizen." Howes quickly learned to appreciate Long's devotion to public broadcasting as well. "You had a responsibility to the public and that was why you were there. And once you lost that interest or that focus, then you became less useful. In fact in her books, you'd finished."[106]

Long, who travelled from Vancouver to Halifax in search of new female talent,[107] was careful about choosing the women who would be her on-air commentators. She wanted them to have a solid, relevant background, not necessarily in journalism but in a profession or activities that would contribute to the informative and educational value of CBC programming. In one undated document, she described the various functions that women could fill in radio, including program production and on-air work. In summing up the advantages and disadvantages of a radio career, she wrote, "It offers all the opportunities and excitement of a new and fascinating artistic career. Jobs are limited in number, but mobile. You must be prepared for irregular hours, a multiplicity of duties, strain of ceaseless competition, unpredictable changes in listener interest, and constant responsibility."[108]

Given these standards, it was never easy for women to break into women's programming as planners, producers or broadcasters. She looked for intellect, determination, an ability to communicate easily and professionalism in her recruits, and she had the disconcerting ability to size up a person in an instant, a trait some applicants found intimidating. One of her stock questions to them was, "What is it you feel you have to say to the women of Canada?"[109] Certainly, her reputation preceded her once her unit was well established. Shirley Brett Foley recalled that the "formidable" Long visited the journalism program at the University of Western Ontario in 1949, specifically to look for women to hire, and recruited and trained her in Toronto for the next six months before sending her to Montreal. "She was very nice, mind you, but she scared me almost to the point of death," the successful commentator told her radio audience during an on-air interview with Long herself several years later.[110]

Colpitts regarded her supervisor not as formidable, exactly, but as tough-minded in her way of taking her commentators under her wing, and instilling high standards, which was her way of protecting them from the inevitable criticism that any on-air personality received. Colpitts, who had been active in amateur theatre in Moncton, was reading children's stories on the air when Long had her audition for the commentator position in 1942.[111] After hearing her recording, Long visited her on a trip to the East Coast, interviewing her with a few sharp questions over a picnic lunch in a local park. Colpitts had used a candy recipe in her audition, and Long asked her exactly when it was recorded, given that sugar was rationed because of the war.[112] Later on, after hearing one of her programs, Long declared that she was delighted with the broadcaster's "good sense of feeling and social responsibility."[113]

Colpitts recalled that Long also understood, and enjoyed, the side of broadcasting that was entertaining as well as educational, and expected her commentators to be "showmen," to engage and interest their audiences as well as pass on useful information.[114] One of the initial challenges was getting CBC listeners used to hearing female voices on the air regularly, a change that did not come easily. In the late 1930s, Nellie McClung, then the only female member of the CBC Board of Governors, advocated for women despite some media opposition.[115] Station managers argued that radio technology was still fairly young and it was difficult to transmit high-pitched female voices and make them sound attractive, an attitude that had become ingrained among advertisers, station managers and the public, despite some technological advances since the 1920s.[116] Long seemed to accept this prejudice at face value even as she was determined to get around it. "I could see that this was a natural handicap, but women had overcome a lot more than an octave in other fields."[117] One way to do that was to emphasize the low tones in their voices, rather than the high ones, a method she passed on to the producers, such as Dorothea Cox, who coached Colpitts in turn.[118] If a woman did not have a low or trainable voice, Long would ask one who did to read her commentaries; producer Elspeth Chisholm, for example, became the on-air voice of Thelma LeCocq, who wrote about fashion.[119]

How well the commentators delivered a script was also important. The CBC's managers were already encouraging their presenters of both sexes to use a more intimate speaking style—much like a conversation at the family hearth—to address their audiences. In their eyes, housewives, alone at home during the day, were, like children, vulnerable to shocking or upsetting radio content, which was generally avoided in favour of programming that soothed and reassured them. This did not always apply to talks,[120] one of Long's ways of educating female listeners about their domestic and public roles, but even then women's voices had to be carefully modulated. She learned this lesson after her first live audition demonstrated that women's voices became "higher and higher," and "thin and strained," when they debated each other. When the two protagonists in this case—Mattie Rotenberg and Margaret MacKenzie—were told to take a break, they began talking with each other cordially about their home lives, and their voices suddenly became more relaxed and natural. "We were all fascinated," Long recalled in her CBC memoir. "The women had suddenly come to life. Their voices, their language had changed. Somehow any two women meeting on any remote jungle path, or on a frozen Arctic shore might pause to exchange the same information in that same warm voice. Standing beside me in the audition room, a woman whispered in an awed voice; 'I like that, it's show!'"[121]

Accordingly, Long taught her protégés to write conversationally, for the ear rather than the eye. That way, they sounded as if they were chatting to their listeners over a country telephone line, a woman-to-woman technique that became known as "Elizabeth's Formula" in the CBC Talks department.[122] Ellen Harris of Vancouver took to it right away, telling the other commentators in one of their mail exchanges, "That's the best piece of advice I ever got."[123] Shirley Brett Foley, however, resisted this style at first for something more "elevated." She recalled Long saying to her, "I'm waiting for the day that Shirley goes on the air and says, 'Oh dear, I have such a cold, and the heat was off in the apartment, and my new hat doesn't look at all the way I thought it would with the dress I told you about last week'— That's the day I'll be able to relax."[124] This speaking style, which one archivist described as being replete with "cloying self-satisfaction,"[125] does, to the modern ear, sound patronizing. It was, however, the commentators' way of trying to connect with their listeners, keep their attention and pass on useful information.

Sometimes they used on-air material, both serious and amusing, from their own home lives in order to establish a rapport with their audiences. Harris, who was married to Richard, a high school teacher, shared their worries about their 11-year-old son, Colin, after he became seriously ill with rheumatic fever.[126] On a lighter note, she recounted 8-year-old Susan's horror when the family dog, Brigadier, ate the Easter eggs the child had bought for the other members of the family.[127] Keeping her listeners was important to Harris, who shared Long's view that good programming involved more than domestic notes, and that a broad audience was important. Harris, who received hundreds of Christmas cards, as well as all kinds of material of interest from listeners, such as magazine articles and clippings, was glad that her program seemed to appeal to many people, including some men. "I am pleased about this because, as one of you said recently: I do not like programmes directed AT WOMEN. Women's interests are very broad in spite of what some people believe and men and women can enjoy many things in common." On this same day, Harris confided on the air that she dreaded getting into a rut and losing touch with her listeners. So, she asked them to help her "houseclean" her program by sending her story ideas and feedback on the kinds of features they liked best—recipes, interviews, commentaries or art reviews. "Your letters, you see, have made me realize that this microphone isn't just a complicated piece of metal and wires and electric currents ... it is very human and it is very alive.... Don't forget this programme is planned for you and you have a very real share in what I do. It isn't a one-way thing at all. It is a programme for you and me working together." One listener, Molly Phillips of Royal Oak, near Victoria, B.C., responded in a letter: "I for one would say leave kitchen affairs to others who specialize in such matters and give us something broader and more cultural." She also told the broadcaster not to bother promoting upcoming features on her shows, inserting a compliment that must have reassured her: "It is much more interesting to turn on the radio and wonder what's coming when the programmes are consistently good, as yours are."[128]

Long was aware that her commentators had to be marketed to their audiences in other ways beyond the material they used on the air. If, for example, she decided that a protégé's name lacked an attractive or comfortingly familiar ring, she would change it. Some of her commentators had their own reasons for using on-air pseudonyms. Colpitts did not want everyone to know that she, a married woman with three children, was working for pay when Long hired her in 1942. The other reason, she recalled, was that Long "thought Margaret Colpitts—Cahll-pits as she pronounced it—was a poor radio name. There were too many 'g's and 'p's and 't's. After searching

Margaret Colpitts on the air as "Joan Marshall" of CBC Radio, with announcer Carl McCaull and technician Ross McNaughton. LAC CBC MISA 0208, with permission of the Canadian Broadcasting Corporation.

through the telephone directory for inspiration, she and Long settled on "Joan Marshall."[129] She also persuaded a reluctant Dolores MacFarlane, a Winnipeg commentator, to change her first name to "Peggy,"[130] while Terry MacLellan of Halifax became "Ann Terry" because it sounded snappier.[131]

How they dressed was also important to Long, likely because a number of her commentators made personal appearances, speaking to women's clubs and other organizations on behalf of the CBC.[132] The Montreal producer Margaret Howes laughingly recalled Long's insistence on keeping up the social appearances that were *de rigueur* for women, even during the war years. "I remember the very first meeting, which practically staggered me, and I thought if I can make it with Elizabeth Long I'll have made it with CBC. Because she required that I should wear a hat. I was very amused about that."[133]

Long admitted to McEnaney that she loved to run people's lives for them, but sometimes hated to give them advice because it was coloured by her own experiences and might not suit them.[134] That did not really stop her, however, from taking an intrusive interest in their personal problems, especially if these issues threatened the quality of their work. Once, she called up Brett Foley's mother to inform her that her daughter was depressed over a failing romance, the broadcaster recalled. "'What about Shirley, and what are we going to do about her?'… She wasn't going to have one of her commentators in any difficulty that she hadn't brought on or that she couldn't do anything about."[135]

Occasionally, Long would ask her commentators to record some of their programs and send them to her, so she could listen and return them with her thorough critiques. Brett Foley recalled dreading their arrival on her desk. "I wouldn't have a shred of confidence left by the time I had finished reading her dissection of my particular week's work…. It was just devastating." Even her more experienced colleagues reacted to Long's critiques in much the same way. "She just had to do this, obviously, and I suppose it was a good thing, I don't know…. She was a very stern master, she really was, a mentor." Although Brett Foley did not recall any praise, Long did send complimentary notes to her commentators, as well as useful news releases and press clippings, her comments running up the side and top margins, and below her signature, as if she never had enough room to say what she wanted to say.[136]

Starting in 1944, she organized regular annual gatherings for them in Toronto, "to exchange ideas and to see each other, to give each other strength," Howes recalled, echoing Long's own rationale. "Because it was a very demanding job to be a morning commentator. It was a very prestigious job too, but it was very demanding."[137] Long realized that they needed a way to support each other, once estimating that the radio programs they wrote amounted to the equivalent of six novels a year.[138] She explained,

"Writing and broadcasting a 15-minute talk five days a week is a heavy assignment, especially when you have to locate every news story for every day, to say nothing of all the other days ahead! So it was useful to have an informal conference where all these commentators could offer their opinions and suggestions, share reliable program ideas ... especially those related to the war."[139] She listened to their complaints about their workloads, telling her CBC managers that they were sometimes caught in conflicts between their national and regional supervisors. She and Howes argued that they need more support, better pay and more publicity, and should not be expected to take on additional duties that wore them down.[140] "Peggy" MacFarlane acknowledged, "I don't think we realized at the time how much she fought for the activities of women in the CBC. We just didn't give her credit for it.... We thought she was sort of a cranky, crusty old doll and we didn't realize she was looking after us all the time."[141]

Aside from training and supporting her local commentators, Long tapped into a network of national experts and correspondents of all backgrounds to provide further news and information for the Women's Interest programs. After witnessing a male commentator stumbling as he tried to describe the Queen's dress during the 1939 Royal Tour, she decided that the CBC must use women to cover such occasions.[142] Years later, she hired Jean Halton, a freelance journalist who was married to CBC correspondent Matthew Halton, to cover the wedding of Princess Elizabeth.[143] During the war, she spent two weeks in Ottawa meeting at the Wartime Prices and Trade Board, helping women's group leaders from across Canada to organize a national consumer committee. WPTB material regularly went to the consumer commentator, Ethelwyn Hobbes, who used them in her broadcasts. Long felt that it was important during the war for homemakers to know what vitamins, food, clothing material and other supplies were available, and to what degree.[144] Dr. Elizabeth Chant Robertson regularly sent out material on nutrition, family health and other domestic matters, and provided feedback to the commentators on their scripts.[145] Juanita Chambers, a Montreal psychologist who offered advice on children and family relationships, was one of the few woman of colour regularly on the radio.[146] Several contributors, including the historian Mary Quayle Innis, wrote radio talks on famous women in history and contemporary life.[147] Other broadcast material came via regular radio letters from ordinary women facing particular challenges living and working in remote areas of Canada, such as Beatrice Ford, a teacher in Nain, Labrador, whose grandmother was Inuit.[148] Long felt that any woman who had the talent and desire could be trained to be a good radio programmer or commentator, and she was impatient with the undercurrent of racial prejudice still common at the CBC and among some of her friends. She remembered getting very annoyed when Talks staff members ignored two bright young Aboriginal women who had come to the unit for six months of broadcasting training. Rather than make the effort to help them, they "agreed to protest such silly little girls being sent to bother them. They were not silly—they were miraculous."[149]

Aside from her regular regional and national commentators, Long hired several women who were essentially news analysts, women known in the CBC as "Bessie Long's stable," whom she encouraged to inform their women listeners about economic and political issues that could have an impact on them and their families. They were told not to take sides in their broadcasts, but to remain unbiased, even though they had strong feelings about women's rights and social justice that came through in their commentaries.[150] One of the earliest was Mattie Rotenberg, who had graduated with a Ph.D. in physics from the University of Toronto, the first woman and first Jew to be awarded the degree. She and her husband, Meyer, a lawyer, had five children, and she did not work in broadcasting while raising her family. Instead, she wrote a women's column for the weekly *Jewish Standard* in the 1930s and founded and directed a day school for Jewish children for 15 years. While she was broadcasting, which was a part-time occupation, she also worked three days a week as a physics lab demonstrator. She told her daughter she would not have worked full time if it meant she could not have a family.[151]

Long evidently took to her from the start, possibly because she was not only bright and informed, but she shared her interest in women's issues, international affairs and peace. Using her scientific background, Rotenberg contributed occasional items to the CBC in the beginning of her radio career, all of them 12 to 15 minutes long and designed to teach her listeners something. "My very first broadcast was called 'College in the Kitchen.' That was of course one of Elizabeth's titles. Trying to refute the argument that it's a waste for women to go to college if they become a housewife ... I pointed out in the first place how much our daily life depends on, say—of course, my interest being in science—on scientific progress. Even the clock we use, and our cooking."[152] The script for the program, which aired in 1939, has her adopting the chatty style that Long encouraged in her commentators, with Rotenberg leading her listeners into a virtual kitchen, pointing out how many useful inventions were the work of university professors. "There's your alarm clock ticking on the shelf—as common and homely an article as we can find. But that ordinary clock is an accurate measuring instrument, which the most advanced scientists of other days couldn't even imagine. I can't begin to tell you how many different kinds of Professors had their work put into that little clock, but there it sits, telling you it's time to start getting dinner ready." This eight-page script continued with a discussion of the important roles academics played in the humanities as well as the sciences, learning that focused on "the things of the mind and of the spirit," such as love and cooperation, that make for a strong home. It ended with her suggesting to her listeners that they follow her lead and plan to send their daughters to college so they could take advantage of this higher learning, no matter what they decided to do with their lives.[153] As simplistic as their approach may have sounded, Rotenberg and Long were encouraging women to get a higher education in the humanities and sciences at a time when they were not generally encouraged to do so, and those who wanted to take medicine were still being barred or restricted through quotas at some universities.[154]

Rotenberg, who was not confined to science topics, broadcast series on women in ancient history; on men and women who contributed to society, such as Elizabeth Fry and her work on prison reform; and on women's rights and responsibilities. In 1945 she won an award from the Canadian Women's Press Club for one of her broadcasts, "The Post-War Woman," which underlined the importance of women understanding world affairs and encouraging their children to become informed adults. She told her listeners, "Trade between nations, tariffs, inflation—these are matters that affect the welfare and happiness of every home—these are not remote questions only for the minds of statesmen.... If a democracy is to succeed, every citizen must be intelligent and responsible; must have the knowledge and information to take part in self-government.... Therefore, as a citizen, the post-war woman must study and learn—she must know—about public affairs. Otherwise what is the use of women's long struggle for the vote?"[155] She felt that sheer ignorance among the people, as well as a dismissal of women's rights, contributed greatly to fascism, and that it was up to women to help ensure that it never take hold again.[156]

In her bid to educate listeners about international affairs, and especially women's rights worldwide, Long assigned Rotenberg several programs on those themes after the war. Long was delighted that the United Nations was holding separate meetings about women's rights. "Even the idea of making it official was a great step forward for the legal status of women, and like every other woman, I was interested to see them in action," she wrote in her CBC memoir. She accompanied Rotenberg to the United Nations, recalling later that the listeners liked her commentator's regular five-minute reports on what was happening there.[157] Rotenberg found that agreement on resolutions on equal pay and other rights for women had to be negotiated carefully at these meetings because of partisan, international politicking from all sides.[158] Even the British House of Commons, which had agreed to the principle of equal pay for its female civil servants back in 1920, still could not bring itself to implement it over 30 years later, she informed her listeners. She told them that a current bid to set a definite date to make it official received only lukewarm support from both Conservative and Labour politicians, who put the matter off, despite the fact that women were jamming the public galleries.[159] Personally, as much as she invoked maternal feminist thinking in her support of strong women's roles in the home, especially during the war,[160] Rotenberg strongly believed in equal pay for equal work, regardless of gender or race, as "the only fair thing from the standpoint of democracy, justice and the welfare of all." She also believed that any married woman, even one with young children, should have the right to work, at least part time, and to receive social benefits, so that she had "the chance to participate in the larger world of which her home is a part." Husbands should share the burden by lending a hand with home and child care, she believed.[161] These ideas were not unusual among white, middle-class women who were working outside the home at the time.[162]

Long's CBC colleagues have also credited her with discovering another prominent broadcaster, Florence Bird, although it appears from Bird's archived papers and autobiography that she took the initiative for her own career. The American-born journalist, a graduate of the elite Bryn Mawr College, chose to write and broadcast under the name "Anne Francis," partly as a nod to a suffragist grandmother, and partly because her husband, John, was also a journalist and she felt they should have separate professional identities. They were in Winnipeg during the war, where she wrote and broadcast home-front material.[163] Afterwards, they moved to Ottawa, where she did news commentaries for the Women's Interest programs, including *Trans-Canada Matinee*, which she said she helped Long plan.[164]

Bird specialized in economics, politics and international affairs, teasing out issues in these fields that were of particular relevance to women. Like Long, Rotenberg and other feminist journalists of her generation, she looked to the postwar United Nations as a model of democracy and equality for all citizens, particularly its Universal Declaration of Human Rights.[165] She was known as a strong supporter of equal pay for work of equal value and other rights for all women, regardless of class or marital status, who worked outside the home. For the Women's Interest programs, she wrote and narrated weekly radio series on the economic status of women, why women worked and the kinds of jobs they did.

On one program, for example, Bird pointed out that women in the workforce were earning far less than men, which she felt was highly unfair. She believed that although men and women were different from each other, they should still be treated the same in the workplace "in the name of common justice," and urged her listeners to help solve the problem. "In Canada today, many women are paid less money for doing the same work as men, and that leaves me with one more question, and I don't know the answer to this one. Here it is: What are you and I, as voters, citizens, or just plain women, prepared to do about it?"[166] The Canadian Institute of International Affairs published a series of pamphlets based on this program series.[167] "I did a lot of research for that," Bird recalled, "and my hair stood on end when

I realized what was happening to women.... I was a strong lobbyist, so there I was, at least one commentator who was not taking political sides, but was just a strong feminist saying, 'This is what is happening to women. It's not good enough. You better do something.'"[168] Bird also devoted a talk to the value of women in the workforce, explaining that they represented 10 percent of the workers in heavy industry, 65 to 70 percent of textile workers, and 50 percent of the workers in retail and in the banks. She argued that "women have made an essential place for themselves in the working world and they are there to stay because they are needed." She not only wanted women's clubs and individual voters to study the matter, publicize the problem and lobby for change,[169] but she also encouraged her colleagues to discuss these issues on the air in the hope that some of their listeners would become activists.

Ellen Harris in Vancouver, for example, read Bird's talks on women's rights on her program, starting with her own strong introduction in favour of them: "It is time we women wakened up to the fact that our place in the world has changed whether we like it or not." Nevertheless, when one young female listener objected that Bird was being "ridiculous" and that women should not compete with men, Harris defended her colleague, adding, "We can do many things as well as the men ... no woman should feel that she is better than a man, and no man should feel that he is better than a woman. We are equals." Most of the listeners who contacted Harris agreed with Bird on the issue of equality in the workplace, including equal pay for equal work, the Vancouver broadcaster reported to them later.[170]

On at least one occasion, however, Bird's script was edited beforehand, either by herself or someone else in the Ottawa studio who clearly thought she was expressing herself too frankly. She meant to point out how the British government accommodated its married female employees, but the following observation was crossed out with red ink: "Personally, I think the Canadian Government might also consider experimenting in this matter. As you know, at the present time, the dominion government does not employ married women in the Civil Service, but, of course, there is always the hope that it may adapt itself to changing conditions ... particularly if other countries like Great Britain and the United States point the way."[171] Since the CBC had the same policy against hiring married women, which would have included Bird, her comments might have been considered too subjective, as well as adversarial to the corporation.[172]

Although she worked regularly for Long, Bird was one of the few female broadcasters who managed to develop a career primarily outside of women's interests, becoming a respected commentator on national and international affairs programs, such as *Capital Report*, where, on at least one occasion, she had to fight for equal pay with her male fellow panellists.[173] As part of her interest in international affairs, Bird covered the United Nations from time to time, for example, explaining for listeners the 1944 meeting at Bretton Woods, New Hampshire, where the delegates agreed to establish the International Monetary Fund and the World Bank.[174] She also travelled extensively in Europe, producing commentaries and documentaries.[175]

Long occasionally sent encouraging notes to Bird about the excellent quality and appeal of her commentaries, notes that reflected what she perceived as the varied intellectual and class characteristics of her national audience. After hearing one of Bird's radio broadcasts, possibly one of her historical overviews of women and work, Long was enthusiastic. She felt that the commentary engaged the listeners, including "fishermen's wives in Newfoundland and prairie women in northern Saskatchewan," but did not intimidate them. "You are terrific. Poised, sure of yourself and sure of women—you see it all in historical perspective. You know progress is inevitable. You don't expect more than women demand and the public learns to accept.... I cannot think of a man broadcaster who is an expert in any given field who could give such a human glimpse of his subject—perhaps because he has not tried too hard to identify with his audience—and perhaps because he need not be the voice of such a great minority as the women workers of the world."[176] Even after Long retired and returned to Winnipeg, she kept in touch, once counselling Bird, who had apparently missed winning an award, not to be discouraged. "How silly to ever doubt your ability, and as long as we can write, we shall! We all walk humbly before the God of the Pen! We all need encouragement. An award helps recognition for a woman, but even CBC here has it by the grapevine that Florence is the only one who does her homework—and producing the others is a bore! Don't tell them I told you."[177]

The on-air presence of Rotenberg and Bird contributed to programming that was designed to inform their listeners about women's postwar perspectives on international affairs as well as domestic ones, a key component of Long's programming goals. She also used her women's club connections to promote international understanding among women through scripted radio letters and exchange broadcasts from abroad, emphasizing the simple, domestic concerns that they had in common. She was initially encouraged by the anthropologist Margaret Mead, who suggested to her that her listeners might be interested in the customs of women and their families in other countries.[178] Long told one interviewer, "I felt human relations the world over could be improved through such a program. There's a bond between women because they have family relations and home interests in common. They share the basic problems, the non-political ones."[179] In her memoir, she gave a more extensive version of the reasons behind her decision. In 1944 the head of the NCWC, Mrs. Edgar Hardy, contacted her after hearing a CBC broadcast featuring several of Long's women commentators attending their own annual meeting in Toronto. Hardy invited her to travel with her to New York to attend a meeting of the Association of Women Radio Commentators of the United States. The theme of the New York conference was "Women of the United Nations," aimed at helping to build international understanding and a lasting peace. Whenever she was asked why she was set on programming women's voices from other countries, Long recalled, "I said because of the war, I knew Canadian women would be interested in women of other countries, and sometimes a few of our immigrants would find it comforting to hear messages from their former homes." But, she added, she secretly cherished the idea that nations should talk to each other sincerely as a way of cooperating in the interests of world peace and international development.[180] Peace issues were important to Long, who felt it would not be accomplished without an end to ethnic and racial animosity.[181] Her perspective was shared by Ellen Harris in Vancouver, who regularly broadcast Long's material or her own on religious and racial intolerance, international human rights and peace issues.[182]

The exchange broadcasts with other countries began only after Long tried unsuccessfully several times to get international women's groups interested in fostering them. In a "pique," she finally lost patience with them and announced at one conference, also in New York, that the CBC was to broadcast the weekly programs, and then she had to make sure that it was done. In 1947 the Radio and Television Committee of the International Council of Women elected her as its convenor and decided, in Long's words, "to create better international understanding through person to person broadcasts, with regular women's programmes including news and views of women of other countries."[183] The ICW was also committed to getting women placed in administrative and planning positions in broadcasting and promoting the uses of radio for educating women at the local level in Asia and Africa.[184] Her position as the ICW's broadcast convenor allowed Long to travel overseas, meeting with women broadcasters, members of various women's councils and nongovernmental organizations attached to the United Nations.[185] After she set up and chaired a similar committee for the NCWC, it elected her vice-president and national chairman of its Arts and Letters Committee.[186] In these capacities, she continued to argue strongly for international communication among women, and for informative radio programming for them over the CBC national network.[187] Ellen Harris, for example, read regular radio letters from a prominent Dutch housewife, who wrote about the postwar reconstruction there and its effects on her family. Harris and Long later visited her in person on separate trips to the Netherlands.[188] Some of the women broadcasters Long got to know overseas visited Toronto.[189]

From all those connections came programming that Long fostered to inform listeners at home and through the CBC's overseas radio service. *New World Calling* featured newsletters from Canadian women who were

married to diplomats or belonged to international organizations, but sometimes from citizens of those countries as well, none of whom were necessarily experts.[190] Long just wanted them to share their experiences or impart
information that listeners would find interesting and entertaining. On one
edition of the program, Long organized women leaders from 17 countries
to answer the question: "What education should I give my daughter that
she may help build a better world?"[191] Long did not confine her interests to
European women, McEnaney explained. "She was an internationalist. She
had contacts all over the world and she had women from Africa and South
America and Asia delivering talks." On another series, she asked the participants to talk about their mothers-in-law, as a way of getting them to discuss
family relationships in a way that might reveal commonalities.[192] Several of
the programs on *Women's World*, which aired on the CBC International Service in the late 1940s, featured heavily scripted and carefully balanced panel
discussions with three women who immigrated to Canada from Latin America and Spain on whether women should become involved in politics and otherwise work outside the home.[193] Long also organized exchange programs
with radio stations around the world, giving her local broadcasters the
option of the material they should use.[194] On at least one occasion, she had
the CBC subsidize what she considered substandard fees sent to Canadian
commentators. In 1954 she arranged to send a monthly commentary by Florence Bird to a women's program on the South African Broadcasting Corporation service, but decided that, because of the exchange rates, the CBC
should pay Bird more than the three pounds the SABC offered.[195]

In 1951 Long was 60 years old, the required age of retirement then for
female civil servants, including permanent employees of the CBC, but she
appeared reluctant to leave. Management kept her on under contract for
another two years, possibly because at least one influential woman's group,
the Canadian Association of Consumers, lobbied on her behalf.[196] In 1953
Helen James took over as supervisor of Women's Interest programming,
with Long staying on as adviser until 1956.[197] Afterwards, most of her time
and energy were taken up with freelance writing and the various club activities that fostered her interests in feminism, international understanding
and peace.[198] At the time, she was helping McEnaney in one of her own latest endeavours, doing public relations for the new Canadian Peace Research
Institute, which later had a political falling out with the more radical Voice
of Women.[199]

Long was still very interested in the working and personal lives of her
former colleagues and protégés, however, once going to the Winnipeg train
station to bestow a wedding gift and a sentimental note on Brett Foley, who
was passing through on her way to Vancouver to get married. "So this was
her.... There was an umbilical cord of some kind that never was cut with her
and her broadcasters."[200] Long's letters to McEnaney, who was still lobbying

for equal rights for women at the CBC, were often peppered with gossip and counsel, particularly about how to use influential individuals or women's groups in the ongoing campaign. Long thought women were "foolish" when they did not apply for promotions that involved greater responsibilities because they were enjoying the jobs they already had. "I failed that way myself. I can see now it is unsound."[201] She rejoined the local branch of the Canadian Women's Press Club but found the members, who were by then a mix of journalists and public relations workers, timid and conventional compared to "McClung, Cora Hind and dozens more. LEADERS all." The current members were not quick to help lobby for CBC women because, in her estimation, they were too intent on being "nice girls.... Well, the big revolution has not come here, nor the revelation that you only will be respected when you do raise hell."[202] Women's progress at the CBC was, in the mid-1960s, still proceeding at a glacial pace; in fact, four senior female programmers, James, Howes, Cox and Helen Carscallen, resigned because their various ambitions were being stalled or they just weren't being heard by management.[203]

The tide was beginning to change, however. In February 1967 Florence Bird was appointed chair of the Royal Commission on the Status of Women in Canada, which had come about because of determined lobbying by women's groups. Bird wrote Long, "This is the toughest, most interesting, and necessary job I have ever tackled. I only hope I can do it."[204] At a Women's Canadian Club meeting in Winnipeg, where Bird gave a speech on the commission's agenda, Long joined her at the head table. Not only did Bird look stunning in a fashionable black and beige ensemble, she told McEnaney, "She listed all OUR PROBLEMS. My opinion is that even to have them listed and identified as something thwarting the advance of women is a good thing because no longer can sentimentalists and unconscious women haters dismiss that special problem as a WHIM."[205]

Long wrote to Bird, asking her not to let the issue of equal pay dominate the commission's investigation, although it was important, pointing out that there was a "certain advantage" in not being in competition for the top jobs. "You and I are both good examples of what lots of fun we had out of our work because we were ONLY WOMEN. We knew we never would make the big money, but we stuck to the rules and then spread LATERALLY. We got into everything that interested us and had a most entertaining life, with the approval of the men because we were no threat to they [sic] succession to their special throne."[206] She told McEnaney that Bird well understood how women could become demoralized at work, however. "Anne Francis [Bird] has all this stuff at hand. As you know, I paid her to become an expert on women workers, and she has kept right on."[207]

Nevertheless, Long bluntly rejected McEnaney's suggestion that she organize a brief to the commission from Prairie press women, because she had little faith in them anymore. "I have already told you how stupid the prairie members are. They would not know how to write a brief if they had any ideas."[208] She was no doubt disappointed that her local branch, once so vibrant and activist, was beginning to fail. There were no regular meetings after 1969 because older members had died or moved, and the younger women preferred to join the Winnipeg Press Club, one of several journalists' organizations across the country that had finally decided to accept female members.[209] Anyway, she told McEnaney, she was too busy establishing the NCWC's Lady Aberdeen Library, a collection of thousands of titles by and about women, housed today at the University of Waterloo. She was also helping to organize a new public library in Winnipeg.[210]

McEnaney went ahead and presented a well-publicized brief to Bird's commission on behalf of the Toronto branch of the Canadian Women's Press Club, complaining about unfair treatment of media women in the press and broadcast fields. She took care to highlight the ongoing inequities in the CBC, where, she said, the men hired their male friends, appointed a few women to senior management as tokens but ignored their advice, and still neglected to include female voices and perspectives on news and farm broadcasts.[211] Helen James's successor, Dodi Robb, made sure the commission hearings and its recommendations received extensive radio and TV coverage on *Matinee* and its TV equivalent, *Take 30*.[212] Long, listening and watching in Winnipeg, was glad to see strong turnouts for the hearings and the rush of calls on open-line radio programs about the issues.[213] The commission recommended equal opportunities for women in the public service in its report, issued in December 1970,[214] and a few years later Bird served as a consultant for a separate internal investigation on the CBC, whose senior managers, she recalled, assured her that there was no gender discrimination there.[215] The report resulted in new procedures aimed at improving the status of its female employees.[216]

In retrospect, Long viewed her time at the CBC with some amusement, especially her earnestness about her work as supervisor of Women's Interest programs. After going over some of her old interview clippings for her memoir, she exclaimed to the recipient, William Macdonald of the CBC, that she had been "so evangelical! Women's talks needed to save the women of Canada. How funny now, but during the war and after perhaps we all were like that. I also had a wonderful time—so much easier to plan what other people will do, than to do it yourself." To McEnaney, she confided, "I am simply in stitches. I was completely mad. Full of talks on women—and everything was grist to my mill. And so positive I was right. I don't see how anyone could bear me ... and unless a person was going to broadcast or give me ideas, I doubt I knew she was in sight at all." Later she added, "I giggle at the sweeping statements I made. I knew all the answers!... When I finish my stint, if I do, I have marked down some clippings for your memoirs, which will be more accurate than mine!"[217]

Elizabeth Long may have taken a self-deprecatory attitude toward her own accomplishments, but the record suggests she made a strong contribution to Canadian feminism during and after the Second World War, from within her own specialized niche. Using the gendered structure of radio to her advantage, and the support of the NCWC and other women's groups, Long, through her commentators, brought both practical domestic advice and news of the wider world to women in their homes. They juggled nostrums about homemaking and child-rearing with information on women's rights in Canada and abroad. Modern-day feminists might find their approach to their listeners, mostly housewives and mothers, somewhat patronizing; yet, under her direction, they promulgated feminist views to a broad yet diverse audience, keeping in mind the constraining social attitudes toward homemakers at the time and being careful not to push them beyond their own limits and uncertainties. At the heart of Long's approach lay her firm conviction that women were generally intelligent, curious and cared about the issues that affected them. In order to carry out her mandate, she hired like-minded on-air personalities, invented some of their personas, coached them on what to broadcast and how to do it effectively, and fostered the feminist outlooks several of them, such as Rotenberg, Bird and Harris, already shared.

A link between the feminist generations is also apparent in Long's personal and professional relationships. It was the suffragist Cora Hind who most influenced her, and she in turn encouraged Florence Bird, who advocated for women's rights and chaired the 1967 status of women commission, one of the most effective government inquiries in Canadian history. Long and her closest associates did not abandon feminism during the mid-20th century, but fostered it firmly, if sometimes carefully, using radio to try to instill confidence and pride in their female listeners, encouraging them to do their best and stand up for themselves on the job and in the home. Given the lack of audience surveys for Women's Interest programming under Long, their impact cannot be measured exactly;[218] however, their feminist attempts to encourage their listeners were liberal and pragmatic, and survived in the women's programming their successors brought to the CBC.[219]

CHAPTER 5

"My Body Belongs to Me, Not the Government"

Anne Roberts, Kathryn Keate and the Abortion Caravan Publicity Campaign of 1970

I n May 1970, shortly after Mother's Day, the *Toronto Daily Star* ran an editorial cartoon featuring a young feminist, chained to a heavy wood chair, being escorted from the House of Commons by a disgruntled RCMP officer. She carried a placard demanding "Free Abortion" and wore a sign over her stomach asserting, "My body belongs to me, *not* the government." Commented the Mountie: "I wish your mother had thought of that!" The cartoonist clearly took his side, regarding her as undisciplined, immature and misguided. To further illustrate his point, he dressed her as a hippie, drew a Disney character on her purse and added the caption: "Taking leave of their census."[1] The cartoon was a sardonic comment on a Parliament Hill protest involving 30 young women who had chained themselves to chairs and railings in the public galleries of the House of Commons, loudly demanding "abortion on demand" and catching police and security officers completely off guard. Their demonstration was the dramatic climax of the Abortion Caravan, a cross-country trek involving women from western and central Canada, and was the first sustained and well-publicized feminist action of the national campaign to decriminalize abortion in Canada.

The Caravan has been featured in detail in several book chapters, theses and feminist publications, some of which have appeared relatively recently as more scholars and activists take renewed interest in the "second wave" of the women's movement. Most of these accounts are based on the activists' oral or written histories of their involvement in the campaign, as are recent media retrospectives produced for its 40th anniversary. While the women discuss, to varying degrees, the extensive news coverage the caravan attracted in 1970, this is not the focus of their stories. They are understandably more intent on recounting this key phase of the

Cartoonist Duncan McPherson's response to the Abortion Caravan disruption in the House of Commons. Copyright: Duncan Macpherson. Reprinted with permission—TorStar Syndication Services.

abortion rights struggle in Canada in the context of the charged feminist politics of the time.[2] This chapter will discuss the media strategies of two feminists who were directly involved in orchestrating publicity for the campaign in light of the print coverage the Caravanners subsequently received. As young journalists in training, Anne Roberts and Kathryn Keate, who is known today as Kathryn-Jane Hazel,[3] straddled the divide between news gathering and activism at a time when the feminist slogan "the personal is political" supposedly cut no ice in the newsrooms of the nation. All reporters, male and female, were expected to avoid any political conflict of interest or activities that would compromise their ability to write the news in a fair and balanced way, a basic tenet of journalistic objectivity that still exists today. Further, they were expected to absorb these attitudes as part of their professional identities for as long as they wanted jobs as reporters and editors. Roberts and Keate, however, were both committed socialist feminists and wanted to combine their activism with their journalism.[4]

By 1970 young women like them were beginning to find a home outside of the women's or so-called lifestyle pages, and were spending more time reporting on social issues and less on fashion and domestic concerns, but many of their male colleagues still resisted their growing demands for gender equality in the newsroom.[5] The fact that women journalists were still not taken very seriously allowed Roberts and Keate to subvert the ideals of neutrality and objectivity during the Abortion Caravan campaign, a freedom that became more difficult for them as their careers progressed and women became more accepted as news reporters. This chapter is primarily based on my interviews with them, on archival documents of the campaign—including important material in Roberts's private papers—and on the newspaper and magazine coverage the Caravan attracted as it travelled across the country.

The Abortion Caravan was born in the feminist ferment of the late 1960s. By that time, more women were attending university, joining the workforce, leaving their marriages and having fewer children. There was an increase in pregnancies among unmarried teenagers and college students, who did not have legal access to birth control until 1969, while pregnant married women who already had several children sought to limit their offspring to a number they could emotionally and financially afford. Reproductive freedom was among the many well-publicized demands that politically liberal women's groups brought to the public hearings of the federal Royal Commission on the Status of Women a year earlier. At the time, abortion for any woman was illegal unless the mother's life was at stake, but many of the briefs to the commission suggested wider, more compassionate grounds for the procedure, including a woman's difficult financial circumstances. A few left-leaning groups and individuals, including university students, did tell the commissioners that free abortions should be available to all women on demand. Both these perspectives were reflected in reader surveys conducted in *Chatelaine*, a general circulation magazine published in both English and French versions, with a majority favouring wider grounds for abortion and a substantial minority favouring abortion solely at the woman's request.[6]

Reproductive freedom was one of the political tenets of the socialist campus groups that were attracting more and more young men and women, already familiar with the anti–Vietnam War and civil rights movements and curious about Marxist-Leninist perspectives. Eventually the female members, tiring of the way the men assumed the leadership roles and tried to dominate them sexually, formed their own caucuses and, in many cases, consciousness-raising groups in which they could share their politics and their personal fears and experiences as women. The so-called sexual liberation era, which to that point seemed to have benefited men more than women, began giving way to the women's liberation movement, its members galvanized by anger at the way society treated them. They questioned every-thing—love, sexuality, marriage, the family, maternity, women's work, includ-ing prostitution, and the many forms of violence that kept women acquiescent to men.[7] To their mind, capitalism was at the root of unequal treatment of the sexes, with patriarchy playing a supporting role.[8] These socialist feminist groups—of which there were about two dozen in Canada in 1970—included the Vancouver Women's Caucus (VWC), which Roberts joined, and Toronto Women's Liberation (TWL), in which Keate became involved. The two groups tried to work together on the abortion campaign, believing that women could not attain equality on the job or in the home unless they had control over their own bodies, and that decriminalizing abortion would put an end to the illegal backstreet operations that threat-ened women's lives and health. They were particularly angry about the new federal legislation governing reproductive rights.

In August 1969, as part of an omnibus bill, the Liberal government of Prime Minister Pierre Trudeau passed a federal law allowing very limited access to abortions, based on a medical model of need—if the woman's life or health was directly at risk—rather than just to save the life of the mother.[9] The new law meant that the pregnant woman had to persuade her own doc-tor that she was physically or mentally unfit to have a child. If she suc-ceeded, the doctor would refer her case to a hospital therapeutic abortion committee (TAC), consisting of at least three other physicians. The provisos of this new law were ambiguous, however. For one thing, it did not define the extent of the threat to the woman's physical and mental health, which gave the doctors more leeway to decide on whether or not she needed an abortion but left the decision in their hands, not hers. The woman could not even appear before them to state her own case. Most of the TAC doctors interpreted the "health" provision as conservatively as possible. Further, while the law stated that only doctors in hospitals could perform abortions, it did not make it mandatory for all hospitals to strike therapeutic abortion committees. In short, a woman could get a timely abortion only if her physi-cian and a TAC in a liberal local hospital quickly agreed that she could have one. Generally, that meant urban, middle-class women with money.[10]

Pro-choice advocates argued that the TAC system did little to prevent less fortunate women, such as married mothers with too many children to support or victims of sexual assault, from continuing to procure back-street abortions, or trying to terminate their pregnancies themselves. They might resort to crude methods such as douching with household bath-room cleansers or similar solutions, or inserting knitting needles, coat hangers or slippery elm through their cervixes, which only endangered their health and their lives.[11] Feminist student activists, who believed any woman, married or not, should be free to have sex, pointed out that the birth control pill and other devices could fail and were not necessarily medically safe; therefore, all women, including those living in poverty, needed access to free, legal abortions to guarantee their freedom of choice over child-bearing.[12]

The Vancouver Women's Caucus, who were determined to take their campaign for the decriminalization of abortion to the federal government in Ottawa, planned the Abortion Caravan very strategically. The twenty feminists participating would leave Vancouver at the end of April and arrive on Parliament Hill just before the Mother's Day weekend, provocative timing meant to underscore their argument that women should be able to choose whether or not to have children. Their vehicles would bear slogans urging that the abortion law be repealed, and one would carry a coffin in symbolic mourning for the women who died from botched illegal abortions every year. The Caravanners would stop at several cities and towns along the way to stage dramatic theatrical skits depicting the suffering women experienced when they tried to persuade doctors to give them abortions. In addition, they would hold public meetings, do interviews with the local media and pick up any woman who wanted to join the motorcade. Their local supporters would feed and billet them. The role of Toronto Women's Liberation was to organize the Caravan activities in their own city and help with the main events in Ottawa. In addition, feminists across the country would hold their own local demonstrations before, on and after the Mother's Day weekend. As political scientist Jane Jensen has written, "The Abortion Caravan of 1970 had the effect of both mobilizing support for abortion rights and providing a dramatic public announcement that a women's movement prepared for radical action had arrived on the scene, with abortion on demand as a key claim."[13]

Media historian Patricia Bradley has documented how news stories about "women's libbers" and their radical politics, challenging rhetoric, colourful street theatre and other agitprop actions were already becoming commonplace in the U.S. media, a double-edged sword for the participants. It guaranteed them attention while presenting the risk that their concerns would be dismissed.[14] The Caravanners understood that risk and planned their media campaign carefully. It essentially consisted of three phases: advance activism and publicity, the cross-country trek, and the demonstrations in Ottawa. Anne Roberts and Kathryn Keate were not in the Caravan motorcade but worked behind the scenes on its behalf. Roberts was involved in the local campaigns in Vancouver and supplied much of the advance publicity for the Caravan as it made its way across the country. She also wrote articles about the campaign for feminist and campus publications, and later as a journalist with the Canadian Press news agency in Edmonton, where she worked during the spring and summers of 1969 and 1970. Keate was a key publicity organizer for the Caravan's volatile demonstrations in Ottawa, writing about her involvement later in *Saturday Night* magazine. She did not arrange this journalism assignment in advance, but agreed to it several weeks after the Caravan was over, when the editor, Robert Fulford, asked her to write a feature story from the perspective of someone who had been involved, in line with the contemporary, subjective trend in first-person New Journalism. It gave her a rare chance to write about her involvement in the mainstream media from the perspective of a feminist activist.[15] This chapter focuses on Roberts and Keate, rather than all the women involved in the publicity, as these two were the only ones who had professional journalism training and who continued full time in the field after the Abortion Caravan was over.

While Roberts's and Keate's childhoods were quite different, their socialist feminist outlooks were similar. Roberts grew up in a conservative Dutch-Calvinist farming community near Grand Rapids, Michigan, but her freethinking parents were well-educated Democrats, union supporters and atheists, which set them apart from their neighbours, as did their occupations. Roberts and her family lived in a house on her grandfather's farm, but her father, Richmond, supervised a metallurgy laboratory at General Motors. Once the youngest of their four children was in school, their mother, Barbara, worked as a librarian, as the editor of a local weekly newspaper, and later as the editor of five advertising weeklies. Although Roberts was not conscious of it at the time, she feels now that her mother was an influential role model as a woman who insisted on working outside the home. Her father "strongly resisted" his wife's decision to work for pay, given the social mores that dictated that men supported their families and married women with children were supposed to stay home. Roberts recalls that her mother always fought those expectations and was "quite a strong person … to be able to kind of forge ahead. It was very important to her." She managed the household schedule with the aid of her children, who were expected to do home and farm chores. As the third child, and the eldest of the two girls, Roberts helped out mainly around the house, even though "I always wanted to be out on the fields and driving the tractor more than doing the dishes."

It was a busy life, but a limited one from her perspective. Given her family's relatively liberal outlook compared to the religious conservatism of the community in which they lived, she felt very much like "a minority, which I think gives you a certain perspective." Later, she attended Michigan State University, where she became involved in the civil rights and anti–Vietnam War movements. By the time she graduated with a degree in anthropology, she considered herself a Marxist. Taking a break from her studies, she worked for a year as a social worker in Detroit, and then, looking for a change, moved to Vancouver to attend graduate school at the University of British Columbia, expecting to become an academic. There she became involved with anti-war and socialist student groups and later with the Vancouver Women's Caucus, an offshoot of Students for a Democratic University. Initially formed by graduate students from Simon Fraser University, the caucus welcomed any women interested in joining, and soon moved downtown to the Labour Temple to accommodate its growing numbers. The members wanted their own group where they were not expected to play second fiddle to the radical men and where they could discuss the issues that concerned them, such as equal pay and job opportunities, and the consequences of bearing children.[16]

Roberts, who was in her mid-20s, recalls, "Being young women, the abortion issue was very important to everyone, the right to birth control, the right to control your own sexuality.... It became very logical to set up our own women's caucus, to look at women's situation, but very much within the context of the radical left and of socialism." Even the term "feminist" was suspect because they associated it with consciousness-raising groups where women discussed their personal relationships with men. "Obviously, patriarchy was an element of it, but our main thing was capitalism ... capitalism and imperialism.... We thought women would never be liberated unless those economic systems were changed and ... the world was made more equitable and democratic and the great differential in power and wealth was changed." Roberts put her energy into women's issues, and anti-poverty and peace projects. In January 1970, for example, the caucus formed a Working Women's Workshop to learn organizing skills and to make connections with women in the union movement.[17] They had already quietly opened a weekly service, referring desperate pregnant women to TAC committees or to sympathetic doctors who would provide safe, if illegal, abortions.[18]

During her time at UBC, Roberts worked on the caucus' newspaper, *The Pedestal*, which operated as a collective, with everyone involved making decisions about what to include in the paper, how to lay out the contents and how to distribute it. The collective model was common for radical women's groups at the time, as it was meant to ensure that there would be no hierarchy and everyone would have an equal role, all of which had to be negotiated together. "It was a very heady time of sharing skills. We all learned about things.... We had endless meetings." She was not conscious of wanting to be a journalist as much as she was aware of the power of the media, having witnessed their impact on the Vietnam War and the civil rights movement. The VWC members wanted coverage of feminist issues, too, but on their own terms. "As a generation, we were very media savvy.... We felt that [the media] was so biased against our point of view that we should get our own word out." Nevertheless, they also courted mainstream media attention through staging demonstrations, even though "we had no confidence that our voices or our views would be accurately reflected. So we also had a huge reliance on our own media."

Roberts found working on *The Pedestal* much more exciting than look-ing for a job as a mainstream journalist, but in the summer of 1969, an opportunity came along that took her away from British Columbia, giving her the technical knowledge she needed to write effective publicity for the abortion campaign later. Through a male friend who had worked for the Canadian Press news agency, she found a summer job at its Edmonton bureau, mainly, she recalls, on the strength of his recommendation and her university education.[19] The CP bureaus in different cities wired news stories and photos to the agency's member newspapers across the country for their own use. The newspapers, in turn, sent their own locally generated news sto-ries to the CP bureaus for distribution. Roberts was happy to divide her time between Vancouver and Edmonton, primarily to be with her partner, a Pakistani Muslim who taught at Simon Fraser University but did his post-doctoral fellowship at the University of Alberta. At the time, there was a great deal of racial prejudice against mixed-race couples, as well as moral disapproval of any pair "living in sin," so she did not talk about her per-sonal life at work, but focused on learning as much as she could about jour-nalism.[20] While she was at CP, Roberts was allowed to do almost everything its "newsmen" were trained to do, and did it so well she earned a raise. She rewrote stories from the local newspapers to send out over the wire to pub-lications across the country, wrote radio copy from the same stories for CP's Broadcast News service, and occasionally did some reporting herself, although not for on-air newscasts. The private broadcasters who subscribed to the service did not consider women's voices authoritative enough, one of several male prejudices against female media workers at the time. Never-theless, after her summer stint at CP, she decided that she wanted to be a journalist.[21]

She never met Kathryn Keate, who was born in Montreal, grew up in Victoria, and after completing her undergraduate degree in English litera-ture at UBC in Vancouver, went on to graduate school at the University of Toronto. Keate was chosen as a key publicist for the Ottawa phase of the Abortion Caravan, partly because of her media background, which she came by naturally. Her father, Stuart Keate, was a veteran newsman and pub-lisher of the *Victoria Times* and, by the late 1960s, of the *Vancouver Sun*. He was a liberal, pragmatic, quietly religious man who admired his young daughter's feistiness, and tried to instill in her and her brother a sense of responsibility for giving back to their community. His wife, Letha, had trained in physical education at Margaret Eaton College, University of Toronto, and then taught recreational activities to unemployed people, in order to keep them healthy and occupied. Like many middle-class women of her generation, she did not work outside the home once she was married. She was a very intelligent person who was always sharp in her assessments of other people and their motivations, Keate recalls.

Her parents accepted her strong-minded nature without letting her get out of control or squelching her, and they encouraged intellectual debates around the dinner table. Her mother, concerned that her "bookworm" daughter wasn't physically active enough, successfully interested her in swimming, dancing and theatre, but when she sent her to charm school at one point, the youngster objected. She "just couldn't handle [the] passive, smarmy, wear a pink dress, have your hair in curls, icky-sticky images of femininity" current during the 1950s and early 1960s. "And my mother would always say, when people would criticize her for letting me run around in overalls, 'Well, I'm working on her character. She can learn all that other stuff later.'"

Keate grew into a bright teenager, already familiar with the writings of Simone de Beauvoir and Betty Friedan, whose feminist books had galvanized middle-class women across North America.[22] "I remember at 17 I felt so liberated, I started describing myself as a feminist and an intellectual. I must've been a real pain in the ass."[23] She made headlines when, as an undergraduate at UBC, she presented a brief to the Royal Commission on the Status of Women, complaining of quotas against women students in some university departments, and of the cultural pressure on them to put their femininity before any other considerations, no matter how bright they were. She also appeared on a local CBC television program, discussing media sexism with other panellists.[24] While she was still at UBC, she spent a few weeks learning about Marxism from the Young Socialist League, and felt that their analysis of capitalism held some merit. She was not familiar with radical women's groups, which were barely beginning to stir on campuses across the country.[25]

Keate learned the journalism craft during the summers, working successively on the *Lethbridge Herald* in Alberta, the Toronto *Telegram*, and the *Evening Times Globe/Telegraph-Journal* in Saint John, New Brunswick. They were all conservative newspapers editorially, although their newsroom editors and journalists tended to be more liberal, and some objected in varying degrees to management's biases. Her father arranged these summer jobs and, in turn, would hire the children of the publishers who hired her, a common mutual arrangement in the industry at the time. These were the offspring who had a talent for journalism themselves, as she recalled. "People in the newsroom were sort of expecting us to be the boss's son or daughter and not do much.... I would've felt badly if we had all been whiners and not willing to work, but all of us were keeners and could be said to be assets to the newsroom." After she graduated from UBC, she went to England and worked for a provincial newspaper group for a few months, but was not given many stories to cover, so she returned to Canada and worked for a while as an editorial assistant on *Monday Morning*, a teachers' magazine issued by Saturday Night Publishing.[26]

By then in her early twenties, she decided to take graduate studies in English at the University of Toronto, where she first attended a meeting of Toronto Women's Liberation (TWL), a Marxist collective. She joined because she wanted to be involved with the Abortion Caravan. She saw a poster for TWL, a common way of recruiting members, and "just showed up at a meeting." She moved into a house that was a political co-op and busied herself as a movement organizer, which included voicing phone announcements over a hotline, another way radicals kept up with each other's activities.[27] Schooled in literature and the arts, as were many young college women, she found that socialist feminist political thought challenged and engaged her. "It was so new and it was so, oh ... complicated and we were getting all these new ideas all at once. I mean there had been just enormous, rapid changes since I'd graduated from high school in 1965. When I look at my high school graduation picture and there I am in my below-the-knee skirt and ribbons in my hair and you know.... You never slept with a boy until you got married. And you never lived with anybody." Most women at the time worked for men in support roles, and needed the permission of male relatives if they wanted to be independent, she recalls. "Your career path was to be a secretary, a teacher or a nurse and you couldn't buy a car or own a house or anything without a [male] co-signer, or run a business." Suddenly, by the end of the 1960s, "all this incredible ferment was happening. You know, changes in the divorce laws. Birth control became legal.... The way women dressed completely changed. Everything was just so different and it happened in such a short period of time."

The TWL group was so large that the members spent much of their time meeting in smaller consciousness-raising groups in each other's homes, where they would talk about the politics of housework, or equality of opportunity in the workforce, and, like many young feminists, started questioning the assumptions behind the so-called sexual revolution. To the minds of many men, the availability of the birth control pill and other protection from pregnancy should have made the women more willing to engage in sex. "So we had no legitimate reason, as far as the men were concerned, for saying no," Keate recalled.[28] By that time, the TWL had set up a birth control clinic at U of T,[29] but access to abortion continued to be a concern, and not just because of the damage that backstreet operations still inflicted on women. "If they were to be independent, they had to be able to control their own bodies. They had to be able to determine when and how they wanted children," and be economically self-sufficient enough to support them.[30] At the same time, Keate would not accept the socialist feminist view of the world without trying to work through all the issues for herself. "I was an independent thinker." Although she essentially agreed with the Marxist analysis of women's oppression—that it boiled down to capitalism, with an overlay of patriarchy—she continued asking the "tough questions." For example, she would challenge the idea that all women were "sisters" and that only they were oppressed. The class system, she felt, made economic victims out of men, because they were expected to provide financially for women, and sex objects out of women, because they were expected to use their bodies to court male protection and care.[31]

Their combined political and news training, then, encouraged both Keate and Roberts to become media activists in the socialist feminist cause. In the fall of 1969, Roberts returned to Vancouver from CP in Edmonton and rejoined the Women's Caucus, which began preparing its local abortion campaign and advance publicity for the Abortion Caravan, due to leave for Ottawa in the spring. Some of the members had recently attended a conference of feminists from western Canada and the United States, where abortion rights were high on the agenda. By December, they had set up workshops on the law and on abortion procedures, as well as the referral service, and made plans to send some of their members in a motorcade to Ottawa to confront Canada's federal lawmakers.[32] They planned stops in Kelowna, Calgary, Edmonton, Saskatoon, Regina, Winnipeg, Thunder Bay, Sault Ste. Marie, Sudbury and Toronto, before arriving in Ottawa, a distance of over 5500 kilometres.[33] They invited other Canadian women to join and assist them as they arrived in their towns and cities on the way to Ottawa, making their politics and intentions clear in their letter to feminist and leftist groups across the country. They wanted abortion taken out of the Criminal Code and wanted publicly funded, community-run clinics that would provide all reproductive counselling and services to replace the hospital TACs. They stressed the importance of sex education in high schools, and of challenging the capitalist culture and male dominance of medical practice and research. They also made it a point to say that they "could not tolerate" any birth control procedure being forced on poor, Aboriginal, racial minority and third world women in the name of medical experimentation or population control.[34]

The entire campaign, including the advance publicity, had to be talked through with other members of the Vancouver Women's Caucus, who were quite aware themselves of how to use the media, Roberts recalls, but were also concerned with the finer points of feminist thinking. "You know, there were lots of discussions, but it wasn't just around media strategy. It was the whole thing. What would be the message of it?... What were the politics of this?" It was controversial because the women had trouble agreeing on whether to focus on one issue, reproductive rights, or link it to others, such as equal pay. "How much to emphasize *just* abortion and abortion reform, or how much this fit into, you know, a whole wider picture of women's liberation. So, there were lots of differences within the group." She recalls that some members of the caucus felt that abortion was beginning to take too much priority over other political issues. "So there was a little bit of tension around that, but … at the time the Caravan was leaving, we would have wanted that to be the front page issue," certainly for *The Pedestal*. Roberts started writing up the first press kits for the abortion campaign—news releases, background information, fact sheets, caucus contacts, and any other material news reporters would need to know in advance before they cover an event. Given her CP training, "I probably just took that work on. I felt confident doing that."[35] They wanted the media to get the public thinking about the power that the medical profession and the state held over women's bodies.[36]

The caucus used *The Pedestal* to publicize the campaign, with the pregnant Justice gracing the front page, along with the headline: "Labouring Under a Misconception: Legalize All Abortion Now!" It was included as a poster in the press kit, along with the Caravan schedule.[37] As the campaign progressed, *The Pedestal* ran the caucus' demands in their letters to the prime minister, Pierre Trudeau, and other government officials, as well as detailed accounts of its marches, meetings and demonstrations in Vancouver. It also published articles and ads about the Caravan, exhorting feminists and their supporters to get involved.[38]

The VWC released its list of demands to the prime minister to the media: the women wanted decriminalization of abortion, including pardons for those convicted of performing them illegally and dismissal of current criminal charges; free reproductive health clinics across the country; and more funded research and medical training on safe birth control, sterilization and abortion. Citing the deaths of 2000 Canadian women a year and injuries to 20,000 others from botched abortions, they accused the government of declaring war on the women of Canada by making them suffer through unwanted pregnancies, regardless of their circumstances. The caucus would "declare war" on the Canadian government in return if its demands were not met by 11 May, after the Abortion Caravan arrived in Ottawa. "We are angry, furious women and we demand our right to human dignity."[39] For their part, the politicians were reluctant to reopen the same drawn-out acrimonious debates that had occurred when they changed the "daringly liberal" law the previous summer, even though there were clearly problems with it.[40] The federal Minister of Health, John Munro, said that revisiting the abortion legislation was not one of his priorities but that he would meet with the women of the Caravan when they arrived in Ottawa.[41]

Before the contingent left Vancouver, the caucus decided to tackle politicians and the medical profession in British Columbia on the grounds that some aspects of health legislation, particularly hospitals and clinics, came under provincial jurisdiction. At least they could argue that they had tried to go through the "proper channels" before they made their way to Ottawa.[42] They held what is believed to be the first pro-choice march in Canada, on Valentine's Day 1970, with Roberts, dressed as the health minister, taking

Anne Roberts, in striped tie and smoking a cigar, portrays the federal health minister, John Munro, as she marches in the Vancouver pro-choice demonstration, 14 February 1970. Photo by the late Saghir Ahmad, with the permission of Anne Roberts, from her private collection.

part. Their demonstration included agitprop theatre depicting TAC doctors denying abortions to several suffering women and a public talk with a sympathetic doctor.

A few weeks later, after a short, unsatisfactory meeting with provincial ministers in Victoria, they briefly invaded the B.C. legislature, displaying large banners and throwing red streamers onto the floor of the House in what would turn out to be a dress rehearsal for the Ottawa campaign. Some caucus members also had a brief verbal sparring match with Prime Minister Trudeau as he passed through the Vancouver airport. The local newspapers, and the alternative press, covered these events quite supportively.[43]

The Pedestal articles did not always include bylines, so Roberts's name did not appear there even though she wrote some of its abortion campaign publicity material. Her work appeared in the student press, as well. *The Peak* (Simon Fraser University) ran an "advancer," with her byline, explaining the events that were to take place in Vancouver on Valentine's Day, the limitations of the current law and the reasons for the abortion campaign and Caravan. She argued that the requirements for a legal abortion were not clear, that the TAC committee protocols unnecessarily delayed the decision until the pregnancy was well advanced, and, since the woman's financial state was not taken into account, that the law discriminated against those who simply could not afford another child. *The Ubyssey* (UBC) ran exactly the same article under someone else's name two days later, which suggests that it was distributed and used freely. Roberts quoted birth control pioneer Margaret Sanger as asserting the need for women to have control over their own bodies, and supplied historical information that lay the blame for laws against abortion on the Roman Catholic Church. A shortened version of her article was produced as a flyer for the Valentine's Day demonstration, and she later wrote news releases about protests supporting Robert Markoff, a local doctor who had been arrested and charged with performing illegal abortions.[44] The following week, *The Peak* quoted Roberts as a caucus member and a "prime organizer" of the Valentine's Day march, demonstrating that her activism took other forms besides writing publicity material. Interviewed during the demonstration, she stayed on message: "Abortion is not a crime, it is our right. Women must be able to control their bodies and choose whether they wish to be mothers. Many thousands of women die at the hands of brutal hack abortionists or from self-induced abortions—these women have been murdered by the state."[45]

Roberts, who returned to Edmonton in late April 1970, got involved with the local Women's Liberation Movement, which was engaged in its own campaign to put pressure on provincial ministers in Alberta regarding the federal abortion law. The Edmonton WLM flyers in her personal papers cited the same Sanger quote and church history that she used in her *Peak* article and in other B.C. campaign material.[46] She had been unable to line up a summer reporting job in Vancouver, even at the *Sun*, whose news editor, she recalled, told her they already had a woman in the newsroom.[47] CP Edmonton, however, was glad to take her back, giving her the opportunity to publicize the Abortion Caravan nationally. She busied herself getting more advance press kits out over the CP wires to the news agency's bureaus and member newspapers across the country. "I gave all the background of how the Abortion Caravan was organized, where it came from, what it was trying to accomplish." The male reporter who had first recommended her for the CP job the year before, and who was also involved in the Left, helped her put the press kit together, but she believes no one else at the office, including the bureau chief, knew what they were doing.[48] She also drafted CP stories about the Vancouver Women's Caucus abortion referral service and another about unnamed doctors who were performing illegal abortions.[49]

While the CP wire service gave this material national distribution, how much of it actually appeared in the newspapers would have depended on their own editors. The stories were written in "pyramid style"; that is, with the most salient details in the lead, and, in descending order, information considered less crucial to the story, in line with the accepted newspaper format. Upon receiving a CP story over the wire, the local newspaper editor would write a headline, decide whether to rewrite the lead paragraph, add local details or edit others. Since the amount of space available for it was another factor, the editor would also decide how much of the less important detail to cut from the bottom of the story, and whether or not to run any accompanying photographs. The same kinds of editorial decisions came into play in reverse; that is, when local reporters on the scene generated their own newspaper stories, these were copied and sent to CP for editing and distribution across the country. Consequently, each newspaper contained more or less of the Caravan's publicity material and comments from the participants, depending on decisions that were made at each editorial desk.[50] Roberts's advance story, a draft of which is in her personal papers, was released via CP before the Caravan left Vancouver, and received a fair amount of media play across the country.[51]

On April 27 the Caravan left Vancouver for Ottawa, with 17 women crammed into a truck, a big yellow convertible, and a Volkswagen van bearing the coffin on top. The front page of *The Pedestal*'s May 1970 issue consisted of photographs of the motorcade, decorated and ready to go, with apt slogans, such as "On to Ottawa" and "Abortion Is Our Right."[52] This time, however, their statistics on abortion, "one thousand and more," became open to question. A CP Vancouver story attributed the figures to the Dominion Bureau of Statistics, a source that was apparently suggested to the caucus earlier by a sympathetic local doctor. According to CP, the DBS said there were an estimated 100,000 illegal abortions in Canada every year, 20,000 women being treated in hospital for complications, and 2000 deaths.[53] The DBS, however, denied it had issued these statistics, saying that it was still trying to compile its figures, and the 20,000 injuries included natural miscarriages and legal abortions. The confusion was not new; even before the 1969 law was passed, Canadian estimates of illegal abortions varied widely, but were commonly assumed to be about 10 percent of the figures given for illegal abortions, injuries and deaths in the more populous United States and Britain.[54] In their brief to Parliament, the Caravanners cited 100,000 to 200,000 illegal abortions and as many as 40,000 resulting injuries.[55] Inevitably, any use of statistics left them open to accusations from reporters, doctors, conservative politicians, anti-abortionist activists and newspaper readers that they were manipulating the figures, or that they were based only on their own surveys.[56] As the Caravan travelled across the country, few news stories quoted any statistics, suggesting that reporters and editors were alerted to the problem of attributing them with any authority beyond the "claim" the women made in their literature or their comments.[57]

While they were on the road, the Caravanners handled media strategy on their own, so it was carefully prepared in advance. The women were armed with one-page fact sheets, which "we feel is necessary so that every time we talk to the press we can make sure we formulate things in a good way and so that we will cover all of the important points." Those points included their attempts to contact Prime Minister Trudeau, Minister of Health Munro, and the Justice Minister, John Turner. Turner refused to respond to their "threats and demands" and would not meet with them. The fact sheet reiterated the problems with the hospital TAC committees, and stressed the importance of women making up their own minds about their sexuality, without interference from male authorities. It also mentioned that researchers were raising questions about the safety of the birth control pill but did not condemn sterilization of, or scientific experimentation on, third world women, racial minority women or those living in poverty. Consequently, that point did not usually reach the media, even though it was in the brief to Parliament.[58]

The caucus initially had strict cooperative rules about who would handle reporters' questions, which would be done by each Caravanner in rotation so that no one would become a media star and all of them would learn how to handle the press. At each stop on their travels, two women—one experienced and another less so—would do the interviews, usually using their own names. Rather than reveal their true identities, the skit performers would adopt the names of famous suffragettes or other radical women of the past, such as Emma Goldman, although the reporters rarely caught on.[59] This policy against media stardom was not strictly enforced, however. Two participants, Dawn Carrell and Marcy Cohen, figured prominently as spokeswomen, which caused some disgruntlement among their peers, even though their comments, and the media coverage, effectively reflected the Caravan's agenda. The pair, whose real names and photos were published in the press, travelled ahead at different points in the campaign, laying the groundwork and helping with local arrangements. Carrell, for example, visited Ottawa in late April before the Caravan left Vancouver, was back in time to join the motorcade, and then left it at Winnipeg to fly to Toronto, accompanied by Cohen.[60]

The advance publicity supplied by Roberts had a domino effect, with stories about the Caravan appearing in a number of newspapers across the country. The Caravanners' demands and the reasons for them figured to varying degrees in the coverage, depending on the newspaper concerned, as did accounts of their public panel discussions, where some local women bravely recounted their experiences of abortion. Almost invariably, the reporters described the Caravanners as "militant," their stories featuring illustrative photos of them with raised, clenched fists, usually standing near the symbolic coffin. The imagery worked well with their declaration of war against the Canadian government. The grim skits may have been more effective with an audience than speech making, however, and certainly attracted media attention. So did their large banners, which also appeared prominently in the newspaper photographs. "We Are Furious Women," "The Women Are Coming" and "Abortions Kill 12,000 Women"—the North America statistic. The story rarely made the front page, but was confined either to the local news pages or the women's pages, well inside the newspapers.[61]

The Caravanners' first public meeting, in Calgary, was uneventful, but garnered some coverage in the local *Herald*, which cited their demands for repeal, pardons and more research and medical education.[62] When they arrived in Edmonton, the local *Journal* sent a reporter, and CP sent Anne Roberts to cover it as well. She found that "quite exciting," she recalls, especially as she knew most of the women involved, including her sister members of Edmonton Women's Liberation.[63] They staged a skit that aimed to demonstrate the "alleged cruelty of the hospital abortion committees, which they claim force women to seek illegal abortions" unless the women had money to pay for them. Roberts either wrote the words "alleged" and "claim" herself or a CP editor inserted them, because to omit them would be considered unfair to the doctors, if not libellous, in journalism practice. She quoted Heidi Fisher, another Edmonton WLM member, who told the rally that the law discriminated against "poor and working women," as those with money could go to Britain or Japan, where abortion was legal. Dodie Weppler of Vancouver explained that the Caravanners were not going to "glorify motherhood" on Mother's Day in Ottawa, but demand that each woman have the right to "choose whether or not she wants to be a mother." Roberts also quoted Marcy Cohen as saying that they were gaining support as they travelled. "Together we are strong and we'll be able to force the government to remove abortion from the criminal code." The story, which appeared in the *Lethbridge Herald* and other papers, was nevertheless balanced with an alternative viewpoint, which is standard practice in mainstream journalism. Roberts included a comment from a young woman who told the rally "that she could not really afford another child but that she believed abortion is murder." A photograph of her holding an anti-abortion placard appeared in the *Montreal Star* version, along with added details from the *Calgary Herald* about the Caravanners' earlier visit there.[64]

After the Caravan left Edmonton, it visited Saskatoon, where derisive laughter and insults from shoppers and young people greeted the women's parade through downtown and their theatre skit as well. The local *Star-Phoenix* did not cite their demands, but did cover the public panel discussion with Caravanner Mary Trew, local law student Norma Simm and obstetrician Thomas Orr. Both Simm and Trew emphasized the inadequacy of the current abortion law for women, while Orr appeared ambivalent, saying at one point that perhaps the fetus had a right to be born. He had replaced another scheduled speaker and was clearly not particularly supportive of the abortion campaign. All in all, the Saskatoon visit resulted in decidedly mixed media messages, despite the Caravanners' publicity efforts.

Reportedly too tired to stage their skit at the next stop, Regina, they drove through the city and held a routine public meeting that night. Six more women from the city joined the motorcade, which now consisted of five vehicles.[65]

In Winnipeg, the coverage of the Caravanners was much better. The *Tribune* highlighted the women's threat of "war" on the Canadian government, and included their demand for community sexual health clinics as well as for repeal of the abortion law in a story that took up half a page.[66] The *Free Press* ran their "furious women" letter to Prime Minister Trudeau in full, the only mainstream newspaper to do so to date, also noting that six women from Winnipeg would be joining the trek.[67]

From Winnipeg, the Caravan headed into Northern Ontario. At Thunder Bay (a.k.a. the Lakehead), they ran into their first substantial opposition. A small group of Catholic anti-abortionists, likely alerted by an advance newspaper story, disrupted their meeting in a local United church, declaring that decriminalization would lead to promiscuity. The women retorted that most of those seeking abortions were married women with too many children. The meeting became so heated that the rector called it to a halt, according to one newspaper report. The other paper ran a photo of the Caravanners, but did not appear to have covered the meeting at all and missed the story.[68] The police were on the alert, which the Caravanners seemed to regard as harassment rather than protection, even though they had been frightened enough to hide their vehicles while they slept over in the town. They sent out a report to the caucus in Vancouver, for media use, saying, "Leaving Thunder Bay, the caravan has since been escorted by police cavalcades of the RCMP and the Ontario Provincial Police, with their bike patrol and a concerned citizens organization, all obviously enjoying the new game of cops and radicals."[69] Recent scholarship has revealed that the RCMP were routinely spying on radical groups, including the Women's Liberation Movement, mainly because a number of its members were aligned with the New Left. The RCMP were already carrying out surveillance on the Caravanners but, according to historians Christabelle Sethna and Steve Hewitt, did not take them as seriously as they did male radicals, and did not lay on enough officers to prevent them from following through with their demonstrations in Ottawa.[70]

The Caravanners received a much warmer welcome in Sault Ste. Marie. The women's editor of the local *Daily Star* had published Anne Roberts's CP news story of their stop-over in Edmonton, and devoted half a page to them when they arrived in the Sault for a routine public meeting. The women complained of the "unpleasantness" in Thunder Bay, which they felt had been deliberately organized, but maintained that otherwise they had attracted much supportive interest along the route. The generally positive reporter, Kay MacIntyre, was intrigued that most of them were young and unmarried, but taken aback by their socialist rhetoric and their "hippy" appearance, "a factor which will not assist them in obtaining an unbiased hearing. There were several quieter girls, well groomed and intelligent, who made a far better but less vocal impression." Nevertheless, hers was one of the only stories from the trek that not only mentioned the necessity of better research on human reproduction but recorded the Caravanners' opposition to governments imposing birth control on Third World women. The story did not mention the police but did point out, as did a related CP report, that Trudeau and his ministers would not be available to see them in Ottawa.[71]

In Sudbury, after another routine public meeting, the local reporter reprinted, without quotation marks, phrases from material Roberts had written for *The Peak*, which was apparently being used as part of the Caravanners' press kit. "The process of obtaining a therapeutic abortion is complicated and prolonged, and forces a woman to degrade herself before a group of men who hold her future in their hands. As long as a woman cannot prove that she will commit suicide if forced to complete her pregnancy, she has only two alternatives: to bear an unwanted child, or seek an illegal abortion."[72] Roberts had laid the media groundwork effectively in that CP and almost all the newspapers in the cities and towns the Caravan visited covered their street theatre performances or panel discussions, or both, using the publicity material she helped supply. Generally speaking, the news stories about the Caravan were even-handed, quoting liberally from the Caravanners and their media material, despite the fact that these radical young women clearly did not comply with conventional feminine standards of speech, behaviour or dress, which was part of their media appeal at a time when women's libbers were still a novelty.

Although she acted as one of the Caravan's publicists and as CP's reporter on the story when it arrived in Edmonton, Roberts did not see these roles as a professional conflict of interest at the time, because she believed in integrating her activism and her journalism. "I did not accept some idea of journalistic neutrality.... I didn't think anyone in our office had any neutrality.... They would just have different biases than I would have." Although she would think harder about her actions now, she still rhetorically raises the question of whether or not it would have been any more ethical for a reporter who was sexist, a committed capitalist or a member of any political party to cover the Caravan. She thought it was important that it be seen "from the women's perspective and from my perspective."

It was also important to Roberts and her sister radicals to break down the barriers against women having "full choice" over their lives—if and when to bear children, the financial security to support them and the facilities they needed, such as childcare. Access to birth control and abortion were key points on the continuum of reproductive choice. The Abortion

Caravan, which was as educative as it was controversial, moved that process along as did the media coverage, as far as Roberts was concerned. "Each time women talked about it openly and frankly, each time someone learned about it, right? Each time, we were challenging a lot of ... *ideas* that people hadn't maybe even articulated. They didn't even know they had them until someone came along and challenged them.... I think with a lot of young women it was quite liberating to know that it was okay to get an abortion or that a whole group of women said it's okay. Right? That they did it publicly. They weren't ashamed. They didn't feel sinful.... And it wasn't just the Abortion Caravan, it was all the different ways that women were challenging things that ... over time were very successful. Yes, I think it did change many, many things."[73]

The Caravan's next stop was Toronto, where Kathryn Keate and the other members of Toronto Women's Liberation had already become involved in the abortion campaign. A six-page planning document outlined why it was necessary to decriminalize abortion, making essentially the same arguments as the Vancouver Women's Caucus. The TWL members wanted to work with the caucus on the Caravan and continue their own campaign in Ontario afterwards, so they made several proposals designed to lay the groundwork for both. They suggested networking among women's organizations, unions, and community and political groups, researching and issuing information pamphlets on abortion, fundraising, planning street theatre and demonstrations, and coordinating efforts to get media coverage. "The present media committee should include someone from the abortion campaign, and should be in charge of making decisions about the press in conjunction with the whole abortion caravan planning committee." One woman even suggested they practise interviewing each other on tape, "so that a lot of women could learn to speak to the press."[74] They didn't reveal to the media the disagreements they were having with a few of the other groups involved, including the New Feminists.[75] The NF was a radical feminist group that had decided patriarchy, not capitalism, was the primary root of women's oppression, and had split from TWL earlier because of this political disagreement. The NF insisted on attending the campaign activities anyway.[76]

By the time the Caravan reached Toronto there were 40 participants in the motorcade, double the original number. The caucus had sent letters to all members of Parliament, complaining of not being able to set up a meeting with Prime Minister Trudeau in Ottawa, and asking for their support.[77] Marcy Cohen accused him of "gross irresponsibility" in declining to meet with them, and again read out their declaration of war. As it turned out, Munro had to cancel his original plan to meet them because he was called to an international health conference in Geneva. Trudeau was packing for a trip to the Far East, and Turner, still irked at the women's demanding language, was reported to have made plans to play tennis rather than attend their rally on Parliament Hill the following Saturday.[78] Margaret Weiers of the *Toronto Daily Star*, who was familiar with women's issues, was one of the few reporters to have the women comment on the four demands they were making, including the need for community reproductive health clinics and scientific research. That evening, the Caravanners held a successful rally in support of the Caravan, which was attended by 500 people, among them New Feminists and other groups, as well as parents with their children.[79] Caucus spokeswomen also appeared on radio programs.[80]

In Ottawa, a local Women's Liberation Movement group, whose members apparently consisted mainly of the "Waffle" or radical left adherents of the New Democratic Party, were active enough to demonstrate for abortion rights outside the annual meeting of the Ontario Medical Association the day the Caravan arrived in town. They also helped organize the march and rally to be held the next day on Parliament Hill.[81] Nevertheless, word had earlier been sent to Toronto that Ottawa feminists were having difficulty organizing media strategy for the Caravan activities on Parliament Hill. Keate was told that a number of them were federal civil servants who were supposed to be politically neutral, and they were afraid to risk their jobs by openly getting involved. Since she was out of work because *Monday Magazine* had just folded, and the winter school term had just ended as well, she was free to go and help out, planning publicity and writing press releases.[82]

She went to Ottawa by train in advance of the Caravan, staying in the home of a woman who was sheltering an American army deserter. At the time, young men were being drafted into the U.S. Armed Forces to fight in the Vietnam War, leading to numerous demonstrations on university campuses. Just after Keate arrived in Ottawa, the police opened fire on anti-war protesters at Kent State University in Ohio, killing four students. The incident upset young radicals everywhere, as most shared a sense of solidarity regardless of their immediate activities. Keate remembers her host coming to the breakfast table with the newspaper, saying, "My God, they're killing us now!" The shootings intensified their own sense of danger at the risks they were about to take by acting on their declaration of war against the Canadian government, but they persisted.[83] In its May 8 press release summing up the Caravan's progress to date, the Vancouver Women's Caucus declared that given the deaths of women from botched abortions, which they blamed on the state, "We see ourselves in a similar situation to the students of Kent, Ohio; correspondingly, peace can be kept not by the murder of innocent women but by listening and acting upon the demands of all oppressed people."[84]

The newspapers, however, paid more attention to the timing of their arrival, the Friday of Mother's Day weekend, juxtaposing catchy pictures and lead paragraphs meant to draw readers' eyes to these unconventional women and their supporters. A reporter for the *Ottawa Journal* led his story with, "Just two days before the nation's tribute to Mother, the anti-unwanted-motherhood leaders gathered in Ottawa to protest against restrictive abortion laws." He also described their small rally of "shirt-and-pants attired women" and their "impromptu" skit at a shopping mall dramatizing the difficulty of getting safe, legal abortions. There was a photo of one woman with a clenched fist, holding a "Free Abortion on Demand" placard, and another of a car driven by the supportive husband of a local Women's Liberation member, with a message scrawled along its side, "If MPs Could Be Pregnant, Would Abortion Be Legal?" His one-year-old daughter could be seen in the car window. The story reported only one of the Caravanners' demands—that the abortion law be repealed—a demand that the prime minister had recently rejected when questioned in the House of Commons. Nevertheless, the Caravanners expected a thousand women from Toronto, Kingston and Montreal to join them for the Parliament Hill rally on Saturday.[85] In Montreal, radical francophone feminists who supported Quebec separatism, and therefore did not recognize the federal government's authority in the first place, sent their best wishes but decided to participate in their own local pro-abortion events.[86] At the same time, the *Montreal Star*'s lifestyles editor, Zoe Bieler, produced two in-depth articles discussing the difficulties of getting doctors and TAC committees in Montreal to approve abortions. The section included a photo of an unmarried young mother holding her infant daughter, on their way to Ottawa. The accompanying article explained that although the woman did not feel ready to have a child, she had decided against a risky illegal abortion, and she wanted to support the Caravan, especially the women who had to face the same decision that she did. The main illustration for the feature was a large drawing of a nude woman, sitting atop a pedestal, snapping the chains that bound her there.[87] In the meantime, feminists in other cities, including Vancouver, Calgary, Edmonton and Winnipeg, also held forceful demonstrations in support of the Caravan that weekend, initiating increased media attention to the abortion campaign.[88]

On the Saturday of Mother's Day weekend, the Caravanners marched to Parliament Hill, where they held an outdoor rally with about 450 supporters, and then a crowded meeting inside one of the buildings to hear the women's brief. When a Montreal doctor, Henry Morgentaler, began to speak, impatient women booed him, because they found him patronizing and, anyway, they wanted to hear from women rather than men. Most of them apparently did not know that he had already set up an illegal abortion clinic in Montreal, the beginning of a long legal battle that eventually led to the decriminalization of abortion in Canada in 1988.[89] Grace MacInnis of the New Democratic Party, the only female MP, suggested at the rally that they take the two years necessary to organize petitions to the House of Commons, but they groaned loudly at her as well because they wanted action right away. They were far more inspired by a fiery address from Doris Power of the Just Society Movement, an anti-poverty organization from Toronto.[90] Power, who was on welfare and already had three children, was eight months pregnant because she had been denied an abortion. Some newspapers ignored Power, but ran an attention-grabbing CP wire photo of Gayle Nystrom, wife of an NDP MP, wearing a sign around her waist bearing the words "This Uterus Is Not Government Property," similar to the ones that other women were wearing. Other photos showed the Caravanners and their predominantly female supporters marching on Parliament Hill with their pro-abortion banners, contrasting them with a counter demonstration put on by an anti-abortion group, Campaign Life. A sidebar in the *Ottawa Citizen* quoted the Caravanners' full brief to the government, containing all its demands, which few other newspapers carried, although CP Ottawa had also listed them. Another *Citizen* article provided some of the colourful rhetoric from abortion supporters, including, "Trudeau says the government has no business in the bedrooms of the nation, but they're sure ready to catch you when you come out." In the *Journal*, a more conservative paper, a Campaign Life spokeswoman voiced her objections to abortion, calling it a "cancer." Several reporters also noted that no Liberal politicians came to hear the Caravanners out.[91] "The angry women of the Cross-Canada Abortion Caravan unfurled their Babies by Choice banners on Parliament Hill on Saturday, but no one from the government was on hand to get the message," the *Globe and Mail* reported.[92]

After the rally, the frustrated and angry Caravan participants and many of their female and male supporters immediately carried their cardboard coffin and crude abortion implements to the nearby official residence of the prime minister, at 24 Sussex Drive, demanding to speak with him before he left on his trip.[93] Most of the news stories about the weekend's events led with the details of this dramatic action, along with photographs. They reported that from 150 to 400 protesters, depending on the account, linked arms and "invaded" the grounds after "minor scuffles" with the few RCMP officers at the gates. The protesters held a sit-in on the lawn during which they roundly cursed the police, calling them "pigs," and booed a representative of the prime minister, who came outside to remonstrate with them. After the RCMP allowed them to leave a wreath, their coffin and the abortion tools behind, they quietly left. According to a retrospective media report, the RCMP persuaded the prime minister that images of the police arresting young women would not play well in the media so soon after the killings at Kent State.[94]

Keate was walking in the crowd near the rear of the march to the prime minister's house, and by the time she reached the gates, they had already broken through the RCMP's defences. Later, in her *Saturday Night* magazine cover story, she gave her unique insider's perspective on her own feelings and those of the other women sitting near her on the lawn at 24 Sussex Drive. They decided to sit down partly because they were concerned for the safety of the children with them,[95] although Caravanner Margo Dunn said they were afraid the police would pull guns on them.[96] Dunn, whom Keate identified in her story as "Elsa," then read aloud the dangerous procedures women sometimes used in trying to abort their fetuses, including inserting knitting needles or injecting a corrosive household cleaner. It made Keate feel sick. Dizzy, she put her head between her knees, listening to the "violent sobbing" of the woman sitting beside her and the "horrified silence" of the others. The police allowed them to leave the coffin and the implements on the doorstep, and then they left, most of them walking with their sodden placards in the pouring rain. Her version was certainly more sympathetic than the other accounts in the mainstream media, and was not as critical of the participants' behaviour toward the RCMP and the prime minister's representative, whom the Caravanners regarded as patronizing. Keate couldn't resist a crack at Trudeau, "the millionaire Catholic bachelor [who] would not be interested in the deaths of more than one thousand women in his country each year from illegal abortions." At the same time, she really wanted her readers to appreciate that the women did not plan or carry through with their Mother's Day actions in a cavalier way, and why it was important to repeal the abortion law.[97]

On Sunday, Mother's Day, the Caravanners did not stage any protests, but met at their temporary headquarters—a disused downtown school—to plan their next move. Given that no government representative had agreed to meet with them, despite the fact that they had travelled halfway across the country, they felt that they had to do something more dramatic to bring public attention to their cause. According to Margo Dunn, they had been entertaining the idea of demonstrating inside the House of Commons all during the trek, and had discussed it with women along the route, but they had not made a definite decision.[98] Keate reported in *Saturday Night* that they talked well into the night, trying to decide how far to take their demands, as they knew the police were watching them. She, along with two other participants, had already been taken to the police station once after an off-duty officer caught them pasting Caravan posters on bank and storefront windows near Parliament Hill. They were not charged, as technically there was no law against doing so. On the Sunday night, the police continuously circled the school building and, near midnight, three plainclothes officers entered and searched their belongings, making Keate and the others nervous. She wrote: "I am more afraid than I have ever been, and I am angry that I am afraid, that I am letting myself be hassled. Discussion has been tense and confused since they searched us. Should we go on with our plans, or do nothing? Should we risk being arrested? Is it worth it? But we must act. Some of the women have travelled 3,000 miles for this campaign. We just can't give up now." One of the women, who had been doing abortion referrals for three years, wept as she insisted that they chain themselves inside the Commons visitors' galleries because they owed it to all the women who had suffered so much from unwanted pregnancies and botched operations. The chains would signify the limits the state put on women's control over their own bodies, and would ensure that the MPs heard their message before security officers could detach them and get them outside. Tense, exhausted and sad, the women decided it was an action they must carry out, regardless of their fears that they could be arrested and perhaps injured. Keate's article was the only mainstream media account that explained the strategy behind their decision to disrupt the House of Commons the next day.[99]

The Caravanners planned their Parliament Hill action carefully. A number of them and their supporters would stage an outdoor protest, marching around the Eternal Flame in a silent vigil, wearing mournful black head coverings and arm bands and carrying the cardboard coffin and the implements of botched abortions. At a certain point, the women were to remove the black head coverings, revealing red ones underneath, meant to symbolize their rage, their declaration of war, and their intention to keep fighting for women's reproductive choices.[100] This demonstration served as a decoy to divert RCMP attention from their other more daring protest inside the public galleries of the House of Commons, until it was too late for them to intervene. Publicity was key, and it was important to make sure that as many reporters as possible were on Parliament Hill at the time, not just members of the press gallery, who would likely cover the House anyway. Contacting them all was Keate's job, mainly because she was willing to do it and knew what to say to get them on the scene. Some of the TWL members had mixed feelings about her involvement, she recalls. "I wasn't appointed necessarily because of my expertise as a member of the media. If anything that sort of made me somewhat suspect.... You know, I had worked as a journalist, the media was seen as being hostile to the women's movement and judgmental and sexist, and I had been part of that. And the fact that I wasn't willing to renounce my wicked past and I actually enjoy journalism on a certain level was really, really hard for them to understand.... I'm not an ideologue and definitely the women's movement *was*, and so journalists were seen as the bad folks. But, anyway, no one else was willing to call up the big bad media."[101]

There was no written news release. Instead, on the Monday morning, Keate phoned Canadian Press, all the newspapers and all the broadcast outlets in the city, using the most "inflammatory" and "outrageous" rhetoric she could.[102] "We knew that if we threatened violence the media would all be interested. So, we said that we were declaring war on the House of Commons. When they'd ask questions, I'd say 'I'm not going to tell you, just be there,' and I gave the time.... And that was it. That was the extent of our media outreach.... I knew not to get into arguments or discussions or anything. I knew how to handle it. So my background had helped." She recalled that the news editors she phoned greeted her announcement with jocular skepticism, but alerted their reporters anyway. The media were not particularly friendly toward women's liberation at the time, regarding them all as "bra burners" and "weird teenagers," she added, even though most of the Caravanners were in their 20s and some were older.

Knowing they would immediately be suspect if they showed up at the Commons visitors' galleries in their usual women's liberation garb, the Caravanners prepared for a costume change. The inside contingent had to look respectable enough to get past the RCMP and the House security commissionaires without questions being asked. They shaved their legs, switched from jeans to dresses and miniskirts, applied makeup, and, in some cases, chose male escorts, flippantly referred to as "beards," to complete their masquerade. Keate remembers that chain belts were a fashion accessory at the time, as were large purses, which were handy for carrying bigger chains and padlocks past the security guards.[103] At the time, the guards could prevent anyone carrying suspicious packages from going into the galleries, but they did not normally search women's handbags.[104]

The three galleries were ranged above and around the floor of the House, allowing a wide view of the seated MPs below. Only the public gallery was open to any visitor. The press gallery was reserved for reporters, and the guards routinely demanded guest passes, signed by MPs, before any of their constituents could enter the government and opposition galleries.[105] Keate's article did not mention how the women managed to get these passes,[106] but she recalled that they phoned the MPs' offices, pretending to live in their ridings. "We worked with the women inside the House of Commons to get passes from the members of Parliament and basically it was a question of us calling them up and pretending to be people from, you know, Saskatoon or Winnipeg or whatever, with fake names."[107] The ruse worked, allowing them to spread out as much as possible throughout the public and members' galleries. In the meantime, the decoy demonstration around the Eternal Flame was proceeding "like a Sunday picnic," Keate said, with a few RCMP officers watching the Caravanners but not interfering in any way, beyond locking the doors to the House of Commons to keep them out. The officers were too late, as the other contingent had already secretly entered the galleries, waiting for their three o'clock deadline, when they would stand up and declare war on the government of Canada.[108]

The journalists seated in the press gallery had a clear view of what happened next. The *Winnipeg Free Press* reported: "Complete disorder and pandemonium took over in the House of Commons as 31 young women arose one after the other in the public and members' galleries and screamed at startled MPs, 'Free abortion on demand.'"[109] The story made front-page news across the country. Most of the reporters paid far more attention to the disturbance in the House from the "screaming" women than to the reasons for their demands for "free abortion," the headlines reflecting the women's anger and their noisy "invasion" of the Commons. What was stunning for most of the journalists and the MPs was the effectiveness of their strategy and the fact that their demonstration forced the House to adjourn for the first time in its history. It was half an hour before it could resume business again. CP reported that the women apparently belonged to "the Women's Liberation Movement, the most radical feminist group in Canada." It mentioned that the women had held a rally on the Hill on Saturday, when "they didn't wear make-up, were in slacks, beads and shawls. It was hard to believe they were the same girls, wearing dresses and smiles, who took their places in the galleries Monday."[110]

They started their "ruckus" a few minutes after Justice Minister Turner gave a noncommittal answer to an MP from the New Democratic Party, Andrew Brewin, who asked him if the abortion legislation would be amended.[111] Brewin may have been standing in for Grace MacInnis, who was absent that day. One of the Caravanners stood up and started shouting out a speech in favour of repeal of the abortion law. She had managed to hook herself up with a microphone to the translation system, which was available at every seat in the galleries and on the floor of the House, so that her demands could be heard by everyone. As soon as a guard reached her, a woman in another area jumped up and began the speech again, and so on, in progression, until most of the women scattered throughout the galleries were yelling their slogans in unison. One security guard shouted, "Get those whores out of here," and others called them "sluts" as they struggled to get the women outside. It was a difficult job, given that about a dozen had chained themselves to their seats. The guards had to call for cutting pliers and hacksaws, which took more time, and it was not a gentle process, with the women yelling and resisting them. At least one of them bit a guard who tried to clap his hand over her mouth to silence her. Although several of the reporters said that the guards were not unduly rough, a few women complained afterwards of being gagged or choked. One of them said, "rubbing a chafed wrist, that 'they took the chains off after nearly breaking our arms.'" Beyond that, they were not injured, as they had feared, and, as it was not against the law for a member of the public to "disrupt the decorum of the House," none were arrested, although a few were questioned and photographed in the Speaker's Chamber.[112]

As the women were ejected from the House, arms linked, tears streaming down their faces and singing women's liberation songs, they ran over to join the other demonstrators, including Keate, who were still marching outside, by this time numbering about 100 in all. Several publications ran a CP wire photo of the Caravanners burning a large facsimile of the abortion section of the Criminal Code, as well as other photos showing shouting women with clenched fists. No photographs or television images of the demonstration in the galleries were taken, as journalists were not allowed then to record the proceedings inside the House of Commons.[113] There was some broadcast coverage of the demonstration outside.[114] Marcy Cohen and other Caravanners explained to reporters that they had decided to disrupt the House after government leaders, including Turner, had refused to meet with them, and they attached themselves to the gallery chairs to represent Canadian women who were chained by the abortion law. Moreover, they would continue their "war" until the law was repealed.[115] Several of the politicians, apparently embarrassed that their names appeared on the women's gallery passes, said they had been forged. Others raised the question of tightening security regulations governing access by the public.[116]

Although the Caravan had received generally good coverage up to this point, the editorial tone immediately shifted. Some newspapers drew parallels between the Caravanners and the militant British "suffragettes," a misplaced stereotype in Canadian context, but one that was commonly used. Almost all the editorials and opinion columns condemned the disruption in the House of Commons, whether or not they agreed that the abortion law was inadequate, or should at least be reviewed. Nevertheless, most of them felt that the women's demanding tone and protest would not, or should not, be enough to force the House to re-examine the legislation, although the usually conservative *Ottawa Journal* suggested that government leaders should at least meet the women as they had requested. One women's page columnist, Pat Wallace of the Vancouver *Province*, felt the "emotional binge" of the "overly-militant" Caravanners had tarnished the respectable reputation that "lucid" and "rational" feminists had earlier earned with their briefs to the Royal Commission on the Status of Women.[117] Letters to the editor ran the gamut from support to outright condemnation. One *Globe and Mail* reader pointed out that it was easy enough to laugh at the Caravanners, just as it had once been easy to laugh at the actions of the suffragettes, but it was time to face the fact that abortion, although not a perfect solution to unwanted pregnancy, was the fairest one for the woman concerned.[118]

Keate herself was among the Caravanners captured in a *Toronto Daily Star* press photograph, shouting, her clenched fist raised, as she marched with the others around the Eternal Flame. The same image made the front cover of *Saturday Night*, doctored so that a spotlight hit her face, to accompany her account in the magazine. The photos inside showed the women

DEMANDING FREE ABORTIONS, a group of women stands with fists upraised in front of the Parliament Buildings in Ottawa yesterday, as they continue protest which began in the House of Commons, forcing an adjournment for a half hour. The women, most of them in their late teens or early 20s, were part of a group of more than 200 who have been conducting an "Abortion Caravan" across Canada.

—*Photo by Errol Young*

Abortion law protesters break up House sitting

WORLD COURT WATCHES ARCTIC POLLUTION LAW

Canada's plan to exercise control over pollution of the Arctic seas and other coastal waters has drawn faint interest from the world's maritime nations. But the World Court at The Hague is watching closely. For a special re-

Kathryn Keate (centre, third from right) joins the Abortion Caravan protest outside the House of Commons, 11 May 1970. Photo by Errol Young. Published with the permission of Errol Young and TorStar Syndication Services.

burning the large facsimile of the current abortion law, and carrying the coffin up the main steps outside the building. Two women in miniskirts, likely members of the gallery contingent, hugged each other.[119] Several readers objected to the actions of the Caravan participants, and the swear words some of them had used, intimating that women only had themselves to blame if men took advantage of them sexually.[120] Although it was not commonly done then, Fulford allowed the salty language to appear in print because, Keate recalls, she quoted it in context. It included a crude invitation from one of several passing male drivers who harassed her as she sat alone with her suitcase in the dark outside her Toronto commune after she returned from Ottawa. Their behaviour was unsettling enough to make her cry, she told her readers. "I can't even walk out alone on the goddamn streets without being hassled. Some liberated woman I am."[121]

Like Anne Roberts, she believes that the publicity she organized in Ottawa benefited the cause and was part of her duty as a feminist, as was her article in *Saturday Night*. She certainly didn't write it for the money. The magazine was then in such dire financial straits that she was paid 50 dollars less than the rate she had been quoted, and she was told by an accountant at the magazine to cash the cheque quickly before it bounced.[122] Although she had worked on several newspapers and on *Monday Magazine* during her university years, Keate did not feel a conflict over her Caravan activism, mainly because she was not working full time as a reporter at that point and did not even consider herself a "professional" journalist. "I had the mind-set and the training and the ability for it but I certainly didn't see that I was recognized as that." In the 1970s, "if you walked into the newsroom and said that, I mean, everyone would have fallen off their chairs laughing. Even just the word 'journalist' was suspect. That was a word that academics used. You were a 'reporter,'" and female journalists, who were mostly still relegated to the women's pages or "fluff" assignments, were taken even less seriously. She would have considered herself a very green wannabe reporter.[123]

Toronto Women's Liberation, however, felt she had engaged in a *political* conflict of interest because of her *Saturday Night* article. "I got hell for that, absolute hell." Two of TWL's leading members called her on the carpet, literally, on the floor of the U of T co-op daycare centre, for a three-hour "struggle session," during which they tried to convince her of the ideological error of her ways. They were particularly angry with her because she had revealed that some of the women involved in the Caravan demonstrations, including herself, had been afraid and tearful. Keate, however, was unbowed. "I told them the same thing I would tell them today. That's what happened, that's what made it a better story, that's what made it accessible to people, and that's what made it more of a triumph. Because it showed that even though women were scared and were frightened and were lonely and had enormous obstacles to overcome, that they did it and they did it through hard work and organization and cooperation and planning and it was a major success. Because of that. Not in spite of that, because of that, because it was part of the whole picture." Keate believes that radicals in general do not understand the function of journalism, or the mindset of journalists, who don't like ideological rules. As an activist, she believes that "you don't censor the struggle, you don't censor what people have to go through to get where they are. They don't understand that it bonds people like nothing else does."[124] Keate had written in *Saturday Night* that it angered and saddened her that feminists had to exert "tremendous pressure" in order to change the "terrible facts of life for women." From her perspective, it was necessary. After the Abortion Caravan was over, she and the other participants had become even more determined to do everything they could to help those who needed safe, legal abortions.[125] Presciently, she had concluded: "It's going to be a long, hard struggle."[126]

Both Roberts and Keate have followed similar career paths since the Abortion Caravan, juggling their need to earn a living with their political convictions, which, ironically, became harder for them to do as women journalists became more accepted in newsrooms but were also bound to follow the rules, written or unwritten.[127] Some months after the Caravan was over, CP fired Roberts after she appeared on CBC TV on behalf of the Edmonton Women's Liberation group and refused to promise her bureau chief that she would stop her political activism. He felt it compromised her identity and work as a CP reporter, and she did not. She recalls that he was a member of a local business group, which she pointed out was a double standard where one's activism was concerned, but he didn't agree. She freelanced for a while and, after her partner died, returned to the United States, where she earned a graduate degree in journalism and reported on social issues for a Chicago-area chain of newspapers. Later she came back to Canada and worked at CBC radio in Edmonton, eventually taking a job as a journalism instructor at Langara College in Vancouver. She has two children with her current partner and has also been a Vancouver school board trustee and a city councillor with the progressive COPE coalition.

She always believed that there was a strong argument for including in all her news stories the perspectives of people who did not share her political beliefs. "Because I did have, still have, enormous confidence in people that if they read all the kinds of points of view and if they really understood what was going on,... most people would adopt a more socially progressive politics.... I felt that I was being fair to everyone, that I wasn't distorting people to achieve an end because I had such confidence that if people were fully informed they would make their best decisions."[128]

Toronto Women's Liberation apparently forgave Keate her political transgressions. Some months after the Caravan ended, she and TWL member Alma Marks appeared on the CBC TV program *Take 30*, explaining socialist feminism to host Adrienne Clarkson and a small group of skeptical women also invited to the studio.[129] Although, unlike Roberts, she was not working as a news reporter during the Caravan campaign, Keate was still bucking the common news industry attitude that no journalist, including one in training, should compromise his or her professional objectivity by becoming an activist of any kind.[130] But that was not her view at the time, nor is it now. Her goal all along has been to live "authentically," in line with her principles. "I want to practise what I believe. If I'm a feminist I want to act like a feminist in all spheres of my life—in the workplace, politically, socially, religiously, personally in my relationships with men and women." During her career she has worked on mainstream newspapers, including the *Daily Colonist* in Victoria, and with CBC Radio in Vancouver. After her marriage broke up and she needed to support her son, she opted for better pay and a more flexible schedule. She worked in public relations at the University of Western Ontario, among other positions. Nevertheless, she has twice quit a job when office demands clashed with her political convictions. All along, she has consistently volunteered her services to a number of political organizations, first the NDP and then the Green Party, as well as environmental, community and Unitarian congregation groups.

She now holds a Ph.D. in communication and in recent years, has taught media studies courses at Vancouver Island University in Nanaimo, BC. Like Roberts, she believes that one's political principles do not necessarily compromise good journalism. "I have gone into interviews with people who I totally disagree with, and I may hate everything they stand for, but I have written articles that have expressed their point of view in an objective way." She likens the devil's advocate role that journalists often adopt to a "struggle session" during which one learns that one's own vision is not necessarily perfect.[131]

American media scholars are currently involved in debates over how much the abortion issue overshadowed other equality issues in the news coverage of the feminist movement, or how much liberal perspectives took precedence over radical ones.[132] In Canada, the media coverage of reproductive rights, including abortion, was generally liberal in tone, even when the Royal Commission on the Status of Women recommended, in December 1970, a compromise that amounted to decriminalizing abortion in the first trimester and an end to the TAC committees, suggestions the government ignored.[133] The socialist feminists behind the Abortion Caravan did not have the advantage of liberal respectability, perhaps, but they won their time in the limelight, mainly because the issue was controversial and they were familiar with the ways in which the news media work. As activists, they understood that reporters look for conflict, impact, timeliness and the proximity of the issue to readers who are familiar with it.[134] Given the focus in most journalism on some form of conflict, the Caravanners' dramatic rhetoric, such as their "war on the Canadian government," was a highlight in several of the stories, complemented by self-conscious photos of the women raising clenched fists, acting out their skits, yelling their demands and hoisting their banners. This is what they intended, as part of their radical, attention-seeking performance, which was fuelled by genuine anger, and these images, constantly repeated, became symbolic of their politics and reflected other images of so-called women's libbers that were quickly becoming a staple of media coverage in the United States, Canada and elsewhere. Descriptions of the way they dressed, and the swear words they used, only underscored the still prevalent expectation that young women should be ladylike, and these young radicals definitely were not, a perspective reflected in the editorial cartoon that opens this chapter.

As a result of the feminist publicity strategy behind it, the Caravan campaign had a high media profile from start to finish, which was notable given that the group started out with 17 women in a three-vehicle motorcade, although they had dozens of supporters at each stop along the way, and hundreds at the Ottawa demonstrations. Reporters took them seriously enough to cover the Caravan because their arguments struck a chord for many women of child-bearing age, who feared unwanted pregnancy but had little power over the outcome. It helped that the Caravanners' publicity campaign was well organized, a definite advantage in courting news coverage. Owing to the concerted efforts of Roberts, Keate and the other women involved, the media were informed of their coming in advance and well briefed on the scene by Caravanners who had practised their scripts and their eye-catching street theatre performances. Consequently, their progress across the country and their demand that abortion be decriminalized was covered by just about every local newspaper, because they knew how to attract attention through their rhetoric and their actions. They were demonstrating that the highly contentious abortion issue was still not settled, that women's right to choose was at stake, and that women were still being harmed because of the situation. In response, the local reporters were much better than only "barely respectful"[135] of their efforts, although their news stories were not as broad-ranging as perhaps the Caravanners had hoped. Of their key demands, only the most dramatic one—abortion on demand—really caught the media's attention because they were expressing a radical solution to an age-old problem, one that would shift child-bearing decisions from doctor to pregnant woman, a revolutionary idea for all concerned. In addition, the law had only been recently changed after a great deal of public debate, and repealing it would mean the end of the hospital TACs. A few reporters did pay attention to the Caravanners' call for legal pardons for convicted abortionists, and also mentioned the need for independent, free community sexual health clinics, a change that would involve the sanction of the provincial governments. Only the individual journalists' interest, and the available space, allowed at least some mention of the need for sex education in medical schools, research on the medical safety of various birth control methods, and the Caravanners' opposition to controlling women's reproductive functions in the name of population control.

It was easier for reporters to refer to them simply as "militant" and focus on the pro and con arguments of the abortion issue itself, mainly because of the logistics and practices of news writing, especially the pyramid style of reporting that often deleted detail and context, and the "fairness and balance" that invited opposing viewpoints. Before the Caravan reached Ottawa, most of these stories were published on the women's pages, which some might argue marginalized them further. Historically, however, these sections have always been the first to carry news of equality rights that might not have been found anywhere else in the newspaper, and that was still true in 1970.[136]

Once the Caravanners became confrontational, bringing their "declaration of war" to the prime minister's residence and the House of Commons, the placement of the stories shifted to the front and inside news pages, as their actions were a direct, blunt challenge to the male political establishment that had tried to ignore them. The journalists, including press gallery reporters, scrambled to cover what was essentially dramatic spot news, having to explain to their readers that these determined women had caught everyone off-guard with the lengths they were prepared to go to in pressing their case for "abortion on demand." Most of the editorials, taking House security and decorum as their benchmarks, condemned their actions but did not necessarily disagree with their sentiments. The same pattern applied to letters to the editor.

Roberts, Keate and the other participants in the Abortion Caravan campaign did not win further reproductive freedoms for Canadian women in the short run, nor could they, given the highly charged nature of the political discussions, right up to the 1988 Supreme Court decision favouring Morgentaler's clinics. Although that decision effectively took abortion out of the Criminal Code, the battle is still not over.[137] Today, the current generation of pro-choice advocates, many of them university students as well, are using the Internet to network with each other, lobbying to end the provincial health regulations that still make access to abortion uneven across the country. The media continue to track the debates.[138]

CHAPTER 6

Collective Visions

Lesbian Identity and Sexuality in
Feminist Periodicals, 1979–1994

I n December 1987, a group of laughing lesbians tumbled out of a closet onto the cover page of *Pandora*, Halifax's feminist-run quarterly. The headline read, "Too Visible?" while, inside, an editorial challenged all readers to accept the fact that the periodical's contributors would continue to write regularly about lesbians and their lives. A few subscribers had complained about lesbian content in an earlier issue, yet no one, the editorial continued, had questioned the amount of copy that *Pandora* devoted to any number of issues primarily of interest to heterosexual women. So why did the word *lesbian* have so much power? "For those who are homophobic, whether the word 'lesbian' appears once or a hundred times, it's too much. For them, the sore point is not the quantity, but its very presence."[1]

From the early 1970s to the turn of the 21st century, activist lesbians in Canada and their supporters used feminist newspapers, devoted to issues and events in the broader women's communities, to engage in far-reaching discussions about identity politics. For lesbians, it was important to take power over their sexuality back from the state, challenge social disapproval in the mainstream press, and express their feelings in ways they felt were true to themselves and their own emotional and erotic experiences. A number of historians, communications scholars and other academics have begun to track this history,[2] including coverage of lesbians in the mainstream media,[3] but they have not extensively analyzed the role of the feminist press as recorder and arbiter of debates about lesbianism.[4] This essay will highlight the roles of several editors and editorial collectives on three of the best-known feminist publications, explain the oppositional political climate in which they operated, and explore the complexity of the debates in their pages about lesbian identity and sexual practices.

Pandora cover, December 1987. Photo by Lori J. Meserve. Published with the permission of Lori J. Meserve and Debbie Mathers, co-coordinator, *Pandora*.

These debates took place as women, lesbians and gay men were winning more legal rights federally, provincially and municipally,[5] but how much flexibility the feminist periodicals had to explore lesbian sexuality in print varied with local conditions. It depended on who was on the collectives; what their interests were; who was available to provide the coverage; what the reaction might be from any and all of their financial sources, including government funding agencies, advertisers and readers; and what other competing issues were in the news. It is clear that feminist publications, which rejected censorship on principle, helped advance the discussions about lesbian identity and sexuality, sometimes with a bluntness that would not have been acceptable in the mainstream press. At the same time, lesbians argued amongst themselves over the acceptable boundaries of their identities, self-expression and sexual practices.

It has always been difficult to determine the exact number of feminist publications in Canada at any given time, due to the constant turnover. There were more than 300, including newsletters, between the late 1960s and the turn of the 21st century, but the total seemed to level out at 40 and 50 between the late 1980s and mid-1990s, with circulations that rarely exceeded 2000 to 2500 readers each.[6] Periodicals that were entirely devoted to lesbian issues alone tended to be short-lived, and, because of systemic discrimination and threats of censorship, unable to attract financial support through public funding and advertising.[7] Gay newspapers, like the movement itself, tended to be male dominated.[8] By comparison, the more enduring and welcoming feminist periodicals offered relative safety for exploring lesbian topics; among them were *Kinesis* (Vancouver, 1974–2001), *Broadside* (Toronto, 1979–1989) and *Pandora* (Halifax, 1985–1994).

For this study, I have conducted oral history interviews with the following editors and coordinators: Emma Kivisild, Esther Shannon, Nancy Pollak and Fatima Jaffer of *Kinesis*; Philinda Masters of *Broadside*; and Bethan (formerly Betty-Ann) Lloyd and Debbie Mathers of *Pandora*. They all identified as lesbians then, as did most of the members of their editorial collectives. These collectives were based on a model of communal responsibility already common among a number of left-wing feminist organizations, with the members sharing their political perspectives and individual abilities. Similarly, the members of the editorial collectives shared their views and skills—such as writing, photography and design—with each other, with their writers, with the women who volunteered to help out on newspaper layout and distribution days, and with their readers. While one woman, or a small team, might take on the everyday tasks of editor or production coordinator, collective members generally expected to operate as equal partners and decide together, during regular meetings, on the content, production and distribution of the periodical.[9]

My oral history interviews, the articles the editors published and surviving archival documents[10] demonstrate how the three publications helped shape and reflect the "counter-public sphere" of feminist and lesbian media expression, and the ways in which they were limited as well. By "counterpublic," communication scholars mean the alternative media representing women and minorities, as opposed to the mainstream or "public sphere." There are concentric circles of feminist "counter-publics" and their media. One could argue, for example, that *Chatelaine*, with its predominantly female readership, was already an "alternative" publication to *Saturday Night* and other general circulation magazines. But the women who published feminist periodicals did so because they felt that the mainstream media, *Chatelaine* included, did not reflect their more radical politics or lesbian realities. Later on, women of colour planned their own feminist periodicals, in which they debated the nature and practices of lesbianism from *their* "counter-public" perspectives.[11]

Kinesis, Broadside and *Pandora* were chosen for this essay mainly for their consistency and relative longevity, although they did not, on their own, represent feminist periodical publishing in Canada as a whole.[12] They were, respectively, two monthly newspapers and a quarterly, they were available in these same formats for at least nine uninterrupted years sometime between 1979 and 1994, and they broadly represented the urban west, central and eastern parts of the country. Their editors and editorial collectives were all dedicated to countering the mainstream media's neglect or negative views of women and feminism. They focused on news and views of the women's movement because they wanted to foster communication among women who were already feminists, or who were attracted to their ideas. Most of the editors, collective members, production coordinators and writers considered themselves activists and were no doubt influenced by current debates on women's issues, although they welcomed different points of view, including those of their readers.[13] Aside from reproductive choice and lesbianism, they covered many other feminist concerns over the years, such as equal pay and fair working conditions, daycare, health, racism, the environment and women's rights abroad.

Public discussions about lesbian rights and responsibilities in these feminist periodicals were always risky, especially from the early 1980s to the early 1990s. During those years, heterosexual feminist activists slowly became more accepting of the lesbians among their ranks, but right-wing politicians cut off government funding to feminist services and publications that advocated freedom of choice on abortion and sexual orientation. The previous federal governments and some provincial ones had initially helped fund a number of programs for women in order to give them a representative voice in the body politic, or run services such as battered women's shelters. Short-term grants funded special projects, a way of attracting more feminist labour for these services and new trainees for the feminist presses. In 1985 the Conservative federal government provided 15 percent of the budgets of several feminist publications, but by the late 1980s was listening to strong lobbying from right-wing politicians, churches and civic groups such as REAL Women that wanted an end to government funding for any feminist service or publication that advocated abortion or lesbianism. The federal office of the Secretary of State, colloquially known as "SecState," made its decision not to fund groups whose "primary purpose is to promote a view on abortion or sexual orientation" official in 1987,[14] which meant that feminist groups applying for funds had to get around the policy or die. *Herizons* (1983–1987 and 1991–), a feminist magazine published in Winnipeg, was forced to close because of this repressive campaign, but began publishing again a few years later without government support.[15]

While some readers did occasionally complain about lesbian content in *Kinesis, Broadside* and *Pandora*, it was the editors and the rest of the collective members who decided what would or would not be published. One cannot use the idea of audience agency and influence with confidence in their cases because relatively few readers tried to become involved in setting the editorial agendas, although when they did, some of their comments were revealing. Only *Kinesis* conducted formal readership surveys every few years, finding in 1984 that a number of respondents wanted more lesbian content, which it provided.[16] In general, stories and issues were covered if the various women's groups informed the periodicals of upcoming events and when there were enough contributors and other volunteers available to do the work. If there were complaints, they often came by telephone or in person, exchanges that have not been recorded for posterity.[17]

Pleasing big advertisers was not a priority for the feminist editors or their collectives, so it was not really an issue when it came to lesbian content. Mainstream businesses were not interested in advertising with them because their periodicals' circulations were modest and they had strict editorial guidelines forbidding sexism or any other form of discrimination in all content, including ads. The publications relied instead on advertising from progressive businesses and organizations, such as feminist bookstores and unions. They all also courted sustaining donations from subscribers and organized fundraising events.[18]

To make their newspapers attractive to look at and handle, and easier to produce, they all went through some design and technological changes.[19] They scrambled to find distributors, usually women's centres, alternative bookstores, organic food shops, gay bars and similar enterprises that catered to their readers but were struggling to survive as well. Every time one of these locations closed down, the feminist periodical concerned was left with a gap in its distribution network that had to be filled.[20] Because of the increasing costs of publication, each experienced crises of various kinds, which meant that they steadily had to increase their advertising and subscription rates, and mailing charges.[21]

The editors and their collectives on *Kinesis*, *Broadside* and *Pandora*, while sharing a belief in the importance of advocacy journalism and a dislike of censorship, also had their particular perspectives on feminist and lesbian issues and their own ways of operating. All of them covered news of legal battles that focused on the human rights of lesbians and gay men as a matter of course, as well as the literature and cultural and sports events that attracted their readers.[22] More contentious in the feminist press were the debates centring on the nature and manifestations of same-sex love between women. But, because these editorial collectives were intent on making room for articles about all the major issues in the women's movement, in part to attract wider female audiences, lesbian content, no matter how controversial, did not dominate their editorial agendas. From time to time, there were brief surges of it, usually owing to special features or inserts. In *Kinesis*, the lesbian content averaged 12 percent, with a high of 21 percent in one issue; in *Broadside*, the average was 4.5 percent, with a

(Left to right) *Kinesis* editors Esther Shannon and Nancy Pollak, with columnist Noreen Shanahan and production coordinator Marsha Arbour having a picnic, c. 1985. Marsha Arbour private collection.

high of 15 percent; in *Pandora*, the average was 8 percent, with a high of 10 percent. *Kinesis* was the most inclined to cover the debates about the nature of lesbian eroticism, followed by *Broadside*, while *Pandora* was the least frankly sexual and focused more on lesbianism as an identity issue.[23]

At the same time, lesbians were particularly attracted to working as editors, collective members, writers and production volunteers on these three publications because they were safe havens where they could be open and relaxed about their sexual orientation in ways they could not be elsewhere.[24] They often socialized together as well.

During the mid-1980s to mid-1990s, the editors and coordinators interviewed for this essay were all living publicly as lesbians. Each one brought to feminist publishing her life experiences; her own journalistic, publishing or production expertise; and different priorities within the range of feminist concerns.

Emma Kivisild, *Kinesis*'s editor from 1984 to 1985, had lived in Vancouver, Taiwan and Toronto with her Estonian refugee parents before the family settled in Calgary. She went to Princeton, where she majored in philosophy, before returning to Calgary, where she wrote for *City Limits*, a politically focused arts magazine. One evening, she covered a talk about radical feminism and, instantly smitten, embraced the movement wholeheartedly. After she moved to Vancouver with friends, she became involved in the local feminist community and, with the help of a short-term government grant to *Kinesis*, learned production skills there before taking the editor's position. She was 22 years old, involved in the punk-arts scene and the peace movement, and just coming out as a lesbian, and she liked to challenge the political perspectives of the older women on the *Kinesis* editorial board. She believed in frank discussions about lesbian identity and sexuality, not playing the topic down in deference to the few straight women involved in the publication. The collective and the newspaper itself gave her and other women a forum in which to express who they were and to discuss the issues that concerned them. "*Kinesis* was the right place, at the right time and the right thing. It was a miracle."[25]

Her successor, Esther Shannon (1985–1988), grew up as a "tomboy" in "a very low-income and quite uneducated family" in Cape Breton, Nova Scotia. After she left home and dropped out of high school, she lived with a male partner among the radical hippies in Halifax, where she had two children. It was at that point that she started reading about feminism. Later, after the couple settled for a time in Powell River, British Columbia, she helped set up the local women's centre, fell in love with a straight woman and realized she was a lesbian. She had always dreamed of being a journalist, and after moving to Ottawa, learned the craft at the feminist periodical *Upstream* (1976–1979) from the journalism students who volunteered there. Travelling on to Vancouver, she was given short government-grant jobs handling subscriptions and other tasks at *Kinesis*, before taking over as editor. "Feminism was my life," Shannon recalled, and so she was most interested in producing news and analysis. "I saw our feminist journalism as a pipeline, and a way to educate the feminist and the women's movement, educate the wider community, and ... essentially build the movement." Shannon recalls a number of readers complaining of too much material about lesbians or, alternatively, about stories that might reflect badly on the community. Her first edition, with a cover photo of a woman in a karate pose, spotlighted the importance of self-defence skills for women, but another cover flag heading announced an additional feature on the inside about women raping other women. "I believe [it] was the first story that was written about that. It blew up. People thought that it was a very inappropriate cover.... That's what the letters were about. I actually thought they were about a lot of anxiety about that dirty laundry out there." All in all, lesbian issues did not take precedence over other feminist topics in *Kinesis*, in her mind. "I feel that we spent as much time on lesbianism as was appropriate."[26]

The next editor, Nancy Pollak (1988–1992), a self-described "army brat," was raised in various southern Ontario towns; lived for two years in West Berlin, Germany; went to high school in Ottawa; and attended the University of Toronto for one year before leaving for Vancouver and "a new leaf." There she worked at Press Gang, a politically radical, cooperative publishing company, where she learned graphic design and typography, among other skills. Initially hired by Vancouver Status of Women on a government grant, she started working at *Kinesis* after Shannon invited her to attend a weekend retreat on Saturna Island, where the attendees critiqued the news-paper's content and took part in skills-training workshops. "That was the beginning of the end, you know, they sucked me in," she laughed. Pollak describes herself as "an example of a feminist who never thought that fem-inist politics were sufficient to explain the world politically, or, you know, human experience, or what I was looking for as a human being.... It was an irreplaceable set of tools and outlooks and ways of seeing and ways of act-ing, but it wasn't all there was." At one point in her life, she had lived briefly in Paris, where she observed how badly Black people from the former French colonies were treated. With her anti-imperialist perspective, she strongly encouraged the *Kinesis* editorial board to reach out to women of colour and, with the input of the newspaper's new Women of Colour Caucus, it formally adopted an affirmative action policy that embraced racial diversity.

The lesbian content of *Kinesis*, Pollak recalled, focused more on news of human rights challenges than on self-reflective essays dealing with iden-tity and relationships. In her time, the editorial board did allow essays and open letters on different topics under the heading "Commentary," but it was also concerned about maintaining the delicate balance between *Kinesis*'s editing policies and contributors' freedom of expression. It did not publish "rants," she said. Its approach to lesbianism was consistent with its way of doing feminist journalism on any topic and was a reason, she thought, why articles about lesbianism as identity and sexual practice were usually found on the arts and cultural pages. Most of the editors, "myself included, would have been fascinated ... and pretty comfortable with [talk of sexuality] in our personal lives, but not knowing how to cover it in the paper except in the cultural pages. It's interesting."

Despite her spirited public defence of articles about lesbianism in *Kine-sis*, Pollak sometimes had to fight her own internal reservations, a visceral reaction of the type common to women like her who grew up gay in an era when lesbianism was socially unacceptable. "I'd been a lesbian all my life as far as my emotional and sexual orientation is concerned.... I didn't come to lesbianism because of the women's movement. And had to, you know, encounter my own internalized homophobia, which I think is very differ-ent when you have been a lesbian from the get go than when you embrace it.... I would sometimes look at *Kinesis* and go, 'Oh my God, look at all this lesbian content.' Which is actually not true. There was relatively little les-bian content in *Kinesis*."[27] This comment is an accurate reflection of her tenure (1988–1992) compared with those of the other editors interviewed for this chapter, a difference that could be attributed to a combination of fac-tors, for example, the political funding pressures over lesbian content; other prominent issues in the news at the time, such as free trade and the decrim-inalization of abortion; and the editorial board's efforts to include more stories about women of colour.[28]

Pollak's successor, Fatima Jaffer, was the first woman of colour to edit *Kinesis* (1992–1994). Jaffer, who was born in Mombasa, Kenya, described her heritage as West African, South Asian and Muslim. After her family moved to Canada, she studied English literature at McGill University; worked on the *McGill Daily*, the campus newspaper; and became involved in the anti-racism movement, which took priority over feminism for her at the time, although "everything I wrote was about women." She took a graduate degree in journalism at the University of Western Ontario with the intention of moving back to East Africa to work there, but found herself looking for a job in Vancouver instead. It was a difficult time because of the racism she faced. "It was so in your face and obvious in those days." So she applied for, and got, a grant-funded assignment at the Vancouver Women's Health Collective, right next door to the Vancouver Status of Women office. With Pollak's support, she started working at *Kinesis* as production coordinator, a paid position, and became involved with the newspaper's Women of Colour Caucus, which they dubbed the "Not Just Another Page Collective," meaning the members wanted their issues integrated throughout the paper. Its presence "was essential to me even beginning to think about accepting the job as editor. I mean, if it hadn't been there, I wouldn't have done it." The caucus, with its 25 to 30 members, not only contributed important input into the newspaper's collective decision making, but also became a safe place for women of colour who were attracted to other women, just as *Kinesis* had been for their white predecessors. "It really was a lot about people going through a process of coming out as lesbians, as well," Jaffer recalled.

Jaffer and her ethnically diverse editorial collective focused on the concerns of women of different racial backgrounds and their rights in Canada and around the world. She wanted to "change the perception of who else are our movers and shakers in the women's movement." As editor, she wrote and actively solicited articles that reflected different racial perspectives on lesbianism as well, including erotic writing that appealed to her. She was particularly attracted to the writing of Makeda Silvera, for example, reviewing her new anthology and interviewing her. As a woman of colour, Jaffer recalled, "it was mind blowing for me, you know, at the time, and I was a relatively new lesbian too, actually."[29]

Of the three periodicals discussed in this essay, *Kinesis* was the mostly strongly associated with a nongovernmental organization that depended on government funding, a situation that became more politicized as time went on. Vancouver Status of Women (VSW), a broad-based feminist advisory group that relied on federal and provincial government grants to survive, issued *Kinesis* as an editorially independent newspaper, paying the editor, who was considered a staff member, a salary. In 1984 the right-wing Social Credit government of British Columbia stripped VSW of its core funding, but the federal Liberals restored it the same year, just before the

Conservative Party defeated them in an election.[30] By the late 1980s, VSW was receiving some federal funding from the SecState.[31] In the spring of 1989, SecState cut VSW's funding by 15 percent and, in a follow-up meeting in the summer, delivered a "discouraging and infuriating" message, then-editor Nancy Pollak wrote in *Kinesis*.

> As we've reported, the Conservative's rationale for cutting Women's Program funding was The Deficit, that handy economic excuse for withdrawing public funds from whatever they don't politically support. Well, the SecState's bureaucrats had economic arguments—VSW and *Kinesis* should be more market-driven; and their political arguments—*Kinesis*'s coverage of lesbian issues and abortion makes it hard for them to defend our funding. There is a wall here, and on the wall is writing. VSW has been warned not to pursue SecState funding for *Kinesis* next year. Regardless of how the organization deals with this warning, the ground under *Kinesis* has shifted."[32]

The collective members would enlist their supporters' help in resisting what Pollak termed "this attack on English-speaking Canada's most comprehensive feminist newspaper," while VSW and other feminist groups would fight back against the extensive budget cuts to women's services.[33] VSW and *Kinesis* together had to find ways of making up the shortfall, which for the newspaper meant raising its newsstand, subscription and advertising rates.[34] After fierce opposition from feminists across the country, the government relented to a limited degree over the extent of the reduction in Women's Program funding, with VSW and *Kinesis* raising further funds through appeals for support, as well as a successful new subscription drive, volunteer recruitment and fundraising events.[35]

Pollak's successor, Fatima Jaffer (1992–1994), said that after further SecState cuts in 1993, VSW assigned her to another position within the agency, as information coordinator, but she continued to edit *Kinesis*. She recalled receiving strong support for its editorial policies from Status of Women's regional director in British Columbia, whom she considered an ally. "I would check with her occasionally and say, 'You know, I'm gonna do this, and you might get some flack, but we're gonna do it.'" After two years at the helm of *Kinesis*, Jaffer stayed on for several more years to help the relatively inexperienced new editor, Agnes Huang. She also recalled that budget cuts continued after the federal Liberals were returned to office in 1993, as they were more interested in short-term project spending than ongoing support to women's groups.[36] In the meantime, the successive federal governments had threatened the financial stability of many smaller publications when the Conservatives included reading material under the federal Goods and Services Tax and when both they and the Liberals cut postal subsidies to Canadian magazines.[37]

The other two feminist publications examined in this essay were not as directly affected by the SecState cuts, but the Conservative government's attitude certainly contributed to a discouraging climate for feminist publishing after it came to power in 1984. In Toronto, Philinda Masters and a group of her friends had formed a nonprofit company to launch *Broadside* (1979–1989) because there was no alternative feminist publication in the city at the time. Masters was born in Toronto, grew up there, and attended the University of Toronto, where she became a reporter on the campus newspaper, *The Varsity*, a stint that included one year as sports editor. After she graduated, she worked at the *Financial Post* for a while, but decided that mainstream journalism was not for her. In the meantime, she had been involved with the Women's Place centre, as well as with the group known as Women Against Violence Against Women (WAVAW). *Broadside* gave her the opportunity to work as a journalist in a completely feminist environment, even if she was not well paid. She became its longest-serving editor, a part-time position, although, in reality, she was working full time. A year before the newspaper folded, she decided to take on a real full-time position at an academic journal, *Resources for Feminist Research*, but she still contributed to *Broadside*.

Masters recalled that in *Broadside*'s early days, there was tension within its predominantly lesbian editorial collective over how much same-sex content to publish, as several members were heterosexual socialist feminists who were more interested in political theory and action. The other members included teachers who were lesbians "when that was not acceptable and it was dangerous to their careers." The collective's decision not to disclose in print the sexual orientation of its members irritated some of the radical lesbians in the city, one of whom wrote a letter asking them, "Why don't you just come out?" and challenging them to publish it. "Of course we're not going to publish it, because that's the whole problem," Masters retrospectively observed. To settle on *Broadside* being a feminist newspaper for all women seemed a good compromise, with a number of its writers tackling such controversial issues as pornography and lesbian sexuality. "We almost never censored stuff," Masters said, a practice that sometimes got them into political trouble with specific feminist groups or readers. At the time, left-wing feminists were roughly divided into radical lesbians primarily opposed to patriarchy, and socialist feminists primarily opposed to capitalism. As for the politics of *Broadside*, "We didn't see ourselves as a lesbian paper, we saw ourselves as a feminist paper which was fueled by the concerns of lesbian politics as well as socialist feminist politics.... We were not really interested in liberal feminism"[38]—that is, bringing about change within the established political system.

Broadside did not rely on SecState for operating funds, but cobbled together its financial support from subscriptions, advertising, donations, fundraisers and a series of short-term government and arts council grants.[39] Because of internal difficulties and staff burnout, *Broadside* suspended publication early in 1989, but the collective asked the federal government to help finance a tenth anniversary edition. The ministry turned down the request because of *Broadside*'s political stance in support of choice on abortion and lesbianism, so the collective turned to the Ontario government's Women's Directorate and supportive donors to publish what would turn out to be the final issue.[40] While SecState policies were not the direct reason for *Broadside*'s folding, the antagonistic political climate played its part in the collective's decision. Masters explained to the newspaper's readers: "Being considered lesbian, having unabashed lesbian content, obviously is enough to give anyone the heebie-geebies. The question is, how does the government get away with such a misogynist agenda? They get away with it partly because the very groups who could put up a fight have already been effectively destabilized. Feminist publications are a powerful tool in this respect, and the less support we get, the better for the status quo." *Broadside*, she added, would always have to rely on some form of government subsidy, "so lack of substantial support from our biggest potential supporter was always a problem." She also felt that it was time that a more racially diverse group of women take over the publication, but no one

Broadside's tenth anniversary—and last—edition, 1989. Uncredited collage, published with the permission of Philinda Masters, former editor and co-publisher of *Broadside*.

stepped forward. Possibly women of colour were more interested in support-ing their own periodical, *Our Lives*, which inherited *Broadside*'s subscrip-tion list but did not survive for very long.[41]

In Halifax, Betty-Ann Lloyd with Brenda Bryan and a small group of women established *Pandora* in 1985 because they wanted to teach and encourage other women to express themselves in print.[42] Born in Calgary, Lloyd had lived in Edmonton, Quebec City, Vancouver and Toronto, as well as in small Maritimes towns. She married early in her life, and after that mar-riage ended, had a son and, in her words, "lived within lesbian community," sharing custody of the child with his father, an equitable arrangement that left her time to devote to *Pandora*. With her background and her experi-ence working on community newspapers, with the CBC and as an instruc-tor in the School of Journalism at King's University College in Halifax, she felt that a common focus for *Pandora* was more important than juggling disparate political views. She saw the importance of presenting it as a "women's" rather than feminist, community paper. Nevertheless, the small collective that ran *Pandora* was primarily feminist, and the newspaper's welcoming environment drew women who were exploring both their poli-tics and their sexuality. It was, Lloyd recalled, a good place to be "finding your voice as a feminist, but primarily as a lesbian. You know, lesbians came out as feminists, women came out as lesbians."[43] She did not consider the publication to be politically radical, except that it took a women's standpoint, including a lesbian-inclusive editorial stance, and that it was published as a feminist collective effort. But she was mindful that Maritimers, including the female readership they were trying to attract, generally felt that sexual explicitness, especially in the first person, was "too much information."[44] Locally, lesbian activists complained that their work and issues went unac-knowledged by the broader feminist community groups, a complaint that was echoed elsewhere in Atlantic Canada at the time.[45] When an otherwise supportive reader complained about two stories that mainly concerned les-bians in *Pandora*'s first issue, September 1985, accusing the periodical of pro-moting lesbianism as form of "sexual gratification," Lloyd was quick to respond editorially that the articles "centred on lesbianism as a lifestyle (not as a source of sexual gratification!)." She went on to say: "In our soci-ety, heterosexuality is assumed and the inclusion of any other lifestyle can seem alarmingly [blatant]. However, I think it is important to keep in per-spective the actual emphasis placed on lesbian lifestyle in *Pandora*."[46]

Pandora's production coordinator, Debbie Mathers, who was born in Montreal but grew up in Halifax, brought her prior experience on alterna-tive local newspapers such as the *Fourth Estate* to the periodical. She and a small editorial committee took over from Lloyd, who went to Toronto to study for a master's degree before returning two years later to volunteer with distribution. Mathers recalled that editorial meetings often included contributors to the publication, and that lesbian issues were included in its editorial mix as a matter of course, but were not overstated: "We just kind of covered the news as it came up. If it was a lesbian thing, it was a lesbian thing. If it wasn't a lesbian thing, it wasn't a lesbian thing." When it did appear as a specific issue, it stood out because of the identity politics concerned, and because, for some readers, it was contentious to begin with.[47]

Unlike *Kinesis* and *Broadside*, *Pandora* was distributed free of charge, with the exception of mailing costs, relying mainly on advertising, fundraising and donations to keep going. Because the collective members wanted to avoid political interference, they did not apply for or receive government funds as a rule, with the exception of a short-term employment grant to hire summer help. At the 1986 feminist periodicals conference, held near Orangeville, Ontario, the delegates pledged themselves to increasing lesbian visibility in their publications.[48] *Pandora*'s run-in with SecState came after it asked for a grant to help it host the next feminist periodical meeting in Halifax in 1987. Because the collective refused to leave abortion and lesbianism off their conference agenda, or even pretend to do so, they did not get the grant and cancelled the conference. For Lloyd, it was "an ethical issue.... I mean this was the whole point of having a feminist periodical, a women's paper, it was about not being silenced. And so we were going to silence ourselves to take money? I don't think so!"[49]

Pandora was subjected to another kind of political punishment that did not centre on its pro-choice position on abortion and lesbianism but rather on its woman-only letters policy, which it clearly stated on its editorial page.[50] In 1991 the Nova Scotia Human Rights Commission forced the newspaper to defend itself and pay its own costs after it refused to publish a letter to the editor from a man, a fathers' rights advocate responding to an article about child custody. The newspaper, which was legally within its rights, eventually won the case, but it was an expensive and gruelling ordeal that drained the *Pandora* women's energy but made a few of them determined to persevere nonetheless. They managed to keep the newspaper going for another couple of years until burnout took its toll.[51] Lloyd and Mathers both recalled that near the end of its run, *Pandora*'s collective was split more or less 50–50 between heterosexual and lesbian or bisexual women, but it was rare to run any lesbian material that was explicitly erotic in the publication at any time.[52] The last collective, which was racially diverse, wanted to cover all kinds of different issues, including lesbianism, but decided that there was not enough feminist energy and support to sustain *Pandora*, and it folded in 1994.[53]

Under the leadership of their editors and collectives, *Kinesis*, *Broadside* and *Pandora* all engaged in discussions about lesbianism, the degree and intensity of the articles depending on their own editorial priorities and the perceived interests of their readers. There was no clear progression on the issues as they presented them; rather, there was an overlapping, complex and continuing interplay of ideas regarding self-recognition, gender politics and erotic behaviour. Essentially, the articles in these periodicals examined the following interrelated questions: who is a real lesbian, what kind of a lesbian is she, and how should she express her sexual desires? The debates, grounded in conflicting interpretations of lesbian feminist theories, centred on issues such as lesbianism as innate or a choice, bisexuality, monogamy versus non-monogamy, butch and femme roles, the differences between pornography and eroticism, striptease and sexual celebration, and whether sadomasochism between women was truly consensual and egalitarian. The discussion ranged from the cerebral to the titillating, with the writers using language that became franker as time went on.

Those women who identified as radical feminists were intent on developing a lesbian sensibility and ways of being that fostered equality between partners rather than the heterosexual, biological determinism that prescribed stifling roles for all women.[54] They saw themselves as rebelling against patriarchy. At the same time, women who wanted to express their lesbianism as freely as possible identified as outlaws rebelling against both patriarchy and feminist orthodoxy. Many women occupied a shifting middle ground, adopting ideas about lesbian identity that suited them. Although anger and bitterness sometimes peppered these discussions, the discourse in the feminist press also relayed clear attempts to compromise and accommodate different points of view.

Taken together, these articles provide a snapshot of lesbian identity and sexuality, though like most media messages, they should be taken as only a reflection of reality, funnelled through the viewpoints of the women concerned. Most lesbians are not necessarily intellectuals, feminist activists, sexual radicals or even openly gay. The women who edited, produced and wrote for these publications embraced some or all of those characteristics, thereby providing the means whereby lesbian identity and sexuality could be publicly discussed.

Regardless of how frank, or not, they were willing to be, when challenged, each of these editors, their collectives and the writers whose articles they published strongly defended lesbians in principle, mainly because, as feminists, they believed that women should have freedom of choice over their own bodies, the same argument they made for abortion rights. Believing, as well, the radical feminist position that "the personal is political," feminist periodicals like *Kinesis* and *Broadside* had historically presented lesbianism as a choice women could make,[55] or as a form of creative feminist theory,[56] not something that was innate to their natures, as others argued elsewhere.[57] Another early feminist publishing goal, outside of politics, was simply to provide basic information about same-sex love, its history and its complications. One *Kinesis* special supplement included topics such as developing healthy, long-term relationships by balancing individual autonomy with togetherness; a historical overview of lesbian sexual politics from the 19th century to the present; health concerns that included instructions on how to avoid venereal disease; the complicated, secret lives of closeted lesbian athletes; and bisexuality among women.[58]

In the first issue of *Pandora*, which began publishing in the fall of 1985—relatively late compared with the others—readers were asked to fill out a teasing "politically correct" questionnaire and send it in with subscription money, a donation or a letter to the editor. Among the 19 questions was: "A woman who has a female lover is: (a) a queer, (b) a dyke, (c) a lesbian, (d) gay, (e) other." There appeared to be no right answer.[59] More seriously, one *Pandora* writer later maintained that straight feminists should understand that lesbianism was not really about sex, but about "a way of life, a culture, that is different from heterosexual culture just as Black culture is different from White culture, Jewish culture is different from Christian culture, working-class culture is different from middle-class culture." Lloyd does not remember who wrote the unsigned article, but it was in line with the perspective she expressed during community workshops she and Brenda Bryan conducted on heterosexism.[60]

Political and personal definitions of the term *lesbian* seemed to abound in the feminist press. When Eve Zaremba, one of the founders of *Broadside*, began writing an essay on lesbian sexuality for a feminist anthology, she found that her friends were giving her different perspectives, so she asked *Broadside* readers for their feedback. Lesbian sexuality was not the same thing as living as a lesbian because this option had become viable only recently for Western women, whereas it was repressed in many other countries, she wrote. Lesbian feminism was a product of the current women's movement. "Sex on the other hand is any overt sexual activity between women," but one did not need to identify as a lesbian or live as one to make love with a woman. So, she borrowed phrases from the American feminist poet Adrienne Rich, describing lesbian desire as "primary intensity between women."[61]

Feminist, lesbian or gay rights conferences provided heterosexual, bisexual and lesbian feminists a more public opportunity to work out their definitions and differences, occasions that were covered assiduously in the feminist press. Contributing writer Alex Keir reported for *Pandora* on the 1985 women's sexuality conference in Toronto, at which the needs of women of all orientations were discussed, as well as the tensions among them. In one workshop, they debated contentious ideas, such as: "Heterosexual women are screwing the enemy ... heterosexual privilege in society ... lesbian privilege in the women's movement ... misogyny—women hating women ... sexual attraction to each other." At one point, Keir wrote, "we split into groups to define lesbian, heterosexual and bisexual. We had a dreadful time of it but managed to narrow it down to words such as: primary relations, self-definition, and political identification."[62]

Only on rare occasions would a self-defined lesbian writer openly acknowledge that she had experimented with heterosexual sex,[63] as distrust of women who slept with both women and men was common among lesbians for both emotional and political reasons. They generally regarded women who identified as bisexual as fence-sitters, but the ones who spoke up publicly insisted that loving both females and males was consistent with the feminist ideal of having control over one's own body and that they should not be shunned or criticized for their feelings.[64] In *Pandora*, collective member Joanne K. Jefferson identified herself as bisexual by choice and wrote that she was tired of feeling that she had to hide aspects of her identity from both lesbians and straight feminists. She wanted acceptance and recognition from both groups. "I want people to acknowledge that we exist, not as sexually selfish or scared people, but as proud, strong people who need to be able to celebrate our identity and culture."[65]

For a few lesbian contributors to *Pandora*, who wrote anonymously about their troubling or romantic personal experiences, basic acceptance was also the most important issue.[66] True to *Pandora*'s usual editorial position, their articles were not overtly sexual, but included, for example, the post-coming-out letters between a lesbian and her mother, and a young woman's delighted account of her first night at Rumours, a local gay club.[67] In the broader Halifax community, overt lesbian affection could be controversial, as two local women learned when they dared to kiss in a local café and were asked to leave. They mounted an exhibit documenting the incident as a form of political protest, which was covered in *Pandora*.[68]

Exactly what form lesbian identity should take prompted more rounds of discussion in the pages of the feminist periodicals. The writers pondered whether one should divorce oneself from unequal, patriarchal models of love and sex, and invent a new kind of egalitarian lesbian lifestyle. What did it mean to call oneself a non-monogamous lesbian feminist, a bar dyke, a butch or a femme? How did belonging to an identifiable group other than white, middle-class and able-bodied affect one's self-definition and way of being as a lesbian? These, too, became highly contentious issues, at least among the lesbians who thought and wrote about them, especially when they expressed sentiments that were not "politically correct," or "p.c.," in the view of the outspoken lesbian-feminists, who held sway at various conferences.[69]

Yet, at those gatherings, there was marked resistance to toeing the radical feminist line, the participants usually agreeing to live and let live without one side labelling the other.[70] As writer Judy Leifschultz argued in *Broadside*, while non-monogamy might have been the theoretical choice of radical lesbian feminists, many women found that it was too emotionally and logistically challenging to have more than one lover at a time, and one's personal desires were more important than community expectations.[71]

By the mid-1980s, lesbians were discussing other kinds of identity politics as well. Writer Mariana Valverde, who covered the 1984 lesbian sexuality conference in Toronto for *Broadside*, reported that there were workshops for women who had their own particular experiences and concerns. "There were Jewish lesbians, fat lesbians, old and young lesbians, lesbians of colour, and lesbian mothers. I didn't attend any of the sessions, since I am white and thin and able-bodied and not especially old or young," she wrote, "but all the reports indicated that these were among the most successful workshops." She quoted one fat lesbian as saying, "It was great. We ate doughnuts, we did exercises, and we *almost* talked about sex."[72]

Still, the editors and writers on all three publications had not yet adequately tackled some difficult questions about lesbianism and feminist theory, such as butch/femme dynamics and the fun-loving "bar dyke" culture that favoured lesbian social life over political analysis.[73] A number of them were open to listening to women very different from themselves, however. In 1985 lesbian activist Darl Wood, a contributor to *Pandora*, reported that, through the influence of the women she met at an international gay rights conference in Toronto, she had to examine her own prejudices against apolitical lesbians, butch/femme relationships, bar dykes and others. "When the feminist movement becomes too introspective, fine-lined and unaccepting of every womyn I, for one, plan to learn all I can from the keen perception of our alienating behaviour as seen by the bar dykes of Canada. Their no-shit and to-the-point-if-you-don't-mind insight leaves me far behind in my own murky rhetoric," Wood declared.[74]

Of all the identities lesbians took on, butch and femme seemed to receive the least notice in these feminist publications until the early 1990s, when their champions stood up to be counted, yet their presence had been clearly evident, even in the lesbian feminist community, for some time. During the late 1980s, several books had been published about the pre-1970s butch-femme culture, when most lesbians outwardly adopted masculine or feminine identified roles. The younger generation in particular seemed eager to reclaim these foremothers as outlaws worthy of emulating, to the chagrin of the lesbian feminists who rejected sex roles as oppressive to women.[75] During the 1980s, partly to counter destructive Hollywood images,[76] lesbians began producing their own feature and documentary films. At the 1988 lesbian film festival in Vancouver, *Kinesis* reported, the audience "loudly applauded" a short film that featured outdoor, butch-femme lovemaking against the seductive topography of the Gulf Islands.[77] The newspaper also noted that lesbian audiences of all political persuasions gave a warm welcome to the National Film Board's historical documentary feature, *Forbidden Love*, in which a number of older lesbians, including those who identified as butch or femme, told their stories. A fictionalized, pulp novel style storyline furnished a parallel narrative to their memories, teasing out romantic images of lesbian love in dangerous times.[78] The iconic photo of the two fictional lesbian lovers was the only illustration of white women that made the cover of *Kinesis* during Jaffer's tenure as editor. "And that was important, you know, because it was a groundbreaking film," she explained.[79]

Real-life lesbians who identified as butch or femme were becoming more visible again, but, regardless of how they dressed and acted, they did not adhere to the same rigid, gender-based protocols that were common before the second wave of the feminist movement. Nevertheless, their presence in the lesbian feminist community was still treated with kid gloves, according to reports and advertising in *Kinesis*. In 1993, promotional material for International Lesbian Week in Vancouver featured "The Butch/Femme Panel. You love them, you bitch about them, you wonder if you are one. Six local femmes and butches share their stories, theories and fashion advice." Writer Karen X. Tulchinsky quoted the organizer, Mary Brookes, who explained, "It's the long-awaited debate. We've all been talking about it, with our friends anyway. One of the reasons we're having the panel is to look at the changes that have happened in the late 1980s and early 1990s that will allow the discussion to happen in a way that was impossible in the 1970s lesbian community." Brookes also cautioned, "This is not the place to criticize the existence of Butch and Femme lesbians. The women on the panel and those in the audience who speak out are vulnerable, and we want the atmosphere to be safe for everyone. We need to be respectful to our butches and femmes. They, like drag queens, have taken the flack, have been on the front lines challenging heterosexual society in ways that have created positive change for all lesbians." Tulchinsky did not question Brookes's comments, which suggested, first of all, that challenging questions were not welcome, having the likely effect of self-censorship among some audience members. The article also misinterpreted lesbian history. It was true that brave lesbians of an earlier era who were open about their sexual preferences and easily identifiable as butches and femmes were often targets of abuse and violence, even from the police.[80] The later generation came out in a relatively safer era, although butches, because they were viewed as masculine masqueraders, certainly felt the brunt of social disapproval more than femmes, or "lipstick lesbians," who were often assumed to be straight.[81] It was equally true, but not mentioned in the article, that radical lesbian feminists of the 1970s and 1980s were open and loud in asserting women's right to love women and fought for the legal changes that made it possible. They were generally intolerant of butch and femme role-playing, however, reflecting a mutual distrust that contributed to the divisions in the lesbian community at large.[82]

Lovemaking was another arena of political debate, leading to a number of difficult questions for women who identified as lesbian feminists. How did the principle of having control over one's own body relate to engaging with someone else's for sexual pleasure? Lustful texts, images, entertainment and even private lesbian behaviour in all its variations prompted a great deal of disagreement in feminist periodicals about the differences between eroticism and exploitation of women. Much of the discussion centred, politically, on what was patriarchal practice in and out of bed, and what was not, given that the only role-models lesbians had were heterosexual ones, which were assumed to be male-dominant. As straight men controlled the adult entertainment industry, distorted lesbian sex and appropriated it for their own pleasure, could lesbians make their own, more equitable erotica? Could a lesbian be a caring, sensitive, equal partner and make sex exciting at the same time? Or did one partner have to have real or illusionary power over the other to make it a truly explosive experience?

In the 1970s, before *Broadside* and *Pandora* existed, *Kinesis* had published a few informative articles and book reviews about lesbian sexuality,[83] but in the 1980s, the debates took on a life of their own because of the increased availability of heterosexual pornography, especially on video. A number of feminist writers were strongly opposed to pornography, while others argued that there was no harm in lesbian eroticism and vehemently disagreed with censorship.[84] In 1981 Joan E. Biren, an American lesbian photographer known as JEB, produced a number of erotic images for her touring slide show. An anonymous *Broadside* writer admitted: "I find the idea of lesbian erotica fascinating and I'm anxious to see in what sense JEB's selection of erotica reflects a lesbian sensibility and art." The writer asked, hypothetically, how one would interpret three photographs of the same two lesbians making love if they were taken by a straight female, a straight male and a lesbian. Would the straight woman photographer's sexual orientation make any difference? Would one want to label the man's photograph pornographic? "And would that element necessarily be missing in the photograph shot by a lesbian? Or a lesbian feminist? Can (or *should*) these questions be answered without knowing who stood behind the camera?" Some of the Canadian feminist periodicals used JEB's romantic photographs to illustrate articles about lesbian sex, as they did with the tamer of the erotic images that another photographer, Tee A. Corinne, produced.[85]

None of the feminist publications were particularly explicit in illustrating these articles, even in features that were about lesbian erotic images. Some readers would love them, some readers would reject them, and there was always an underlying concern about police raids and censorship of gay and lesbian publications deemed too revealing. Many feminists—heterosexual and lesbian—who were debating pornography versus eroticism were aware that censorship was a method of social control most often used against sexual minorities. Pollak of *Kinesis* recalled women in Vancouver arguing, "We don't like censorship and we don't like a lot of porn. You know. Which is an interesting balancing act."[86] In Toronto, there were raids at the Toronto gay magazine *The Body Politic*, and Canada Customs was delaying or preventing mainly gay and lesbian material from crossing the border, including sex manuals and magazines.[87]

Susan G. Cole, a *Broadside* founder who opposed male heterosexual pornography because she believed that it harmed women, had a conversation about safe lesbian eroticism with the American writer Kate Millett, who was in Toronto for the conference on female sexuality in 1984. Cole asked her: "How probable is it that women will be able to use so-called erotica as part of the exploration of our sexuality? And how possible is it to come up with images when they [male pornographers] own them?" To which Millett, who drew illustrations to accompany some of her erotic poetry, replied frankly that it was important for women to redefine their own bodies, especially the "cunt," take it back, and possess it authentically, on their own terms. *Broadside* quoted her in a defining caption, or "call-out," in the middle of the article: "Sometimes when I draw things I am sexually aroused, and part of that arousal goes into what I'm doing and is available when you see the picture. There's an element of arousal in appetite, which is what I think erotic art is about—it celebrates appetite. But my drawings are not all that suggestive.... They are, finally, about a relationship."[88]

Cole, in her keynote address to the 1984 conference, said that the aggression and hierarchy of male pornography had scared lesbians when it came to lovemaking, leaving them

> without a language, without rules.... It's hard to open your mouth in those paeans of ecstasy to "wild abandon," it's hard to open your heart, it's hard to open your legs, when you don't feel safe.... I believe that there is such a thing as a world-changing erotic life worth struggling for. I think there is a place where we could bask for one exquisite moment in freedom; where we could act on desire and not be afraid; where we could create with another woman that electromagnetic field, that real sexual energy, palpable sexual energy, that would shock, literally shock, the rest of the patriarchal world to a standstill.[89]

Cole later admitted that she did not know what her own term, *eroticizing equality*, meant, but it would involve the word *energy* rather than *power* and hold on to the concept of love as an integral component of a lesbian relationship.[90]

Every woman wanted good sex, including feminists, she argued in *Broadside*, but "the kind that feels good, the kind that empowers women, the kind that redefines sexuality on our own terms." As far as lesbians were concerned, "Given the definition of sexuality under patriarchal construction, the best we've been able to do in the feminist struggle has been to fiddle ever so slightly with a few roles, give lesbians a chance to be 'tops' as well as 'bottoms,' without challenging the hierarchical construct in the first place. Actually, the very best evidence we have that sexuality is socially constructed and not biologically determined is the fact that not only have some lesbians resisted the ideology of forced heterosexuality, but have resisted the male/dominant female/submissive role demands by changing places at will."[91] Cole's stance on pornography, Masters recalled, generally reflected that of the editorial collective, but the few members who disagreed with her still thought it was important that *Broadside*'s writers be free to express their opinions.[92]

It was apparent, from reports from the same conference and subsequent ones, that lesbians wanted to talk more about "our hottest sexual experiences" than the nitty-gritty of sexual politics.[93] Ingrid MacDonald, who had recently joined the *Broadside* collective, covered a talk by Mariana Valverde at the 1985 gathering. For Valverde, who was just about to publish her book *Sex, Power and Pleasure*, all attempts to describe sex and sexuality were metaphoric. "Talking about sex is hard because there's no inherent meaning in the sexual acts themselves. Although we might think a certain act has meaning or that a certain act is, for example, considered degrading, that means that meaning is coming from the constellation of social events around the act." MacDonald found such presentations too cerebral and tame. She quoted Connie Clement, a sex educator, as referring to the vagina as "a warm, moist couch, or a soft, desirable fold, and no longer as the vast cavity into which tampons get lost." But MacDonald said she would recommend describing it as a "burning, clenching couch or a throbbing, devouring fold." She concluded, given the tone of the keynote talks at the conference, "that our sexuality is still more 'out there' than 'down there'.... I hankered for a taste of something frank or vulgar to be discussed. While allowing that a balance must be struck between turning an audience on and freaking them out, there seemed to be only a cautious entry made into our volatile sexuality." The delegates felt safe enough discussing what had become familiar topics, such as coalitions between women of different sexual identities, bisexuality and pornography, but there was "a conspicuous absence of a kind of sexuality that may be too close to the street for the tastes of some. There seems to be a silence around butch/femme, class, safe sex practices, race, leather, S./M., and voyeurism." She had essentially the same complaint about the following year's conference.[94]

In contrast, talks by lesbian sex advocates were a popular draw, even when the speakers implicitly blamed feminism, among other factors, for dysfunctional relationships. JoAnn Loulan, an American who billed herself as a lesbian sex therapist and published highly popular books, visited Toronto in 1985 and Vancouver in 1988 with stand-up performances that were half therapy and half comedy. Basing her comments on a survey of 1566 lesbians in her various audiences, she tackled the frequency of childhood sexual abuse among them (38 percent) and the internalized self-hatred that led to difficult relationships. She claimed that after the first throes of passion, "when the jaws of life couldn't pry your bodies apart," lesbian couples tended to have sex far less often, especially after they had been together for about three years. *Kinesis* reported: "She believes we've made an unconscious contract with straight society—with the church, our parents, the feminist movement—that we will stop doing what is uniquely lesbian. We will stop having lesbian sex, which is the source of our power.... She urges us to commit 'premeditated sex,' to unleash our erotic imaginations on our sex lives and to be lesbians with passion."[95]

But Cy-Thea Sand, a regular contributor to *Kinesis*, was concerned that the recent focus on hot sex in the lesbian community was becoming less of a conversation and more a set of rules and credentials. "In the 70s, many women felt that the only way to be a true feminist was to sleep with women. I now sense a pressure for *real* lesbians to be sexual dynamos, uninhibited Amazons forever searching for the ultimate sexual high. While lust as a public subject is extremely important for women—when they are doing the talking, that is—the private, complex, personal nature of the topic may be getting lost." It would take time, she felt, for lesbians to fully understand the import of the words of the African-American poet Audre Lorde, who wrote about lesbian desire as "a measure between the beginning of our sense of self and the chaos of our strongest feelings." Was it possible, Sand asked, that lust was connected with another impulse women often stifled, their anger?

> The questions we need to ask are as varied and individual as the women who comprise our communities. I don't want our questions short-circuited or undermined in a frantic, unwise attempt to fill in the silences of decades.... The bottom line in this 'speaking sex' exercise should be women's increased independence and sense of worth. To this end we have to take responsibility for the content of our desires and step by self-defined step give them life. In this process there will be a diversity of sexual language, a diversity which should excite us and also enable us to promote tolerance and respect even as we speak in different languages.[96]

For some lesbian feminists, it was difficult to tolerate or respect behaviour that they felt essentially exploited other women. Certain elements of bar dyke culture, for example, encouraged lesbians to be voyeurs. In 1989 a local gay club in Vancouver, Talk of the Town, held striptease evenings for lesbians, events that prompted an indignant "Commentary" article in *Kinesis* from JoAnn P., who wondered, "How can lesbians behave like the men they have so openly criticized for such behaviour?" She was upset that a number of her friends were eager to go, but, because she was writing about it, she decided to take in one of the shows herself. Some members of the audience behaved worse than the strippers, she declared, acting "like wild women who hadn't seen a naked woman in a long time." She estimated the crowd at between 50 to 60 lesbians, with only about half a dozen of them really trying to engage with the strippers, at least one of them proffering dollar bills in her mouth in exchange for visually close contact with the performer's breasts. "Frankly, I was appalled. Is that exploitation or not?" JoAnn P. was a recovering addict who found it difficult to accept that her fantasy of lesbian community as "one of love, care and *respect* for other women" had turned into disillusionment, now that she was clean and sober.[97] According to Pollack's records of the editorial board minutes, the collective expected "criticism from readers" in response to JoAnn P.'s commentary, but apparently that was not the case. Only one letter, which supported her position, was published.[98]

Although women like JoAnn P. had deep reservations about such entertainment, "sexpertease" nights were a regular feature of International Lesbian Week (ILW) in Vancouver in the 1990s, and were advertised in *Kinesis* during Pollak's and Jaffer's tenures. One promo promised: "Sensual, erotic, steamy and raunchy. This show is too hot to touch. Treat yourself to a little heat. The evening of entertainment your mother warned you about."[99] As one organizer, Mickey McCaffrey, explained to contributing writer Karen X. Tulchinsky, "There have been some women in the past to have been offended by some of the content of the show—but it's the most popular event. Tickets traditionally sell out within a few days. There have been line-ups around the block of women hoping to get in at the last minute."[100]

The pages of *Kinesis* also revealed that there were many women who were clearly hungry not just to be teased, but to view erotic lovemaking from a lesbian point of view, which was still relatively rare. In 1988 the newspaper covered "Drawing the Line," a well-attended "interactive" exhibit of 100 photographs. It challenged each viewer to gaze at increasingly explicit images, mostly of the same two lesbians making love, and then, with a coloured marker, to draw a line on the wall beside the image that was most challenged the viewer's sensibilities. The exhibit, produced by the lesbian Kiss&Tell collective, depicted a range of sexual intensity, from gentle loving to S&M scenarios, using different costumes, actions and backdrops. This was rare, wrote Pat Feindel, a member of *Kinesis*'s editorial board. "To see them is to realize, to *feel* the absence of images like this—images of sex between lesbians, sex that is honest and alive. I felt overwhelmed by an awareness of that absence, that silence. I also felt moved, exposed and excited to see the images hanging there. I have been given a gift."[101] By the time the exhibit was over, there were not just lines drawn but many scrawled comments next to different photographs, testifying to the diversity of opinion among the attendees. Emma Kivisild, the former *Kinesis* editor, was a member of Kiss&Tell and one of the models in the photographs. "Everyone wrote all over the walls and that was kind of an amazing thing.... We were really worried about what our community was going to say to us because we had S&M content."[102] Feindel did not describe those particular photographs in detail but clearly felt they should be open to discussion, while the most explicit image *Kinesis* published from the exhibit showed one of the models leaning over the edge of a bed, in the act of placing her head between the legs of her partner, who was seated on the floor.[103]

Of all the issues that lesbian feminists debated, S&M was probably the most troubling one, politically and emotionally, almost from the beginning. For some lesbians, passion really did mean unleashing their sadomasochist desires, or at least their curiosity. A collection of stories, entitled *Coming to Power*, appeared on the scene in 1981, complete with illustrations. In a *Broadside* review, Mariana Valverde expressed bemused skepticism at the authors' erotic claims.

> It would seem that lesbian sadomasochistic sex is super-powerful, ecstatic, out of this world, and indestructibly orgasmic, every single time, over and over. Sound familiar? Yes, that's how lesbians used to describe lesbian sexuality, burying lust under a mountain of adjectives and enveloping sex in a cloud of superlatives. We used to go around telling the whole world that they (i.e. straight women) just hadn't ever had proper sex. The women writing about their experiences and fantasies in this book seem to be telling other lesbians and feminists that they (i.e. "vanilla" lesbians and straight women) just haven't lived if they haven't tried s/m.

Although she was not offended by the book as a whole, she was not particularly impressed with the quality of the writing as "the plots and characters are mere excuses to get to the juicy parts.... And the prose relies on all the clichés of heavy breathing, electric tensions, beads of sweat, deep and wet cavities, butterflies, waves crashing, and the rest." Valverde's real concern was the nature of the sexual power expressed in S&M, even if the sex was consensual and the women loved each other. While she would defend their right to do it, she questioned whether or not they had really considered its patriarchal cultural roots, even while they claimed that it was consistent with lesbian feminist ideals regarding self-determination. She also cautioned practitioners not to refer to non-practitioners as "puritanical" and "repressed," and not to assume that their sexual edginess made them the ipso facto leaders of the lesbian feminist community. "Guilt has never worked as a political tactic, and if those of us whose sexual practices are contentiously described as vanilla (i.e. boring) are constantly guilted for being part of the problem, then it will be very difficult to unite the lesbian feminist community—not to mention the women's movement at large—in defence of this minority."[104]

Other writers in *Broadside,* Lorna Weir and Eve Zaremba, blamed gay male radicals for encouraging lesbians to reject feminism and embrace butch-femme roles and S&M. Even so, they wrote, feminists needed to pay more attention to lesbians who prided themselves on being sexual outlaws, not shut them out. "It is unfortunately true that many feminists aren't comfortable with lesbian sexuality, and also that feminist dykes have behaved with a degree of arrogance toward the bar and street dykes," they wrote. "The assumptions that butch-femme relationships vanished from this earth c. 1970 and that lesbians are 'naturally' feminists were self-deluding. Finally whatever the last word on S/M may be, the debates to date have already been fruitful in jolting lesbian feminism from its silence in matters sexual. In order to build solidarity and work with other groups of lesbians, feminists must recognize their existence, learn to appreciate their experience and treat them with respect. The fact that this attitude is not always reciprocated is no excuse on our part. We must make sure that the level and content of our mutual discourse remain constructive and open."[105]

That perspective was shared by several *Kinesis* editors, who had started publishing debates and other articles about S&M in the early 1980s, coverage that might partly be attributed to experimental, edgy attitudes in Vancouver's large arts community.[106] Contributors argued over whether S&M between lesbians was more consensual than the heterosexual version, and could be used as a tool to "demystify power," in the best feminist sense.[107] Some readers, passionately against the pornographic images that presented women in submissive, and sometimes violent, relationships with men, were not happy to see articles about lesbian S&M in *Kinesis.*[108]

The debate had the potential of causing much emotional and political damage in the lesbian feminist community, so most women who were attracted to S&M simply did not talk about it openly. Kivisild explained that one's sexuality was considered very political in those days; moreover, nasty rifts among lesbians over sexual practices that some considered male-identified could be "devastating," mainly because their own peer groups might be their only safe havens in a straight world. "Feminism and sexual practices were very, very closely linked.... I don't think for everyone, but it was a community, so I think for a lot of women who had done lots and lots of work as feminists and who were S&M practitioners, it was just the idea that they were going to be kicked out. They couldn't handle it."[109] Pollak recalled that because many feminists were also beginning to discuss the effects of pornography and child sexual abuse on women at around the same time period, sadomasochism was "a total hot button issue in the women's community."[110] Jaffer explained that "we had to fit it within a feminist context.... There were very many feminists very against the whole S&M thing. And then you had the people who'd been sexually abused as children, who were saying 'This is actually a healing therapy, it's about control of violence, it's not about violence, it's about permission and consent, it's about being respectful.'"[111] Other women saw it simply as a new frontier of sexual experimentation, one that they quickly abandoned. Esther Shannon said that she and a number of lesbians she knew tried S&M, but found it "just too elaborate" and not spontaneous enough.[112]

General acceptance or at least tolerance of those lesbians who did take to it was slow in coming, especially with loudly "out" S&M participants.[113] For their part, the more radical practitioners tended to react angrily to criticism of their fashion style or public behaviour. In 1988 *Kinesis* columnist Nora D. Randall confessed to feeling intimidated by the S&M contingent who marched in leather and metal dress during a parade supporting the rights of sex workers in Vancouver. She felt uncomfortable with the "freak show" of S&M and "leather dykes," with their short, jelled hair, and by the sex trade workers, who dressed in their street-walking clothes and wore their hair "ratted." Although she made it quite clear in the same article that she worked through her visceral feelings and came to appreciate them all as "my people" by the end of the evening, there were still indignant letters of complaint to the editor. Dykes for Dykedom wrote: "We have both been shit on for what we wear, what we do, and as S.M. dykes for how we flaunt our sexuality. We've been shit on for being femmes, shit on for being butches, and now, shit on for what we do with our hair." Randall, who tended to be a bridge-builder, apologized, saying she obviously had not explained well enough that she was trying to unlearn her internalized fears and prejudices during the march, and she invited more dialogue.[114]

Judging from the pages of *Kinesis*, it was only years later that supporters of S&M openly presented it, during public entertainments for lesbians, as an acceptable sexual activity, although they still anticipated criticism. In 1994 a "sexpertise" show during International Lesbian Week in Vancouver included an S&M scene. A host apparently introduced it as a consensual act and told the audience, "so don't say anything," a directive aimed at squelching any immediate objections or criticism. This revelation came from Shannon e. Ash, who was writing for *Kinesis* a review of a feminist book of essays that were critical of S&M, a perspective she generally shared. In a two-page, detailed overview, she listed a number of new trends, including the claim among its advocates that S&M was both "hot sex" and an overt rebellion against feminist orthodoxy more than an expression of consensual feminist choice. Ash wondered about the lesbians she knew who were strong social justice and peace advocates but defended S&M, a practice that could include fascist and racist fantasies and sex-play. She wasn't quite ready to believe that they were just accepting "a misguided political notion of liberal tolerance and libertinism," and thought it might be worthwhile to take up one essayist's suggestion of reinstituting sexuality discussion groups in the lesbian community.[115]

Certainly, there were lesbians who insisted on choosing to be sexual their way, no matter what feminists or anyone else had to say about it, including women of different racial backgrounds who had begun to get in on these discussions. In June 1991, when Pollak was editor, *Kinesis* ran five full pages from a transcription of a multiracial panel discussion on lesbian sexuality called "Sexploitations," whose members challenged their audience to resist every form of censorship and moral judgment, and to express themselves freely in their sexual activity. It quoted Patrice Leung, a filmmaker who was particularly critical of judgmental attitudes she said she found in the lesbian community. "Despicable as they are, I have witnessed within our happy lesbian community use of dogma, rhetoric and labelling as a means of monitoring each other's behaviour, especially each other's sexual behaviour. This in fact mirrors the control tactics use by our homophobic detractors.... Make no mistake, we lesbians are fascists and bigots, we are not holier than they." She urged lesbians not to go along with "group think.... Your choices will never have the approval of every faction, clique, caucus, posse, harem and potluck in the lesbian community. So please yourself." She herself could not speak for all lesbians, she said. "Or all lesbians of colour, or all Chinese lesbians of colour, or all Chinese lesbians of colour who wear glasses. I represent myself and I am the sum of my parts. I am not a label. I am a human being. I will not toe the party line. My sexuality is mine alone to choose. I fight heterosexuals every day for that."[116]

Although *Kinesis*, *Broadside* and *Pandora* published serious and challenging articles on lesbian identity and sexuality, there was lighthearted humour in their pages as well. In February 1982 Judy Leifschultz wrote the following "community standards" directive in *Broadside*: "Sadomasochistic sex is unacceptable this month, but biting is and continues to be part of our progressive sexuality...."[117] In 1986 *Kinesis* published unique spins on the conventional lesbian coming-out story in a "True Confessions" page by writers obviously using assumed names. Pixie Woods revealed her heterosexual fantasies, Vicky B. Goode confessed to wanting to have sex in public, and Micki Prude bewailed the fact that no matter how seductively she dressed, her nipples did not perk up at the critical erotic moment, but became inverted, like "a pair of shy buds demurely receding like night flowers at daybreak."[118] The graphics became more humorous as well. *Kinesis* ran a photo of the 1993 International Lesbian Week (ILW) parade in Vancouver, complete with a placard in the foreground that read: "Play Healthy Eat Your Honey." A drawing in the bottom left-hand corner with the greeting, "Happy ILW from *Kinesis*," featured an interracial couple, sensuously dancing buttock to crotch, one of them in a skirt, the other in pants, both of them wearing open-toe sandals with heels.[119] Even *Pandora*, in its later years, got in on the fun, publishing a send-up of a straight advice column, limericks, comic strips and sexual wordplay.[120] In 1993 Brenda Beagan of Halifax joined a lesbian march in Washington, D.C., contributing a two-page feature to *Pandora* that included a photograph of bare-breasted women, a relatively rare image for that publication.[121] Whether amusing, defiant, argumentative or thoughtful, the treatment of lesbian identity and sexuality in *Kinesis*, *Broadside* and *Pandora* was not consistent, nor was the subject given more coverage than any other leading feminist concern, despite its contentiousness. The lesbian feminists who wrote about it were not prudes; rather, they were trying to work out new ways of loving women that were not based on traditional male–female relations, which they saw as flawed. As they sorted some of these questions out, they criticized each other but also made clear attempts to discuss and accept their differences. Rebels all, they challenged each other as much as they did the patriarchy.

Controversial practices such as butch/femme role-playing, displaying erotica and engaging in sadomasochism were not typical of all lesbians, but were highly interesting to those who considered themselves to be intellectuals, rebels and trendsetters. The editors and writers who disagreed with the sexual radicals felt it equally important to debate the issues openly but in ways that would not be destructive to the lesbian community as a whole. Because the members of the press collectives and their contributors tended to be politically engaged with lesbian feminism, they paid relatively little editorial attention to women who had always identified as butch or femme, or who had no real politics at all, just a desire to live their lives as safely as they could. It took them time to reach out to lesbians of colour, whose perspectives were strongly sharpened by their experiences as racial minority women.[122]

All of the editorial collectives and other contributors to *Kinesis*, *Broadside* and *Pandora* brought their own experiences and outlooks to the discussion of lesbian identity and sexuality, as far as each publication could support them. Together, they managed to provide news and views of the Canadian women's movement, and of lesbian life, when few other resources were readily available. Each publication persevered in its own way, in a climate of official government disapproval that threatened its funding or activities to varying degrees. While *Kinesis* and, to a lesser extent, *Broadside* were operating under politically charged financial pressures, the more economically independent *Pandora* had to contend with the relative conservatism of its local constituency. The women who ran and wrote for these three periodicals operated in a set of concentric, counter-public media spheres, often bumping into each other in their arguments and declarations, while visibly marking the shifting borders of lesbian existence, as they understood and embraced it.

CHAPTER 7

"When a Woman Speaks"

Aboriginal Women and Their Rights in Alanis Obomsawin's Documentaries, 1975–2007

O n a warm, sunny day, Agatha Marie Goodine, a 108-year-old Cree elder, walks slowly through the tall grass, talking to the women and children who accompany her about the value of womanhood. Leaning on her walking stick, she waves her hand, explaining, "The Great Spirit created a woman and made her mother of many children. The Great Spirit has affection and sympathy for the woman. And when a woman speaks, she should be highly respected and so should her children because they are so precious."[1]

This message, near the end of one of Alanis Obomsawin's earliest films, has been an underlying theme in much of her work over her 40-year career at Canada's National Film Board. When Obomsawin focuses on women and girls, they are often mothers, women's rights activists, warriors and peacemakers. They nurture and teach their people, help fight for their own rights and those of other community members, and act as intermediaries and negotiators in times of conflict. She also tackles with compassion the social problems Native men, women and children have encountered on and off the reserve.[2]

This chapter focuses on Obomsawin's vision of Aboriginal womanhood, exploring how, as a filmmaker, she has documented the women's contributions to Native life and rights, including female equality, over the last 30 years. If, as Gail Guthrie Valaskakis had argued, the stories Native people tell about themselves contribute to their own sense of history and identity, shifting and changing with times and circumstances,[3] specific attention to Aboriginal women's contributions to that interplay of cultural and political forces is essential to the media record. Several of Obomsawin's films will be considered here in the context of her personal story, women's rights struggles in Aboriginal communities, the documentary tradition and

Alanis Obomsawin editing one of her films. Photo by André Pichette. Published with the permission of the National Film Board of Canada. All rights reserved.

politics of the National Film Board, and the federal government's film and television broadcasting priorities. Native women have always been "caregivers, educators, and energizers in Native communities and their economic visibility and political presence has grown significantly since the 1960's,"[4] Valaskakis once wrote, and this is reflected in Obomsawin's documentaries, which present a complex vision of women's value and power. The filmmaker admires their courage, despite the many hardships they have endured, which are the legacies of systemic racial and gender discrimination. "They have suffered a lot, and yet at the end they are still strong, they are still standing," she says.[5]

In one of her first documentary films, *Mother of Many Children* (1977), she established her view of Aboriginal womanhood across Canada and advocated for the right of First Nations women to keep their status, property and succession rights under the Indian Act after marrying non–First Nations men, a legal struggle that was just then getting under way. In one of her more recent films, *Waban-Aki: People from Where the Sun Rises* (2006), Obomsawin returned to her home village in Quebec to record its residents' history and to revisit marriage and equality rights, this time under the 1985 Indian Act, which Aboriginal women recently challenged in the courts because it still disenfranchised some of their grandchildren.

Her perspectives on women as community leaders and defenders are apparent in her best-known film, *Kanehsatake: 270 Years of Resistance* (1993), which documented the Mohawk standoff with the Quebec police and the Canadian army in the summer of 1990. While her main intent was to capture the perspectives of the Mohawk community, she paid more attention than most of the mainstream media to the central role the women played as mediators, peacekeepers, spokeswomen, roadblock guards and organizers of provisions and health care. In *My Name Is Kanentiiosta* (1995), she expanded on the experiences of one young mother from the nearby reserve of Kahnawake, who was arrested at Kanehsatake as the standoff ended. The police detained her longer than necessary because she insisted on using her Aboriginal name for the court records. In *Rocks at Whiskey Trench* (2000), Obomsawin retrospectively produced a related documentary that highlighted the courage of the women of Kahnawake during the Kanehsatake crisis. In order to escape an army assault on their own reserve, they formed a motorcade and drove themselves, their elderly parents and their children through a rock-throwing gauntlet of hate-spewing white residents who were out to injure or kill them.

Obomsawin's first director's rough cut for *Kanehsatake* consisted of twelve hours of footage, which she edited down to four hours, then three hours, and finally to just under two hours, a process of deletion that she found so painful, she resolved to make several documentaries rather than just the one, which she did over the next few years.[6] She designed the shorter films from the Kanehsatake conflict to be shown in schools, so that young people would see, in the words of Ottawa journalist Nancy Baele, "the generosity and courage of the people behind the barricades."[7]

Obomsawin has received many honours for her accomplishments during her career. Film scholars see her as an educator, a storyteller and an advocate for Native rights,[8] all of which also fall neatly into the categories of both documentary and alternative journalism. She sees herself as a "documentarian" who does not speak for Aboriginal people but wants them to be heard through her films.[9] After Kanehsatake, Obomsawin recorded further conflicts between Native people and the authorities, notably the crisis over Mi'gmaq fishing rights at Esgenoôpetitj/Burnt Church, New Brunswick, in which she interviewed Native men and women and their white protagonists and allies. Another film documented the Mi'gmaq people's successful attempts at river conservation.[10]

Obomsawin's long-time focus on educating her viewers, Aboriginal and non-Aboriginal alike, by documenting historical and contemporary events is not foreign to a journalistic appreciation of her work. Storytelling is an essential component of the craft, as the people mainstream journalists see as "sources" or even "characters" often play key roles in their stories. Such characters are even more present in Obomsawin's films, as, she explains, "If you are going to make a good documentary, you have to tell a story."[11] Her special emphasis on the importance of the individual voices of the people she interviews is not only intrinsic to the Abenaki oral tradition; in her words, "they are the most important part of the film."[12] But her own subjectivity is equally important as a component of the Aboriginal and gender sensitivity that operates within the "counter-public" or "subaltern" sphere of news media culture, where minority communities, who are not considered part of the mainstream "public sphere," can find a voice. She is both a participant and an interpreter of Native issues in her films.[13]

In the view of Randolph Lewis, who has written the only book about her work to date, "If multiple perspectives are always [*sic*] provided in her films, Obomsawin makes clear which one she endorses."[14] Although she is not bound by conventions of journalistic objectivity, Obomsawin does pay some attention to "fairness and balance" in that she will sometimes interview people who oppose Aboriginal perspectives, usually to underscore a point about racism. She is especially reluctant to do so, however, if she feels the mainstream media have already privileged these people.[15] She rarely portrays conflicts or disagreements among Native people themselves, but prefers to emphasize the importance of their history and their shared experiences, especially for the sake of the younger generation, who learn less and less as their elders die and need to understand where they came from.[16]

"The kinds of decisions you make are often influenced by your past," she once explained. "So, if you are denied your past, you don't have much of a future. And you have a difficult present because you are always trying to figure out why you do certain things in life. Or if you are disturbed, or feel you don't belong anywhere. There are reasons for that and you have to find them out." Documentary filmmaking, she believes, "changes society. It brings knowledge of the others that you always call 'the others.' And all of a sudden you realize that they feel like you, and they have stories that are similar, and they need you, and you need them." So, what is "subaltern" to the academic is essential and central to Obomsawin; or, in bell hooks's terms, the margin is actually at the centre, and the accompanying perspective is necessarily oppositional to the mainstream.[17]

A member of the Abenaki tribe and the bear clan, Obomsawin was born in Lebanon, New Hampshire, on 31 August 1932, where her mother was working at the time. When she was six months old, her mother took her across the border into Quebec, where her father worked as a bush guide. She spent her early childhood with relatives at Odanak, her parents' Abenaki village and reserve on the St. Francis River, near Sorrel, northeast of Montreal. Because both her parents had to work elsewhere, she lived with her aunt and uncle, and learned the songs and stories of her people from Théophile Panadis, her mother's cousin. While she was still a child, she rejoined her parents, who were then in Trois-Rivières, Quebec. They were the only Aboriginal family there, and she was often bullied and beaten up by her classmates and scorned by her teachers at the French public school. Her unhappy adolescence was punctuated with racist catcalls and abuse, and, although she did learn to stand up for herself, it was a painful time. It took her a while to get over her anger,[18] even if she did manage to hang on to her self-confidence.

"I never believed what I was told I was. I knew that there was a lot of wrong there. Every time I tried to do something they would tell me, 'Oh you can't do this, you're an Indian!' The more they said that to me, the more I said, 'Well I am going to do that anyway.' I was just a fighter. I just wanted to make changes."[19] By the time she was a young woman, Obomsawin was fluent in French, but not in English, which she learned while living and working in Florida as a childcare giver and model. Later, in Montreal and New York, she developed a career as a singer and storyteller of Aboriginal stories, especially for children, and travelled across the country, visiting residential schools and singing for Aboriginal people in prisons. After she was profiled in a film documentary, she started working at the National Film Board in the 1960s, first as an adviser on films about Native people, then as a filmmaker in her own right.[20]

The National Film Board, which is a government-funded and publicly owned institution, was established in 1939 under the leadership of John Grierson, a Scot trained in Britain, who regarded documentary film as a tool of education for citizenship and social change. During the Second World War, the NFB produced propaganda films that were meant to strengthen the home-front morale of Canadians. After the conflict was over, the agency made and distributed animated films, and documentaries about Canada and its peoples, for audiences at home and abroad. In the era before television, NFB films were shown at school and community gatherings of all kinds, while the shorts were often screened in movie houses alongside Hollywood features, an aspect of the film industry already dominated by Americans. The NFB's filmmakers were expected to embrace Grierson's value system, combining creativity with the ethos of public service.[21]

At the time Obomsawin was hired, the NFB's focus, particularly its depictions of Aboriginal peoples and other minorities, tended to be ethnographic in nature, usually filmed through the lenses of predominantly white, liberal observers.[22] Obomsawin was encouraged by Grierson,[23] who, film scholar Jerry White believes, had an influence on the educative way she tells stories, and who was a close enough friend to become godfather to her daughter, Kisos, adopted when she was one week old.[24] Grierson believed in the power of propaganda as persuasion, a principle a number of the NFB's filmmakers adopted, along with the practice of conferring with their filmed subjects before, during and after production. This was evident in the *Challenge for Change* (CC) series, which began in 1967 as an experiment in social change activism, and endured until 1980. It included the Indian Film Crew (IFC) program, devoted to training Aboriginal filmmakers who would be expected to promote social change in their own communities across the country. Although Obomsawin did not produce CC films of her own, she employed some of the IFC trainees, notably on *Amisk* and *Mother of Many Children*.[25] During her first few years at the NFB, she made multimedia education kits and short films and spoke about Aboriginal issues in other people's documentaries, including *Our Dear Sisters* (1976), one of the films in the NFB's *Working Mothers* series. In this film, which was produced by Kathleen Shannon of the feminist Studio D, she discussed her own experiences as an Aboriginal filmmaker and single, working mother, patiently acknowledging her little daughter, who hovered in the background and then scrambled onto her lap during the interview. When Kisos was young, Obomsawin brought her to the office and on location because, she said, this was in line with Native family traditions. Even when filming people of other tribes, she knew that everyone felt responsible for all the children, including hers, so she did not have to worry about her.[26]

By that time, the NFB's perspective had shifted, as academics, policy advisers and filmmakers insisted on challenging established knowledge and, in the case of documentaries, became more interested in "the autobiography of the marginal subject,"[27] that is, films about women, Aboriginals and other minorities, but from their first-person, often adversarial points of view rather than through the lenses of predominantly white, male directors. In 1974 Kathleen Shannon had spearheaded the establishment of Studio D, an anglophone "women's room," while her francophone counterparts continued for the next dozen years to remain integrated, although they, too, demanded equality with male filmmakers and their projects.[28] Believing that "the personal is political," the women of Studio D were intent on bringing issues such as systemic inequities and violence against women to public attention, using women's narratives and consciousness-raising techniques with their audiences.[29]

Obomsawin declined to join Studio D, which was the only women's filmmaking unit in the world,[30] because her films dealt with the difficulties experienced by all Aboriginal people—men, women and children. She was not dedicating her storytelling solely to women's lives. "I didn't want to be closed in a frame like that because I was concerned about the whole family. I could not say that I would only work with women."[31] She feels the same way today, but adds: "I will stand with any feminist who fights discrimination against women," such as their treatment under the Indian Act.[32] While Obomsawin's perspective is her own, it is important to note that, despite the pro-woman activism among some Aboriginal women, it is unusual for any of them to call themselves "feminist," as they relate the term to white women's political concerns. Furthermore, it can still be dangerous for them to insist on their rights, especially in their own communities. In some instances, they have been accused of betraying their people if they do not make loyalty to their Aboriginal nation the priority, while some Native leaders have been known to use unsubstantiated assertions about "tradition" to try to keep the women compliant.[33]

Obomsawin sees Aboriginal women's traditional roles and skills as contributing to their strength and that of their communities, but feels that the original Act dismissed their influence over Native affairs and took away their rights. It also robbed the men of their traditional roles of fighter, hunter and protector, but granted them a disproportionate amount of patriarchal power in their communities while women's rights were weakened.[34] This is a similar view to that taken by the Native Women's Association of Canada (NWAC), especially in the period leading up to the 1985 amendments to the Indian Act, which were supposed to do away with gender discrimination.[35] "Where else in Canada," Obomsawin asks today, "do you see women and their children lose their heritage and property rights because of who they marry?"[36]

Obomsawin has always produced, directed and written, and usually narrated, her own films herself, so that her voice as an Aboriginal woman is strongly heard as are those of other women, even as they are juxtaposed with those of men and children. Film scholar Zuzana Pick emphasizes the importance of her "insider" voice through the interviews she conducts,[37] while Lewis believes that her use of the female voice gives her and the women she films the kind of authority that used to be reserved for males in white culture.[38] As she tailors and voices her scripts to tell her stories her way, Obomsawin is actually assuming the traditional role of the Abenaki woman as teacher, as well as operating as a documentarian. She is still one of the few women Native filmmakers to present a counterview to the coverage of Native issues by the mainstream news media. She borrows from traditional Native views of Aboriginal women and puts them front and centre, which counters the news media's tendencies to ignore them,[39] underestimate their influence or stereotype them as either "Indian princesses" or "squaws." Scholars analyzing media coverage of Aboriginal rights also tend to ignore female influence, or mention it only in passing,[40] even though it can be considerable, depending on the community. Perhaps that is because few non-Aboriginal academics and journalists understand the importance of the tradition of female power.[41] Those who are Aboriginal themselves do.

The late Gail Valaskakis, who was the daughter of a woman tribal member of the Lake Superior Chippewa Indians, was raised on a reservation in Wisconsin, and was familiar with North American Aboriginal cultures through both her heritage and her academic training. She explained traditional roles for Native women in terms of their spiritual connections to Mother Earth and Grandmother Moon, and to the birth of all things. The dominant white society has misconstrued traditional Native beliefs about the power of the female, transforming her into a simplistic and "romanticized idea of nature's pristine beauty, the Indian princess and her earthy, beast-of-burden sister, the squaw." While Native women have sometimes reappropriated such essentialist images as the "powwow princess," she explained, "their identity is also constructed in the discourse of [living and ongoing] Native traditionalism and treaty rights, including women's relationship to the land, to nature, and to each other." Still, "their struggle with Indian identity—and Indian men—is complex, confusing and painful," especially when the women have to fight for their rights, or for freedom from abuse. But in relation to the dominant society, the men and women are "yoked together in the community of subalterns and in cultural heritage. And women play a special role in the continuation of that community." The woman is its foundation and heart. If she is weak, so are her people.[42]

Mother of Many Children

Despite the mixed success of the Indian Film Crew program, there was a dearth of NFB films by and about Aboriginal people from their own point of view, a fact that Obomsawin researched herself and brought to the attention of the NFB's administration in 1979. Her own films were among the very few exceptions. Obomsawin's *Mother of Many Children* was shot in 1975, during International Women's Year,[43] and released in 1977 after a resurgence of the Native rights movement across North America. Some activists reclaimed traditional roles and dress and reasserted their sovereignty rights in opposition to government legislation, such as the Indian Act in Canada. The Act established Indian status through paternity rather than blood or matrilineal descent, gave male tribal chiefs more authority than clan mothers, and imposed patriarchal measures that detracted from the rights of married women.[44] The women were divided among themselves over whether to oppose the very existence of the Act and its impact on Aboriginal communities, or try to change it to assure them better legal protections. At the time, white feminists were challenging gender norms by fighting for equal rights through changes in labour legislation and other laws, better social services for women, and an end to sex role stereotyping in the media. A number of Native women felt they should do the same, but that did not mean sacrificing their heritage.[45] Rather than protest traditional ideas of Aboriginal womanhood, Obomsawin explained and celebrated them, while also supporting more legal rights for Native women. She became politically aware, in the first place, because of her own experiences. "I think it was just my life as an Aboriginal woman that made me want change," she once told an interviewer.[46] She further explains, however, that her resolve to fight against discrimination through her filmmaking is primarily sparked by the many injustices toward Aboriginal people, including the women, that she still witnesses today.[47] Obomsawin believes that life is sacred for everyone, and human rights are paramount.[48]

Mother of Many Children opened with her own poem: "From earth— from water / our people grow to love / each other in this manner. / For in all our languages / there is no he or she / We are the children of / the earth and of the sea."[49] Much of the film explored female experience: the coming-of-age rituals for girls, childbirth, and especially the work that they did in their families and their communities as mothers. They fished, worked the land, learned to use medicinal herbs, sewed, and wove baskets. The women telling their stories were from many Aboriginal nations: Abenaki, Ojibway, Cree, Mohawk, Métis, Innu and Inuit, among others. Several of the women recalled their girlhoods; their coming-of-age rituals; how mothers, grandmothers and aunts taught them the skills they needed to survive; of facing hard times and trying to help their families and communities overcome problems such as poverty, banishment to white-run, residential schools, alcoholism and illness. Native women also worked for pay to help support themselves and their families, making prints, weaving baskets and sewing for a cooperative in Montreal, and working as civil servants with Indian Affairs in Ottawa, as teachers of Aboriginal children, and as social workers helping Native people in cities overcome addictions to alcohol and drugs.

Of all her documentaries, this is the one that most explores Aboriginal womanhood. She wanted to do a film about the women and their traditional roles because no one else had ever done it before, and she wanted to depict the experiences of as many women, representing different Aboriginal peoples, as possible.[50] Rather than highlight famous Native women, "I wanted to pay homage to women at home, who survive, who take care of children— people you don't really know. I wanted to show the beginning of life to the end through as many women as I could—in terms of culture, traditions, and language."[51] As the narrator, as well as writer, producer and director of this film, Obomsawin explained on the sound track that in matriarchal clans, men and women were considered equal, even though their duties were different. They worked as a team in order to survive and one sex was not considered better than the other. It was only recently that some communities adopted the idea that the majority opinion ruled, rather than community consensus, as was traditional. It was often the women elders who still decided in the end what the community needed, and their male appointees would speak for them in council. The same kind of insistence on the strong contributions that Aboriginal women made to their communities led a number of Native women to fight for their marriage rights under the Indian Act. During this film we see the beginnings of Native women's activism in federal politics and in their communities. Mary Ann Lavallee, a Cree from the Cowessess reserve in Saskatchewan, exhorted a Native women's conference to start fighting for what they wanted: "It takes women to get things going and to get things done," she told them.[52] Part of the activists' strategy was to make sure that government, media and the public were aware of these issues. Lavallee had appeared at a hearing of the Royal Commission on the Status of Women in 1968 decrying the dismissive way in which Aboriginal women were treated, and Mary Two-Axe Earley and other Mohawk women presented briefs objecting to discrimination under the Indian Act against women who married non–First Nations men. At the time, such a woman lost her Indian status and her rights on the reserve, but if a man married a non-status woman, he kept his status, and his wife gained her own. Some Native activists opposed intermarriage in the first place or argued that space and amenities were already limited on the reserves.[53]

By the mid-1970s, the issue was being fought in the courts. Obomsawin devoted a segment of *Mother of Many Children* to one woman's struggle to keep her status after she had married a white man. Jeannette Corbière Lavell, an Ojibway, recently recounted that many chiefs opposed the move to change women's status under the Indian Act, and refused them any help or funding. Women were being harassed and even "booted off" the reserves, she recalled, by Native leaders working in concert with bureaucrats from the federal Department of Indian Affairs. "Indian Affairs was brainwashing our chiefs."[54] The issue of women's status under the Indian Act has always been contentious among Aboriginal people, but Obomsawin does not give in to any of their attempts to control her agenda, any more than she did with a white bureaucrat at the National Film Board later on. She has since revealed that one chief who opposed any gender status changes in the Indian Act tried to stop her from including an interview with Corbière Lavell in *Mother of Many Children*, saying he would forbid her from speaking to any of his people if she did not listen to him. "So he is not in the film," she said.[55]

Mother of Many Children documented Corbière Lavell's court challenge from her own perspective. In the film, she explained that the white judge in the county court where she first took her case mocked her argument that she wanted equal rights to live on the reserve with her people. He dismissed the value of reserve life altogether before he ruled against her case, upholding what was then section 12(1)(b) of the Indian Act. She won her case when she took it to the Ontario Court of Appeal, but the province's attorney-general appealed that decision to the Supreme Court of Canada, which ruled against her by a close margin, five to four. The women's fight to keep their status was successful up to a point. The Act was changed in 1985 to give them and their children back their status, but it did not include all their grandchildren, an issue to which some First Nations women, and Obomsawin, would eventually return.

In her early years as a filmmaker, Obomsawin received a lot of advice and help from the NFB's producers, technicians and other specialists,[56] but she also ran into problems getting funding for her films, as well as racism because of her insistence on telling stories from an Aboriginal point of view.[57] During the 1970s, the film board was still dominated by men who tended to see any primary focus on race or gender as peripheral to the art of filmmaking, even while they felt obliged to follow federal policies that demanded gender and racial inclusion in NFB productions. Moreover, as a government-funded agency, it was always a lightning rod for more conservative critics inside and outside of Parliament, who were quick to question its filmic messages and recommend budget cuts, reorganization and more commercial priorities.[58] Obomsawin revealed later that she had encountered great difficulty completing *Mother of Many Children*, a reflection of the government's resistance to Aboriginal perspectives, in this case on womanhood. Getting financing for the film was a problem she compared to "standing up in a canoe." The film board would not give her the money unless she found outside funding as well, and the Department of Indian Affairs turned her down. "I have letters saying, 'Forget it.' Indian Affairs doesn't want to put money into it; they don't want a film on women." She finally went to Ottawa and repeatedly persuaded the Secretary of State to give her money, which it did, financing the film piecemeal, sequence by sequence.[59]

In 1984 the NFB survived a government-appointed committee report that suggested that the federal government allocate more resources to commercial feature filmmaking and turn the NFB into a research and training centre. The recommendation came from the Federal Cultural Policy Review (Applebaum-Hébert Committee) in 1982, whose members felt that the CBC's televised documentaries had much wider audiences than those of the NFB, which were rarely televised or shown in theatres. They were usually rented or bought for educational or individual use. While the federal government was willing to provide more support to private filmmakers, it still insisted that the NFB had an important public role. The Minister of Communications, by then in charge of the NFB, made it known that bilingualism, multiculturalism and regionalism were all key to Canadian national identity, and that citizens of all backgrounds, particularly Aboriginals and racial and ethnic minorities, should be given the opportunity to tell their stories in their own ways, and watch them as well.[60] From Druick's perspective, this decision, focused as it was on the importance of diversity, reflected shifting demographics and related concerns about racism, an increase in First Nations autonomy, and the threat of Quebec separatism.[61]

Obomsawin's career reflected that political trajectory and benefited from it as well, but not right away. Some bureaucrats were still suspicious of her motives as an Aboriginal filmmaker when she made *Incident at Restigouche*, about Quebec police raids on a Mi'gmaq community over fishing rights, which was filmed in 1981 but not released for another three years because of difficulty getting funding. A member of an NFB program committee had told her not to interview white people, but she ignored the directive, even interviewing the Quebec cabinet minister responsible for ordering the raids, with whom she was quite angry.[62] When the same NFB committee member later chided her, she recalled, she insisted that no one was going to tell her whom to interview. "And if you feel that I, as a Native person, cannot interview white people, we'll go through everything the Film Board has done with Native people, and see who interviewed them."[63]

Nevertheless, she staunchly defended the NFB against charges in some quarters that it was losing its documentary vision. She said that its detractors included not just outsiders who were simply telling lies about it, but some independent filmmakers who had been trained there and were still being commissioned to do films. "It is pretty dishonest, I think." Asked what she would do if she were in charge, she strongly indicated that communication between management and staff needed to be improved. She would do something about that. "People would talk and argue things out.... Then we could fight for certain things together." She still saw the NFB as the "voice of the country. They make films that could not be made anywhere else." If Canadians lost the NFB, she asked rhetorically, "Who would allow the people to tell their stories?"[64]

Waban-Aki

In 2006 Obomsawin returned to the question of women's legal rights when she profiled Odanak, the Abenaki village where she spent her earliest years, to document the people and their history. Her film also traced the economic relationship between the sexes. Abenaki men, who traditionally made their own birch-bark canoes, were hunters, trappers and nature guides. They also cut down the ash trees and planed off the thin wooden strips the women needed to make handicrafts, particularly the woven baskets they sold to tourists. In this film, several women explained in detail the intricate craft of weaving the colourful ash baskets braided with sweet grass that helped them earn their livelihoods for so many years. Later, they were forced to sell the baskets in the government store and lost money, especially in the American market. In the film both men and women talked about this history and the political issues facing them today, particularly that of retaining Indian status for future generations.[65]

The Ottawa premier of *Waban-Aki* was held on International Women's Day 2007, with Obomsawin and several other Aboriginal women as guests. As the film demonstrates, much of Aboriginal women's traditional power is tied to childbearing and providing for their families and communities, the theme she had first highlighted in *Mother of Many Children* 30 years earlier. Obomsawin told her Ottawa audience, "Remember that (women) are the life givers and there is no higher power than this."[66] They are also important to the community economy. At various points in the film, Obomsawin demonstrated that womanhood is powerful in its own way mainly because women are also mothers and clan mothers. The medicine woman's power is stronger than that of a medicine man because she has the ability to bear children; a young man needs the mother's permission to court her daughter. In the tradition of the Abenaki people, one's Native identity comes from the mother, but this is not true under the patriarchal structure of the Indian Act, which is still being felt in Aboriginal communities.[67]

Although a number of women who married non-status men were reinstated as "Indians" under the 1985 Indian Act, the law also said that if one of their children married a non-Native person, the grandchildren would not be considered status Indians. It is an anomaly Native people refer to as the "double-grandmother" clause as it did not apply to the grandchildren of the men who married non-status women. Since the 1985 Indian Act came into effect, the various tribes have also been given more power to determine who is or is not a member, a complicated system that has resulted in about 17 categories of "Indian," with resulting conflicts on and off the reserves, and even within the same family.[68]

In *Waban-Aki*, Obomsawin devoted a long sequence to this issue. Violet Thomas spoke out strongly when she declared that the Indian Act does not allow Aboriginal women to decide their identity for themselves. It "does not honour the [matrilineal] lineage of our peoples ... [and] does not embrace [traditional] teachings of who we are and where we come from as indigenous women of the land. [It] "disgraced and now dishonours our women." For these women, the issue is more than whether or not property rights and other privileges can be passed on to the next generations. It is also a question of the identity that they feel was stolen from them, and will be taken from their grandchildren, because of the gender discrimination in the original Indian Act.

An Aboriginal woman who fell in love with a non-status man had two choices. One was to have children with him outside of marriage and declare on the birth certificate that the father was unknown, a strategy that allowed her and her children to keep their Indian status but played into white stereotypes of the Aboriginal woman as morally loose. The other choice was to marry but lose her status and that of her children. In *Waban-Aki*, Obomsawin talks to Aboriginal women who bore children out of wedlock so they all would keep their status, and those who married non-Native men and lost it. One of them is Jeannette Corbière Lavell, who attended the Ottawa premiere of the film. In *Waban-Aki*, Obomsawin retold the story of Corbière Lavell's challenge to the Indian Act back in the 1970s, using footage first shot for *Mother of Many Children* and a new sequence showing Corbière Lavell discussing today's situation with younger activists. Several women and their adult children who also married non-status spouses are unhappy that the grandchildren of the family have already suffered because of their choices. Diane Nolette, who married a white man, as did three of her sisters, summed up the way in which Bill C-31, the 1985 amendment to the Indian Act, categorizes the varying status of Native people under its subsections—6(1), 6(2), 6(3): "We are classified by numbers: one, two, three. As Indians we are Indians. Not numbers. But we carry the label." In one sequence, children and younger adults told the camera how they personally were categorized—as a one, or a two, or a three—divisions that have led to an emotionally destructive hierarchy of "Indianness" among them. Obomsawin told the audience at the Ottawa opening of the film that she found it upsetting to hear the young people call each other by numbers.[69] "It produces racism among ourselves," she later explained.[70]

Another real fear is that Aboriginal young people have fewer Status Indian partners to choose from, and that the Abenaki and other Aboriginals recognized under the Indian Act will simply "die out" through intermarriage, an eventuality that many Native people unhappily regard as legal assimilation. As narrator of the film, Obomsawin cited the most recent statistics underlying these concerns among her own people—38,000 Abenaki registered in Canada and 23,000 in the United States where once, in the early settler days, there were hundreds of thousands of them.[71]

In March 2010, after a legal direction from the British Columbia Court of Appeal, the Conservative federal minority government introduced an amendment to the Indian Act that would give all the grandchildren equal rights. Sharon McIvor, a self-described Aboriginal "feminist" lawyer and justice advocate, had successfully filed a constitutional challenge to the Indian Act, citing sex discrimination as prohibited under section 15 of the Charter of Rights and Freedoms. She also believes that Native women's rights are existing, traditional rights that are protected under sections of the Canadian constitution that specifically shield Aboriginal peoples from discrimination, as well as under provincial human rights acts and international law. McIvor (Salish) is a member of the Lower Nicola Indian Band, which has a reserve near Merritt, British Columbia. Her clan has a matrilineal tradition, but she was not registered under the Indian Act when she was born in 1948, and she married a non-status man. Under the 1985 version of the Act, she became a "re-instatee" under section 6(1). But because his father was not registered, her son was entitled only to 6(2) status under the Act as a "half-Indian." As her son then married a non-registered woman, this means that their children were not registered at all. McIvor attended the *Waban-Aki* premiere in Ottawa to try to raise money to cover court costs for her case. In its decision, in the spring of 2009, the B.C. Court of Appeal ruled that the Indian Act still discriminated on the basis of gender. It gave the federal government a year to change the law so that all the grandchildren of Aboriginal women in mixed marriages would have legal access to the reserves. In other words, both Aboriginal women and men who married non-status partners would be able to pass their status down two genera-tions. The federal government responded in the spring of 2010, however, with amendments that continued to base degrees of Indian status heritage on the sex of the grandparent who married a non-status partner, prompt-ing criticism from McIvor and several legal commentators.[72] In *Waban-Aki*, Obomsawin took a position in favour of women and their rights. We do not hear from Native people who oppose any changes to the Act, or the ways in which the bands can designate Indian identity.[73]

The Kanehsatake Films

Obomsawin underlines the value of women's traditional roles in other ways, specifically in her films about Aboriginal land and other rights. Several scholars have explored these films, especially her work on the Oka/Kanehsa-take crisis of 1990, one of the most newsworthy events in Canada's media history. But these studies tend to either downplay or ignore her view of gen-der relations in Aboriginal communities, even though her consciousness of female power, and of discrimination against Native women, has been both implicit and explicit in them.[74] Several feminist scholars, however, have examined the role of masculinity and the significance of the term "warrior" both in the news media and among the Mohawk, for whom it has a contested meaning.[75] As Valaskakis explained, journalists tended to represent the warrior as a militaristic monolith, usually armed and dressed in army fatigues, with a bandana covering his face. But, in reality, there are politi-cal and cultural divisions among different factions of the Warrior Society and other groups on reserves, who see the true warrior as a peaceful arbi-trator.[76] In Obomsawin's documentaries about the Kanehsatake conflict, we see women both as negotiators for peace and fighting alongside the men, trying to protect their children, their communities and their land.

"The Oka crisis" and "Mohawk crisis" are the usual mainstream refer-ences to the volatile standoff among the Canadian government and military, the Quebec police, the white community of Oka, and the adjoining Mohawk community of Kanehsatake with their allies from nearby Kahnawake and other Native communities. Briefly, the local town council of Oka tried to take over traditional Mohawk land, which included a cemetery, to extend a golf course and build a luxury housing development. During the winter, the clan mothers of the community kept a watchful vigil in the cemetery area, known as "the Pines." By summer, when the Oka council took out an injunction against them and prepared to take over that land, the women asked Mohawk warriors to set up barricades blocking off the area. When the Quebec police moved in to remove the barricades, there was gunfire and one of the officers was killed. Although Obomsawin does not attribute blame in any of her films about the conflict, the Quebec coroner eventually ruled that the bullet came from a Mohawk position.[77]

Over the course of the summer, 78 days, the situation escalated into a prolonged armed standoff, first with the Quebec police and then with the army. In solidarity with the people of Kanehsatake, their Mohawk allies at nearby Kahnawake blockaded the Mercier Bridge between their land and the island of Montreal, a blockade that lasted close to a month. Mohawk leaders met with negotiators from the Quebec and federal governments at a local monastery, considered to be neutral ground. The Mohawk wanted the army and police to leave the areas around Kanehsatake and Kahnawake, but the talks broke down. After the army moved in, 60 protestors, many of them Natives from outside Kanehsatake, barricaded themselves inside the treatment centre there in a final standoff. In the end, they agreed to leave, thinking their negotiators would be allowed to escort them. But the army went back on its word, and the men and women were arrested as they walked out. The police charged them with participating in a riot, wearing a disguise and obstructing the police. Some of the men were charged with firearms offences. In the end, all but three of them were acquitted.[78]

"Oka" was more than an isolated, dangerous dispute, however. It brought simmering tensions over Native land rights in Canada to a head, and signalled to governments at all levels that Native land could not be appropriated with impunity without a struggle. In Obomsawin's words, "This was a turning point for the Mohawk people. No more land-taking."[79] Personally, the summer of 1990 catapulted Obomsawin emotionally back to her difficult years in Trois-Rivières. "The racism was so apparent, I felt disgusted, to tell you the truth. Everything that was going on there made me return to a really ugly time in my life." Although she knew there were some mainstream journalists who did their best to report on these events fairly, Obomsawin said later that she was appalled by some of the more sensational media coverage. "Or if there was no news, they made it up. They interpreted what was happening—that I found very difficult to take. It's so dangerous."[80] It is one of the reasons it is so important to her that the story be told through the eyes of the Mohawk people who were there, and, in the case of the women discussed in this chapter, those who were brave enough to stay until the very end.[81]

When she first heard that shots had been fired between the Mohawk and the police in the Pines at Kanehsatake, Obomsawin dropped the work she was doing on another film and drove to the scene. The next day, she returned with a cameraman and eventually persuaded the police to allow her behind the barricades. Several crew members who worked with her that summer found the assignment too dangerous and left, but, despite her own fears while working in that "hell," her love of human rights prompted her to stay until it was over. She recorded hundreds of hours of video and audio of the conflict between the Mohawk people and the police and army, and also used news footage and stills held at various media archives.[82] From all this material, she made several documentaries. The first was *Kanehsatake: 270 Years of Resistance* (1993), followed by *My Name is Kahentiiosta* (1995) and then *Rocks at Whiskey Trench* (2000). This analysis will consider the role the women played together, as the events occurred in real time, not as a chronological filmography.

Kahentiiosta, a young woman from the nearby Mohawk reserve of Kahnawake, came to Kanehsatake to help out early in the conflict. She was featured briefly in *Kanehsatake*, as one of the people who occupied the treatment centre, but, in *My Name Is Kahentiiosta*, she was the sole narrator. Her voice and point of view were central to the action in that film, and she told her story in ways that reflected her own and Obomsawin's view of Mohawk womanhood. After a brief historical explanation of the white incursion on Mohawk territory in the St. Lawrence Seaway area, footage of the crisis at Kanehsatake fills the screen.

Over shots of male warriors, and of women linking arms across a road, Kahentiiosta explained their gender roles this way: men provide, organize and defend, while women are the mothers of the earth. "We feel for what she provides," she said, which in this case meant becoming protective of the people and the land. In the film, we see her with other women crowded into the back of a pickup truck, bandanas covering their faces, as the police raided the Pines. The Mohawk men told the women to get into the truck when shots were exchanged with the police. "We didn't think [the police] would shoot," she said. Later, after the army was called in to Kanehsatake, we see footage of the women mounting all-terrain vehicles to scout the area, warning of the presence of soldiers, and reminding the Mohawk men not to shoot first. Kahentiiosta, dressed in camouflage with a scarf around her neck, was seated behind another woman on an ATV. From her perspective, the community was being invaded and everyone must do their part to protect it, including the women. "I knew that we were losing more land." As the army advanced, Kahentiiosta, still dressed in camouflage, helped dismantle a Mohawk barricade before the soldiers took it over.[83]

Her appearance in warrior attire in the action sequences was in stark contrast to her interview clips, where she was seated outside, wearing a comfortable dress, the picture of a more conventional mother. She explained that circumstances forced her to be tough when necessary. She decided to keep her two sons with her at Kanehsatake to teach them the value of facing danger to defend their territory. She wanted them to grow up strong. "I don't want my children killed. But I want them to see the struggle we're going through. This isn't for us. This isn't for me. I'm not here because I want to be. I'd rather be home like everybody else."[84]

In Kanehsatake, the action after the opening sequences in the Pines shifted to the negotiators, including several women. The Mohawk and other Aboriginal leaders appeared as the police and then the army moved in. Talks began with the government while the residents of the reserve and their supporters stood firm, trying to get the police and army to withdraw, and to get food and medical supplies onto the site. While the narrative of this film did not specifically highlight the role of women, Obomsawin's film clips included Ellen Gabriel, one of the leading Mohawk spokeswomen and negotiators, who is seen several times as the film progresses, along with women negotiators from other reserves. Gabriel recalled her own reaction when the police first arrived on the scene. She explained that the women had to confront them because their traditional obligation was "to protect our land, to protect our mother." In another interview clip, she explained that she's always felt the Mohawks behaved honourably and in a way that minimized the violence, although they knew something bad would happen. Later in the film, she is shown on the scene, firmly telling reporters that the Mercier Bridge barricade would not come down until the police withdrew. "We are talking about our rights. This is our territory and the government has to acknowledge that." At a ceremonial gathering at the beginning of the talks between Mohawk and government negotiators, she stood, raising and lowering a lone feather. "I am proud to be Mohawk.... When we started this blockade something had to come out of it that would progress our cause and unite our people." In the Mohawk language, she wished the gathering peace.[85]

As the negotiators tried to work out a resolution to the crisis, the army took up positions in Oka and on the outskirts of Kanehsatake and Kahnewake. Armed Mohawk warriors, many masked, wearing camouflage and carrying guns, got ready to defy them. One of them, "Wizard," explained to Obomsawin on camera that as a Mohawk man, it was his traditional responsibility to protect the people. But, when the army started to advance along one of the main roads, both men and women confronted the soldiers. One woman asked, "Where are you going—to our houses to kill us?" and another demanded, "Pull back!" Gabriel told the media that the military broke a promise that they would tell the Mohawk of the soldiers' movements in advance. "They are on Mohawk land and they must leave."[86]

A few days later, the negotiations broke down. The provincial spokesman said the Mohawk would not give up their weapons. The Mohawk called their own news conference to say negotiators had reached agreement on everything but sovereignty and whether charges would be laid against their fighters. Another negotiator, Minnie Garrow of Akwesasne, a Mohawk reserve near Cornwall, Ontario, assertively explained that the people were native to the land and were not trying to take white people's territory. They were facing an army ready to assault them when all they were doing was trying to protect their burial ground from a golf course. "You must keep that in mind. Have you forgotten?"[87] But even the negotiators were not safe. The Quebec police detained one of them, Mavis Etienne, for five hours. She told news reporters that she was arrested for being behind the barricades, defying a government injunction that they come down, and for intimidation and "stuff like that." She added that since the white negotiators were also behind the Mohawk barricades, the police should arrest them as well.[88]

In the meantime, the Mohawk of nearby Kahnawake, in support of their Mohawk neighbours and in fear of an army invasion, had barricaded the Mercier Bridge, which separated the reserve from Montreal. They also blockaded several roads in the area. In *Rocks at Whiskey Trench*, Obomsawin again presented these events in the context of the historical struggle of the Mohawk against white people's incursions on their land. An older woman, Selma Karioniakatste Delisle, repeated one of the filmmaker's recurring themes in a brief clip. "Women are the title holders to the land and we will never give that up."[89] The film recalled that the people of Kahnawake had been blockading the Mercier Bridge between their reserve on one side and the island of Montreal on the other, as well as the roads to the reserve, for some weeks. The residents and merchants of the neighbouring town of Châteauguay were angry at the disruption in their work commutes and local trade. Every day, a number of them harassed the Mohawk men, women and children and tried to prevent them from bringing food and supplies onto the reserve by boat. In one scene, a Mohawk woman, holding her infant daughter and accompanied by her young son, struggled to push her way under the locked arms of burly, taunting white men so she could get to the river bank and return to the reserve. At night, dozens of hooligans gathered to burn Mohawk warriors in effigy.

When the negotiations with the government broke down and the army moved on Kanehsatake, the leaders of Kahnawake were afraid that soldiers were going to enter their reserve as well, and that people might be killed. So they sent old people, women and children away in a convoy of 75 cars. They said that they thought it would be safe because the area was relatively quiet at the time. But the army officers stationed at the bridge stopped the convoy, searching every vehicle for weapons. These delays gave the local troublemakers time to gather on the nearby roadway known as

Whiskey Trench. Once all the cars were searched, the authorities told the Mohawk women to start driving past the angry crowd, and not to stop for anything. Throwing large rocks and other objects, the mob viciously attacked the convoy as it passed. The Quebec police and the RCMP who lined the roadway intervened only when the attackers tried to swarm the cars to get at the people inside, but did not try to stop them from throwing rocks from the roadside and an overpass above it. Few bystanders seemed to care about the lives of the people inside the cars, let alone their dignity.

In *Rocks at Whiskey Trench*, the alarming footage of this attack, which had appeared briefly in *Kanehsatake* several years earlier, was juxtaposed with present-day comments from the people who had endured the barrage. The women, some elders and the children, now teenagers, spoke of how they had feared that they and the family members were going to be killed as the large rocks crashed against their vehicles, many smashing through the windows, bruising and cutting the adults and children inside. Several of them wept, upset at the memories, and some adults were still struggling with guilt that they left the reserve that day rather than try to stay and protect their families there. Raising the question of "who was responsible," Chief Peggy Mayo explained that if the leaders of Kahnawake had known they were sending these women, older people and children into such danger, they never would have tried to get them out that way. Other interviewees blamed the army and the police for not intervening more strongly in the attack, some suggesting that their ineffectualness was deliberate.

The Quebec police refused to comment, Obomsawin explained later, but she did record her own interviews with the mayor of Châteauguay, and, even more effectively, one of the Québécois men involved in the attack at Whiskey Trench. Arms folded defensively, he blamed the Natives, the police and the army—everyone but the people who threw the rocks. His dismissive assertion that nothing changed after the attack for either the local residents or the Mohawk serves to underline the fact that despite attempts among the people of the reserve and some whites to heal the rift between the two communities, racial discrimination still existed. There were, according to some appreciative Aboriginal speakers, also isolated incidents of kindness or help from a police officer or soldier, providing a modicum of journalistic balance while not sacrificing Obomsawin's essential narrative about racial brutality to notions of equal representation from "both sides."[90]

If anything, the Whiskey Trench experience cemented the women's love of their community and strengthened their pride. Near the end of the film, Allison Jacobs, executive secretary and communications agent at Kahnawake, wept, declaring, "I'm proud to be Mohawk. I think that no matter how hard the governments or outside communities try, they could never beat that out of us, not even with a rock."[91]

When the Mercier Bridge was reopened, following negotiations between the people of Kahnawake and the army, Ellen Gabriel was uneasy. Appearing in the film *Kanehsatake*, she complained to the media that soldiers with tanks and machine guns had now surrounded the Mohawk people. She insisted that they would not surrender because they had done nothing wrong and they would not be intimidated. But once the barricades across the bridge came down, the police and army could do what they liked, she said, adding that they were trying to break the Mohawks' spirit and create divisions among the people. "And this is what they call peaceful resolution."[92]

In other film clips from *Kanehsatake*, we see other Aboriginal women involved in the crisis becoming, if anything, more resolved to hold their ground. It is not always clear if they there or come from elsewhere. Obomsawin films one young woman, identified only as Chicky, at length, allowing her to express her anger. "Somebody had asked me, 'how far are you willing to go?' and I said 'six feet under' and I think that's what's going to happen." She believed that this was just another attempt to keep Native people in their place, and she was ready to face jail "in honour" if necessary, and to teach her children and grandchildren to fight when she came out. She was raised as a pacifist, she said, "but this has changed me. I've never been violent. I've never thought to hit out, to strike out, but now, don't look at me sideways because I know I'll never bow down to them because they just step on your hands. If this is civilized, I'd rather stay on this side of the barricades."[93]

After the military surrounded the treatment centre at Kanehsatake, Elaine Montour, who was almost hit with an army flare, lashed out, yelling, pushing and slapping at the two soldiers in front of her. In the meantime, as the authorities ordered a peace camp of supporters in the area to leave, several women got into shouting matches with the police. One woman objected loudly when her husband was arrested for defying an order to move on, and she was frogmarched to a police cruiser, crying that her child was alone in her car. At other moments in the film, we see several women restraining male warriors, who are taunting and threatening the soldiers as they move in on Mohawk land. Other women are cooking and organizing food and other supplies.[94] Yet, as Obomsawin, the narrator, explains, the conflict over the land is not settled. At one point, near the end of the crisis at Kanehsatake, Obomsawin herself spoke to the media as, discouraged and exhausted, she walked down a road leading away from the area, carrying her directional microphone. She told the reporters there that if the government made an honest promise in writing to settle Native land claims, the standoff would be over. The clip is not in her films but appeared on local Montreal newscasts the same evening. Beyond that comment, she did not want to do media interviews, because, she explained later, "I didn't want to say anything that might jeopardize the Warriors. It was not time to make any statements."[95]

Kahentiiosta and her son, from Alanis Obomsawin's film *My Name Is Kahentiiosta* (1995). Photo by Shaney Komulainen. Published with the permission of the National Film Board of Canada. All rights reserved.

As the army advanced, Kahentiiosta went to the treatment centre, which soldiers soon enclosed with razor wire. As she and some of the others gathered around a camp fire, she cradled her five-year-old son, warning him not to touch a dangerous-looking army flare sticking out of the ground that had apparently been fired over the barbed wire. As military helicopters circle overhead, she gently rocked and sang to her child to comfort him and calm his fears.

Later, she was among those thrown to the ground and arrested as the people left the treatment centre. During the melee, a fourteen-year-old girl was wounded in the chest with a bayonet while she was trying to protect her four-year-old sister. Several other people reached Oka, where they demanded to know where the police had taken their arrested family members. Chicky reappeared, demanding, "When is this going to end? When are we going to have our fucking rights? This is not finished." At the courthouse in St. Jerome the next day, as a prisoners' van arrived, Mohawk women berated the police for treating them roughly, saying that they wouldn't leave the land and that they would be around for years.[96]

The night before, when the occupants walked out of the treatment centre, Kahentiiosta was accused of hitting a soldier, thrown to the ground, handcuffed, arrested and detained. In *My Name Is Kahentiiosta*, she explained that she had asked two other women to take her son to safety, but they were also stopped by the soldiers and arrested in front of him. As they all boarded the army bus, her boy tried to get away, but a soldier caught him and put him inside it. Kahentiiosta could not comfort him because she was handcuffed behind her back, a story she told in voice-over, with drawings, since there was no camera present. Her other son was also on the bus, which drove to the Farnham Military Base. The detainees spent the night in the vehicle while waiting for their court appearances the next day. Around 1 a.m. her handcuffs were removed. At the base, she told her children they must leave her there and go home with her grown niece. Kahentiiosta said goodbye to them before the soldiers took her away. The provincial police questioned, photographed and fingerprinted her. They told her to change from camouflage into street clothes for her court appearance. She changed her clothes, but she gave her name as Kahentiiosta. "They wanted a Canadian name, I guess, so I just looked at my lawyer and I didn't say anything else," she said on film. Her lawyer told her that if she did not give her "Canadian" name she would be detained longer, but she still refused. He said she would be alone among the men at the base, and might be beaten up or even raped. This advice appeared to be an attempt to intimidate her into compliance. But she still refused, while all the other women were released. Another lawyer tried to persuade her to give her English name, she recounted later. She said that she told him, "They took enough from us. We have been through enough.... I want this name on the record. If they don't respect it, well, you know, we'll have to deal with it later."

A courtroom drawing showed her standing apart from the other women who were being released, looking unhappy. They wanted to stay with her, she recalled. Tearfully, she told the camera how she had to send her niece, who had come to get her children, away from the jail. While she was being detained, she covered her face when the army tried to make a film record of her presence. When she next appeared before the judge, he tried to tell her that everyone was afraid to come to court, but she told him that it was especially hard for Native people because it was not their court. They were defending their land. After her lawyer produced her birth certificate, the judge released her and the other women with conditions, one of them being that they had to stay away from Oka. Her refusal to give the authorities her "Canadian" name was a short-lived but important symbolic act of defiance, part of the lesson she wanted to teach her children about the value of Native identity. She felt the Mohawk won in the end, because the Pines are still there. They succeeded in stopping the expansion of the golf course.[97]

Before the film *Kanehsatake* ends, there is footage of an anniversary parade and gathering at Oka in July 1992 after all but three of the people arrested had been acquitted. Ellen Gabriel marched with the others, carrying a child on her back, and, as the credits rolled, men and women marched out of the courthouse together, smiling and waving.[98] Obomsawin did not mention in her films that both Gabriel and Kahentiiosta were, according to Lewis, "seasoned activists and veterans of other conflicts."[99] She also did not record the disagreements among the different Native groups at Kanehsatake during the standoff, or the resentment some of the residents felt against those from Kahnawake and Akwesasne, who they thought were exacerbating the conflict, not helping efforts to reach a settlement. While Obomsawin does not dwell on these and other internal conflicts, other Aboriginal media workers have been more forthcoming. One of the more fruitful accounts came from Beverley Nelson and Kassennahawi Marie David, who were broadcasters for the Kanehsatake radio station during the crisis, and also acted as media contacts for mainstream journalists. In a co-authored article, with academic Lorna Roth, they said as Aboriginal journalists they had trouble getting press accreditation from the army and were given limited access to non-Native sources.[100] David confirmed that during the crisis the women helped negotiate for a peaceful settlement; were the liaisons among the police, army and their community; ran the radio station; and organized food, medicine and other supplies. She also discussed the divisions among those who follow traditional ways, and others who behave according to more white-influenced structures where men take the initiative. She revealed that some of the Native male negotiators did not want Gabriel and other women taking the lead in the talks with the governments, and froze them out.[101] Although Gabriel took a noticeable role in the film *Kanehsatake*, she said for herself later that she would have liked to have seen more interviews of people from her community, adding that the people inside the treatment centre who figured in the film were not from Kanehsatake. But her criticism is muted and couched within her appreciation and praise of Obomsawin for having the courage to stay there during the standoff, documenting these events for future generations.[102]

Obomsawin's films about the Kanehsatake crisis have reached much larger audiences than would have been possible before then. Up until the 1990s, her films were mostly shown in universities, schools and Aboriginal communities, although audiences became broader once her work became available on videotape and was featured at film festivals. Still, the mainstream press took little notice of Canadian documentary films unless they were deemed controversial, and even then the CBC balked at showing *Kanehsatake*.[103] Its management tended to regard NFB documentaries in general as competition and as not "objective" enough for a public broadcaster. Obomsawin has argued that all films have a perspective, and she made hers for Aboriginal and non-Aboriginal people alike. "I don't know about the CBC. I do have a point of view, as they point out. But they have a point of view also, obviously—they just don't call it that." Mounting a new documentary TV program, *Witness*, in the fall of 1993, the CBC soon changed its policy about broadcasting films with minority perspectives, and agreed to show the film *Kanehsatake*, followed by a panel discussion.[104]

By the 1990s, the NFB, then regulated under Heritage Canada, had made as its priorities women, children and "special interest groups," mainly Aboriginals, racial minorities and immigrants.[105] Specialty television channels, a more culturally aware understanding of Canada and Canadians under the 1991 Broadcasting Act, and a shift in the NFB's focus to more first-person diversity all contributed to broader audiences for these films. At the same time, a number of new television venues have developed for documentary films, including the ones Obomsawin directs—not just CBC News Network (formerly Newsworld), which specializes in news and public affairs, but more educational television channels, as well as a number of specialty channels, including the Aboriginal People's Television Network, the History Channel and TLC (formerly The Learning Channel). In addition, the NFB now enables viewers to access its films from its website.

All these changes are in line with the specifications of the 1991 Broadcasting Act, which emphasizes the need to reflect and reach the diversity of the national audience. The NFB, which at that point suffered more budget cuts and a reorganization, also shifted its focus to diversity in film subjects, making broadcasting arrangements between it and the CBC easier to manage.[106] In the meantime, other Aboriginal women and women of colour, trained in Studio D, got behind the camera to tell their own stories, as part of the 1990s commitment to diversity and first-person voices. In the end, Studio D was closed to make room for the Reel Diversity program, reflecting the lives of both men and women of diverse backgrounds. Various government programs, such as Telefilm and the Canadian Television Fund, also were designed to encourage the recording of diverse voices. Now young Aboriginal filmmakers, such as Tracey Deer, working with independent film companies and the NFB, can showcase their documentaries on Native identity issues, including those faced by women and girls.[107]

Valaskakis had noted the importance of the many ways in which Aboriginal women construct their identity "in the intertwined discourses of grandmothers, and mothers, daughters and others. In narratives that situate, reclaim and transform the past, Native women express the identity, community and empowerment of the present."[108] This is exactly what Obomsawin's documentaries reflect on the cultural level—a vision of Native women as powerful and empowering, both in the past and the present. But, as she herself notes, the nature of documentary production, including struggles to get financing, make immediacy in their coverage virtually impossible,[109] leaving the field open to news reports that simplify and stereotype Native issues, rather than provide in-depth context, especially from an Aboriginal perspective. As a form of alternative journalism, however, her documentary films present a counter-narrative to the negative news media images of Aboriginal women as rabble-rousers, an aspect of the squaw stereotype, as well as to the meek model of the beautiful "Indian princess." Obomsawin shows us strong women, and provides the context for their anger and their need to take action against incursions on their land and rights. While some journalists ignore Aboriginal spokeswomen by rendering them "absent" from community leadership and influence, she presents them as authoritative sources whose words must be heard.

CONCLUSION

Every woman's byline is the distinctive signature of her work in the media. That is how she is known, whether she uses a pen name, an on-air alias or her real name. In establishing her reputation, she must choose where and how she will invest her talent and energies, and how much she is willing and able to use her particular niche to advocate on behalf of other women. Becoming an activist was not an easy choice for any of the media workers in this series of historical essays, whether they joined a women's organization or championed various causes on their own. They all had to face gender discrimination that was relentless in every era and especially difficult for the advocates in the later period, who were challenged because of their support of abortion, lesbianism or Aboriginal women's rights. These experiences politicized them, leading to convictions that, for most of them, had to be weighed against the necessity of making a living. Each one had to decide where she could wield the most subversive or active influence: in the mainstream media, the alternative media, or both. She also had to decide what name to use, her own or one she made up, a choice that reflected how she saw her public self.

From the 1870s to the turn of the 20th century, some exceptional women found a limited place in the mainstream media, as long as they did not threaten the public sphere of men too overtly. Agnes Maule Machar, writing as "Fidelis" in a series of intellectual periodicals, was able to argue, from a Christian perspective, that bright, middle-class women should be allowed to go to university. In making this daring demand, she was stretching, not trying to obliterate, the conceptual boundaries of what was then considered the female sphere, arguing that well-educated women would operate more effectively within it, according to God's plan. Similarly, her arguments in favour of protective legislation for working-class women stemmed from her concern for their health as current or potential mothers. Although it is true that she was also committed to social reforms as a matter of fairness and justice—a point she made in her support of equal pay— her byline might well have been dismissed or erased if she had made an argument for full equality between women and men.

When advertising revenue became the greatest factor in the survival of the press, it opened up new opportunities for women in journalism but also limited their scope as activists. The ones who wrote their own columns and edited women's pages in the daily newspapers were expected to attract female readers and ads from the businesses that catered to them. Four Toronto writers positioned themselves accordingly as arbiters of women's affairs and fashions, adopting feminine pen names— "Kit,"[1] "Faith," "Madge" and "Sama." Clearly, they were not supposed to compete with male journalists by engaging in discussions about business or politics, but rather to contain themselves to feminine matters that did not threaten gender relations or compromise their own newspaper's ability to make a profit. The Toronto writers were not all happy with this imposed condition of their employment, and two of them were outspoken enough to say so, letting their readers know how their choice of topics was limited by the business imperative of providing fashion news of all kinds. Yet the role they were expected to assume as concerned, motherly advisers to their readers enabled them to become critics of modes and practices that threatened women's well-being and to advocate for some forms of healthier and more comfortable dress. But they could only go so far. Negotiating this conflict was as much of a balancing act for them as riding that new-fangled invention, the bicycle.

Francis Marion Beynon, on the other hand, had the freedom to use her own name in expressing her feminist views because they were consistent with those of her employers and the editors of the *Grain Growers' Guide*, the Prairie weekly. Although it was, in many respects, a conventional women's page, Country Homemakers gave Beynon a platform from which to argue for the issues closest to her heart, including women's suffrage and peace. When these two goals collided over the conscription issue during the First World War, she found herself painfully and increasingly out of step with many of her associates, precipitating her decision to leave for New York and a career as a writer. Wartime politics and her own ambitions, rather than outright censorship, were the forces that isolated her from her readers in the end, and all but obliterated her byline from the Canadian record.

Elizabeth Long was well known among her CBC colleagues and protégés as a force to be reckoned with behind the scenes when it came to women and their rights. As supervisor of Women's Interest programs during and after the Second World War, Long had a practical appreciation of the kind of radio material her homemaking listeners wanted—domestic and childrearing advice plus information on current events outside their homes. She was happy to provide it all through the expertise and talent of the women she trained as broadcasters, directing them to change their names as on-air performers if that would make them more comfortable or win them attentive listeners. She also encouraged her commentators and program hosts to take up the cause of women's rights on and off the air, and to broaden their listeners' knowledge of what other women around the world were doing. She was a liberal feminist activist, subversively using her sex-segregated radio department to fight for equality of opportunity for all women.

The next generation of women media workers and activists juggled their political convictions with professional admonitions not to become involved in any cause if they expected to be recognized as real reporters. They had two choices, comply or risk exclusion, a painful prospect just when newsrooms across the country were finally ready to end the sex segregation that had barred female journalists for decades. But some women did try to negotiate the boundaries between conventional journalism and advocacy, and that included Anne Roberts and Kathryn Keate, both of whom used their real names rather than try to hide their involvement in women's liberation groups. The chapter devoted to them shifts the focus to another aspect of media work, public relations, specifically the feminist publicity strategy behind the Abortion Caravan, a pro-choice motorcade that travelled from Vancouver to Ottawa in the spring of 1970. Roberts and Keate, who both identified as socialist feminists, took lead roles behind the scenes in successfully attracting the media's attention to the Caravan and its demand that the federal government remove abortion from the Criminal Code. In doing so, they used their knowledge of newsgathering techniques while subverting traditional notions of journalistic objectivity, potentially risking their own careers.

Other young committed feminists like them decided that mainstream journalism would never fairly reflect women's rights issues, and therefore started their own alternative newspapers. This group included the editor-coordinators behind *Kinesis* in Vancouver, *Broadside* in Toronto and *Pandora* in Halifax. They either signed their own names to their editorials and articles, or, in the spirit of feminist collectivity, wrote in the names of their editorial boards. Most of the women they assigned to write articles about lesbianism and those whose letters they published were bravely open about their identities as well; only a few hid behind cautious pen names or outright anonymity. In the 1980s to mid-1990s, feminist services and periodicals, which had been partly supported through government grants, found themselves losing the ideological battle to right-wing conservatives who wanted them silenced, especially if they dared support abortion or lesbian rights. The feminists behind these three newspapers fought back. Each

editorial collective, in its own way, was pro-choice in its politics and defiantly published articles and supported debates about lesbian rights, identity and sexual practices. That some were more frank than others was a
reflection of how the editors assessed the level of acceptance among their
local female readerships.

Documentary filmmaking is another form of media that has been used
for advocacy on social issues. Filmmaker Alanis Obomsawin has made powerful statements on behalf of Native women's identities and rights. Although
she considers herself a documentary maker, rather than a journalist, and
does not identify with the term *feminist*, Obomsawin, proudly using her
own Abenaki name, has always been an activist on behalf of Aboriginal
communities, where the women have a strong presence. She advocates for
their marriage rights under the Indian Act, and depicts them as strong
defenders of Native land and identity in times of conflict, supporting their
traditional roles as being essential to the survival of their people. As a film
director for the publicly owned National Film Board of Canada, Obomsawin
had to fight gender and race prejudice from time to time, especially from
bureaucrats who held the purse strings, to ensure she could make her films
about Aboriginal women, men and children. Her work has found a home in
the NFB, not just because of her skills but also because of the shifts in its
mandated commitment to public service, education, creativity and diversity over the years.

All these different women, using various forms of media in their
activism, have something to teach the next generation, to whom I have dedicated these essays. In every era, they were laughed at or dismissed for
being advocates for women's rights and identities, but they persisted regardless, each in her own fashion, some of them more radically than others. It
is important that today's students know and understand this history, and
appreciate that it was always mediated by the political, economic and cultural priorities of the media industry in each time period.

There is plenty of scope for further research on the history of women
in "journalism," again, broadly defined. Biographies of the famous women
could lend a great deal of insight into their different ways of newsgathering, as could studies of the female rank and file, especially after the Second
World War. Another generation of female media workers came of age in
the 1960s and had to battle its way to gender equality over the ensuing
years, a struggle that is not over yet for its successors.[2] Further, there is a
need to explore how women from different ethnic and racial backgrounds
were able to function, the kinds of challenges they met, and how they were
able to use conventional media or their own alternative forms of it in the
service of social change.[3] There is research to be done, for example, on the
Black activist Carrie Best of Nova Scotia beyond her own compilation of her
newspaper column from the 1960s.[4] In 1962 Charlotte Perry of Windsor,

Ontario, apparently became the first Black woman to be accepted as a member of the Toronto branch of the Canadian Women's Press Club, something I discovered through one of Elizabeth Long's letters to a colleague.[5] It would certainly be worthwhile to further examine the history of WTN, the Women's Television Network, where, in its feminist days of the early 1990s, women of different racial backgrounds played key on-air and production roles.[6]

The term *journalism* must embrace women of different backgrounds, times, circumstances, politics and media forms. Their writing, broadcasting, filming and other forms of media work can tell historians, communications researchers and other scholars a great deal about the political, economic and cultural changes in society over time, contributing far more than just a footnote to our knowledge and understanding.

NOTES

Introduction

1 Hanno Hardt, "Without the Rank and File: Journalism History, Media Workers and Problems of Representation," in *News Workers: Toward a History of the Rank and File*, ed. Hanno Hardt and Bonnie Brennen (Minneapolis: University of Minnesota Press, 1995), 1–29.

2 Magda Fahrni, Suzanne Morton and Joan Sangster, "Feminism and the Making of Canada: Historical Reflections/Le feminisme et le façonnement du Canada: Reflexions sur l'histoire,"*Atlantis*, 30:1, 2005, 4.

3 Liesbet van Zoonen, *Feminist Media Studies* (London: Sage, 1994), 40.

4 Barbie Zelizer, *Taking Journalism Seriously: News and the Academy* (Thousand Oaks, CA: Sage, 2004), chapter 2. The contributors to Zelizer's more recent anthology highlight the intersections between history and communication, including the traditions of journalism. Barbie Zelizer, ed., *Explorations in Communication and History* (New York: Routledge, 2009).

5 William J. Buxton and Catherine McKercher, "Newspapers, Magazines and Journalism in Canada: Towards a Critical Historiography," *Acadiensis*, 28:1, Autumn 1998, 103.

6 Anthony Westell, *The Inside Story: A Life in Journalism* (Toronto: Dundurn Press, 2002); A.B. McKillop, *Pierre Berton: A Biography* (Toronto: McClelland and Stewart, 2008).

7 Catherine McKercher, *Newsworkers Unite: Labor, Convergence, and North American Newspapers* (Lanham MD: Rowan and Littlefield, 2002); Florian Sauvageau and David Hemmings Pritchard, *Les journalistes canadians: Un portrait de fin de siècle* (Sainte-Foy, QC: Presses de l'Université Laval, 1999).

8 Gene Allen, "News across the Border," *Journalism History*, 31:4, 2006, 206–216.

9 Marc Edge, *Asper Nation: Canada's Most Dangerous Media Company* (Vancouver: New Star Books, 2007) and Edge, *Pacific Press: The Unauthorized Story of Vancouver's Newspaper Monopoly* (Vancouver: New Star Books, 2001).

10 Mary Vipond, "Going Their Own Way: The Relationship between the Canadian Radio Broadcasting Commission and the BBC, 1933–1936," *Media History*, 15:1, 2009, 71–83; Vipond, "'Comrades in Arms': War Work at the CBC,'" a paper presented at the annual conference of the Canadian Communication Association, 2008.

11 Russell Johnston, *Selling Themselves: The Emergence of Canadian Advertising* (Toronto: University of Toronto Press, 2001).

12 Cecil Rosner, *Behind the Headlines: A History of Investigative Journalism* (Don Mills, ON: Oxford University Press, 2008).

13 Dwayne R. Winseck, *Communication and Empire: Media, Markets and Globalization, 1860–1930* (Durham, NC: Duke University Press, 2007).

14 Ross Eaman, *Historical Dictionary of Journalism* (Lanthan, MD: Scarecrow Press, 2009).

15 Maurine Beasley, "Recent Directions for the Study of Women's History in American Journalism," *Journalism Studies*, 2:2, 2001, 207–220.

16 Beasley, "Recent Directions," 218.

17 Franca Iacovetta, "Gendering Trans/National Historiographies: Feminists Rewriting Canadian History," *Journal of Women's History*, 19:1, 2007, 206–213; Joan Sangster, *Transforming Labour: Women and Work in Post-war Canada* (Toronto: University of Toronto Press, 2010), introduction.

18 See, for example, Marlene Epp, Franca Iacovetta and Frances Swyripa, eds., *Sisters or Strangers? Immigrant, Ethnic and Racialized Women in Canadian History* (Toronto: University of Toronto Press, 2004), introduction.

19 Fahrni, Morton and Sangster, "Feminism and the Making of Canada," 3–6; Sangster, *Transforming Labour*, 12–13.

20 Sangster, *Transforming Labour*, 9–12. On the progress of women in the "white-collar" professions, including journalism, see, for example, Mary Kinnear, *A Female Economy: Women's Work in the Prairie Provinces, 1870–1970* (Montreal; Kingston: McGill-Queen's University Press, 1998); Jayne Elliott, Meryn Stuart and Cynthia Toman, eds., *Place and Practice in Canadian Nursing History* (Vancouver: University of British Columbia Press, 2008); Alison Prentice and Marjorie Theobald, *Women Who Taught: Perspectives on the History of Women and Teaching* (Toronto: University of Toronto Press, 1991); Gertrude J. Robinson, *Gender, Journalism and Equity: Canadian, U.S. and European Perspectives* (Crestkill, NJ: Hampton Press, 2005); Marjory Lang, *Women Who Made the News: Female Journalists in Canada, 1880–1945* (Montreal; Kingston: McGill-Queen's University Press, 1999).

21 See, for example, Joan Sangster, introduction, part 4, "Women's Activism and the State," in *Framing Our Past: Canadian Women's History in the Twentieth Century*, ed. Sharon Anne Cook, Lorna R. McLean and Kate O'Rourke (Montreal; Kingston: McGill-Queen's University Press, 2001), 201–211; also Sangster, *Transforming Labour*, 235.

22 Jacquetta Newman and Linda A. White, *Women, Politics and Public Policy* (Toronto: Oxford University Press, 2006), chapter 4.

23 Cheryl Gosselin, "Remaking Waves: The Québec Women's Movement in the 1950s and 1960s," *Canadian Women's Studies*, 25:3/4, Summer 2006, 34–39.

24 Lang, *Women Who Made the News*. For a popular history, see Kay Rex, *No Daughter of Mine: The Women and History of the Canadian Women's Press Club 1904–1971* (Toronto: Cedar Cave Books, 1995).

25 Janice Fiamengo, *The Woman's Page: Journalism and Rhetoric in Early Canada* (Toronto: University of Toronto Press, 2008); Sandra Gabriele, "Gendered Mobility, the Nation and the Women's Page," *Journalism: Theory, Practice and Criticism*, 7, 2006, 174–196. Peggy Martin, *Lily Lewis: Sketches of a Canadian Journalist: A Biocritical Study* (Calgary: University of Calgary Press, 2006).

26 Jane Rhodes, *Mary Ann Shadd Cary: The Black Press and Protest in the Nineteenth Century* (Bloomington: University of Indiana Press, 1998).

27 Anne-Marie Kinahan, "'A Splendid Army of Organized Womanhood': Gender, Communication and the National Council of Women of Canada, 1893–1918." Ph.D. dissertation, Carleton University, 2005, chapter 3.

28 Lang, *Women Who Made the News*, chapter 8.

29 Lang, *Women Who Made the News*, chapter 3.

30 Anne-Marie Kinahan, "Commodifying Women's Citizenship: Gender, Consumption, and Everywoman's World," a paper presented at the annual meeting of the Canadian Communication Association, Ottawa, 2009; Kinahan, "Finding the Political in the Domestic: Feminist Media History and Canadian Women's Magazines," a paper presented at the biannual meeting of the Canadian Association of Cultural Studies, Montreal, 2009; Kinahan, "Creating the Citizen/Consumer: Early 20th Century Canadian Women's Magazines and the Female Audience," a paper presented at the annual meeting of the Canadian Communication Association, Vancouver, 2008.

31 Maria Dicenzo, "Feminist Media and History: A Response to James Curran," *Media History*, 10:1, 2004, 43–49; referring to Curran, "Media and the Making of British Society, c. 1970–2000," *Media History*, 8:2, 2002, 135–154.

32 Michelle Elizabeth Tusan, *Women Making News: Gender and Journalism in Modern Britain* (Champagne: University of Illinois Press, 2005); Jan Whitt, *Women in American Journalism: A New History* (Champagne: University of Illinois Press, 2008); Patricia Bradley, *Mass Media and the Shaping of American Feminism, 1963–1975* (Jackson: University Press of Mississippi, 2003) and Bradley, *Women and the Press: The Struggle for Equality* (Evanston, IL: Northwestern University Press, 2005); Deborah Chambers, Linda Steiner and Carole Fleming, *Women and Journalism* (London; New York: Routledge, 2004).

33 Lang, *Women Who Made the News*, 216–217.

34 Lang, *Women Who Made the News*, chapter 9.

35 Lang, *Women Who Made the News*, chapter 4.

36 Anne F. MacLellan, "Women, Radio Broadcasting and the Depression: A 'Captive' Audience from Household Hints to Story Time and Serials," *Women's Studies*, 37:6, 2008, 616–633; Barbara M. Freeman, *The Satellite Sex: The Media and Women's Issues in English Canada, 1966–1971* (Waterloo, ON: Wilfrid Laurier University Press, 2001), chapter 2.

37 Valerie Korinek, *Roughing It in the Suburbs: Reading* Chatelaine *Magazine in the Fifties and Sixties* (Toronto: University of Toronto Press, 2000).

38 Barbara M. Freeman, "From No Go to No Logo: Lesbian Rights in *Chatelaine* Magazine, 1966–2004," *Canadian Journal of Communication*, 4:31, Fall 2006, 815–841.

39 Joan Sangster, for example, argues persuasively that the commission's recommendations regarding women in the workforce were limited because its liberal feminist perspective produced little in the way of class analysis. Sangster, *Transforming Labour*, chapter 7.

40 Freeman, *The Satellite Sex*, chapters 2 and 9.

41 Barbara M. Freeman, "The Day of the Strong-Minded Frump Has Passed: Journalists and News of Feminism in Canada," in Cook, McLean and O'Rourke, *Framing Our Past*, 385–391.

42 Simma Holt, *Memoirs of a Loose Cannon* (Hamilton, ON: Seraphim Editions, 2008); Stephen Clarkson, ed., *My Life as a Dame: The Personal and the Political in the Writings of Christina McCall* (Toronto: House of Anansi Press, 2008). See also Pamela Wallin, *Since You Asked* (Toronto: Random House of Canada, 1998); and Linda Kay, *The Reading List* (Lanham, MD: Hamilton Books, 2005).

43 Freeman, *The Satellite Sex*, chapters 2 and 9.

44 Freeman, "The Day of the Strong-Minded Frump Has Passed."

45 Barbara Godard, "Feminist Periodicals and the Production of Cultural Value: The Canadian Context," *Women's Studies International Forum*, 25:2, 2002, 209–223; Barbara Marshall, "Communication as Politics: Feminist Print Media in English Canada," *Women's Studies International Forum*, 18:4, 1995, 463–474.

46 Gail Vanstone, *D Is for Daring: The Women behind the Films of Studio D* (Toronto: Sumach Press, 2007).

47 Robinson, *Gender, Journalism and Equity*, 54; on the glass ceiling, see chapter 5.
48 Robinson, *Gender, Journalism and Equity*, 1.
49 Fiamengo disputes other scholars' interpretations of her Christian perspective, for example. Janice Fiamengo, "Agnes Maule Machar, Christian Radical," in *The Woman's Page*, 29–57.
50 Lang, *Women Who Made the News*, 219; on Alice Fenton Freeman, see Jill Downie, *A Passionate Pen: The Life and Times of Faith Fenton* (Toronto: HarperCollins, 1996); Freeman, "The Day of the Strong-Minded Frump has Passed."
51 Barbara M. Freeman, *Kit's Kingdom: The Journalism of Kathleen Blake Coleman* (Ottawa: Carleton University Press, Women's Experience Series, No. 1, 1989).
52 Janice Fiamengo, "Gossip, Chit-Chat and Life Lessons: Kit Coleman's Womanly Persona," in *The Woman's Page*, 127–128.
53 Freeman, *Kit's Kingdom*.
54 Nancy Fraser, *Unruly Practices: Power, Discourse and Gender in Contemporary Social Theory* (Minneapolis: University of Minnesota Press, 1989) and Fraser, "Rethinking the Public Sphere: A Contribution to the Critique of Actually Existing Democracy," in *Habermas and the Public Sphere*, ed. C. Calhoun (Cambridge, MA: MIT Press, 1992), 109–142.
55 Barbara M. Freeman, "Laced In and Let Down: Women's Fashion Features in the Toronto Daily Press, 1890–1900," in *Fashion—A Canadian Perspective*, ed. Alexandra Palmer (Toronto: University of Toronto Press, 2004), 291–314.
56 In 1941, the rate of married women in the workforce was 4 percent representing 12 percent of the female total. A decade later, it was 11 percent, or 30 percent of the female total, and by 1962, the rate was 22 percent, or almost half the female total. Veronica Strong-Boag, "Canada's Wage-Earning Wives and the Construction of the Middle-Class, 1945–1960," *Journal of Canadian Studies/Revue d'études canadiennes*, 29:3, Autumn 1994, 7.
57 Freeman, *The Satellite Sex*, 216–217.
58 Freeman, *The Satellite Sex*, chapters 2 and 9.
59 Philinda Masters, "A Word from the Press: A Brief Survey of Feminist Publishing," *Resources for Feminist Research/Documentation sur la recherche féministe*, 20:1 and 2, Spring/Summer 1991, 27–35; Godard, "Feminist Periodicals"; Marshall, "Communication as Politics."
60 Carolyn Kitch, "Changing Theoretical Perspectives on Women's Media Images: The Emergence of Patterns in a New Area of Historical Scholarship," *J&MC Quarterly*, 74:3, 1997, 477–489.
61 Sherna Berger Gluck, "Women's Oral History: Is It So Special?" in *Thinking about Oral History: Theories and Applications*, ed. Thomas L. Charlton, Lois E. Myers and Rebecca Sharpless (New York and Toronto: AltaMira Press, 2008), 138.
62 Mary Chamberlain, "Narrative Theory," in Charlton, Myers and Sharpless, *Thinking about Oral History*, 145.
63 In the 1970s, I was a news reporter for CBC radio and TV, and then private radio. No matter where I worked, some male colleagues sneered at my insistence that it was important to cover the women's movement. Others supported me. On at least one occasion, and possibly more, I submitted a news article to the Ottawa publication *Upstream*, but I was not otherwise involved in feminist publishing.
64 Elizabeth Lapovsky Kennedy, "Telling Tales: Oral history and the Construction of Pre-Stonewall Lesbian History," in *The Oral History Reader*, ed. Robert Perks and Alistair Thomson (London; New York: Routledge, 1998), 344–355.
65 Kate Taylor, "'My First Battle—It's Always Education,'" *Globe and Mail*, 8 May 2009, R3.
66 Valerie Raleigh Yow, "Biography and Oral History," in Charlton, Myers and Sharpless, *Thinking about Oral History*, 183–222.
67 For an overview, see Gill Jagger, *Judith Butler: Sexual Politics, Social Change and the Power of the Performative* (London; New York: Routledge, 2008).

68 Josette Brun, ed., *Interrelations femmes-medias dans Ameriques française* (Sherbrooke: Presses Université Laval, 2009).
69 Josette Brun and Barbara M. Freeman, "L'après-8 mars au Canada anglais et au Québec: Une célébration contrastée." *Sciences de la Société journal*, Presses Universitaires du Mirail, Toulouse, France, 2007, 149–163.
70 Lana Rakow, "Feminist Historiography and the Field: Writing New Histories," in *The History of Media and Communication Research: Contested Memories*, ed. David W. Park and Jefferson Pooley (New York: Peter Lang, 2008), 118.

Chapter 1

1 Photograph of Agnes Maule Machar, Queen's University Archives, V23-P-3, 166-3. The physical description of Machar comes from the following sources: Fraser Sutherland, *The Monthly Epic: A History of Canadian Magazines, 1789–1989* (Markham, ON: Fitzhenry and Whiteside, 1989), 62; Carole Gerson, "Three Writers of Victorian Canada," in *Canadian Writers and Their Works*, ed. Robert Lecker, Jack David and Ellen Quigley (Downsview, ON: ECW Press, 1983), 215; Constance Backhouse, *Petticoats and Prejudice: Women and Law in Nineteenth-Century Canada* (Toronto: Osgoode Society/Women's Press, 1991), 277. See also Dianne Hallman, "Cultivating a Love of Canada through History: Agnes Maule Machar, 1837–1927," in *Creating Historical Memory: English-Canadian Women and the Work of History*, ed. Beverly Boutilier and Alison Prentice (Vancouver: University of British Columbia Press, 1997), 25–26, 31. Machar's dates are usually given as 1837–1927, but the birthdate on her tombstone is 1836. Brian S. Osborne, *The Rock and the Sword* (Kingston, ON: Heinrich Heine Press at Grass Creek, 2004), 292–293.
2 Janice Fiamengo, *The Woman's Page: Journalism and Rhetoric in Early Canada* (Toronto: University of Toronto Press, 2008), 5; Sarah Curzon and Sara Jeannette Duncan contributed occasional articles on women's rights to *The Week* in the 1880s. See, for example, S.A. Curzon, "Platform Women," *The Week*, 1:26, 29 May 1884, 408; also Sara Jeannette Duncan, "Woman Suffragists in Council," *The Week*, 3:17, 25 March 1886, 261. The common use of initials or masculine pen names has made it difficult to identify any other female contributors. Machar wrote occasionally for the church press, which is not considered in this study. However, regardless of denomination, those publications were also dominated by middle-class male writers presenting official church views, even in evangelical churches where women took on more leadership roles. When these periodicals were designated family or home journals, the readers tended to be women. Lynne Marks, "'A Fragment of Heaven on Earth'? Religion, Gender, and the Family in Turn-of-the-Century Canadian Church Periodicals," *Journal of Family History*, 26:2, April 2001, 252. In Upper Canada, the colonial newspapers, church presses and other published material, many borrowing from British and American publications, had already set a media precedent regarding public discourse about gender roles. See Cecilia Morgan, *Public Men and Virtuous Women: The Gendered Languages of Religion and Politics in Upper Canada, 1791–1850* (Toronto: University of Toronto Press, 1996).
3 Sutherland, *The Monthly Epic*, 20–21; Gerson, "Three Writers," 198.
4 Curzon, who often argued for women's equality as a matter of justice as well as maternal privilege, was quick to defend women activists like herself and their causes. She edited and wrote for the *Canadian Citizen and Temperance Herald*, and occasionally for more general circulation publications, such as *The Week*, usually as S.A. Curzon. See Beverley Boutilier, "Women's Rights and Duties: Sarah Anne Curzon and the Politics of Canadian History," in Boutilier and Prentice, *Creating Historical Memory*, 53–57; and Heather Murray, "Great Works and Good Works: The Toronto Women's Literary Club, 1877–1883," *Historical Studies in Education/Revue d'histoire de l'éducation*, 11:2 (Fall/automne 1999), 1–15, at http://

www.edu.uwo.HSE/99murray/html, 3 February 2006; Alison Prentice et al., *Canadian Women: A History*, 2nd ed. (Toronto: Harcourt Brace Canada, 1996), 196.

5 Duncan, who was just starting her literary career, appeared ambivalent about equal rights for women, preferring to write clever, sometimes satiric observations on suffragists and their issues, perhaps in a youthful attempt to impress rather than engage. There are several studies of Duncan and her writing, both her fiction and journalism. Misao Dean, *A Different Point of View: Sara Jeannette Duncan* (Montreal: McGill-Queen's University Press, 1991); Janice Fiamengo, "The Uses of Wit: Sara Jeannette Duncan's Self-Fashioning," in *The Woman's Page*, 59–87. See also Thomas E. Tauskey, *Sara Jeannette Duncan: Novelist of Empire* (Port Credit, ON: P.D. Meany Publishers, 1980); and Tausky, ed., *Selected Journalism: Sara Jeannette Duncan* (Ottawa: Tecumseh Press, 1978).

6 Janice Fiamengo challenges some of the assertions of earlier writers regarding Machar's religious perspectives. See Fiamengo, "Agnes Maule Machar, Christian Radical," in *The Woman's Page*, 29–57. Ruth Compton Brouwer, "The 'Between-Age' Christianity of Agnes Machar," *Canadian Historical Review*, 65:3, September 1984, 347–370; Brouwer, "Moral Nationalism in Victorian Canada: The Case of Agnes Machar," *Journal of Canadian Studies*, 20:1, 1985, 90–108. See also Nancy Chenier, "Agnes Maule Machar: Her Life, Her Social Concerns and a Preliminary Bibliography of Her Writing," M.A. thesis, Carleton University, 1977.

7 Dianne Hallman, "Cultivating a Love of Canada through History," 25–26, 31; Hallman, "Agnes Maule Machar on the Higher Education of Women," *Historical Studies in Education/Revue d'histoire de l'éducation*, 13:2, 2001, 165–182; Hallman, "Rights, Justice, Power: Gendered Perspectives on Prohibition in Late Nineteenth-Century Canada," *History of Intellectual Culture*, 1:2, 2002, 1–14, at http://www.ucalgary.ca/hic, 16 February 2010; Dianne M. Hallman, "Religion and Gender in the Writing and Work of Agnes Maule Machar, 1837–1927," Ph.D. dissertation, University of Toronto, 1994.

8 See, for example, Ramsay Cook, *The Regenerators: Social Criticism in Late Victorian English Canada* (Toronto: University of Toronto Press, 1985), 186–191; Backhouse, *Petticoats and Prejudice*, chapter 9. On Machar's fiction specifically, see Mary Vipond, "Blessed Are the Peacemakers: The Labour Question in Canadian Social Gospel Fiction," *Journal of Canadian Studies*, 10:3, 1975, 32–43; Gerson, "Three Writers"; Janice Fiamengo, "'Abundantly Worthy of Its Past': Agnes Maule Machar and Early Canadian Historical Fiction," *Studies in Canadian Literature*, 27:1, 2002, 15–31. Regarding Machar's place in Kingston's history, see Brian S. Osborne, "The World of Agnes Maule Machar: Social Reform, Nation, Empire, Nature," Kingston Historical Society, at http://www.heritage.kingston.org/wok/machar.html, 18 January 2006, and in Osborne, *The Rock and the Sword*, 285–295.

9 Marilyn G. Flitton's introduction to her work, *An Index to The Canadian Monthly and National Review and to Rose-Belford's Canadian Monthly and National Review, 1872–1882* (Toronto: Bibliography Society of Canada/University of Toronto Press, 1976), x–xii. On the politics of Canada's press at the time, see Carman Cumming, *Secret Craft: The Journalism of Edward Farrer* (Toronto: University of Toronto Press, 1992), introduction.

10 Ruth Compton Brouwer, "Transcending the 'Unacknowledged Quarantine': Putting Religion into English-Canadian Women's History," *Journal of Canadian Studies*, 27:3, Autumn 1993, 47–61. More recently, Lynne Marks has argued that social historians in English Canada especially still tend to ignore religious influences on families, except for some regional or single-denominational studies. Marks, "'A Fragment of Heaven on Earth'?" 251–252. Examples of historians' interest in the shifts in religious beliefs include David Marshall, "'Death Abolished': Changing Attitudes to Death and the Afterlife in Nineteenth-Century Canadian Protestantism," in *Age of Transition: Readings in Canadian Social History, 1800–1900*, ed. Norman Knowles (Toronto: Harcourt Brace Canada, 1998), 370–387.

11 Morgan, *Public Men and Virtuous Women*, 10. This perceived duality was generally upheld by doctors, who positioned themselves as the scientific experts on women. See Wendy Mitchinson, *The Nature of Their Bodies: Women and Their Doctors in Victorian Canada* (Toronto: University of Toronto Press, 1991), chapter 1.

12 For a brief discussion on the intersections between maternal and equality feminism, and the importance religion played in the lives of these social reformers, see Prentice et al., *Canadian Women*, 189–190.

13 See, for example, Fidelis, "Woman's Work," *Rose-Belford's Monthly and National Review* (hereafter *RB*), 2, September 1878, 298. She was particularly romantic about the nuns and Salvation Army women who worked in the slums. Fidelis, "Our Lady of the Slums," *The Week*, 8:15, 13 March 1891, 234–235.

14 Marks, "'A Fragment of Heaven on Earth'?" 253–254.

15 Fidelis, "Higher Education for Women," *The Canadian Monthly and National Review* (hereafter *CM*), 7, February 1875, 150.

16 Sutherland, *The Monthly Epic*, 28–32.

17 Historical overviews of the Canadian magazine industry at the time are more popular than scholarly in nature, but very useful for their detail. See Sutherland, *The Monthly Epic*; Noel Barbour, *Those Amazing People: The Story of the Canadian Magazine Industry, 1778–1967* (Toronto: Crucible Press, 1982); Peter Desbarats, *Guide to Canadian News Media* (Toronto: Harcourt Brace Jovanovich Canada, 1996); and Flitton, *An Index*, viii–xii.

18 See, for example, Fidelis, "Higher Education for Women," *CM*, 7, February 1875, 144–157; Fidelis, "Unhealthy Conditions of Women's Work in Factories," *The Week*, 8 May 1896, 566–569.

19 At around the same time, Desbarats founded a similar publication, *L'Opinion publique*, as well as the *New York Graphic*, the first illustrated daily in North America. Michéle Martin, *Images at War: Illustrated Periodicals and Constructed Nations* (Toronto: University of Toronto Press, 2006), 16, 29–31; Desbarats, *Guide to Canadian News Media*, 9. Carman Cumming, *Sketches from a Young Country: The Images of Grip Magazine* (Toronto: University of Toronto Press, 1997).

20 Monika Franzen and Nancy Ethiel, *Make Way! 200 Years of American Women in Cartoons* (Chicago: Chicago Review Press, 1988).

21 Studies on Canadian cartoonists and politics in the Victorian period include David Spencer, "The 'Art' of Politics: Victorian Canadian Political Cartoonists Look at Canada–US Relations" at http://facstaff.elon.edu/dcopeland/mhm/mhmjour6-1.pdf, 21 March 2006. Spencer's other works include "Bringing Down Giants: Thomas Nast, John Wilson Bengough and the Maturing of Political Cartooning," in *Communications in Canadian Society*, 6th ed., ed. Craig McKie and Benjamin Singer (Toronto: Thompson Books, 2001), 67–80; "Fact or Fantasy: Pictorial Visions of War in the French and English Press in Canada 1914–1917," in *Picturing the Past: Media, History and Photography*, ed. Bonnie Brennen and Hanno Hardt (Chicago: University of Illinois Press, 1999), 182–205; and "Double Vision: The Victorian Bi-Cultural World of Henri Julien," *International Journal of Comic Art*, 2:2, Fall 2000, 1–32.

22 Cumming, *Sketches*, 195. *Grip* also opposed divorce but deplored wife abuse. Cumming notes, however, that the Toronto *News* did a better job of campaigning for battered wives and for underpaid factory women. Cumming, *Sketches*, 196–198.

23 Christina Burr, "Gender, Sexuality and Nationalism in J.W. Bengough's Verses and Political Cartoons," *Canadian Historical Review*, 83, 5 December 2002, 515.

24 Burr, "Gender, Sexuality," 506–507. See also her analysis of Bengough's cartoons on social reforms. Burr, *Spreading the Light: Work and Labour Reform in Late-Nineteenth-Century Canada* (Toronto: University of Toronto Press, 1999), chapter 4.

25 Hallman, "Cultivating a Love of Canada," 42.

26 Flitton, *An Index*, xx. At *The Week*, it was possible to earn five dollars for a short story. Hallman, "Religion and Gender," 249. There are some figures available for other magazines that did pay its contributors, but most were so precarious financially that payment might have been sporadic, especially for nonfiction. Payments appear to range between four and fifteen dollars, whereas American publications paid about one dollar per word. See Barbour, *Those Amazing People*, 45, 63–65, 70; Sutherland, *The Monthly Epic*, 44–45.

27 Fidelis, "The New Ideal of Womanhood," *RB*, 2, June 1879, 673. This was standard advice for aspiring female writers. Margaret E. Sangster told her readers that "no profession open to women offers less in the way of stability than writing does." Margaret E. Sangster, "A Sermon to Girls: To Those Who Desire to Write for the Papers," *New Dominion Monthly*, November 1876, 435–437.

28 Hallman, "Agnes Maule Machar," 167–168.

29 Elizabeth Jane Errington, "Ladies and School Mistresses: Educating Women in Early Nineteenth-Century Upper Canada," in Knowles, *Age of Transition*, 121–140. Carole Gerson, "Locating Female Subjects in the Archives," in *Working in Women's Archives: Researching Women's Private Literature and Archival Documents*, ed. Helen M. Buss and Marlene Kadar (Waterloo, ON: Wilfrid Laurier University Press, 2001), 12–13.

30 Susan E. Houston and Alison Prentice, *Schooling and Scholars in Nineteenth Century Ontario* (Toronto: University of Toronto Press, 1988).

31 Elizabeth Jane Errington, *Wives and Mothers, School Mistresses and Scullery Maids: Working Women in Upper Canada 1790–1840* (Montreal; Kingston: McGill-Queen's University Press, 1995), 211–216; also Errington, "Ladies and School Mistresses," 121–140.

32 Brouwer, "Moral Nationalism," 92.

33 Errington, *Wives and Mothers*, 133.

34 Errington, *Wives and Mothers*, 168.

35 This assessment is apparently based on the fact that the Machar family kept a country residence as well as a house in town. Backhouse, *Petticoats and Prejudice*, 277. According to the 1832 church report, Machar received an annual salary of 200 pounds from his 400–500 member congregation and another 78 pounds from the government. The church coffers amounted to about 300 pounds annually, with expenditures of 260, apparently not including the payments toward a heavy debt incurred by the construction of the church. An addition was added five years later and a manse was finally built in 1842. Osborne, *The Rock and the Sword*, 80–84. One might compare Machar's salary of 278 pounds in 1832 with the 2500 pounds per annum paid to a provincial court judge in 1817. By 1837, renting a two-storey house would have cost Machar in the neighbourhood of 75–80 pounds per annum, not including fuel. Errington, *Wives and Mothers*, 139–140.

36 Hallman, "Cultivating a Love of Canada," 27.

37 Brouwer, "Moral Nationalism," 92.

38 Errington, *Wives and Mothers*, 161, 169–183. Personal piety more than charity seemed to take precedence among Irish Roman Catholic women, who were encouraged to consider the Virgin Mary as their model of perfect womanhood, especially in the home. See Brian Clarke, "The Parish and the Hearth: Women's Confraternities and the Devotional Revolution among the Irish Catholics of Toronto, 1850–1885," in Knowles, *Age of Transition*, 357–370.

39 Errington, *Wives and Mothers*, 25, 236; Morgan, *Public Men and Virtuous Women*, 147; Prentice et al., *Canadian Women*, 66.

40 Errington, *Wives and Mothers*, 234.

41 It is possible that her parents and her brother had some household help when they could get it, likely one maid or possibly two, as was standard then. See Errington, *Wives and Mothers*, 157, 235.

42　Errington, *Wives and Mothers*, 172–174.

43　Thirty thousand dollars from her estate was used to establish a home for impoverished, elderly women in Kingston. Osborne, *The Rock and the Sword*, 292–293.

44　Brouwer, "The 'Between-Age Christianity' of Agnes Machar," 349; and George Monro Grant, "Education and Co-Education," *CM*, 3, November 1879, 509–518, reprinted in *The Proper Sphere: Woman's Place in Canadian Society*, ed. Ramsay Cook and Wendy Mitchinson (Toronto: Oxford University Press, 1976), 124–135. See also Cook, *The Regenerators*, 188–189.

45　Brouwer, "Moral Nationalism," 92–92.

46　Her other known pen names were Canadensis, which would signal her nationalism, and her initials, A.M.M., and possibly A.A.M. and F, which would give her another level of anonymity when she wanted it. Ethelwyn Wetherald, "Some Canadian Literary Women—II—'Fidelis,'" *The Week*, 5, 5 April 1888, 300. Her Fidelis byline first appeared with a poem Machar wrote in *The Canadian Monthly and National Review* in October 1872, about a decade before her mother died. See Fidelis, "The Battle of the Huns," *CM*, 2, October 1872, 361–362.

47　Sutherland, *The Monthly Epic*, 59–62; Cumming, *Sketches*, 23–25.

48　See, for example, Fidelis, "The Enlarged Conception of Women's Sphere," *The Week*, 7:45, 10 October 1890, 713. A reader of a Presbyterian publication assumed she was male. See Brouwer, "Moral Nationalism," 107, fn 23.

49　This is a point Ann Dagg makes with regard to the pen names and self-effacing language used by female nonfiction book authors of the 19th century, which applies to journalism as well. Ann Dagg, "Canadian Voices of Authority: Non-Fiction and Early Women Writers," *Journal of Canadian Studies*, 7:2, Summer 1992, 111–112.

50　Fidelis, "Voices Crying in the Wilderness," *The Week*, 8:11, 13 February 1891, 169–170; Fidelis, "A Pressing Problem," *RB*, 2, April 1879, 455–469; Fidelis, "The New Ideal of Womanhood," *RB*, 2, June 1879, 659–676; Agnes Maule Machar, "The Higher Education of Women," *The Week*, 7, 27 December 1889, 55–56.

51　Brouwer, "The 'Between-Age' Christianity of Agnes Machar," 356; Cook, *The Regenerators*, 186–191; Vipond, "Blessed Are the Peacemakers," 43; Gerson, "Three Writers," 217. See the discussion regarding the political debate about protective legislation between Machar and another NCWC activist, Carrie Derick, in Backhouse, *Petticoats and Prejudice*, 277–288.

52　Hallman, "Agnes Maule Machar," 165 citing Prentice et al., *Canadian Women*, 169; Hallman, "Religion and Gender," 259.

53　On the Mills, see Nicholas Capaldi, *John Stuart Mill: A Biography* (Cambridge: Cambridge University Press, 2004); Ann P. Robson and John M. Robson, eds., *Sexual Equality: Writings by John Stuart Mill, Harriet Taylor Mill and Helen Taylor* (Toronto: University of Toronto Press, 1994).

54　Fiamengo, *The Woman's Page*, 5.

55　Fidelis, "A Pressing Problem," *RB*, 2, April 1879, 468.

56　Fidelis, "Higher Education for Women," *CM*, 7:4, February 1875, 150; Fidelis, "Woman's Work," *RB*, 1, September 1878, 299–300. Janice Fiamengo, "Rediscovering Our Foremothers Again: Racial Ideas of Canada's Early Feminists, 1880–1945," in *Rethinking Canada: The Promise of Women's History*, 5th ed., ed. Mona Gleason and Adele Perry (Don Mills, ON: Oxford University Press, 2006), 150–153; Hallman, "Cultivating a Love of Canada," 38–40.

57　Morgan, *Public Men and Virtuous Women*, 152. See also Errington, *Wives and Mothers*, 170.

58　See especially Brouwer, "The 'Between-Age' Christianity of Agnes Machar" and "Moral Nationalism"; Hallman, "Agnes Maule Machar" and "Rights, Justice, Power"; also Backhouse, *Petticoats and Prejudice*, chapter 9.

59　Flitton, *An Index*, xiii.

60 Janice Fiamengo, "Even in This Canada of Ours Suffering, Sympathy and Social Justice in Late-Victorian Social Reform Discourse," PhD. dissertation, University of British Columbia, 1996, 56. Adam knew several women activists through his membership in a mixed-gender literary club, and was more open to women's rights than Smith. See Murray, "Great Works and Good Works." Regarding Adam as editor, see Flitton, *An Index*, xix.

61 Agnes Machar to Louisa Murray, 11 April 1884, file 15, Louisa Murray Papers, York University Archives, North York, ON. Cited in Hallman, "Cultivating a Love of Canada," 36. See also Hallman, "Religion and Gender," 249.

62 Paul T. Phillips, *The Controversialist: An Intellectual Life of Goldwin Smith* (Westport, CT: Praeger, 2002), 50, 92–99.

63 See, for example, the several anonymous "Newfangle" exchanges in *Rose-Belford's Review*, July to December 1879, listed in Flitton, *An Index*, 149–150.

64 Fidelis, "The New Ideal of Womanhood," *RB*, 2, June 1879, 667–668. *Blackwood Magazine*'s indulgence in local satire shifted to weightier matters later. David Finkelstein, "'Long and Intimate Connections': Constructing a Scottish Identity for *Blackwood's Magazine*," in *Nineteenth-Century Media and the Construction of Identities*, ed. Laurel Brake, Bill Bell and David Finkelstein (Basingstoke, Hampshire: Palgrave, 2000), 326–338.

65 See, for example, R. Brend'Amour, "The Young Mother," *Canadian Illustrated News*, 28:26, 29 December 1883, 408.

66 Fidelis, "The New Ideal of Womanhood," *RB*, 2, June 1879, 659–660. See also Errington, *Wives and Mothers*, 26–27.

67 Fidelis, "Higher Education for Women," *CM*, 7, February 1875, 153.

68 Veronica Strong-Boag, "Canada's Women Doctors: Feminism Constrained," in *A Not Unreasonable Claim: Women and Reform in Canada, 1880s–1920s*, ed. Linda Kealey (Toronto: Women's Educational Press, 1979).

69 Murray, "Great Works and Good Works."

70 Osborne, *The Rock and the Sword*, 196–198, 282–284.

71 Fidelis, "A Few Words on University Co-Education," *RB*, 8, March 1882, 313–315. She made essentially the same arguments when Queen's opened to women. See Fidelis, "Woman's Work," *RB*, 1, September 1878, 295–311.

72 Murray, "Great Works and Good Works." Prentice et al., *Canadian Women*, 196.

73 J.W. Bengough, "The Learned Doctor Welcoming Ladies to the Provincial University," *Grip*, 11 Oct. 1884. For the story of the gender war that ensued, see Sara Z. Burke, "New Women and Old Romans: Co-education at the University of Toronto, 1884–95," *Canadian Historical Review*, 80:2, June 1999, 219–241. My thanks to Sara Z. Burke for her help in identifying Wilson in this cartoon.

74 The "bluestocking" became a common stereotype in the 18th century, when female activists such as Mary Astell demanded equal rights to education. See Honoré Daumier, *Intellectuelles (Bas Bleus) et Femmes Socialistes* (Paris: Editions Vilo-Paris, 1974). For a Canadian reference, see Alison Prentice, "Bluestockings, Feminists, or Women Workers? A Preliminary Look at Women's Early Employment at the University of Toronto," *Journal of the Canadian Historical Association*, New Series, 2, 1991, 231–261.

75 Fidelis, "Woman's Work," *RB*, 1, September 1878, 296; D. Fowler, "Harriet Martineau," *CM*, February 1878, 172–185, citations on 176.

76 Alexis Easley, "Authorship, Gender and Power in Victorian Culture: Harriet Martineau and the Periodical Press," in Brake, Bell and Finkelstein, *Nineteenth-Century Media*, 154–164.

77 Her emphasis and spelling. Fidelis, "Woman's Work," *RB*, 1, September 1878, 302.

78 Fidelis, "Woman's Work," *RB*, 1, September 1878, 304.

79 Mitchinson, *The Nature of Their Bodies*, chapter 1; Strong-Boag, "Canada's Women Doctors," 110–112.

80 Fidelis, "Higher Education for Women," *CM*, 7, February 1875, 154.
81 Fidelis, "Higher Education for Women," *CM*, 7, February 1875, 154; Hallman, "Agnes Maule Machar," 178.
82 Brouwer, "Moral Nationalism, 99; Marks, "'A Fragment of Heaven on Earth'?" 254. See also Prentice et al., *Canadian Women*, 191–192.
83 Eric Sager, "Women Teachers in Canada, 1881–1901," *Canadian Historical Review*, 88:2, June 2007, 201–236; Alison Prentice and Marjorie Theobald, *Women Who Taught: Perspectives on the History of Women and Teaching* (Toronto: University of Toronto Press, 1991); Errington, *Wives and Mothers*, 209–210; Jayne Elliott, Meryn Stuart and Cynthia Toman, eds., *Place and Practice in Canadian Nursing History* (Vancouver: University of British Columbia Press, 2008); Jean Thomson Scott, "The Conditions of Female Labour in Ontario," in *Toronto University Studies in Political Science*, First Series, No. 3, ed. W.J. Ashley (Toronto: University of Toronto, 1889), 18–25. Republished in Cook and Mitchinson, *The Proper Sphere*, 172–182.
84 Fidelis, "Higher Education for Women," *CM*, 7, February 1875, 144–157; and "Woman's Work," *RB*, 1, September 1878, 295–311.
85 Minnie Phelps, "Women as Wage-Earners," in *Woman: Her Character, Culture and Calling*, ed. Rev. B.F. Austin (Brantford, ON: Book and Bible House, 1890), 51–55, reprinted as "Unequal Pay for Equal Work, 1890," in Cook and Mitchinson, *The Proper Sphere*, 182–186; Scott, "The Conditions of Female Labour in Ontario."
86 On this point, see Alice Kessler-Harris, *A Woman's Wage: Historical Meanings and Social Consequences* (Lexington: University Press of Kentucky, Blazer Lecture Series, 1990).
87 Fidelis, "The New Ideal of Womanhood," *RB*, 2, June 1879, 675.
88 Fidelis, "Higher Education for Women," *CM*, 7, February 1875, 144–157; and "Woman's Work," *RB*, 1, September 1878, 295–311.
89 Prentice et al., *Canadian Women*, 134. The lowest annual salaries for the female staff in Toronto remained static for two decades, ranging between $200 and $225 from 1871 to 1891. The more senior of them did better, earning up to $400 in 1871 and $675 twenty years later. Rural teachers' salaries were at about the same level as the lowest amounts just cited, probably reflecting the discrepancy in salaries paid to teachers with only a third-class certificate from county model schools and those paid to teachers with a minimum second-class certificate from Normal schools. National Council of Women of Canada, *Women of Canada: Their Life and Work*, Compiled by the National Council of Women of Canada at the Request of the Hon. Sydney Fisher for distribution at the Paris International Exhibition 1900, 118–119.
90 Vincenz Katzler, "Women's Work," *Canadian Illustrated News*, 12:23, 4 December 1875, 360. Library and Archives Canada, *Canadian Illustrated News* online, at http://www.collectionscanada.gc.ca/databases/cin/001065-101.03-e.php, 17 May 2009.
91 Figures from Prentice et al., *Canadian Women*, 130.
92 Murray, "Great Works and Good Works."
93 Fidelis, "A Pressing Problem," *RB*, 2, April 1879, 463; Agnes Maule Machar, "The Higher Education of Women," *The Week*, 7, 27 December 1889, 55–56.
94 Fidelis, "Voices Crying in the Wilderness," *The Week*, 8:11, 13 February 1891, 169–170.
95 Fidelis, "A Pressing Problem," *RB*, 2, April 1879, 455–469.
96 On the WCTU in Ontario, see Sharon Anne Cook, *Through Sunshine and Shadow: The Woman's Christian Temperance Union, Evangelicalism and Reform in Ontario, 1974–1930* (Montreal; Kingston: McGill-Queen's University Press, 1995). WCTU figures from Prentice et al., *Canadian Women*, 192–193.
97 National figures in Lady Ishbel Gordon of Aberdeen and Temair, "The National Council of Women of Canada: What It Means and What It Does" (SI. unknown 1900), 15. Toronto statistics in "Report of the Corresponding Secretary," National Council of Women of Canada, *Annual Yearbook of the National Council of Women*

of Canada, April 1894, 19–20. For the history of the NCWC and its goals, see N.E.S. Griffiths, *The Splendid Vision: Centennial History of the National Council of Women of Canada* (Ottawa: Carleton University Press, 1993); Veronica Strong-Boag, *Parliament of Women: The National Council of Women of Canada* (Ottawa: National Museums of Canada, 1976); Beverly Boutilier, "Helpers or Heroines? The National Council of Women, Nursing and 'Women's Work' in Late Victorian Canada," in *Caring and Curing: Historical Perspectives on Women and Healing in Canada*, ed. Dianne Dodd and Deborah Gorham (Ottawa: University of Ottawa Press, 1994), 17–47; Backhouse, *Petticoats and Prejudice*, chapter 9; Anne-Marie Kinahan, "'A Splendid Army of Organized Womanhood': Gender, Communication and the National Council of Women of Canada, 1893–1918," Ph.D. dissertation, Carleton University, 2005, and Kinahan, "Cultivating the Taste of the Nation: The National Council of Women of Canada and the Campaign against 'Pernicious' Literature at the Turn of the Twentieth Century," *Canadian Journal of Communication*, 32:2, 2007, 161–179.

98 In 1889, in Toronto, the average single woman over 16 years of age, working 54 hours a week or 259 days a year, made an annual wage of $216.71. After living expenses, she had $2.43 left. The typical working mother over 16, who worked an average of six more days a year, made $285.90—$14.23 less than she needed to support herself and her family. Cited by Lori Rotenberg, "The Wayward Worker: Toronto's Prostitute at the Turn of the Century," in *Women at Work, 1850–1930*, ed. Janice Acton, Penny Goldsmith and Bonnie Shepard (Toronto: Canadian Women's Educational Women's Press), 48–49.

99 For specific details on pay and working conditions, Brian McIntosh, "Sweated Labour: Female Needleworkers in Industrializing Canada," in Knowles, *Age of Transition*, 179–191; Christina Bates, "Shop and Factory: The Ontario Millinery Trade in Transition, 1870–1930, " in *Fashion: A Canadian Perspective*, ed. Alexandra Palmer (Toronto: University of Toronto Press, 2004), 113–138; Susan Trofimenkoff, "One Hundred and Two Muffled Voices: Canada's Industrial Women in the 1880's," *Atlantis*, 3:1, Fall 1977, 69–80; Fidelis, "A Pressing Problem," *RB*, 2, 18 April 1879, 459.

100 Strong-Boag, *Parliament of Women*, 195–198; Backhouse, *Petticoats and Prejudice*, chapter 9.

101 Fidelis, "Unhealthy Conditions of Women's Work in Factories," *The Week*, 13:24, 8 May 1896, 568.

102 Fidelis, "Unhealthy Conditions of Women's Work in Factories," *The Week*, 13:24, 8 May 1896, 569.

103 Fidelis, "The Second Canadian Women's Council," *The Week*, 12:28, 7 June 1895, 656.

104 Fidelis, "The Women's National Council and Certain Critics," *The Week*, 12:41, 6 September 1895, 967.

105 Fidelis, "Healthy and Unhealthy Conditions of Women's Work," *The Week*, 13: 18, 27 March 1896, 421.

106 Backhouse, *Petticoats and Prejudice*, 276–288.

107 Fidelis, "Healthy and Unhealthy Conditions of Women's Work," *The Week*, 13: 18, 27 March 1896, 422.

108 See, for example, Edward Jump, "The Patent Gridiron [The Domestic Question as Developed at Recent Meetings]," *Canadian Illustrated News*, 12:1, 4 January 1873, 13. Library and Archives Canada, *Canadian Illustrated News*, at http://www .collectionscanada.gc.ca/databases/cin/001065-101.03-e.php, 17 May 2009.

109 Canada Census 1891; Magda Fahrni, "'Ruffled' Mistresses and 'Discontented' Maids: Respectability and the Case of Domestic Service, 1880–1914," *Labour/Le Travail*, 39, Spring 1997, 69–97; Lorna R. McLean and Marilyn Barber, "In Search of Comfort and Independence: Irish Immigrant Domestic Servants Encounter the Courts, Jails and Asylums in Nineteenth Century Ontario," in *Sisters or Strangers? Immigrant, Ethnic and Racialized Women in Canadian History*, ed. Marlene Epp, Franca

Iacovetta and Frances Swyripa (Toronto: University of Toronto Press, 2004), 133–160; Marilyn Barber, "The Women Ontario Welcomed: Immigrant Domestics in Ontario Homes, 1870–1930," in *The Neglected Majority*, Vol. 2, ed. Alison M. Prentice and Susan Mann Trofimenkoff (Toronto: McClelland and Stewart, 1985), 102–121. Marilyn Barber "Below Stairs: The Domestic Servant," *Material History Bulletin*, 19, Spring 1984 (Ottawa: National Museum of Man).

110 Fidelis, "The Women's National Council and Certain Critics," *The Week*, 12:41, 6 September 1895, 968.

111 Fidelis, "Healthy and Unhealthy Conditions of Women's Work," *The Week*, 13:18, 27 March 1896, 423.

112 NCWC, *Women of Canada: Their Life and Work*, 102–109. Government was also slow to react to the problem, but eventually tighter laws and the belated efforts of social reformers and trade unions did bring about some improvements from the late 1800s onward. McIntosh, "Sweated Labour," 192–196.

113 Backhouse, *Petticoats and Prejudice*, 272.

114 Boutilier, "Helpers or Heroines?" 17–47.

115 This was particularly true of its debate over whether to include an audible version of the Lord's Prayer as well as silent prayer when opening its annual meetings and in her boosting of wholesome magazines for women and children sponsored by the NCWC's founder, Lady Aberdeen. Fidelis, "The Second Canadian Woman's Council," *The Week*, 12:28, 7 June 1895, 657; Fidelis, "The Prayer Question at the Meeting of the Women's National Council," *The Week*, 12:31, 28 June 1895, 729; Fidelis, "Two New Magazines," *The Week*, 11:13, 23 February 1894, 302. On the NCWC campaign for wholesome literature, see Kinahan, "Cultivating the Taste of the Nation."

116 Fidelis, "Woman's Work," *RB*, 1, September 1878, 310.

117 Early members of the WCTU, for example, "faced audiences unaccustomed and frequently hostile to the idea of women speaking in public." Prentice et al., *Canadian Women*, 193.

118 Her emphasis. Fidelis, "Higher Education For Women," *CM*, 7:4, February 1875, 150.

119 See "The Law and the Lady" in *Grip*, 34, September 1892, 202, reprinted as "Women Invade the Professions 1892," in Cook and Mitchinson, *The Proper Sphere*, 167–169; also, NCWC, *Women of Canada*, 61; Garth Grafton, *The Globe*, 1 July 1885, 6. It would be another twenty years, in 1899, before the determined Clara Brett Martin, Canada's first female lawyer, was able to join a law firm in Toronto. Backhouse, *Petticoats and Prejudice*, chapter 10.

120 "The Female Righter," *Grip*, 10:24, 4 May 1878, reprinted in Cook and Mitchinson, *The Proper Sphere*, 7–8.

121 M, "The Woman Question," *RB*, 2, May 1879, citations on 568 and 575.

122 Murray, "Great Works and Good Works."

123 Fidelis, "The New Ideal of Womanhood, *RB*, 2, June 1879, 674.

124 Murray, "Great Works and Good Works."

125 Married women in Ontario had earlier won limited rights to control their own property, which were expanded in 1897, but they were not given the municipal franchise. Prentice et al., *Canadian Women*, 194–196.

126 Cumming, *Sketches*, 35.

127 Bengough, "Grand Triumph for the Woman Suffragists," *Grip*, 24 November 1883. See also Bengough, "Woman's Sphere," *Grip*, 16 March 1889. The CWSA became the Dominion Women's Enfranchisement Association in 1889, again with Stowe as its leader. Prentice et al., *Canadian Women*, 199–200, 205–209, 216.

128 Cumming, *Sketches*, 194.

129 Cook, *Through Sunshine and Shadow*, 99–102; Agnes Maule Machar, "The Citizenship of Women," *Woman's Century*, 3, March 1916, 9.

130 Hallman, "Cultivating a Love of Canada," 42.

Chapter 2

1 *Daily Mail,* 16 May 1891, 11.
2 Janice Fiamengo, "Gossip, Chit-Chat, and Life Lessons: Kit Coleman's Womanly Persona," in *The Woman's Page: Journalism and Rhetoric in Early Canada* (Toronto: University of Toronto Press, 2008), 121–152.
3 Barbara E. Kelcey, "Dress Reform in Nineteenth-Century Canada," in *Fashion: A Canadian Perspective,* ed. Alexandra Palmer (Toronto: University of Toronto Press, 2004), 229–248.
4 See for example, Elizabeth Sifton, "Montreal's Fashion Mile: St. Catherine Street, 1890–1930," in Palmer, *Fashion,* 203–226. Russell Johnston, *Selling Themselves: The Emergence of Canadian Advertising* (Toronto: University of Toronto Press, 2001).
5 *Evening News,* 1 April 1893, 7.
6 *Evening News,* 1 April 1899, 7, and 24 June 1899, 7.
7 *Evening News,* 14 April 1900, 12.
8 For example, see Barbara M. Freeman, *Kit's Kingdom: The Journalism of Kathleen Blake Coleman* (Ottawa: Carleton University Press, 1989), chapter 1; Jill Downie, *A Passionate Pen: The Life and Times of Faith Fenton* (Toronto: HarperCollins, 1996), 70.
9 Freeman, *Kit's Kingdom,* chapter 1; Downie, *A Passionate Pen,* chapter 9.
10 Alexandra Palmer, "Introduction," in *Fashion,* 3–14; Cynthia Wright, "'Feminine Trifles of Vast Importance': Writing Gender into the History of Consumption," in *Gender Conflicts: New Essays in Women's History,* ed. Franca Iacovetta and Mariana Valverde (Toronto: University of Toronto Press, 1992), 229–259.
11 Thorstein Veblen, "The Economic Theory of Woman's Dress," in *Essays in Our Changing Order,* ed. Leon Ardzrooni (New York: Viking Press, 1945), 67–74; and Veblen, *Theory of the Leisure Class* (New York: Macmillan, 1912); Lois W. Banner, *American Beauty* (New York: Alfred A. Knopf, 1983); Elizabeth Wilson, "Fashion and the Postmodern Body," in *Chic Thrills,* ed. Juliet Ash and Elizabeth Wilson (Berkeley; Los Angeles: University of California Press, 1993), 3–16.
12 Helen Damon-Moore, *Magazines for the Millions: Gender and Commerce in the* Ladies' Home Journal *and the* Saturday Evening Post, *1890–1910* (New York: State University of New York, 1994), 3.
13 Amy Aronson, *Taking Liberties: Early American Women's Magazines and Their Readers* (Westport, CT: Praeger, 2002); Carolyn Kitch, *The Girl on the Magazine Cover: The Origins of Visual Stereotypes in American Mass Media* (Chapel Hill: North Carolina Press, 2001); Mary Ellen Zukerman, *A History of Popular Women's Magazines in the United States* (Westport, CT: Greenwood Press, 1998); Ellen Gruber Garvey, *The Adman in the Parlour: Magazines and the Gendering of Consumer Culture, 1880s–1910s* (New York: Oxford University Press, 1996); Jennifer Scanlon, *Inarticulate Longings: The* Ladies' Home Journal, *Gender, and the Promise of Consumer Culture* (New York: Routledge, 1995).
14 Alex Goody, "Consider Your Grandmothers: Modernism, Gender and the New York Press," *Media History,* 7:1, 2001, 47–56.
15 Marjory Lang, *Women Who Made the News: Female Journalists in Canada, 1880–1945* (Montreal; Kingston: McGill-Queen's University Press, 1999), chapter 6, citation on page 164.
16 Sandra Gabriele, "Gendered Mobility, the Nation and the Woman's Page: Exploring the Mobile Practices of the Canadian Lady Journalist," *Journalism,* 7, 2006, 174–196.
17 Susan Henry, "Changing Media History through Women's History," in *Women in Mass Communication: Challenging Gender Values,* 2nd ed., ed. Pamela J. Creedon (Newbury Park, CA: Sage, 1993), 341–362.
18 Lang, *Women Who Made the News,* introduction.
19 Freeman, *Kit's Kingdom,* introduction and chapter 5.

20 "The Little Woman," *Vancouver Daily World*, 6 July 1895, 2.
21 Downie, *A Passionate Pen*, 93. Faith began her career as a freelancer, writing a regular letter from Toronto as Stella for the Barrie, Ontario, *Northern Advance*. Downie, *A Passionate Pen*, chapters 5 and 6.
22 Henry Morgan, *Canadian Men and Women of the Time* (Toronto: William Briggs, 1912), 287; Sandra Gwyn, *The Private Capital* (Toronto: McClelland and Stewart, 1984), 281. On the politics of the *Globe*, see J.M.S. Careless, *Brown of the* Globe, 2 vols. (Toronto: Macmillan, 1959, 1963). On the pen name Sama, see "From a Woman's Standpoint," *Toronto Empire*, 11 March 1893, 6.
23 See, for example, *Globe*, 26 December 1891, 10, and 30 April 1892, 11. On Madge, see Lang, *Women Who Made the News*, 34, 37, 45–46; Ross Harkness, *J.E. Atkinson of the* Star (Toronto: University of Toronto Press, 1963), 16, 45; Wayne Roberts, "Rocking the Cradle for the World: The New Woman and Maternal Feminism, Toronto 1977–1914," in *A Not Unreasonable Claim: Women and Reform in Canada 1880s–1920s*, ed. Linda Kealey (Toronto: Women's Educational Press, 1979), 39. See her column, *Toronto Daily Star*, 15 October 1904, 17.
24 Gene Allen, "News across the Border," *Journalism History*, 31:4, 2006, 206–216; Mary Vipond, *The Mass Media in Canada*, 3rd ed. (Toronto: Lorimer, 2000), 16; Paul Rutherford, *A Victorian Authority: The Victorian Press in Late Nineteenth Century Canada* (Toronto: University of Toronto Press, 1982), 113.
25 See "The Globe's Special Page for Women," *Globe*, 9 April 1891, 11. Examples of foreign fashion letters include those "Canadienne" wrote from London and "J.L." wrote from Paris in the *Empire*, 15 and 22 April 1893, 7; see also the *Toronto Daily Star*, 8 January 1898, 5.
26 On political alliances, independence and the shift to consumerism, see Carman Cumming, *Secret Craft: The Journalism of Edward Farrer* (Toronto: University of Toronto Press, 1992), introduction, 63–66, 156–158. On literacy, see Rutherford, *A Victorian Authority*, 24–35; on advertising revenue and circulation estimates, see Johnston, *Selling Themselves*, 28, 39. Joseph Atkinson discovered, when he took over the *Star* in 1899, that the true daily circulation of that newspaper was not 14,000 readers as he had been led to believe, but half that amount. The *Daily Mail* had a circulation of 31,000 in 1887, which had dipped to 24,000 by 1890, and there were fears the *Globe* would catch up, according to Cumming, *Secret Craft*, 170–171. The *Daily Mail* was still the leading newspaper in 1892; the amalgamated *Mail and Empire* at an estimated 41,000 circulation came second to the *Globe* at 47,000 by 1900. Minko Sotiron, *From Politics to Profit: The Commercialization of Canadian Daily Newspapers, 1890–1920* (Montreal; Kingston: McGill-Queen's University Press, 1997), 24, 53–54; Vipond, *The Mass Media in Canada*, 17.
27 Rutherford, *A Victorian Authority*, chapter 3; Johnston, *Selling Themselves*, chapters 1, 6.
28 Vipond, *The Mass Media in Canada*, 20.
29 For a typical example of a women's page with advertising, see "Woman's Kingdom," *Daily Mail*, 30 April 1892, 5.
30 Freeman, *Kit's Kingdom*, 52–53.
31 See Christina Bates, "Shop and Factory: The Ontario Millinery Trade in Transition, 1870–1930," in Palmer, *Fashion*, 113–138.
32 Amanda Vickery, "Golden Age to Separate Spheres? A Review of the Categories and Chronology of English Women's History," *The Historical Journal*, 36:2, 1993, 383–414; Gabriele, "Gendered Mobility."
33 The subtitle of "Woman's Kingdom" was "Kit's Gossip and Chit-Chat." See the illustration in Freeman, *Kit's Kingdom*, 50.
34 There are few reliable records of the salaries newspaper men and women made at the time. Freeman, *Kit's Kingdom*, 10, 55. Kit complained that syndication editors were paying male journalists ten dollars for political columns and women two

dollars for fashion columns. See *Mail and Empire*, 3 June 1899, 16. Faith made an estimated two dollars for her column when she started, forcing her to keep her full-time job as a teacher. Downie, *A Passionate Pen*, 92.

35 Freeman, *Kit's Kingdom*, 55. On contemporary advice for women journalists, see Linda Steiner, "Construction of Gender in Newsreporting Textbooks, 1890–1990," *Journalism Monographs*, No. 135, October 1992, Association for Education in Journalism and Mass Communication, U.S.A.

36 See, for example, Lynne Warren, "'Women in Conference': Reading the Correspondence Columns in *Woman*, 1890–1910," in *Nineteenth-Century Media and the Construction of Identities*, ed. Laurel Brake, Bill Bell and David Finkelstein (Basingstoke, Hampshire: Palgrave, 2000), 122–134.

37 Mary Ellen Roach and Kathleen Ehle Musa, *New Perspectives on the History of Western Dress* (New York: NutriGuides, 1980), 52–53.

38 Freeman, *Kit's Kingdom*, 95.

39 Kit's response to "Balmaceda," *Daily Mail*, 14 November 1891, 5.

40 A.J.W. to Madge Merton, *Globe*, 6 June 1891, 11.

41 Freeman, *Kit's Kingdom*, chapter 1; Downie, *A Passionate Pen*, chapter 8.

42 Freeman, *Kit's Kingdom*, 52–53.

43 *Empire*, 9 January 1892, 5.

44 *Empire*, 30 January 1892, 5.

45 *Empire*, 20 June 1891, 5.

46 *Empire*, 4 July 1891, 5.

47 *Empire*, 26 June 1895, 11.

48 *Empire*, 20 January 1894, 11. See also her accounts of later excursions to the same store. *Empire*, 2 June 1894, 11, and 22 September 1894, 11.

49 *Empire*, 17 March 1894, 11. Sama of the *Globe* also wrote up department store openings for the *Globe*, 22 September 1894, 7. Ads for the same stores appeared in the *Globe*, 22 September 1894, 15, and 21 September 1894, 6. On department store advertising, see Sotiron, *From Politics to Profit*, 59–60.

50 *Daily Mail*, 30 July 1892, 5.

51 *Daily Mail*, 22 November 1890, 5.

52 See the illustrations in the *Daily Mail*, 12 March–16 April 1892, 5.

53 Anne Hollander, *Seeing through Clothes* (New York: Viking Press, 1978), 311, xii.

54 For example, in the *Empire*, 24 August 1894, 11.

55 *Globe*, 14 January 1893, 5.

56 *Daily Mail*, 24 September 1892, 5ff. to 30 December 1892, 5.

57 Freeman, *Kit's Kingdom*, 8–9.

58 Response to Marion Aspodel, *Daily Mail*, 14 April 1894, 6.

59 *Mail and Empire*, 6 July 1895, 5.

60 *Mail and Empire*, 20 July 1895, 6. See also the *Mail and Empire*, 13 July 1895, 5, 6, and 27 July 1895, 5.

61 *Mail and Empire*, 20 July 1895, 6. See also the *Mail and Empire*, 13 July 1895, 5, 6, and 27 July 1895, 5.

62 See, for example, her response to "Matilda," *Daily Mail*, 30 May 1891, 5; see also her responses to "Jinks" and "Mary," *Daily Mail*, 8 August 1891, 11.

63 *Mail and Empire*, 2 November 1895, 5, and 9 November 1895, 5.

64 *Globe*, 17 February 1894, 7.

65 See Cynthia Cook's discussion of fancy-dress balls for both women and men in Cook, "Dressing Up: A Consuming Passion," in Palmer, *Fashion*, 41–67.

66 See, for example, Sama's column in the *Globe*, 8 April 1893, 6.

67 These theories originated with Thorstein Veblen, George Simmel and others. See Angela Partington, "Popular Fashion and Working-Class Affluence," in Ash and Wilson, *Chic Thrills*, 145–146. Kathy Peiss is a modern scholar who has challenged these theories, saying working-class women developed their own styles. See Peiss,

Cheap Amusements: Working Women and Leisure in Turn-of-the-Century New York (Philadelphia: Temple University Press, 1986); also Peiss, *Hope in a Jar: The Making of America's Beauty Culture* (New York: Metropolitan Books, Henry Holt and Company, 1998).

68 Marilyn Barber, "The Women Ontario Welcomed: Immigrant Domestics for Ontario Homes," in *The Neglected Majority: Essays in Canadian Women's History*, Vol. 2, ed. Alison Prentice and Susan Mann Trofimenkoff (Toronto: McClelland and Stewart, 1985), 105–106.

69 Banner, *American Beauty*, 25–26, 198–199. Valerie Steele, *Fashion and Eroticism: Ideals of Feminine Beauty from the Victorian Age to the Jazz Age* (New York; Oxford: Oxford University Press, 1985), 138–141; Carol Dyhouse, *Girls Growing Up in Late Victorian and Edwardian England* (London: Routledge and Kegan Paul, 1981), 34–36. On women and work in Canada, see Alison Prentice et al., *Canadian Women: A History*, 2nd ed. (Toronto: Harcourt Brace Jovanovich, 1996), chapter 2.

70 Madge's response to "Dunbar," *Globe*, 13 June 1891, 11.

71 *Daily Mail*, 5 September 1891, 5.

72 Response to another "Bridget," *Daily Mail*, 17 June 1893, 8.

73 Barber, "The Women Ontario Welcomed," 102–105.

74 *Globe*, 28 November 1891, 11.

75 *Empire*, 24 November 1894, 4.

76 *Daily Mail*, 28 March 1891, 5.

77 *Daily Mail*, 25 April 1891, 5, and 28 February 1891, 5. The birds mode persisted, much to Madge's disgust. *Toronto Daily Star*, 18 August 1900, 19.

78 *Globe*, 24 March 1894, 6.

79 *Globe*, 24 October 1891, 11.

80 She wrote, with humour, of her own attempts to look fashionable for her presentation to the governor general and his wife at a ball in Ottawa in the *Mail and Empire*, 12 February 1898, part 2, 4.

81 *Daily Mail*, 20 June 1891, 5.

82 *Daily Mail*, 16 November 1889, 5. See also Faith Fenton's description of Princess Alix's trousseau, *Empire*, 1 December 1894, 1.

83 *Globe*, 17 October 1891, 11.

84 Steele, *Fashion and Eroticism*, 102–103. James Laver, "Taste and Fashion since the French Revolution," in *Fashion Marketing*, ed. Gordon Willis and David Midgley (London: George Allen and Unwin, 1973), 380–381.

85 Prentice et al., *Canadian Women*, chapter 2.

86 *Daily Mail*, 16 May 1891, 5.

87 Banner, *American Beauty*, 5. Hollander argues that celebrities sanctioned rather than started new trends. Hollander, *Seeing through Clothes*, 311.

88 Banner, *American Beauty*, 129, 158–169, 174. The Gibson girl had a sister in the Girl of the Golden West, a Calamity Jane figure. Banner, *American Beauty*, 168. See "C.D. Gibson's Typical American Woman," *Empire*, 9 December 1893, 11.

89 *Empire*, 5 January 1895, 11.

90 *Mail and Empire*, 15 July 1899, part 2, 4.

91 *Empire*, 18 March 1893, 7.

92 *Empire*, 27 May 1893, 7; Barbara M. Freeman, "'The Day of the Strong-Minded Frump Has Passed': Journalists and News of Feminism in Canada," in *Framing Our Past: Canadian Women's History in the Twentieth Century*, ed. Sharon Anne Cook, Lorna R. McLean and Kate O'Rourke (Montreal; Kingston: McGill-Queens University Press, 2001); Lang, *Women Who Made the News*, 219. Cummings was national corresponding secretary of the NCWC. See National Council of Women of Canada, *Annual Yearbook of the National Council of Women of Canada*, April 1894, 1.

93 Banner, *American Beauty*, 9–15, 23.

94 Wright, "'Feminine Trifles of Vast Importance,'" 237.
95 Kelcey, "Dress Reform," 229–248; Prentice et al., *Canadian Women*, chapter 5.
96 Kelcey, "Dress Reform," 229–248.
97 Roach and Musa, *New Perspectives*.
98 Steele, *Fashion and Eroticism*, 146; Roach and Musa, *New Perspectives*, 57–62; Stella Mary Newton, *Health, Art and Reason: Dress Reformers of the 19th Century* (London: John Murray, 1974), 130.
99 Banner, *American Beauty*, 147.
100 Barbara Ehrenreich and Deirdre English, *For Her Own Good: 150 Years of the Experts' Advice to Women* (New York: Doubleday, 1978), 98. The statistic that corsets exerted 21–88 pounds of pressure originated in John S. and Robin M. Haller, *The Physician and Sexuality in Victorian America* (Urbana: University of Illinois Press, 1974), 168.
101 Kelcey, "Dress Reform," 234–236.
102 Steele, *Fashion and Eroticism*, 162–185; see also Valerie Steele, *Fetish: Fashion, Sex and Power* (New York; Oxford: Oxford University Press, 1996), 58–60.
103 *Globe*, 22 April 1893, 6.
104 Newton, *Health, Art and Reason*, 117.
105 *Globe*, 18 February 1893, 7.
106 *Montreal Herald*, 1 April 1899, 12.
107 *Toronto Daily Star*, 7 July 1900, 10.
108 *Empire*, 27 January 1894, 11. See the ad for the Health Brand vest, entitled "A Social Departure," *Daily Mail*, 30 April 1892, 8.
109 Emphasis mine. *Daily Mail*, 14 November 1891, 5.
110 See, for example, the editorial praising the hygienic benefits of shorter hems. *Daily Mail*, 21 April 1891, 4.
111 Kelcey, "Dress Reform," 237–239.
112 *Globe*, 2 June 1894, 6.
113 *Globe*, 18 March 1893, 5. See also Faith Fenton's column about an earlier visit from Mrs. Miller in the *Empire*, 9 January 1892, 5; Kit described a "mud-less gown" introduced by a Mrs. Ingersoll of Boston, *Daily Mail*, 21 November 1891, 5.
114 Hollander, *Seeing through Clothes*, 340; Garvey, *The Adman in the Parlour*, chapter 6.
115 Kate Luck, "Trouble in Eden, Trouble with Eve: Women, Trousers and Utopian Socialism in Nineteenth-Century America," in Ash and Wilson, *Chic Thrills*, 200–212.
116 Kelcey, "Dress Reform," 240–244.
117 *Globe*, 6 June 1891, 11.
118 *Empire*, 26 January 1895, 11.
119 *Empire*, 25 August 1894, 11.
120 Sally Sims, "The Bicycle, the Bloomer and Dress Reform in the 1890s," in *Dress and Popular Culture*, ed. Patricia A. Cunningham and Susan Voso Lab (Bowling Green, OH: Bowling Green State University Popular Press, 1991), 125–145.
121 *Empire*, 11 April 1891, 5. See also Sama's column in the *Globe*, 16 June 1894, 6.
122 *Mail and Empire*, 25 July 1896, 24; *Daily Mail*, 21 June 1890, 5.
123 *Mail and Empire*, 17 August 1895, 5.
124 *Globe*, 8 August 1891, 11.
125 *Globe*, 7 November 1891, 11.
126 *Globe*, 12 September 1891, 11.
127 *Daily Mail*, 22 August 1891, 5.
128 *Daily Mail*, 12 September 1891, 5.
129 Hollander, *Seeing through Clothes*, 357; Steele, *Fashion and Eroticism*, 130; Sims, "The Bicycle, the Bloomer and Dress Reform," 143.

Chapter 3

1 All Canadians were officially considered "British subjects," not "Canadian citizens," at the time. For a recent discussion of enemy alien legal status during the war, see James Farney and Bohdan S. Kordan, "The Predicament of Belonging: The Status of Enemy Aliens in Canada," *Journal of Canadian Studies/Revue d'études canadiennes*, 39:1 (Winter 2005), 74–89. See also Donald Avery, "Ethnic and Class Relations in Western Canada during the First World War: A Case Study of European Immigrants and Anglo-Canadian Nativism," in *Canada and the First World War: Essays in Honour of Robert Craig Brown*, ed. David MacKenzie (Toronto: University of Toronto Press, 2005), 272–299. At the time, Winnipeg was Canada's third-largest city, with an estimated population of 163,000 by 1916. Only 67 percent of Winnipeg's established populace had British roots, while Eastern European immigrants to the city outnumbered recent British newcomers. Allan F.J. Artibise, "Divided City: The Immigrant in Winnipeg Society, 1874–1921," in *The Canadian City: Essays in Urban and Social History*, ed. Gilbert A. Stetler and Allan F.J. Artibise (Ottawa: Carleton University Press, 1984), 300–336.

2 Most historians have based their accounts on an article by Ramsay Cook, who surmised that Chipman was likely being pressured by the Press Censor. Ramsay Cook, "Francis Marion Beynon and the Crisis of Christian Reformism," in *The West and the Nation: Essays in Honour of W.L. Morton*, ed. Carl Berger and Ramsay Cook (Toronto: McClelland and Stewart, 1976), 187–208. Anne Hicks wrote that Beynon had an "angry public disagreement" with her prominent suffrage comrade, Nellie McClung, over the limited franchise, and was "forced" to quit her job at the *Guide* after an "editorial falling out" over her public views on conscription. Hicks, "Introduction" to *Aleta Dey* (London: Virago, 1988), xiii. In an earlier article, she merely referred to Cook's version of Beynon's departure. See Hicks, "Francis Beynon and the *Guide*," in *First Days, Fighting Days: Women in Manitoba History*, ed. Mary Kinnear (Regina: Canadian Plains Research Center, University of Regina, 1987), 48. Thomas Socknat believes Beynon resigned rather than suppress her beliefs. Thomas Socknat, *Witness against War: Pacifism in Canada 1900–1945* (Toronto: University of Toronto Press, 1987), 66–69. Ian McKay believes that it was the "fiercely militaristic climate" in Winnipeg that prompted both Beynon and her sister Lillian Thomas to leave for New York. Ian McKay, *Reasoning Otherwise: Leftists and the People's Enlightenment in Canada, 1890–1920* (Toronto: Between the Lines Press, 2008), 311. Barbara Roberts, basing her ideas on Cook's further assumptions, also believed that Beynon was active in the Anti-Conscription League and attended its rallies. Roberts also wrote that Beynon likely "fled" to New York, fearful that her health or life was threatened by right-wing militarists. Barbara Roberts, "Women against War," in *Up and Doing: Canadian Women and Peace*, ed. Janice Williamson and Deborah Gorham (Toronto: Women's Press, 1989), 48–65, 52; Roberts, "Women's Peace Activism in Canada," in *Beyond the Vote: Canadian Women and Politics*, ed. Linda Kealey and Joan Sangster (Toronto: University of Toronto Press, 1989), 285; Roberts, *A Reconstructed World: A Feminist Biography of Gertrude Richardson* (Montreal; Kingston: McGill-Queen's University Press, 1996), 184. Cook also speculated strongly that Beynon was the target of a "blackball" attempt by patriotic colleagues in the Canadian Women's Press Club. Cook, "Francis Marion Beynon," 200–202. Marjory Lang wrote that Beynon was "silenced" and then "resigned" from the *Guide*, but found no evidence of a rift with the press club in its records. Marjory Lang, *Women Who Made the News: Female Journalists in Canada, 1880–1945* (Montreal; Kingston: McGill-Queen's University Press, 1999), 227–228 and n48. Barbara Kelcey and Angela Davis speculated, without explanation, that she left the *Guide* because she felt unable to help farm women enough. Barbara E. Kelcey and Angela E. Davis, eds., *A Great Movement Underway: Women and the Grain Growers' Guide, 1908–1928* (Winnipeg: Manitoba Record Society Publications, Vol. XII, 1997), xiv.

3 Archives of Manitoba, Lillian Beynon Thomas Papers (hereafter LBT), MG9 A53;
Quill Club, MG 10 c3; Political Equality League of Manitoba P192 (formerly MG 10
C30), 1912–1924; Canadian Women's Press Club Papers, Winnipeg Branch, MG 10
A1, M612 and M13; Hudson's Bay Company Archives, United Farmers of Mani-
toba Papers, MG 10 E1. Archives of the University of Manitoba, United Grain Grow-
ers' Ltd. Fonds (UGG) and Public Press Limited, MSS 76. Saskatchewan Archives
Board, Violet McNaughton Papers, A1. Library and Archives Canada, J.S.
Woodsworth Papers, MG27-III C7, Volumes 2, 15, Correspondence from A. Vernon
Thomas. Queen's University, George F. Chipman Fonds, Location 2141, and T.A.
Crerar Fonds, Location 2117.

4 One comparative Canada–U.S. study does consider both the *Grain Growers' Guide's*
editorial position and readers' letters to Beynon's columns during the provincial suffrage campaigns on the Prairies up to 1916. The study does not discuss the conscription debate and its connection with the federal female franchise campaign of
1917–1918. See Tracy Kulba and Victoria Lamont, "The Periodical Press and Western Woman's Suffrage Movements in Canada and the United States," *Women's
Studies International Forum*, 29, 2006, 265–278.

5 Socknat, *Witness against War*, 60–65; Roberts, *A Reconstructed World*, 182–183.

6 Russell Johnston, *Selling Themselves: The Emergence of Canadian Advertising*
(Toronto: University of Toronto Press, 2001), introduction; on the *Guide*, see 261–266.

7 David MacKenzie, ed. *Canada and the First World War: Essays in Honour of Robert
Craig Brown* (Toronto: University of Toronto Press, 2005); Jeffrey Keshen, *Propa-
ganda and Censorship during Canada's Great War* (Edmonton: University of Alberta
Press, 1996).

8 Alison Prentice et al., *Canadian Women: A History*, 2nd ed. (Toronto: Harcourt
Brace Canada, 1996), 189–190.

9 McClung points the finger at E. Cora Hind in particular. Nellie L. McClung, *The
Stream Runs Fast* (Toronto: Thomas Allen, 1945), xiii, 139.

10 Socknat, *Witness against War*, 69.

11 Lillian Laurie, "Home Loving Hearts," *Weekly Free Press and Prairie Farmer* (hereafter *PF*), 21 June 1911, 2.

12 See, for example, Lillian Laurie, "Home Loving Hearts," *PF*, 4 March 1908, 14; Lillian Laurie, "Matters of Interest to Western Women," *Manitoba Free Press* (hereafter
MFP), 25 April 1908, 23.

13 Biographical information from Archives of Manitoba, LBT, MG9 A53, File 1—Biographical Material and File 2—Personal Correspondence. File 3—Business Correspondence, letter from LBT to Austin Weir, 19 May 1960.

14 Hicks, "Francis Marion Beynon and the *Guide*," 41–47; Cook, "Francis Marion
Beynon." On women in advertising at the time, see Johnston, *Selling Themselves*,
75–76.

15 Cook, "Francis Marion Beynon," 187, 191–192; Socknat, *Witness against War*, 69–74;
Keshen, *Propaganda and Censorship*, 22–23; Roberts, *A Reconstructed World*, 182.

16 A Mary Dafoe, likely his daughter, was a witness at the Thomases' wedding; Lillian
and Francis Beynon apparently babysat his youngest girls, Marcella and Elizabeth. LBT Papers, File 1, Thomases' wedding certificate 27 September 1911; File 2,
Marcella Dafoe to Lillian Thomas, 1 May 1960. Murray Donnelly, *Dafoe of the Free
Press* (Toronto: Macmillan of Canada, 1968), 37.

17 Chipman and his wife were members of the short-lived Quill Club (1908–1909), a
writing group that included Vernon Thomas, his then-future wife Lillian Beynon, and
Francis Beynon. Quill Club, minutes of meetings, 14 November 1908 to 13 November 1909.

18 Francis Marion Beynon, "Homemakers Convention," Country Homemakers, *The
Grain Growers' Guide* (hereafter *CH-GGG*), 10 June 1914, 9; letter from E.A. Thomson, "Own Their Club Room and the Lot Whereon It Stands," *CH-GGG*, 15 October

1913, 10. Mary P. McCallum, "Women as an Organized Force," *The Grain Growers' Guide* (hereafter *GGG*) 26 June 1918, 12. Susan Jackel, "First Days, Fighting Days: Prairie Presswomen and Suffrage Activism," in Kinnear, *First Days, Fighting Days: Women in Manitoba History*, 53–75.

19   Francis Marion Beynon, "Use the Advertisements," *CH-GGG*, 25 April 1917, 10. See "Five Valiant Servants Wanting Country Employ," *CH-GGG*, 26 June 1912, 13, 36; the ads, from Robert M. Moore and Co. and the T. Eaton Co. Limited, appeared among many other commercial ads on page 36. Sewing patterns for "Dainty Afternoon Models," *CH-GGG*, 24 July 1912, 9. A rare fashion feature appeared in *CH-GGG*, 10 September 1913, 9.

20   Francis Marion Beynon, "Women Don't Want to Be Supported, Thank You," *CH-GGG*, 17 December 1913, 10. On the Prairies, all women who were property owners or were householders in their own names could vote in municipal elections, but a woman could not vote if the property was in her husband's name. Vernon and Lillian Thomas split the ownership of their home so that she could vote municipally. Lillian Laurie, "Lillian Laurie's Page for Women and Girls," *PF*, 9 August 1916, 7, and Lillian Laurie, "Lillian Laurie's Page for Women and Girls," *PF*, 13 September 1916, 7.

21   See for example, the letters of advice and support from Francis Beynon to Violet McNaughton in the early days of the Women Grain Growers' Association and letters to her from Lillian Thomas regarding the federal suffrage campaign. Violet McNaughton Papers, Saskatchewan Archives Board, A1, files E-92(1), E-23 and E-18. For an overview of their relationship with McNaughton, see Georgina M. Taylor, "'Ground for Common Action': Violet McNaughton's Agrarian Feminism and the Origins of the Farm Women's Movement in Canada," Ph.D. dissertation, Carleton University, 1997, especially chapters 3 and 4. On their early suffragist connections with Richardson, see also Roberts, *A Reconstructed World*, 105–116.

22   Lang, *Women Who Made the News*, chapter 8; Jackel, "First Days, Fighting Days"; and Taylor, "Ground for Common Action." There are also several biographies of Nellie McClung that cover this period, including Mary Hallett and Marilyn Davis, *Firing the Heather: The Life and Times of Nellie McClung* (Saskatoon, SK: Fifth House, 1993), especially chapter 6; Roberts, *A Reconstructed World*, chapter 3.

23   Quill Club Papers; Political Equality League of Manitoba, 1912–1924, files 1, 2 and 3. Canadian Women's Press Club Papers, Winnipeg Branch, M613, Copy of CWPC National Report 1913–1914, report of the corresponding secretary, 1913–1914 (Jessie E. Dickins) and M612, Minutes of the CWPC Winnipeg branch 1910 annual meeting, 5 November 1910.

24   Jeffery Taylor, *Fashioning Farmers: Ideology, Agricultural Knowledge and the Manitoba Farm Movement, 1890–1925* (Regina: Canadian Plains Research Center, 1994); John J. Fry, *The Farm Press, Reform and Rural Change, 1895–1920* (New York; London: Routledge, 2005).

25   Norman Lambert, "How the Grain Growers Grew," *GGG*, 26 June 1918, 5–6.

26   Jeffrey Taylor, *Fashioning Farmers*, 117.

27   Archives of the University of Manitoba, United Grain Growers' Ltd. Fonds (UGG), MSS 76, "UGG: A Short History and Chronology." Compiled by Jeffrey Long; Box 30, Folder 1, Grain Growers' Grain Company (hereafter GGGCo) 1909 Annual Report, 33–34, 36–37, 40.

28   Box 3, GGGCo minutes of the directors' meeting 16 July 1907; Box 30, File 1, 1909 GGGCo 1909 Annual Report, 9–10, 41–42. George F. Chipman, "Ten Years at the Front," and "Sixty Thousand Farmers in Business," *GGG*, 26 June 1918, 2, 7.

29   Bold type in the original quotation. UGG, Box 30, File 1, GGGCo 1909 Annual Report, 40.

30   These links can be traced in the minutes from the directors' and shareholders' meetings of the Grain Growers' Grain Company and Public Press Limited (hereafter

PPL) and their annual reports, as well as the records of the Manitoba Grain Grow-
ers' Association (MGGA). UGG, Boxes 3, 30, 41; MGGA, Box 15; Chipman, "Ten
Years at the Front," 2. Regarding support of the female franchise, see MGGA,
Box 15, File 5, Report of the Proceedings of the Ninth Annual Convention of the
Manitoba Grain Growers' Association, 24–26 January 1912, 4–5. On its earliest,
pro-suffrage stance, see Kulba and Lamont, "The Periodical Press."

31 UGG, Box 3, Minutes of GGGCo shareholders' meeting, 16 July 1910; Box 30,
GGGCo 1910 Annual Report, 6. See also Chipman, "Ten Years at the Front," 2. Box 7,
minutes of the GGGCo shareholders' meeting, 12 November 1913.

32 The aims of the *Guide* as a farmers' paper and an antidote to the "partisan press"
are set out in UGG, Box 30, File 1, GGGCo 1909 Annual Report, 17–18, 28, 40–41.

33 When in 1912 its former editor, E.A. Partridge, proposed a merger of the *Guide*
with *The Voice*, which represented the views of organized labour, his colleagues put
a stop to the plan, for to amalgamate with "socialists of the extreme type" would
have "dealt a death blow" to the *Guide*. George F. Chipman Fonds, Box 1, File 4, Political Correspondence, unsigned letter to W.J. Tragillus, 10 September 1912; E.A. Partridge to W.J. Tragillus, 5 September 1912.

34 The *Guide* published 664 pages between June 1908 and June 1909 and 2196 pages
between January 1917 and January 1918, according to its advertisement "Made-To-
Order Paper," *GGG*, 26 June 1918, 11.

35 Queen's University Archives, George F. Chipman Fonds 2141, Box 1, File 1, Family
Correspondence 1906–1921, Chipman to "Aunt Sue," 8 August 1911. File 4, Political Correspondence 1911–1913, T.A. Crerar to Chipman, 31 May 1911; Grain Growers Grain Co. Papers, minutes of the GGGCo. directors' meeting, 24 September
1915; minutes of the Public Press Ltd. directors' meeting, 6 August 1913.

36 There was no constitutional guarantee of freedom of the press in Canada and no
precedent except English common law. The War Measures Act of 1914 gave the
federal cabinet broad powers to censor the spoken and written word. Publications
could mention that they were complying with censorship regulations, but they
could not run blank pages to indicate they had done so, nor could they criticize
Chambers's lists of dos and don'ts that he sent out to editors. Reporters at the front
were constrained by military authorities there. Chambers, who tended to favour senior journalists he knew personally as his regional agents, appointed J. Fred Livesay,
manager of the Western Associated Press, a news wire service, to monitor the publications on the Prairies and in British Columbia. Livesay, an occasional guest of
the Winnipeg women's press club, was the husband of one of its leading members,
Florence Randall Livesay. Keshen, *Propaganda and Censorship*, 5–6, 14, 66–76.
CWPC Winnipeg Branch, Minute Book 1915–1922, Reel M612, minutes of 11 February 1915 and 23 March 1917.

37 Keshen, *Propaganda and Censorship*, 66.

38 J.L. Granatstein, "Conscription in the Great War" in MacKenzie, *Canada and the
First World War*, 62–75, especially 67–69.

39 It was not until May 1918 that tougher censorship regulations were enforced that
specifically forbade any attempt to "persuade or induce any person to resist or
impede" the Military Service Act or do anything "which tends to weaken or in any
way detract from the united effort ... in the prosecution of the war," regulations
that appeared to be aimed more at dissension in Quebec than anywhere else. Cited
in Keshen, *Propaganda and Censorship*, 66; on the *Clarion*, see Keshen, *Propaganda and Censorship*, 89; on the Military Service Act and *The Voice*, see Socknat,
Witness against War, 63, 66.

40 Editorial, "Conscription and Patriotism," *GGG*, 6 June 1917, 5. Banned American
newspapers included several of the Hearst publications. Keshen, *Propaganda and
Censorship*, chapters 1, 3.

41 Francis Marion Beynon, "Between the Editor and Readers," *CH-GGG*, 12 June
1912, 9.

42 Francis Marion Beynon, "Women Don't Want to Be Supported, Thank You," *CH-GGG*, 17 December 1913, 10.

43 Francis Marion Beynon, "What I've Been Reading Between the Lines," *CH-GGG*, 21 August 1912, 9; directive to readers, "The Mail Bag," 26 November 1913, 9; Roberts stated that her readers became increasingly "hostile" to her wartime politics. Roberts, "Women against War," 52. Some letters that appeared in Canadian newspapers were either censored or planted, according to Keshen, but it is difficult to ascertain if this was true of the *Guide*. Keshen, *Propaganda and Censorship*, 79. Samples of readers' views and some of Beynon's replies include the following: Mrs. G.H. Smith, "No Doubt about the Result of War," *CH-GGG*, 14 June 1915, 10; Constant Reader, "Proud of U.S. Attitude," *CH-GGG*, 5 July 1916, 9; H. Morrell, "Conscription Principle Right," and response from F.M.B.," *CH-GGG*, 9 February 1916, 10. Mrs. A.G. Hanson, "From a Canadian by Adoption," *CH-GGG*, 17 January 1917, 10; P. St. John. "Disagrees with Mrs. McClung," *CH-GGG*, 24 January 1917, 14; S.E. Nodwell, "Another Word for the Foreign-Born," *CH-GGG*, 11 July 1917, 9; her answers to Bert Sautne, "Take the Other Fellow's Life but I'll Keep My Money," *CH-GGG*, 27 June 1917, 9, 26; and to Walter Crowe, "Conscript Wealth Also," *CH-GGG*, 4 July 1917, 9.

44 Ad for "Woman and Labor," *GGG*, 13 November 1912, 25. By 1913, the *Guide* was carrying a full-page ad for various books. "Progressive Literature," *GGG*, 12 February 1913, 4. The book was also available to her through the women's press club's own library. CWPC Winnipeg, Reel M612, Minute Book, 1909–1915, minutes of the annual meeting, 23 October 1913; minutes of 26 February 1914; minutes of 25 November 1915.

45 It was part of a series she wrote on the book. Francis Marion Beynon, "Woman and War," 31 July 1912, 9. See also Beynon, "Explanatory," *CH-GGG*, 10 July 1912, 9; "The Woman's Movement," *CH-GGG*, 17 July 1912, 9; "The New Man," *CH-GGG*, 14 August 1912, 9.

46 Terry Copps, "The Military Effort, 1914–1918," in MacKenzie, *Canada and the First World War*, 36.

47 Editorials, "The War" and "Farmers Must Be Active," *GGG*, 19 August 1914, 5.

48 Editorials, all captioned "The War," *GGG*, 16 September, 21 October, and 18 November 1914, 5; editorial, "More Canadian Troops," *GGG*, 25 November 1914, 6.

49 See, for example, "Why Europe Is Fighting," "War Is Hell," and "What Canada Is Doing," *GGG*, 14 October 1914, 7–9, 18, 22; "A Belgian Woman's Letter," "Britannia Rules the Air," and "Sinking of the Aboukir, Hogue and Cressy," *GGG*, 4 November 1914, 7–9; "The First Canadian Contingent," *GGG*, 25 November 1914, 7; Arthur Bullard, "The British War Machine," 5 May 1915, 7, 19; "The Naval Battle," *GGG*, 14 June 1916, 5.

50 Arch Dale illustration, "The Dance of Death," *GGG*, 14 October 1914, 6.

51 See, for example, the cartoon "A Bubble That Will Shortly Burst," *GGG*, 16 August 1916, 6.

52 Francis Marion Beynon, "War Clouds," *CH-GGG*, 12 August 1914, 8.

53 Francis Marion Beynon, "No Christmas Spirit," *CH-GGG*, 9 December 1914, 16; Francis Marion Beynon, "The War as a Peace Agency," and Nelson Harding illustration, "Nineteen Centuries after Christ," from the *Brooklyn Eagle*, *CH-GGG*, 9 September 1914, 8.

54 Robert Carter, "The Triple Alliance," from the *New York Sun*, *CH-GGG*, 16 September 1914, 8. On the war as un-Christian, see Roberts, *A Reconstructed World*, 119–122.

55 Editorial, "News of the War," *GGG*, 28 March 1917, 6; "The United States Draws Sword," *GGG*, 11 April 1917, 5; "War and Democracy," *GGG*, 18 April 1917, 5; A.J.C. Stevenson, "The War Situation Today," and the *Guide* Special Correspondent, "Our Ottawa Letter," *GGG*, 6 June 1917, 32, 34; "United States War Measure," *GGG*, 25 April 1917, 40.

56 Keshen, *Propaganda and Censorship*, chapter 1. Mrs. S.V. Haight, "A Director's Report," Farm Women's Clubs page, *GGG*, 25 August 1915, 21; "Henders' Presidential Address," *GGG*, 12 January 1916, 7.

57 Copps, "The Military Effort, 1914–1918," in MacKenzie, *Canada and the First World War*, 36.

58 F.M.B.'s response to Pennsylvania, "A Woman's Opinion of War," *CH-GGG*, 2 June 1915, 10.

59 "Resolutions Adopted by the International Congress of Women, 1915." This document may have been circulated among a number of leading feminists in Canada. Copy in McNaughton Papers, A1 E-52(1).

60 Roberts, "Women against War," 56, and "Women's Peace Activism in Canada," 283. See also Roberts, *A Reconstructed World*, 129–132, 138–140.

61 Francis Marion Beynon, "Preparedness," *CH-GGG*, 19 April 1916, 10.

62 Frances Marion Beynon's "Answer," to a reader, Gingham Girl, "Peace Not Possible," *CH-GGG*, 26 July 1916, 9. On the attempts of the international suffragists to stay in touch despite enemy lines during the war, see Roberts, *A Reconstructed World*, 136.

63 Francis Marion Beynon, "Penalizing Bachelorhood," *CH-GGG*, 12 January 1916, 10, and "Conscription," *CH-GGG*, 30 May 1917, 10. The *Guide* did not specify who should be recruited first. "Make Conscription General," *GGG*, 23 May 1917, 5; also "Distribute the Sacrifice," *GGG*, 30 May 1917, 5; "Conscription and Patriotism," *GGG*, 6 June 1917, 5; "The Conscription Question," 27 June 1917, 5.

64 Francis Marion Beynon, "The Waste of War," *CH-GGG*, 3 March 1915, 10. On women pacifists and war relief work, see Roberts, *A Reconstructed World*, 121–122.

65 Frances Marion Beynon, "The Returned Soldier," *CH-GGG*, 19 January 1916, 10. Copps, "The Military Effort, 1914–1918," in MacKenzie, *Canada and the First World War*, 38–39. The Patriotic Fund was established by an act of parliament and raised six million dollars in its first three months. By 1916, it supported 25,000 soldiers' families. Keshen, *Propaganda and Censorship*, 5.

66 F.M.B.'s response to Wolf Willow, "Should Be Patriotic Tax," *CH-GGG*, 22 December 1915, 8; and "Can You Send Furs for the Italian Soldiers and at Once?" *CH-GGG*, 27 October 1915, 10; letter from Adelaide M. Plumptree, "Much MisGuided Help," *CH-GGG*, 21 July 1915, 10.

67 Francis Marion Beynon, "Charities and Taxation," 20 December 1916, 10. On women's activities and labour during the war, see Joan Sangster, "Mobilizing Women for War," in MacKenzie, *Canada and the First World War*, 157–193, especially 176.

68 On Tag Days, contributors wore tags with the name of the charity to which they had donated. CWPC Winnipeg Branch Minute Book 1915–1922, minutes of 27 April 1916.

69 Francis Marion Beynon, "The Waste of War," *CH-GGG*, 3 March 1915, 10. On benefits for soldiers, see Desmond Morton, "Supporting Soldiers' Families: Separation Allowance, Assigned Pay, and the Unexpected," in MacKenzie, *Canada and the First World War*, 194–229.

70 Although Gertrude Richardson, who was also a pacifist, wrote for a time in the official publication of the National Council of Women, *Woman's Century*, it generally supported the war. Roberts, *A Reconstructed World*, 125, 207.

71 Front page editorial, "When the War Is Over," *GGG*, 18 November 1914, 1. Peace activists argued that war was contrary to Christ's Sermon on the Mount. Letter from W.E. DeForest, "World Federation and Peace," *GGG*, 11 November 1914, 9.

72 Editorial, "Methodists Condemn Militarism," *GGG*, 25 November 1914, 12, 19. Later, the Canadian church officially supported national registration, Union government and conscription, prompting J.S. Woodsworth to resign as a minister. It also promised to bring in prohibition. Keshen, *Propaganda and Censorship*, 22–23.

73 Editorials, "Where Both Sides Lose," and "Death and Destruction," *GGG*, 14 October 1914, 5.

74 Editorial, "Who Pays for the War?" *GGG*, 15 September 1915, 5–6; editorial, "Increased Soldiers' Pensions," *GGG*, 17 May 1916, 5. See the resolutions of the "Neepawa District Association," *GGG*, 8 December 1915, 12, and the letter from Jas. Seaman, "Patriotic Appeal," *GGG*, 20 October 1915, 12. See also the resolutions from SGGA District 7 and District 10, *GGG*, 5 January 1916, 14; editorials, "A Square Deal for Soldiers," *GGG*, 19 January 1916, 5–6; "Patriotic Taxes," *GGG*, 26 January 1916, 5–6; and "Problems of War Time," 22 March 1916, 6. Editorial, "Raising Patriotic Revenue," 4 April 1917, 5.

75 Editorial, "For the Public Weal," *GGG*, 21 October 1914, 5.

76 Editorial, "Make Conscription General," *GGG*, 23 May 1917, 5. Francis Marion Beynon, "The Flag," *CH-GGG*, 13 June 1917, 9.

77 Beynon's signature did not appear under the article but it was written in her style. "Peace Talk," *CH-GGG*, 5 January 1916, 8.

78 Keshen, *Propaganda and Censorship*, 13, 42.

79 Francis Marion Beynon, "Mrs. McClung's New Book," *CH-GGG*, 24 November 1915, 10. Nellie McClung, *In Times like These* (Toronto: McLeod & Allen), 1915.

80 See for example, Roberts's discussion of Laura Hughes in "Women against War."

81 Francis Marion Beynon, "After Suffrage, What?" *CH-GGG*, 23 February 1916, 10, and "Re-Organization of the P.E.L.," *CH-GGG*, 1 March 1916, 10.

82 In Manitoba and British Columbia, Thomas's readers were told, "any person" who could vote provincially could also vote federally. For Alberta, Saskatchewan and the Yukon, however, the relevant clauses of the Elections Act stipulated that "any male person" could vote federally. Lillian Laurie, "Women and the Vote," *PF*, 9 August 1916, 7. See also Lillian Laurie, "Women Federal Voters," *MFP*, 14 October 1916, 21.

83 This article was unsigned but written in her style and appeared on her page. "The Federal Franchise," *PF*, 3 January 1917, 7. See also Lillian Laurie, "The Federal Franchise," *MFP*, 3 February 1917, 3. An account of one of her talks was published as "Women's Session of Grain Growers—Explains Federal Franchise," *PF*, 17 January 1917, 7. Later, Thomas told her readers to write to the prime minister, urging his government to apply the female federal franchise in Canada to all women who had it provincially. "Keep on Writing," *PF*, 14 April 1917, 19.

84 Lillian Beynon Thomas to Violet McNaughton, 17 September 1916. See also Lillian Beynon Thomas to Violet McNaughton, 21 December 1916. Both letters in McNaughton Papers, A1 E-18.

85 L.B.T., "An Explanation," and letter from Geo. Langley, *CH-GGG*, 2 August 1916, 9; L.B.T. "More about Voting," *CH-GGG*, 9 August 1916, 9. Beynon did not mention her sister's contributions to her page when she returned, however. Francis Marion Beynon, "Home Again," *CH-GGG*, 30 August 1916, 9. She gave a talk to her press club colleagues about her writing course in New York. CWPC Winnipeg Minute Book 1915–1922, minutes of 5 October 1916.

86 Francis Marion Beynon, "An Important Admission," *CH-GGG*, 18 October 1916, 9. See also Lillian Laurie, "Federal Women Voters," *MFP*, 14 October 1916, 21. Francis Marion Beynon, "The Pugsley Bill," *CH-GGG*, 9 May 1917, 10. Editorials, "Shall the Women Vote," *GGG*, 23 May 1917, 5, and "Force of Public Opinion," *GGG*, 30 May 1917, 5–6. Editorial, "Manitoba's New Election Law," *GGG*, 2 May 1917, 5; Francis Marion Beynon, "Another Old Theory Exploded," *CH-GGG*, 14 July 1917, 9. Lillian Laurie, "Pugsley's Franchise Bill," *MFP*, 28 April 1917, 12. See also Lillian Laurie, "Mr. Pugsley's Franchise Bill," *PF*, 2 May 1917, 7. Lillian Laurie, "Women or Persons," *MFP*, 2 June 1917, 20; the pro-suffrage cartoons, probably by Arch Dale, appeared in the Country Homemakers, *GGG*, 31 January 1917, 10.

87 Stella L. Richardson, "Concerning Manitoba Women," Farm Women's Clubs page, *GGG*, 26 January 1916, 27.

88 Francis Marion Beynon, "Persecution for Originality," *CH-GGG*, 7 March 1917, 10.

89 Francis Marion Beynon, "Potato Picking Time Is Coming," *CH-GGG*, 16 October 1912, 10.

90 Francis Marion Beynon, "The Foreigner," *CH-GGG*, 11 February 1914, 10.

91 Francis Marion Beynon, "The Foreign Woman's Franchise," *CH-GGG*, 27 December 1916, 10.

92 Nellie McClung, "Mrs. McClung's Reply" and response from F.M.B. *CH-GGG*, 24 January 1916, 10. Some of her readers agreed with McClung's original view, while others opposed it. That day, Beynon published a letter agreeing with McClung from Wolf Willow, "Foreign Women Should Be Excluded." Other readers took exception to McClung's views. Mrs. G.A. Hanson, "From a Canadian by Adoption, *CH-GGG*, 17 January 1917, 10, and E.P. St. John, "Disagrees with Mrs. McClung," Mail Bag, *GGG*, 24 January 1917, 14.

93 Lillian Laurie, "Mrs. McClung and the Dominion Franchise," *MFP*, 16 December 1916, 24; Nellie L. McClung, "Mrs. McClung's Letter," *MFP*, 6 January 1917, 18, and Lillian Laurie, "Mrs. McClung for All Women," *MFP*, 20 January 1917, 20; also Lillian Laurie in *PF*, 27 December and 3 January 1917, 7; and "Mrs. McClung's Letter," *PF*, 10 January 1917, 7. Thomas wrote a similar column about McClung's position in the *Canadian Thresherman and Farmer*, cited in Roberts, *A Reconstructed World*, 159.

94 Lillian Thomas to Violet McNaughton, 21 December 1916, McNaughton Papers, A1 E-18.

95 General circulation letter dated 28 March 1917 from the Federal Franchise Committee, co-signed by Nellie L. McClung, chairman. Copy in Violet McNaughton Papers, A1 E-18. The idea of the ethnically limited franchise may not have originated with McClung, but with Arthur Meighen, a Conservative cabinet minister. Roberts, *A Reconstructed World*, 151–161.

96 Editorial, "Shall the Women Vote," *GGG*, 23 May 1917, 5; editorial, "Woman Suffrage," *MFP*, 22 February 1917, 9; editorial, "Woman Suffrage," *PF*, 28 February 1917, 9; editorial, "Women and the Dominion Franchise," *MFP*, 26 March 1917, 11.

97 The *Guide* Special Correspondent, "Our Ottawa Letter," *GGG*, 23 May 1917, 31.

98 Editorial, "Have We Shot Our Bolt?" *MFP*, 22 February 1917, 22.

99 Editorial, *MFP*, 17 January 1917, 9, cited in Keshen, *Propaganda and Censorship*, 13, fn 46.

100 McNaughton Papers, A1 E-23, Francis Marion Beynon to Violet McNaughton, 20 February 1917.

101 Aside from his pacifism, Thomas was also a strong defender of French language rights. Woodsworth Papers, Vol. 2, Vernon Thomas to J.S. Woodsworth, 13 May 1917 and 5 August 1917. He later told Woodsworth that he was in the second-last class eligible for military recruitment, but that he would go to prison rather than enlist. As it was, he could be jailed just for writing what was on his mind if he were in Canada, referring to the censorship legislation passed in the spring of 1918. Thomas to Woodsworth, 18 June 1918.

102 Hicks asserts that Thomas wrote several articles about "pacifism," but I have found none that appeared in the *Manitoba Free Press* or the *Prairie Farmer* any later than the editorial of 12 July 1916, noted above. Hicks, Introduction to *Aleta Dey*, xiii–xiv. The PEL had a regular column in *The Voice* about the suffrage campaign. Roberts, *A Reconstructed World*, 134. See, for example, Socknat, *Witness against War*, 66. Although she does not cite the letter in question, Roberts recounts that Thomas, while living in New York, was among the suffragists who supported Gertrude Richardson's Christian Peace Crusade. Roberts, *A Reconstructed World*, 208–211.

103 LBT papers, File 2, note to Mrs. A.V. Thomas from Nellie L. McClung , 21 April 1917, and File 1, undated, signed certificate from the executive of the Political Education League, referring to her departure; CWPC Winnipeg Branch, Minute Book

1915–1922, minutes of 27 April 1917; CWPC Reel M613, Winnipeg Branch Guest Book, LBT's entry for 26 April 1917.

104 McNaughton Papers, A1 E-23, Francis Marion Beynon to Violet McNaughton, 20 February 1917. Library and Archives Canada, J.S. Woodsworth Papers, MG27-III C7, Volume 2, A. Vernon Thomas to J.S. Woodsworth, 13 May 1917.

105 Francis Marion Beynon, "Crossing an Imaginary Line," *CH-GGG*, 16 May 1917, 9.

106 The writer was likely Beynon, who wanted to get her readers discussing the idea. See "Wealth Conscription First," *CH-GGG*, 10 January 1917, 10.

107 "Manitoba Farmers' Parliament," *GGG*, 17 January 1917, 11; editorials, "The Brandon Convention" and "Farmers Mean Business," *GGG*, 17 January 1917, 5. The SGGA and UFA also supported the platform. Leona Barrett, "Farm Women's Clubs," *GGG*, 18 April 1917, 33.

108 "Manitoba Farmers' Parliament," *GGG*, 17 January 1917, 34, 40, 42. See also United (Manitoba) Grain Growers' Association Papers, Box 15, File 10, 1917 Yearbook and Report of the Proceedings of the Fourteenth Annual Convention of the Manitoba Grain Growers' Association, 10–13 January 1917.

109 Francis Marion Beynon, "Toleration," *CH-GGG*, 17 January 1917, 10.

110 *Guide* Special Correspondent, "Our Ottawa Letter," *GGG*, 23 May 1917, 31.

111 Keshen, *Propaganda and Censorship*, 66.

112 Francis Marion Beynon, "The Flag," *CH-GGG*, 13 June 1917, 9; editorial, "Make Conscription General," *GGG*, 23 May 1917, 5.

113 Editorial, "Make Conscription General," *GGG*, 23 May 1917, 5. See also editorials, "Corporate Tax Increased," *GGG*, 2 May 1917, 5, and "Distribute the Sacrifice," *GGG*, 30 May 1917, 5. On the MGGA, see "Manitoba Farmers' Parliament," *GGG*, 17 January 1917, 34, 40, 42. Francis Marion Beynon, "Money Should Be Conscripted First," *CH-GGG*, 14 July 1917, 9.

114 T.A. Crerar Fonds, Series II, Box 34, File Correspondence 15–31 May 1917, Crerar to J.J. Morrison. Secretary of the United Farmers of Ontario, 31 May 1917. Neither the *Guide* nor Beynon was entirely out of step with progressive thinkers. Even Sir Wilfrid Laurier, the federal opposition leader, and his Liberals, who were divided over conscription, also, at one point, suggested that there be a referendum before men were made to enlist in the military. The United Farmers of Ontario, among other groups, demanded it, as did western labour leaders and feminist pacifists such as Gertrude Richardson. Ramsay Cook, *The Politics of J.W. Dafoe and the Free Press* (Toronto: University of Toronto Press, 1963), 76; "U.F.O. on Conscription," *GGG*, 13 June 1917, 10; Socknat, *Witness against War*, 64; Roberts, *A Reconstructed World*, chapter 4.

115 Editorial, "Conscription and Patriotism," *GGG*, 6 June 1917, 5.

116 Editorial, "The Conscription Question," *GGG*, 27 June 1917, 5.

117 See, for example, Francis Marion Beynon, "Money Should Be Conscripted First," *CH-GGG*, 14 July 1917, 9, and her answers to Bert Sautne, "Take the Other Fellow's Life but I'll Keep My Money," *CH-GGG*, 27 June 1917, 9, 26; and to Walter Crowe, "Conscript Wealth Also," *CH-GGG*, 4 July 1917, 9.

118 Francis Marion Beynon, "Military Training," *CH-GGG*, 20 June 1917, 9. A relatively even-handed account of the NCWC meeting was written in Beynon's style but had no byline. "The National Council of Women," *GGG*, 20 June 1917, 8, 31. The resolutions were contained in a letter from Emily Cummings, vice-president of the NCWC, 9 July 1917. Copy in Violet McNaughton Papers, A1, E-41.

119 Francis Marion Beynon, "Just Suppose," *CH-GGG*, 6 June 1917, 9. After the public debate with McClung, Beynon had ended the discussion in her pages because, she said, it might discourage American families from moving to Manitoba, although it is not clear if she was being pressured by the Manitoba Immigration Department, or was just afraid it was causing too much dissension in suffrage ranks. After she left Winnipeg, she told her readers that she did not want her successor to have to

deal with the debates that had occurred among them when she was editor. F.M.B., "Concluding Discussion of Franchise," *CH-GGG*, 28 February 1917, 10; see, for example, Wolf Willow, "A Good Free Trader," republished in *CH-GGG*, 14 March 1917, 10; letter from S.E. Nodwell, "Another Word for the Foreign-Born," published in *CH-GGG*, 11 July 1917, 9; Francis Marion Beynon, "Explanation," *CH-GGG*, 8 August 1917, 9.

120 J.S. Woodsworth Papers, Volume 15, A. Vernon Thomas to J.S. Woodsworth, 28 June 1917.

121 Francis Marion Beynon, "Persecution for Originality," *CH-GGG*, 7 March 1917, 10.

122 Editorial, "Current Events—Freedom of Speech Imperilled," *The Voice*, 8 June 1917, 1; Cook, "Francis Marion Beynon," 200.

123 Francis Marion Beynon, "Freedom," *CH-GGG*, 20 June 1917, 9; J.S. Woodsworth Papers, Volume 15, A. Vernon Thomas to J.S. Woodsworth, 28 June 1917.

124 There is no evidence in federal records that the Chief Censor's office had warned Chipman about Beynon's columns; that she had been under the same secret service surveillance that targeted some left-wing individuals and groups, such as the Anti-Conscription League; or even that pro-war ruffians had threatened her. According to Keshen, Crerar actually helped protect most peace activists from prosecution. Cook, "Francis Marion Beynon," 207, n68; Keshan, *Propaganda and Censorship*, 67, 84–92; Roberts, "Women against War," 51, erroneously citing Socknat's Ph.D. dissertation, 125; Roberts, *A Reconstructed World*, 182–184. Neither Beynon nor her family members and associates mentioned her being threatened by anyone in any of their surviving letters and other documents.

125 There is no record of advertisers or readers demanding her dismissal in the records of the Public Press Limited or its parent company. After she left the *Guide*, one unhappy reader demanded that her replacement as women's editor stay out of politics, and especially refrain from defending enemy aliens. Crerar passed his letter along to Chipman with little comment. Crerar Fonds, Series II, Box 36, Correspondence for 1–15 August 1917, copy of 17 July 1917 letter from Tom Payne of La Riviere to Crerar, enclosed with letter from Crerar to Chipman, 13 August 1917.

126 CWPC Winnipeg Minute Book 1915–1922, minutes of 5 October 1916.

127 Francis Marion Beynon, "Follow the Gleam," *CH-GGG*, 2 May 1917, 10. The novel was Margaret Widdemer, *Why Not?* (New York: Hearst, 1916).

128 Francis Marion Beynon, "Goodbye," *CH-GGG*, 27 June 1917, 9. On the issue of recruiting single men first, see Francis Marion Beynon, "Penalizing Bachelorhood," *CH-GGG*, 12 January 1916, 10.

129 Her last column appeared in *CH-GGG*, 8 August 1917, 9.

130 Vernon Thomas may have written the letter in instalments. He gave the date of her arrival as 30 June, but dated this letter to J.S. Woodsworth 28 June 1917.

131 Editorials, "Conscription and Patriotism," *GGG*, 6 June 1917, 5; "A Square Deal All Round," *GGG*, 29 August 1917, 3; "The War and Rich Men," *GGG*, 5 September 1917, 8; "Stand of Farmers' Candidates," *GGG*, 10 October 1917, 5; "Sir Wilfrid Laurier's Manifesto," 14 November 1917, 3.

132 Francis Marion Beynon, "The Approaching Election," *CH-GGG*, 1 August 1917, 9.

133 *Guide* Special Correspondent, "Our Ottawa Letter," *GGG*, 11 July 1917, 4.

134 These items were not signed but written in her voice. "Difference" *CH-GGG*, 25 July 1917, 9; "The Human Leech," *CH-GGG*, 8 August 1917, 9.

135 Editorials, "Coalition Government," 6 October 1915, 6; "Distribute the Sacrifice," *GGG*, 30 May 1917, 5; "National Political Muddle" and *Guide* Special Correspondent, "Our Ottawa Letter," *GGG*, 6 June 1917, 24; editorials, "The Western Elections," *GGG*, 11 July 1917, 3; "The Liberal Opportunity," *GGG*, 18 July 1917, 5; "The Political Situation," *GGG*, 25 July 1917, 3; "The Big Convention," *GGG*, 1 August 1917, 3; *Guide*'s Special Correspondent, "Our Ottawa Letter," *GGG*, 1 August 1917, 4, 30. The same sentiments against partyism appeared on Beynon's page, but it is not

clear if this was a contribution from her, even though her replacement, Mary McCallum, had not yet started at the *Guide*. The column was signed Editor, Country Homemakers, *CH-GGG*, 18 July 1917, 9.

136 Donnelly, *Dafoe of the* Free Press, 79; Cook, *The Politics of J.W. Dafoe and the* Free Press, 77. Crerar Fonds, Series II, Box 34, Correspondence for 1–18 April 1917, Laurier to Crerar, 10 April 1917; Crerar to Laurier, 18 April 1917; Box 36, Correspondence for 1–15 August 1917, Crerar to Gordon Waldron and Crerar to John Bain, both on 3 August 1917; Crerar to H.W. Wood, 2 August 1917 and Wood to Crerar, 4 August 1917.

137 Editorial, "The War Election Franchise Act," *GGG*, 12 September 1917; see also editorial, "The War Election Franchise," *GGG*, 19 September 1917, 5. Editorials, "The Fusion Movement," *GGG*, 3 October 1917, 3; "Free Press Lectures Candidates" and "Stand of Farmers' Candidates," *GGG*, 10 October 1917, 5.

138 Chipman Fonds, File 5, Political Correspondence, January–March 1918, Chipman to T.A. Crerar, 30 January 1918.

139 T.A. Crerar Fonds, Series 11, Box 35, Correspondence file for 1–30 June 1917, C.W. Rowley to Crerar, 11 June 1917, and Crerar's response, 12 June 1917, regarding the Grain Board appointment; F.J. Colyer to Crerar, 17 June 1917, regarding Borden's cabinet deliberations. Correspondence file for 1–15 August 1917, Borden telegram to Crerar 15 August 1917 summoning him to Ottawa on "matters of highest importance." Box 36, Correspondence file for 15–31 August 1917, H.B. Cowan to Crerar, 23 August 1917, regarding media reports; Correspondence file for 1–15 October 1917, various telegrams regarding his appointment to and from Crerar's friends and associates. He was sworn in as Minister of Agriculture 12 October 1917. Box 37, Correspondence for 23–31 October 1917 holds several letters in which Crerar tells his correspondents that the more contentious planks of the farmers' platform, such as the tariff, will have to wait until the war is over. See, for example, Crerar to John L. Rooke, 30 October 1917.

140 Editorial, *GGG*, "Union Government and Farmers, " *GGG*, 24 October 1917, 3. See also editorials, "*Guide* and Union Government," *GGG*, 7 November 1917, 3, and "Support Farmers' Candidates," *GGG*, 21 November 1917, 5. Later, Chipman intimated in a letter to Crerar that they had not consulted the Public Press's management board before taking an editorial stance in support of Union government. Chipman Papers, Box 1, File 9, Chipman to Crerar, 29 March 1919.

141 It was a promise that was not always honoured at recruitment appeal tribunals, and a few months after the election, the government started drafting farmers' sons. Editorials, "Conscription and Production," *GGG*, 21 November 1917, 5, and "Conscripting Farm Labour," *GGG*, 9 January 1918, 3; Chipman Fonds, Box 1, Political Correspondence, File 6, Chipman to Crerar, 13 June 1918.

142 Editorial, "Union Government Program," *GGG*, 24 October 1917, 3.

143 Crerar Fonds, Series II, Box 37, Correspondence File for 15–22 October 1917, Margaret McWilliams to Crerar, 20 October 1917, saying she was not sure if she should speak for the "organized women" of the west or Winnipeg but she felt that they regarded the new coalition with hope and sympathy and would support and help him.

144 Beynon to McNaughton, 5 October 1917, McNaughton Papers, A1 E-23.

145 Crerar Fonds, Series II, Box 37, Correspondence File for 1–15 October 1917, J.B. Parker to Crerar, 16 August 1917; Crerar to Parker, 3 October 1917; Crerar to T.A. Springmann, 4 October 1917.

146 Beynon to McNaughton, 24 November 1917. McNaughton Papers, A1 D-1(1); Roberts, *A Reconstructed World*, 191–192. This was likely E. Austin Weir, who was in Winnipeg between 1913 and 1924, working for several western newspapers, including the *Grain Growers' Guide*. See, for example, E.A. Weir, "The Country Agent," *GGG*, 26 December 1917, 9. He later worked for CNR radio, the Canadian

Radio Broadcasting Commission and the Canadian Broadcasting Corporation. Library and Archives Canada, E. Austin Weir Fonds, R2327-0-5-E, Biography/Administrative History. Much later, when compiling his papers, he corresponded briefly with Lillian Beynon Thomas regarding one of her early plays and his family life. LBT Papers, File 3, Business Correspondence 1900–1960, Letter to LBT from Austin Weir, 16 May 1960, and her reply, 19 May 1960.

147 Francis Marion Beynon, "A Message of the Women Grain Growers of Western Canada," *The Voice*, 7 December 1917, 5. Cook has cited it as "A Message *to* the Women Grain Growers of Canada," but that is incorrect. Cook, "Francis Marion Beynon," 207, n72. Beynon wrote a similar column in the *Canadian Forward*, cited in Roberts, *A Reconstructed World*, 201–202.

148 Beynon to McNaughton, 11 January 1918, McNaughton Papers A1, D-1(1).

149 Editorials, "The Voice of the West" and "Farmers in Parliament," *GGG*, 26 December 1917, 3.

150 A.V. Thomas to J.S. Woodsworth, 17 December 1917. Thomas's letter to Woodsworth and Beynon's to Violet McNaughton bear the same address, 426 Stirling Place, Brooklyn, New York. Beynon to McNaughton, 24 November 1917 and 11 January 1918. McNaughton Papers A1, D-1(1). On McClung's American tours, see Hallett and Davis, *Firing the Heather*, chapter 6. McClung expressed her views regarding Laurier in an article she wrote just before the election, entitled "Loyalty," *GGG*, 5 December 1917, 18.

151 LBT Papers, File 5, unmarked clipping, "Winnipeg Women's Page Editor Is Writer of Play," c. 1932; File 3, R. Rocker to LBT, 16 August 1943, and LBT to Rocker, 10 February 1944; AH Each and Co. to LBT, 1 November 1946. McClung received the news of Vernon Thomas's death from Lillian herself. File 2, letter from Nellie L. (McClung) to Lillian Beynon Thomas, 14 September 1950.

152 Editorials, "The Voice of the West" and "Farmers in Parliament," *GGG*, 26 December 1917, 3.

153 Mary Kinnear, *A Female Economy: Women's Work in the Prairie Provinces, 1870–1970* (Montreal; Kingston: McGill-Queen's University Press, 1998), 143–150.

154 Cook, *The Politics of J.W. Dafoe and the* Free Press, 81–83; CWPC Winnipeg Minute Book 1915–1922, minutes of 22 November and 13 December 1917. Reel M613, pamphlets and clippings. Cook, "Francis Marion Beynon," 200.

155 Both women's names appeared on the original membership list for 1917, but were not on the revised list compiled for the annual meeting later in the year. CWPC Membership lists for 1917 in 1915–1922 Minute Book. The closest local branch to New York was the one in Toronto.

156 Cook, "Francis Marion Beynon," 207, n68, citing from CWPC Winnipeg Branch Minute Book, 1915–1922, minutes of 20 September 1917.

157 CWPC Winnipeg Branch Minute Book, 1915–1922, minutes of 20 September 1917; 4, 8, and 11 October 1917; and special business meeting to deal with membership, 25 October 1917. See also CWPC Winnipeg Branch Minute Book, 1915–1922, minutes of 10 March 1921; national secretary's annual report for 1920–21, n.d., but attached to clipping, "Miss Cornell Made President of Winnipeg Press Women's Club," 26 May 1921. On the origins of the press club's railway jaunts, see Lang, *Women Who Made the News*, chapter 3.

158 Lillian Thomas was back in the club as a member by 1928 and also served on the CWPC's executive in later years. See Microfilm M612, papers of the CWPC Winnipeg Branch Minute Book, 1922–29 and 1930–1940 minute book records. LBT Papers, File 5, Newspaper Clippings and Theatre Programs c. 1932–1946, "Playwright Honoured at Reception," *Winnipeg Tribune*, 30 April 1932 says CWPC gave her a reception after first night of "Under the Maples." Copy in Scrapbook, File 7. File 3, Business Correspondence 1900–1960, telegrams from E. Cora Hind and Miriam Green Ellis wishing her luck in 1933 Dominion Drama Festival in Ottawa on behalf of their female colleagues at the *Free Press*.

159 Francis Marion Beynon's own introduction to *Aleta Dey* (London: C.W. Daniel, 1919). Hicks, Introduction to *Aleta Dey* (1988) and "Francis Beynon and the *Guide*." Oral family history that "Donald" (no last name given) was Beynon's fiancé should be confirmed by other evidence, which in this case does not seem to exist. Hicks interprets Beynon, writing in her column on wartime grief, as making a personal comment, while I read it as a more general one. In October 1916, at Beynon's request, the press club offered condolences to a former member whose brother died in the war, but not to Beynon herself. When Violet McNaughton quizzed her on her love life in a private letter less than two years after her fiancé supposedly died, Beynon replied that there was no romantic interest in her life and did not mention a lost love. The journalist also told her readers that it would be too personal to discuss her private circumstances in her columns. Hicks, "Francis Beynon and the *Guide*," 48–49; Canadian Women's Press Club Papers, Winnipeg Branch, MG 10 A1, Minute Book 1915–1922, minutes of 5 October 1916; Saskatchewan Archives Board, Violet McNaughton Papers, A, File D-1(1), Beynon to McNaughton, 11 January 1918. Francis Marion Beynon, "Goodbye," *CH-GGG*, 27 June 1917, 9. Cook spoke to Beynon's brother but does not mention her love life. Cook, "Francis Marion Beynon," 205, n10. McKay discusses *Aleta Dey* as a pacifist tract, more than as autobiography, in his *Reasoning Otherwise*, 311–314.
160 A.V. Thomas to J.S. Woodsworth, 5 August 1917.
161 Beynon to McNaughton, 17 March 1919, McNaughton Papers, A1 D-1(1).
162 Beynon to McNaughton, 5 October 1917. McNaughton Papers, A1 E-23.
163 Hicks, "Francis Marion Beynon and the *Guide*," 48; preface to *Aleta Dey*; LBT Papers, File 2, letter from Charles Thomas to LBT dated 19 May 1951 and letter from LBT to Charles Thomas, 10 June 1951. CWPC Winnipeg Branch, Box 6, Scrapbook 1958–1968, clippings of two obituaries for Lillian Beynon Thomas, 3 September 1961.
164 Roberts, "Women's Peace Activism in Canada," 276–277.
165 R.R. Warne, "Nellie McClung and Peace," in Williamson and Gorham, *Up and Doing*, 36, and Janice Fiamengo, "A Legacy of Ambivalence: Responses to Nellie McClung," *Journal of Canadian Studies*, 34:4, Winter 1999/2000, 4.
166 For a useful historiographical overview, see Nancy Forestell, "Mrs. Canada Goes Global: Canadian First Wave Feminism Revisited," *Atlantis*, 30:1, 2005, 7–20.
167 Chipman Fonds, Political Correspondence, File 6, an exchange of letters between Chipman and Crerar, 18, 23, 24 April 1918.

Chapter 4

1 Library and Archives Canada (hereafter LAC), Marjorie McEnaney Papers, R2389-09-E, Vol. 2, Long, Elizabeth—Letters to M. McEnaney, File 4, Long to McEnaney with copy of her reply to Jean Morrison, 6 October 1961, her emphasis; copy of McEnaney to Long, 12 October 1961. Long believed that her successor, Helen James, "threw out all the historical material I was saving when she moved into my office as a surprise for me," but offered no evidence for her accusation. McEnaney Papers, Vol. 2, Long, Elizabeth—Letters to M. McEnaney, File 2, Long to McEnaney, 17 November 1966. Late in life, she privately claimed that James masterminded a takeover of Women's Interests from her, again without evidence. LAC CBC Papers, RG 41, Box 405, File 23-1-6, Elizabeth Long to William Macdonald, 11 April 1970. At the 1953 conference of CBC Talks Supervisors, Long and McEnaney suggested that the CBC keep recordings of important and historical events. McEnaney Papers, Vol. 2, File: CBC Talks and Public Affairs—Reports and Minutes of some meetings and conferences 1951–58, minutes of CBC Talks and Public Affairs conference, 15–19 June 15, 1953, 5.
2 Margaret Howes's interview with Jean Bruce was done in segments over time as ISN 304774, n.d., October and 20 November 1980; and ISN 304776, 10 March 1981.

They will be treated here as one interview. Marjorie McEnaney interview with Jean Bruce, ISN 304779, 5 March 1981; Margaret Colpitts ("Joan Marshall"), interview with Jean Bruce, ISN 304762, November 1980; Florence Bird ("Anne Francis") interview with Jean Bruce, ISN 304761, LAC Canadian Broadcasting Corporation Head Office Collection, R1190-3-X-E, Neil Morrison interview with Alison Taylor, ISN 265660.

3   Josephine Langham, "Tuning In: Canadian Radio Resources," *Archivaria*, 9, Winter 1979–1980, 105–124.

4   McEnaney Papers, Vol. 2, Long, Elizabeth—Letters to M. McEnaney, File 4, Long to McEnaney, 21 February 1962.

5   Mary Vipond, *Listening In: The First Decade of Canadian Broadcasting, 1922–1932* (Montreal; Kingston: McGill-Queen's University Press, 1992); Vipond, "The Canadian Broadcasting Commission in the 1930s: How Canada's First Public Broadcaster Negotiated 'Britishness,'" in *Canada and the British World: Culture, Migration and Identity*, ed. Phillip Buckner and R. Douglas Francis (Vancouver: UBC Press, 2006), 270–287; Vipond, "Going Their Own Way: The Relationship between the Canadian Radio Broadcasting Commission and the BBC, 1933–1936," *Media History*, 15:1, 2009, 71–83; Vipond, "Censorship in a Liberal State: Regulating Talk on Canadian Radio in the Early 1930s," *Historical Journal of Film, Radio and Television*, 30:1, March 2010, 75–94. The experiences of the more recent generations of women broadcasters have been the focus of the corporation's equity reports, as well as scholarly work. *Report of the CBC Task Force on the Status of Women* (Toronto: Canadian Broadcasting Corporation, 1975); Barbara M. Freeman, *The Satellite Sex: The Media and Women's Issues in English Canada, 1966–1971* (Waterloo, ON: Wilfrid Laurier University Press, 2001), chapter 2; Gertrude J. Robinson, *Gender, Journalism and Equity: Canadian, U.S. and European Perspectives* (Crestkill, NJ: Hampton Press, 2005).

6   Anne F. MacLellan, "Women, Radio Broadcasting and the Depression: A 'Captive' Audience from Household Hints to Story Time and Serials," *Women's Studies*, 37:6, 2008, 616–633.

7   Michele Hilmes, "Desired and Feared: Women's Voices in Radio History," in *Television, History and American Culture: Feminist Critical Essays*, ed. Mary Beth Haralovich and Lauren Rabinovitz (Durham, NC; London: Duke University Press, 1999), 17–35; MacLellan, "Women, Radio Broadcasting and the Depression." On the CBC, for example, commercialized serials aimed at female audiences were not handled by the Talks department.

8   CBC Papers, RG 41, Box 405, File 23-1-6, Elizabeth Long's CBC memoir, chapter 5, "Women Daily Commentators Meet."

9   Joan Sangster, Introduction, Part 4, "Women's Activism and the State," in *Framing Our Past: Canadian Women's History in the Twentieth Century*, ed. Sharon Anne Cook, Lorna R. McLean and Kate O'Rourke (Montreal; Kingston: McGill-Queens University Press, 2001), 201–211.

10   LAC CBC Papers, RG 41, Box 405, Box 23-1-6, Elizabeth Long to W.A Macdonald, 15 September and 5 October 1967, and 11 April 1970; Long's memoir, 12 chapters.

11   Elizabeth Long interviews with Marjorie McEnaney, ISNs 248134, 248152, c. 1960; Elizabeth Long interview with Shirley Brett (Foley), ISN 267606, 13 July 1954. Long, who later told McEnaney that she was barely getting by on her pension, insisted on being paid for the seven-minute *Matinee* interview, which was edited down to three and a half minutes for the program. She received $25. McEnaney Papers, Vol. 2, Long, Elizabeth—Letters to M. McEnaney, File 1, Long to McEnaney, "Sunday," n.d. c. 1966; File 4, copy of letter from Long to Jean Morrison, 6 October 1961; File 2, exchange of letters between Long and McEnaney, 12 and 15 October 1961; LAC CBC, RG 41, Box 405, file 23-1-6, memo from producer Gail MacDonald in Toronto to Ken Black in Winnipeg, arranging the interview with the "prickly" Long,

11 October 1961. LAC Jean Hunter Morrison Papers, R1859-0-X-E,Vol. 2, File: CBC 25th Anniversary 1961, women's programming document for *Matinee*, 2 November 1961, script with audio cues but no transcript.

12 LAC, Jean Bruce Fonds, R5638-0-8-E; Jean Bruce, "Women in CBC Radio Talks and Current Affairs," *Canadian Oral History Association Journal*, 5:1, 1981–82, 7–18. LAC Elspeth Chisholm Fonds, R4875-0-7-E and R4875-1-9-E. Morrison interview with Taylor; Alison Taylor, "Window on the World: A History of Women in CBC Radio Talks and Public Affairs, 1936–1966," Master of Arts thesis, Carleton University, 1985.

13 Joan Sangster, "Telling Our Stories: Feminist Debates and the Use of Oral History," *Women's History Review*, 3:1, 1994, 5–28. Thomas L. Charlton, Lois E. Myers and Rebecca Sharpless, eds., *Thinking about Oral History: Theories and Applications* (New York; Toronto: Altamira Press, 2008).

14 The CBC commissioned her to do this project, and she asked several people to help her remember the details, including her first supervisor, Hugh Morrison. LAC Hugh Morrison Papers, R2207-0-X-E,Volume 7, File: Correspondence with Elizabeth Long 1967–68, exchange of letters between Long and Morrison, 1967–1968. LAC CBC Papers, RG41, Box 405, File 23-1-6, Elizabeth Long to W.A. Macdonald, 15 September and 5 October 1967, and 11 April 1970; the unsigned note, her memoir, and a copy of Canadian Broadcasting Corporation, "Pass the Orchids, Please!" *CBC Radio Magazine*, 12:3, Ottawa, April 1956, 6–7.

15 LAC Elizabeth Long Papers, R2179-0-2-E and University of Waterloo Library, Doris Lewis Rare Books Room, Elizabeth Long Papers, WA14; LAC Marjorie McEnaney Papers, especially Volume 2, correspondence from Elizabeth Long, Files 1–4. See also Marjorie McEnaney, *Who Stole the Cakes? A Memoir by Marjorie Winspear McEnaney* (Erin, ON: Boston Mills Press, 1981).

16 LAC Florence Bayard Bird Papers, R4801-0-0-E, and Florence Bird, *Anne Francis: An Autobiography* (Toronto: Clark, Irwin, 1974); LAC Mattie Rotenberg Papers, R4878-0-9-E; University of British Columbia Library, Special Collections, Ellen Harris Papers. Margaret Colpitts's papers were held by her family, with copies in the private collection of CBC Ottawa broadcaster Julie Ireton, who is married to her grandson. The family has arranged to deposit them with the Provincial Archives of Nova Scotia.

17 LAC Neil Morrison Papers, R2551-0-4-E; Ernest L. Bushnell Papers, R6602-0-X-E; Rene Landry Papers, R6202-6-4-F; Hugh Morrison Papers, R2207-0-X-E; Jean Hunter Morrison Papers, R1859-0-X-E; CBC Papers, RG41.

18 Provincial Archives of Manitoba, Canadian Women's Press Club Papers, Microfilm M612, papers of the CWPC Winnipeg Branch, Box 1, Minute Books 1922–1929, 1930–1940; LAC Media Club of Canada Papers (Canadian Women's Press Club), R2800-0-3-E; copies of Women's Press Club of Toronto Papers, University of Waterloo Library, Doris Lewis Rare Books Room, GA94.

19 CBC, RG 41, Box 405, Elizabeth Long to William Macdonald, 11 April 1970.

20 The birthdate here is from Province of Manitoba, Vital Statistics Agency, online records for Elizabeth Dundas Long, her sister Janet Evelyn Long and brothers Thomas Mackay Long and Alfred George Long. Her mother was Margaret Mackay. Elizabeth Long's obituary named her father as Alfred J. Long. "Deaths—Elizabeth Dundas Long," *Winnipeg Free Press*, 11 January 1978, 57. The same obituary appeared in the *Winnipeg Tribune*, 11 January 1978, 18.

21 McEnaney Papers, Vol. 2, Long, Elizabeth—Letters to M. McEnaney 1962–1965, File 3, Long to McEnaney, 10 October 1962.

22 McEnaney Papers, Vol. 2, File: Long, Elizabeth—Profiles, clipping of Thelma Le Cocq, "Profile: Elizabeth Long," *Food for Thought*, March 1958, 262–266. Le Cocq was identified in the article as a freelance journalist and advertising copywriter and a long-term friend of Long.

23 McEnaney Papers, Vol. 2, Long, Elizabeth—Letters to M. McEnaney 1962–1965, File 3, Long to McEnaney, 10 October 1962.

24 McEnaney Papers, Vol. 2, Long, Elizabeth—Letters to M. McEnaney 1962–1965, File 3, Long to McEnaney, 13 June 1964.

25 "Deaths—Elizabeth Dundas Long," *Winnipeg Free Press*, 11 January 1978, 57. Wesley College, then affiliated with the University of Manitoba, was later incorporated into the University of Winnipeg. See "MHS Centennial Organization: University of Winnipeg," The Manitoba Historical Society, at http://www.mhs.mb.ca/docs/organization/universitywinnipeg.shtml, 18 March 2009.

26 Long interview with McEnaney, ISN 248152.

27 McEnaney Papers, Vol. 2, Long, Elizabeth—Letters to M. McEnaney, File 1, Long to McEnaney, 20 November 1967; see also File 3, Long to McEnaney, 10 October 1962. One CBC colleague later mentioned that she may have lost a fiancé in the trenches but likely did not know the full story. Mattie Rotenberg interview with Jean Bruce, ISN 304778, March 1981.

28 McEnaney Papers, Vol. 2, Long, Elizabeth—Letters to M. McEnaney, File 3, Long to McEnaney, 13 February, c. 1964.

29 Le Cocq, "Profile," 262; CWPC Winnipeg Branch, Box 1, Minute Books 1922–29; Long's CBC memoir, chapter 1.

30 CWPC Winnipeg Branch, Box 1, Minute Books 1922–29, minutes of 19 April 1922 and attached, undated clipping regarding its Christmas party in December 1921.

31 CWPC Winnipeg Branch, Box 1, Minute Books 1922–29, 1930–1940.

32 Marjory Lang, *Women Who Made the News: Female Journalists in Canada, 1880–1945* (Montreal; Kingston: McGill-Queen's University Press, 1999), 257; Kennethe M. Haig, *Brave Harvest: The Life Story of E. Cora Hind* (Toronto: Thomas Allen, 1945).

33 CWPC Winnipeg Branch, Box 1, Minute Books 1922–29, 1930–1940.

34 McEnaney Papers, Vol. 2, Long, Elizabeth—Letters to M. McEnaney, File 2, Long to McEnaney, 3 December 1966.

35 LAC Elizabeth Long Papers, Miscellaneous Correspondence, Cora Hind to Elizabeth Long, 19 December 1936. McEnaney Papers, Vol. 2, Long, Elizabeth—Letters to M. McEnaney, File 1, Long to McEnaney, 14 March 1967. In a column she wrote at the time, Long noted that most women's page editors lacked the time and staff to think up new and interesting ideas, mainly because they were constantly expected "to interview the public." Elizabeth Long, "Woman's Page Aid to Fine Front Page," *C.W.P.C. Newspacket*, 2 November 1936, 4.

36 CBC Papers, RG41, Box 405, File 23-1-6, Long's CBC memoir, chapter 1; photo of Long and announcement that she had left Winnipeg for the CBC, *C.W.P.C. Newspacket*, 1 February 1939, 1; "CBC Figure Is Honored at Reception," *Globe and Mail*, 24 March 1956, 19. On Whitton, who later became the first female mayor of Ottawa, see P.T. Rooke and R.L. Schnell, *No Bleeding Heart: Charlotte Whitton a Feminist on the Right* (Vancouver: University of British Columbia Press, 1987).

37 In 1933 the Canadian-born Murray, who had headed the BBC's publicity department, was appointed the CBC's general manager because it was felt he understood the place it should take as a Canadian public network in a field dominated by commercial broadcasters and American programming. Vipond, "Going Their Own Way," 76–77, 80–81.

38 Morrison interview with Taylor; McEnaney interview with Bruce; Helen James interview with Bruce, ISN 304767, October 1980. Hugh Morrison, a previous Talks supervisor, likely had a say in the decision to hire her. He travelled the country to interview prospects, such as Mary Grannan of Fredericton, N.B., whom he hired to do the children's programs. "New Member from Maritimes Has a Variety of Gifts," *C.W.P.C. Newspacket*, 1 May 1939, 2.

39 Marjorie Minnes, "What Happened at the Triennial," *C.W.P.C. Newspacket*, 1 September 1938, 3. Long headed the conference hospitality committee. Eva Calder,

"Committee Plans for Your Pleasure," *C.W.P.C. Newspacket*, 2 May 1938, 2. The offer could have come from the first Talks supervisor, Douglas Buchanan. Taylor, "Window on the World," 63.

40 Le Cocq, "Profile," 262.

41 She thought women, and particularly Queen Elizabeth II, were better suited to be heads of state with diplomatic duties than were men. Long interview with McEnaney, ISN 248134, c. 1960. From the evidence in Long's papers, I believe this interview actually took place in Toronto in July or August 1962. McEnaney Papers, Vol. 2, File 4, Long to McEnaney, 25 August 1962. Le Cocq, "Profile," 262–266; Media Club of Canada Papers, Vol. 12, copy of Kathy Hassard, "Clubs May Waste Time but They Get Results," *Vancouver Sun*, 5 August, no year, 2, a profile of Long after she retired.

42 Vipond, "Censorship in a Liberal State," 77, adopting a discussion of liberalism in Canada from McKay, "The Liberal Order Framework: A Prospect for the Reconnaissance of Canadian History," *Canadian Historical Review*, 81:4, 2000, 617–645; Vipond, *The Mass Media in Canada*, 3rd ed. (Toronto: Lorimer, 2000), 40–42. On early broadcast content in Canada, see Vipond, *Listening In*, chapter 3.

43 In 1941, the Canadian rate of married women in the workforce was 4 percent, representing 12 percent of the female total; a decade later, it was 11 percent, or 30 percent of the female total; and by 1962, the rate was 22 percent, or almost half of the female total. Veronica Strong-Boag, "Canada's Wage-Earning Wives and the Construction of the Middle-Class, 1945–1960," *Journal of Canadian Studies/Revue d'étude canadiennes*, 29:3, Autumn 1994, 7.

44 MacLellan, "Women, Radio Broadcasting and the Depression." "Martha Deane" was the popular Mary Margaret McBride, who later broadcast under her own name. Susan Ware, *It's One o'Clock and Here Is Mary Margaret McBride: A Radio Biography* (New York: New York University Press, 2005).

45 LAC Kate Aitken Papers, R4490-0-0-E, Vols. 5, 6, 7, CFRB Scripts. Claire Wallace started at CFRB, but was broadcasting a regular home-front commentary "They Tell Me," paid for by the federal government, on the CBC by 1942. She later returned to CFRB. University of Waterloo Library, Doris Lewis Rare Books Room, Claire Wallace Papers, WA16.

46 MacLellan, "Women, Radio Broadcasting and the Depression," 629–632.

47 Le Cocq, "Profile," 263; Colpitts interview with Bruce.

48 Production staff functions were considered separate at the time, although they sometimes overlapped. The planners or organizers gathered the people and information key to a particular program, and vetted the script, while the producers were in charge of studio direction as it went to air. The broadcasters narrated the script, hosted the program and interviewed guests. In 1944 the CBC divided its English-language network in two: the Dominion network (consisting of one CBC station and 34 affiliates) and the Trans-Canada network (six CBC stations and 28 affiliates). Its international shortwave service began in 1945. Ross Eaman, "Canadian Broadcasting Corporation," revised by Sasha Yusufali, *Canadian Encyclopedia*, http://www.thecanadianencyclopedia.com, 30 March 2009.

49 Long's CBC memoir, chapter 1, "I Join the CBC Staff," 1.

50 Elizabeth Long, "From Press to Radio! Why?" *C.W.P.C. Newspacket*, 1 September 1939, 3.

51 The quote is a paraphrase of her remarks during a visit to CWPC's Ottawa branch. Alison Hardy, "Ottawa Girls Find Life Easier with Less [sic] Gowns," *C.W.P.C. Newspacket*, 1 Feb 1939, 4.

52 Le Cocq, "Profile," 262; Morrison interview with Bruce.

53 McEnaney interview with Bruce; James interview with Bruce; Dolores MacFarlane interview with anonymous man on behalf of Bruce ISN 304772, February 1981. See also Le Cocq, "Profile," 262; Hassard, "Clubs May Waste Time."

54 Shirley Brett Foley interview with Elspeth Chisholm, ISN 9504, 4 August 1983.

55 Long interview with McEnaney, ISN 248134.

56 McEnaney Papers, Long, Elizabeth—Letters to M. McEnaney, File 1, Long to McEnaney, 2 April 1967; McEnaney interview with Bruce.

57 McEnaney Papers, Long, Elizabeth—Letters to M. McEnaney, File 2, Long to McEnaney, 3 December 1966. In her CBC memoir, she gives a similar but less acerbic version, adding that the Montreal staff, instead of ignoring her, became her friends after that. Long's CBC memoir, chapter 3, "Learning What Radio Is About."

58 Before arriving at the CBC, Morrison had worked with the Canadian Association of Adult Education, one of several organizations that provided advice, information, participation and feedback from their radio listeners' groups on the various issues of the day. He had also written scripts for listener participation programs in the Farm Broadcast Department, among other duties. Neil Morrison interview with Jean Bruce, ISN 304763, November 1980; Morrison interview with Taylor; LAC Neil Morrison Papers, Vols. 1–2; 4–6 and 10 document his supervision of Talks and Public Affairs; Vipond, *The Mass Media in Canada*, 40.

59 Morrison interview with Bruce.

60 McEnaney Papers, Vol. 2, Long, Elizabeth—Letters to M. McEnaney, File 1, Long to McEnaney, "Thursday," c. March–April 1967.

61 CBC RG 41, Vol. 405, 11 April 1970, Long to Bill Macdonald.

62 Morrison interview with Bruce.

63 Neil Morrison Papers, Vol. 6, File: Correspondence and memos re: staff January–December 1944, Morrison to Ira Dilworth, B.C. Regional Representative, 28 January 1944, regarding producer Ada McGreer. Long had complained before that McGreer did not consult with her. File: Policy re: internal organization 1939–61, 24 June 1943, memo from E. Long. Morrison recommended reassigning her. File: Correspondence and Memos re: Staff 1945, Morrison to the Director General of Programmes, 18 January 1945.

64 Neil Morrison Papers, Vol. 10, File: Programming and policy, Public Affairs Department 1944, Morrison to Joan Dangelzer, Montreal, 17 May 1944.

65 Neil Morrison interview with Bruce; Morrison interview with Taylor. Harris Papers, Box 13, Folder 13–10, Long to Harris, 19 May 1947. Neil Morrison Papers, Vol. 4, File: Correspondence and memos re: staff 1945, 19 April 1945, Morrison to Helen Magill, Winnipeg; File: Correspondence and memos re: staff as National Supervisor, Talks and Public Affairs 1953, David Walker in Winnipeg to Neil Morrison, undated.

66 Morrison interview with Bruce.

67 James interview with Bruce. James did speak out against discrimination in the CBC and, partly because of it, eventually quit working there, as did several other women. Bruce, "Women in CBC Radio Talks," 17–18; Taylor, "Window on the World," 88–89, and chapter 5.

68 Hilmes writes that this was the case on American commercial stations. Hilmes, "Desired and Feared," 27–28.

69 Howes interview with Bruce.

70 Hilmes is including serials as well as information programming here. Hilmes, "Desired and Feared," 29.

71 Nicole Morgan, *The Equality Game: Women in the Federal Public Service, 1908–1987* (Ottawa: Canadian Advisory Council on the Status of Women, 1988).

72 Based on 1945 data. Neil Morrison Papers, Vol. 5, File: Supervisor, Talks and Public Affairs Correspondence re: position 1945–49, letter of complaint from Morrison to management, marked 1945, complaining that he made $400 less than his predecessor, and was making only $300 more than the $3000 Long made. R.P. Landry to Morrison, 20 June 1945, saying that the Labour Board had approved a new salary structure, giving him a raise to $4410 a year.

73 CBC, "Pass the Orchids, Please!" 7.

74 Brett Foley interview with Chisholm.

75 Le Cocq, "Profile," 264. LAC Neil Morrison Papers, Vol. 10, File: Women's Talks, Programming, n.d. 1944–54, Long to Morrison, 16 February 1948, noting the lobbying attempts to get one Toronto broadcaster higher pay.

76 James interview with Bruce. The commentators' freelance pay rates seemed to vary a great deal depending on the years concerned and the length and frequency of the broadcasts. Colpitts recalled initially being paid $30 during the war for five 15-minute programs per week, but according to Morrison's records, she and Ethelwyn Hobbes both made $50. Colpitts interview with Bruce; Neil Morrison Papers, File: Talks Department Budget 1943–48. Ellen Harris, who had three 15-minute programs and two 5-minute ones per week, made $55 per week in 1948. Harris Papers, Box 4, Folder 4-22, March 1948, précis slip attached to a Harris script for the CBC Talks Archives. It appears commentators were paid separately for single items sent to the network. Harris Papers, Box 13, Folder 13-9, a Talks Archives record of $10 payment for a 13-minute interview script on immunization with attached script, 3 October 1945. Florence Bird (a.k.a. Anne Francis) normally received $40 for five 3-minute women's commentaries. James interview with Bruce; Brett Foley was uncertain but thought she might have made $25 a week as a beginner in 1949 and $100 per week when she left in 1958. Brett Foley interview with Chisholm. In contrast, Claire Wallace said she made $65 a week for five 15-minute commentaries over CFRB in 1936, which had on-air advertisements. During the war, when she worked full time for the government of Canada on a home-front program, aired over the CBC, she received $170 per week, partly because her work involved extensive travel. A raise to $200, which her critics considered unwarranted during wartime, resulted in a national controversy that her career barely survived. University of Waterloo Claire Wallace Papers, W16, File 172: "The Affair Financial" and File 196: Scrapbook 1952, copy of Claire Wallace, "The Mike in My Life," *Chatelaine*, March 1952. Her scripts and other Second World War material are in Files 1942–49 and File 171: Scrapbook, "Travels across Canada: Broadcasting for National War Finance 1942–1944."

77 Jennifer A. Stephen, "Balancing Equality for the Post-War Woman: Demobilizing Canada's Women Workers after World War Two," *Atlantis*, 32:1, 2007, 122–132.

78 On the debate in Canada's magazines on this issue, see Strong-Boag, "Canada's Wage-Earning Wives," 5–25.

79 Bruce, "Women in CBC Radio Talks"; Taylor, "Window on the World," chapter 5.

80 LAC Long Papers, File: Profiles, Le Cocq, "Profile," 263. As a newspaper woman, she had supported all the usual women's features, including social news, as long as they were well written and interesting. Long, "Woman's Page Aid."

81 McEnaney interview with Bruce.

82 McEnaney interview with Bruce.

83 Long Waterloo Papers, W14, File 15, Speeches, scripts, etc. by Elizabeth Long, her memo to commentators regarding Simone de Beauvoir, 15 September 1953. De Beauvoir, who visited several Communist countries starting in 1955, was intrigued with communism, and supportive of its ideals, but was not blind to its faults. Simone de Beauvoir, *The Second Sex* (New York: Knopf, 1952) and *All Said and Done* (New York: Putman, 1974). Communism was a pressing issue during the McCarthy era on both sides of the border. Richard Cavell, "Introduction: The Cultural Production of Canada's Cold War," in *Love, Hate and Fear in Canada's Cold War*, ed. Richard Cavell (Toronto: University of Toronto Press, 2004), 3–32; also Reg Whitaker and Gary Marcus, *Cold War Canada: The Making of a National Insecurity State, 1945–1957* (Toronto: University of Toronto Press, 1994).

84 Long passed consumer news on to her commentators; for example, Harris Papers, Box 4, Folder 4-4, 26 November 1947, program script #378, encouraging listeners to join the new Canadian Association of Consumers, "created out of the demand of the women themselves." Box 13, Folder 13-11, 3 January 1950, memo from Long

regarding a House of Commons debate on truth in commodities advertising. Canada's first Housewives Consumers Association was decidedly left wing and the target of an anti-communist media campaign in the 1950s. See Julie Guard, "Canadian Citizens or Dangerous Foreign Women? Canada's Radical Consumer Movement 1947–1950," in *Sisters or Strangers? Immigrant, Ethnic and Racialized Women in Canadian History*, ed. Marlene Epp, Franca Iacovetta and Frances Swyripa (Toronto: University of Toronto Press, 2004), 161–189. Canadian historians tend to treat the Consumers Association critically as being more liberal than left-wing, although it included members of both persuasions. Joan Sangster, "Consuming Issues: Women on the Left, Political Protest and the Organization of Homemakers, 1920–1960," in Cook, McLean and O'Rourke, *Framing Our Past*, 246; Joy Parr and Gunilla Ekberg, "Mrs. Consumer and Mrs. Keynes in Postwar Canada and Sweden," *Gender and History*, 8:2, August 1996, 212–230. On early American consumerism in the context of commercial radio, see Kathy M. Newman, "Poisons, Potions, and Profits: Radio Rebels and the Origins of the Consumer Movement," in *Radio Reader: Essays in the Cultural History of Radio*, ed. Michele Hilmes and Jason Loviglio (New York: Routledge, 2002), 157–181.

85 The *C.W.P.C. Newspacket* ran news roundups from various branches that mention Long and her commentators among other members. Long was active in the Toronto CWPC, giving several talks on radio. See the editorial, "Our Radio Issue," *C.W.P.C. Newspacket*, 1 May 1940, 2; Marjorie Minnes, "1940 Regional Conference Under C.W.P.C. Auspices Is Voted Best on Record," and "Toronto Branch Shares Quarters Two Other Groups," *C.W.P.C. Newspacket*, 1 August 1940, 1, 2; Beryl Cameron, "Clubhouse in the Wind for Toronto," *C.W.P.C. Newspacket*, March 1949, 3. Long was a member of the national CWPC Memorial Award Committee in 1943. "Memorial Award," *C.W.P.C. Newspacket*, November 1942, 1, 4. The Maritimes commentator, Margaret Colpitts, was a member of several organizations, including the CWPC. Colpitts interview with Bruce; Eileen C. Cushy, "Celebrates Golden Jubilee," *C.W.P.C. Newspacket*, March 1949, 4; Ellen Harris joined the Vancouver branch. Phyllis Nemetz Snyder, "'Hang' Member Vancouver Club, but Honor Her," *C.W.P.C. Newspacket*, October 1948, 3.

86 Records of correspondence between Long and the leaders of these associations can be found in LAC CBC Papers, RG 41 Vols. 178, 179, Trans-Canada Matinee, File 11-18-1 International Council of Women; File 11-18-2 National Council of Women; File 11-18-2-2 Canadian Association of Consumers; File 11-18-2-3 Programmes; File 11-18-2-4 Programmes—Women's Interests Trans-Canada Matinee; Long Waterloo Papers; McEnaney Papers, Long, Elizabeth—Letters to M. McEnaney, File 1, Long to McEnaney, 2 April 1967.

87 Morrison interview with Bruce; Morrison interview with Taylor. This policy is documented in Neil Morrison Papers, Vols. 1–6, 10. In one letter, before he became her supervisor, Long cautioned him to side-step the rivalries among these associations when asking them to help plan programs for women's listening groups, and suggested the CBC should formulate a policy. LAC Neil Morrison Papers, Vol. 1, File: Correspondence, chronological January–May 1940, Long to Morrison, 4 April 1940. See also Vol. 2, File: Correspondence, chronological 1944, 7 June 1944, Morrison to Maud Ferguson, Ottawa, regarding women's groups there; 10 July 1944, Joan Dangelzer to Morrison, about her work organizing Montreal women's groups. File: Correspondence, Chronological 1945, Morrison to Helen Magill, 5 February 1945, regarding a radio program organized for the Local Council of Women in Winnipeg. File: Correspondence, Chronological 1945, Morrison to the CBC chairman 3 June 1946 regarding Long's success in having several national women's groups declare their appreciation of the CBC.

88 James interview with Bruce.

89 N.E.S. Griffiths, *The Splendid Vision: Centennial History of the National Council of Women of Canada* (Ottawa: Carleton University Press, 1993), 228–229. Long

served as vice-president of both organizations. Long Waterloo papers, Inventory entry. Margaret Colpitts, Florence Bird and Elizabeth Long all served terms as convenor of the NCWC's Arts and Letters Committee. McEnaney Papers, Long, Elizabeth—Letters to M. McEnaney, File 4, Long to McEnaney, 28 August 1957; File 2, Long to McEnaney, 16 January 1967. At different times, Colpitts also served as the NCWC's national chair for publicity and as chair of its Trades and Professions Committee, and as the president of the Nova Scotia Council of Women. She also attended the 1957 meeting of the International Council of Women in Montreal as a Canadian delegate. Long Waterloo Papers, Box 84-131, undated biographical typescripts about Colpitts, and Box 132-175, File 42, ICW conference, list of delegates. Long Waterloo Papers, Box 132-175, File: Catherine MacIver, copy of "CBC Talks Producer," *Regina Leader-Post*, 21 April 1947.

90 Conferring with women's groups was in line with government policy at the time, which found a place in print as well as broadcast media. See Barbara M. Freeman, "Mother and Son: Gender, Class and War Propaganda in Canada, 1939–1945," *American Journalism*, Special Issue on World War II, 12:3, Summer 1995, 260–275.

91 LAC Neil Morrison Papers, Vol. 10, File: CBC programming, policy and scheduling, n.d. 1940–45, clipping of laudatory editorial on women's programming, *Winnipeg Free Press*, 22 December 1943.

92 Long's CBC memoir, chapter 8, 9, "Program Set-Up and Speakers." See also L.B. Kuffert, *A Great Duty: Canadian Responses to Modern Life and Mass Culture, 1939–1967* (Montreal; Kingston: McGill-Queen's University Press, 2003), chapter 2.

93 LAC Neil Morrison Papers, Vol. 10, File: CBC programming, policy and scheduling, 1940–45, 31 July 1944, Elizabeth Long to Morrison, with copies to Helen Magill and Elspeth Cameron, a memo on several radio network afternoon series of interest to women. File: "Women's Talks," programming, n.d. 1944–54, several pamphlets about women's programming, including a draft plan for *Matinee*, originally meant to run 45 minutes each afternoon on the CBC's Trans-Canada Network.

94 Long's CBC memoir, chapter 9, "Program Set-Up and Speakers." See also chapter 10, "What Women Were Thinking." The commentators, she recalled, never did broadcasts about postwar family budgeting as it "seemed best to leave them to work out their own financial plans together." Long's CBC memoir, chapter 11, 2.

95 McEnaney Papers, Vol. 1, File: CBC Radio Talks for Women, "Radio Talks for Women" pamphlet. In Vancouver, Ellen Harris's *Morning Visit* aired from 1944 to 1952. UBC Special Collections, Ellen Code Harris Papers, finding aid. Harris's show was apparently dropped after the spring of 1952, according to her records. Harris Papers, Box 13, Folder 13-13, 9 July 1952, Doug Nixon, BC Programme Director, to Harris; 16 July 1952, Harris to Nixon. CBC policy to "change programmes and personnel from time to time" was the reason, according to a 31 July 1952 letter from Kenneth Caple, B.C. Regional Representative, to Harris; letter 12 September 1952 from Harris to listeners, explaining that the CBC had dropped her. It's not clear if it was broadcast, published or sent anywhere; letter 6 November 1952 from Robert Harlow, Talks Producer, to Mrs. G. Showers, explaining that Harris had found work elsewhere; other letters of objection from listeners are in the same file.

96 Long's CBC memoir, chapter 4, "Happier Wartime Living."

97 Long, "Women Morning Commentators Meet."

98 Ellen Harris, for example, ran into trouble with a difficult female director in Vancouver. Harris Papers, Box 13, Folder 13-9, Harris to Long, 10 December (1945), saying she would like a more formal written contract outlining her duties in relation to her local producer; Long memo to Harris, 13 August 1946, hinting at upcoming staff changes that would make Harris more comfortable. Folder 13-10, 23 September 1946, Long to Harris, telling her she had a "fairly free hand" in organizing her own broadcast material as long as her scripts were vetted just before the program went to air; 26 October 1946, telling Harris to invent a domestic reason to leave the studio right after her show so that any criticism of her work would have

to be in writing; 31 October 1946, Long counselling her not to try to involve male supervisors in her disputes with "a bad tempered woman," as men generally refused to intervene in a disagreement between two females. "You will simply have to fight it out for yourself" and be patient until the spring when, presumably, staff changes would occur. Long to Harris, 19 May 1947, noting Harris's satisfaction with new male production staff.

99　Howes interview with Bruce; Le Cocq, "Profile," 262–264; Harris Papers, memos from Long to Harris, Box 13, Folder 11, 25 February and 21 April 1948 on program meetings by mail; Folder 13-9, 8 June 1945, on local story leads; 17 September 1945 on government press releases in the mail; 9 October 1945, 5 and 14 November 1946, and 23 June 1947 on using other commentators' scripts. According to Long to Harris, 27 February 1946, the CBC held a three-month copyright on each script, after which the rights reverted to the freelancer who wrote it. Folder 13-11, 5 January 1949, Long sent Harris CBC regulations, which, among other things, forbade commentators to use trade names on the air. According to Long to Harris, 18 August 1949, it was all right to invent by name a "typical" patient when explaining medical treatments; 7 November 1949, Long to her women commentators and producers regarding pre-recorded shows.

100　Harris Papers, Box 13, Folder 13-9, Long to Harris, 27 November 1945 and 27 February 1946, and Harris to Long, 10 December (1945), regarding a possible increase in her workload from three 15-minute programs a week to two additional 5-minute talks a week as the rest of the local commentators were doing at the time. This was Long's way of preventing the Vancouver program director from hiring a different woman commentator on Tuesdays and Thursdays, when Harris was not on the air, which Long thought would harm audience shares for them both. Folder 13-10, 7 October 1946 and 19 August 1947, Long to Harris, regarding her agreement to take on the extra work. Folder 13-11, 11 February 1949, Long to Harris saying the CBC could not give her extra money to hire a stenographer.

101　Harris Papers, Box 13, Folder 13-6, 4 November 1944, letter from Harris to her mother, saying she had household help once or twice a week and neighbours helped care for her two children when needed. Box 5, Folder 5-5, 27 May 1948, program script #508 explaining that another friend helped her type scripts. Folder 13-3, Colpitts, writing as Joan Marshall, to Harris with advice on handling a workload of five programs a week; also Colpitts, commenting on her work in radio and later television in Bill Stewart, *A Picture by Christmas: Early CBC Television in Nova Scotia* (Halifax: Nimbus Books, 2002), 63.

102　Shirley Brett Foley's farewell broadcast, *Trans-Canada Matinee*, ISN 38963, 30 May 1958. In another interview, Brett Foley used the word "legs" instead of "feet" but the intent was the same. Brett Foley interview with Chisholm.

103　Colpitts interview with Bruce. Ireton Private Collection, Colpitts's son Bob, and daughter Peggy Wightman, interviews with Ireton; the script of "One Woman, Two Names," a radio documentary Ireton wrote and narrated for a CBC Radio network program, *Sunday Edition*, July 2004. Few of Colpitts's commentaries have survived in her papers. The material Ireton acquired from the CBC Halifax archives includes a partial transcript of "Democracy in the Home," the first edition of the TV program *The Joan Marshall Show* and an excerpt from an archived interview with her husband, Wendell Colpitts, who was a teacher and high school administrator. Also in the Ireton collection are an untitled script about the blind man, 10 January 1950; another about the Spring Hill mining disaster c. 1956. There are several biographical articles, including copies of the following: Nancy Lewis, "Drama, Civic Interest Were Key to Broadcasting Career," *Halifax Mail-Star*, 27 March 1965; CBC publicity material, 13 September 1950; Colpitts's typescript for *CBC Times*, 24–30 September 1950; another biography dated 15 May 1962, and a CBC Radio press release, 15 March 1968. In Long's Waterloo Papers, Box 84-131, there are undated biographical typescripts that Colpitts might have sent her.

104 Harris Papers, Box 4, Folder 4-1; 5 November 1947, program script #363, and booklet, "Evening Classes 1947–48, 39th Session of the Vancouver Night Schools," issued by the Vancouver Board of Trustees.

105 Harris Papers, Box 5, Folder 5-25, 6 December 1948, program script #594.

106 Howes, who was born and raised in Edmonton and was a graduate of the University of Alberta, had spent years working with the Christian Student Movement and the YWCA, and was a volunteer organizer of citizen feedback groups for the CBC's Citizens' Forum, before Neil Morrison hired her as a public affairs producer in 1946. Howes interview with Bruce.

107 See, for example, Neil Morrison Papers, Vol. 5, File: Business Trips, Staff—reports and memos 1938–50, 11 January 1941 memo from Long to Morrison on her recent four-day trip to Winnipeg, during which she consulted with her former press club colleagues and tried to arrange for Lillian Beynon Thomas to mend an apparent rift with the CBC and do talks. Other memos regarding her trips are in the same file. See also "Winnipeg Branch Entertains Many Noted Visitors," *C.W.P.C. Newspacket*, 1 March 1942, 4; "Winnipeg's Big Party" and C.W.P.C. Gadabouts," *C.W.P.C. Newspacket*, May 1943, 1; Jean Champion, "Newspaper Experience Valuable," *C.W.P.C. Newspacket*, November 1943, 3.

108 McEnaney Papers, Vol. 2, File: Working Women Papers, copy of Elizabeth D. Long, "Radio as a Career for Women," undated.

109 Le Cocq, "Profile," 262–263.

110 Brett Foley interview with Chisholm; Long interview with Brett Foley on *Matinee*.

111 Colpitts interview with Bruce.

112 Colpitts interview with Bruce.

113 Neil Morrison Papers, Vol. 5, File: Business Trips, Staff—reports and memos 1938–50, memo from Long, undated.

114 Colpitts interview with Bruce.

115 McEnaney Papers, Vol. 3, File: McClung, Nellie—reference materials 1912–1940, copies of clippings, "More Women Radio Announcers Favoured," *Globe and Mail*, n.d. and "Kindly Preserve Radio Public from More Feminine Announcers, " *Trail, BC, Times*, 24 November 1937; Langham, "Tuning In," 120. McClung was on the CBC Board of Governors from 1936 to 1942. "Obituary—Nellie McClung, Writer, Women's Rights Leader," *Globe and Mail*, 3 September 1951, 33; "Music in the Air Harnessed and Nellie Holds the Reins," *C.W.P.C. Newspacket*, 2 November 1936, 4. Long had met her years before on a Prairie press women's junket. Long interview with McEnaney, ISN 248152.

116 Hilmes, "Desired and Feared," 20–25.

117 Le Cocq, "Profile," 263 and Long's CBC memoir, chapter 1.

118 Colpitts interview with Bruce; Brett Foley interview with Chisholm.

119 Elspeth Chisholm interview with Jean Bruce, ISN 304786, July 1981.

120 L.B. Kuffert, "What Do You Expect of This Friend? Canadian Radio and the Intimacy of Broadcasting," *Media History*, 15:3, 2009, 303–319.

121 Long's CBC memoir, chapter 1.

122 Long, "A Welcome Guest in Every Home," *CBC Times*, 2, July 1950; Le Cocq, "Profile," 263. Colpitts interview with Bruce; Brett Foley interview with Chisholm. Long's radio tips were circulated among her CWPC colleagues as well. Georgina Murray, "Appealing Radio Program Likened to Conversation on Rural Telephone Line," *C.W.P.C. Newspacket*, 1 May 1940, 2. Murray, the daughter of B.C. newspaper legend Margaret "Ma" Murray, joined the CBC Talks staff a year earlier. "B.C. Member Is Latest Convert to the CBC," *C.W.P.C. Newspacket*, 1 May 1939, 2; also no author, "Successful Broadcasting Calls for Intimate Style; Avoid Platform Oratory,' *C.W.P.C. Newspacket*, 1 August 1941, 3–4.

123 Ellen Harris Papers, Box 4, Folder 4-11, January 1948, "Program Meeting by Mail." See, for example, Box 13, Folder 13-9, Elizabeth D. Long to Ellen Harris, 23 October 1945, on writing simplified scripted introductions for interviews with medical

experts, with Long's corrections on the attached script Harris had sent the network, dated 3 October 1945. Also, CBC RG 41, Vol. 177, 10 January 1955, Long to Peggy MacFarlane.

124 Shirley Brett Foley on *Matinee*, 1958.
125 Langham, "Tuning In," 120, 122.
126 Harris Papers, Box 4, Folder 4-15, 6 February 1948, program script #429. This file includes letters from Harris's son's physicians; his registration number at the Mayo Clinic in Rochester, Minnesota; and a first-person manuscript Harris wrote, "Your Son Has St. Vitus Dance," undated. Box 13, Folder 13-10, 15 and 21 November and 17 December 1946, Long encouraged her to gather broadcast material on health issues from Rochester, and to introduce herself to women radio hosts in the city, both of which she did.
127 Harris Papers, Box 4, Folder 4-23, 24 March 1948, program script #462.
128 Harris Papers, Box 4, Folder 4-27, 16 April 1948, program script #479. Phillips to Harris, 28 April 1948. Colpitts also asked her listeners for feedback. Taylor, "Window on the World," 110.
129 Bruce interview with Colpitts. It was not unusual for women to feel guilty about taking jobs outside the home, or to want to avoid criticism for doing so. For an analysis of social attitudes toward them, especially just after the war, see Joan Sangster, *Transforming Labour: Women and Work in Post-War Canada* (Toronto: University of Toronto Press, 2010), introduction.
130 According to MacFarlane, Long thought "Dolores" was too "Spanish." She might have meant it did not go well on air with a Celtic surname. MacFarlane interview with anonymous man for Bruce.
131 Dorothea Cox interview with Jean Bruce, ISN 304753.
132 Brett Foley interview with Chisholm. Harris Papers, Box 13, Folder 13-15, 13-16, 13-17, various invitations to speak at women's and other functions.
133 Howes interview with Bruce. On wartime fashion, see Susan Turnbull Caton, "Fashion and War in Canada 1939–1945," in *Fashion: A Canadian Perspective*, ed. Alexandra Palmer (Toronto: University of Toronto Press, 2004), 249–269.
134 Long interview with McEnaney, ISN 248134, c. 1960–1961; on her intellectual curiosity, see also McEnaney Papers, Vol. 2, Long, Elizabeth—Letters to M. McEnaney, File 4, Long to McEnaney, 13 July 1962.
135 Brett Foley interview with Chisholm.
136 Brett Foley interview with Chisholm.
137 Howes interview with Bruce; "Radio Gals' Get-Together," *C.W.P.C. Newspacket*, November 1943, 4, with a photograph of Jean Hinds, Winnipeg; Jean Howarth, who was about to take up the post in Vancouver; Marcelle Barth, Montreal; Monica Mugan, Toronto; "Joan Marshall" (Margaret Colpitts) of the Maritimes; and Ethelwyn Hobbes, network consumer commentator.
138 She was quoted in a roundup of CWPC Toronto news. Jean Love, "Kate Aitken in Britain," *C.W.P.C. Newspacket*, August 1945, 4.
139 Long, "Women Morning Commentators Meet." These comments were also included in Long's CBC memoir, chapter 5, 2.
140 McEnaney Papers, Vol. 2, File: CBC Talks and Public Affairs—reports and minutes of some meetings and conferences 1951–58; minutes of CBC Talks and Public Affairs conference, 15–19 June 1953, 11; minutes of the annual conference, CBC Talks and Public Affairs, Toronto, 10–14 May 1954, 2–3, 5; minutes of the annual conference, CBC Talks and Public Affairs, 2–6 May 1955, 6.
141 MacFarlane interview with anonymous man for Bruce, February 1981.
142 Long's CBC memoir, chapter 2, "Our Royal Tour."
143 Ellen Harris Papers, Box 13, Folder 13-10, memo from Long to her women commentators, 30 October 1947 regarding royal wedding with biography of Matthew Halton attached; Box 4, Folder 4-3, 17 November 1947, program script #372 and

19 November 1947, program script #374. The folder includes a news release from *United Kingdom Information—This Week in Britain*, with questions and answers headlined "More Facts about the Royal Wedding," 27 October 1947. Attempts to offer regular BBC programming had foundered on technical and cultural difficulties, but appealing to the "Britishness" of Canadian listeners became a tradition, at least in special events programming. Vipond, "The Canadian Broadcasting Commission."

144 Long's CBC memoir, chapter 4.

145 Harris Papers, Box 13, Folder 13-11, 11 February 1949, Long to Harris saying Chant Robertson was pleased with her work; for example, Harris Papers, Box 4, Folder 4-27, 19 April 1948, program script #480.

146 Morrison interview with Bruce. Long apparently stayed in touch with Chambers, as did Mary McEnaney, Marjorie's sister. McEnaney Papers, Vol. 2, File: Retirement from CBC—personal letters to M. McEnaney, 1958, Mary McEnaney to Marjorie McEnaney, 22 February 1958. To my knowledge Carrie Best of Glasgow, Nova Scotia, host of *The Quiet Corner*, was the only other woman of colour regularly on the air in Canada during the 1950s and early 1960s. Her program was heard on four stations in the Maritimes. She was a well-known human rights advocate and newspaper columnist. Carrie Best, *That Lonesome Road* (Halifax: Clarion 1977); *All in a Day*, an interview about Carrie Best, CBC Radio, Ottawa, 11 February 2011, at http://www.cbc.ca/allinaday/2011/02/11/a-stamp-for-carrie-best/. When Charlotte Perry, a Black journalist Long met in Windsor, Ontario, was finally accepted as a member of the Toronto CWPC in the early 1960s, Long applauded the news. McEnaney Papers, Vol. 2, Long, Elizabeth—Letters to M. McEnaney, File 4, Long to McEnaney, 17 February 1962.

147 Long Waterloo Papers, File 22, Mary Quayle Innis's series of radio talks, *Political and Social Status of Women*, featuring leading women from around the world, January 1951 to September 1953. Long felt that listeners liked variety and Innis's talks were popular with them. See Harris Papers, Box 13, Folder 13-11, 6 March 1951, Long to Harris.

148 Long Waterloo Papers, File 64: Beatrice Ford, "My Life in Labrador" script, 12 August 1955, broadcast from St. John's, Newfoundland.

149 McFarlane interview with anonymous man for Bruce; McEnaney Papers, Vol. 2, Long, Elizabeth—Letters to M. McEnaney, File 3, Long to McEnaney, 25 October 1963.

150 Bruce, "Women in CBC Radio Talks," 14. CBC RG 41, Vol. 177, 20 February 1946, Long to Doug Nixon; 25 November 1946, Long to Jean Howard; Vol. 174, 21 January 1948, Long to Florence Bird.

151 Rotenberg interview with Bruce; Nessa Rapoport, "Recollections of Mattie Levi Rotenberg," Jewish Women's Archive, at http://jwa.org/discover/recollections/rotenberg.htm, 3 July 2008.

152 Rotenberg interview with Bruce with interview notes. A number of Rotenberg's scripts are in LAC Mattie Rotenberg Papers, Vol. 1 and 2.

153 Rotenberg Papers, Vol. 1, File 140, script for "College in the Kitchen," 15 November 1939.

154 Alison Prentice et al., *Canadian Women: A History*, 2nd ed. (Toronto: Harcourt Brace Canada, 1996), 241–243; Julia Cataudella, "When Women Came to Queen's," *Canadian Medical Association Journal*, 161:5, 7 September 1999, at http://www.cmaj.ca/, 14 November 2008.

155 Rotenberg Papers, Vol. 1, File 150, script for "The Post-War Woman," 1945, published in full, along with a separate article about the award, in the press club's newsletter. Mattie Rotenberg, "The Post-War Woman," and Kathleen McDowell, "Mattie Rotenberg Wins C.W.P.C. Award," *C.W.P.C. Newspacket*, August 1945, 3–4. Her series *Women's Way* was aired during the winter of 1946–1947 on the CBC's Trans-Canada Network. File 1: Copy of CBC brochure "Radio Talks for Women."

156 Rotenberg Papers, Vol. 1, File 146, script for "It's a Woman's War."

157 Long's CBC memoir, chapter 7, "Opening Day at Lake Success."

158 Rotenberg interview with Bruce; see, for example, Rotenberg Papers, Vol. 1, File 148, "Women Face the Future," 26 November 1945; Vol. 2, File 159, "Women of the New World," 5 November 1947; also UN scripts in Files 207, 208, 250–254, 261, May 1950–1951.

159 Rotenberg Papers, Vol. 2, File 310, untitled script, 19 May 1952.

160 See, for example, Rotenberg Papers, Vol. 1, script 141, "There's No Substitute for a Mother," 18 November 1940; also files 5–9, scripts for January 1940.

161 Rotenberg Papers, Vol. 1, File 143, 22 April 1944; File 155, her script for a debate on Citizens' Forum: "Do Jobs and Families Mix? Should Married Women Work?" 29 October 1947. Other scripts concerning equal pay, social benefits for housewives and the importance of education for girls are in Vol. 1, Files 140–154.

162 Stephen, "Balancing Equality for the Post-War Woman," 125–127.

163 Bird interview with Bruce; Bird, *Anne Francis*, 181–199.

164 Bird interview with Bruce.

165 CWPC members discussed it among themselves as well. See, for example, the editorial "Those Women's Pages," as well as "Is Woman's Page Put to Full Use in Our Democracy?" and Dorothy Howey and Kay Rex, "Two Press Women Talk about Copy for Women," in *C.W.P.C. Newspacket*, March 1949, 2, 3.

166 LAC Bird Papers, File 3-1, Economic Status of Women, Why Women Work and Women and Jobs: Scripts 1948–51. Quote from Anne Francis (Florence Bird), "Economic Status of Women in Canada," No. 4 in the series, November 1948. She broadcast another series on women, crime and rehabilitation. LAC Bird Papers, Vol. 3, File 3-14.

167 Bird, *Anne Francis*, 209–210. See for example, Anne Francis (Florence Bird), "The Rights of Women," *Behind the Headlines Series*, 10:4. Canadian Association for Adult Education and the Canadian Institute of International Affairs, 1950.

168 Barbara M. Freeman private collection, Florence Bird interview with Freeman, 18 November 1992.

169 LAC Bird Papers, Vol. 3, File 3-1, Economic Status of Women, Why Women Work and Women and Jobs: Scripts 1948–51; Anne Francis (Florence Bird), "Why Women Work: The Rival," 16 December 1949; also "Ontario Bill #120. An Act to Ensure Fair Remuneration to Female Employees," April 1951; Francis, "Economic Status of Women in Canada," 9 October 1948.

170 Harris Papers, Box 5, Folder 5-22, 12 November 1948, program script #578, Harris's introduction and a copy of Francis (Bird), "Economic Status of Women in Canada," originally written 9 October 1948 for broadcast before 13 November 1948; Folder 5-23, 19 November 1948, program script #583, Harris's response to criticism of Bird; Folder 5-26, 10 December 1948, program script # 598, Harris noting most listeners' agreement with Bird. Other examples of Bird's scripts used by Harris are in Folder 5-24, 22 November 1948, program script #584, and 26 November 1948, program script #588; Folder 5-25, 3 December 1948, program script #593; Folder 5-26, 13 December 1948, program script #599; Box 9, Folder 9-10, 1 October 1951, radio letter #10, Anne Francis, "Economic Status of Women: Employment of Married Women in Canada (1)." Folder 13-11, 11 February 1949, Long to Harris telling her she could either use Bird's broadcast scripts as they were or adapt them into her own scripts.

171 LAC Bird Papers, Vol. 3, File: 3-1 Economic Status of Women: Scripts 1948–51. "Economic Status of Women, the Perfect Wife," dated November 1948 for use before 10 December 1948.

172 Landry Papers, Vol. 5, CBC Pension Committee Meetings file, meeting of 5 April 1956, section 9; Morgan, *The Equality Game*.

173 Bird interview with Freeman.

174 Bird interview with Bruce. For more information on the Bretton Woods agreement, see http://jolis.worldbankimflib.org/Bwf/whatisbw.htm (31 March 2011).
175 Bruce, "Women in CBC Radio Talks," 13–14.
176 LAC Bird Papers, Vol. 3, File 3-1: Economic Status of Women: Scripts 1948–51, Script for "Why Women Work: New Year Calling," 30 December 1949; File 3-15, Correspondence from Bessie Long, letter from "Bessie L." on CBC letterhead dated only "Friday"; Long to Bird, 26 November 1951, another letter congratulating Bird for an unspecified program that Long felt only a woman would have the courage to do.
177 In another letter, Long urged Bird to get to know the ICW women. LAC Bird Papers, Vol. 3, File 15, Elizabeth Long to Florence Bird, 7 September 1960. Bird had also joined the CWPC. LAC Media Club of Canada, Vol. 38, File 38-3, 1946 membership list; Vol. 41, File 41-13, CWPC Triennial Report 1951–1954, membership list.
178 Le Cocq, "Profile," 264.
179 Hassard, "Clubs May Waste Time."
180 Long, "Women Morning Commentators Meet." CBC Papers, Vol. 178, Trans-Canada Matinee, File 11-18-2, National Council of Women, Elizabeth Long to Mrs. Edgar Hardy, President, National Council of Women of Canada, 31 May 1946 and other correspondence with her between 1941 and 1946; Long, "Women in Radio," talk to NCWC meeting, Regina, Saskatchewan, 9 June 1947.
181 Long interview with McEnaney, ISN 248134.
182 Harris Papers, Box 4, Folder 4-1, 4 November 1947, program script #362, prejudice against Jews and the Japanese; Folder 4-27, 14 April 1948, program script #477, interview with Muriel Lester, Secretary of the International Fellowship of Reconciliation; Box 5, Folder 5-16, 1 October 1948, script #549, disc of Eleanor Roosevelt on human rights; Folder 5-17, 13 October 1948, program script #557, update from the UN; Folder 5-22, 11 November 1948, program script #577, interview with Reginald W. Sorenson, British MP and vice-president of the National Peace Council; Box 7, Folder 7-8, 15 September 1949, Long to her commentators regarding a Women's Institutes essay competition; Folder 7-7, 18 November 1947, regarding a Gwen Wilkins radio talk on India's female health minister; Folder 7-24, 19 April 1950, regarding another Wilkins radio talk on the upcoming meeting of the UN Status of Women Commission; Folder 7-28, 19 June 1950, program script #923, on the International Labour Organization's campaign for "equal pay for work of equal value." Folder 13-11, 2 December 1949, Long memo to commentators with a Wilkins script attached on the female Nobel Prize winners.
183 LAC Long Papers, Newspaper clippings 1969–1971, copy of Margaret Aitken column "Between You and Me," n.d.
184 Long Waterloo Papers, File 1: Correspondence, Elizabeth Long, "The International Standing Committee on Radio and Television of the International Council of Women." *E.B.U. Review*, "Part B, General and Legal," published bi-monthly by the administrative office of the European Broadcasting Union, Geneva Switzerland, No. 63, September 1960, 19–21.
185 LAC RG41, CBC Papers, Trans-Canada Matinee, File 11-18-1-1: International Council of Women, report by Elizabeth D. Long, "Tour of Six European Countries May–June 1948," 18 pages. There are also various memos regarding international women's broadcasts over the CBC. See also Long's CBC memoir, chapter 8, "Seven Weeks in Seven Countries." She occasionally wrote background material herself. Harris Papers, Box 13, Folder 13-11, Elizabeth D. Long to commentators and producers, "Background Material—Educational Movies in Togoland," 1 October 1951. LAC Neil Morrison Papers, Vol. 10, File: "Women's Talks," Programming, n.d. 1944–54, Elizabeth Long, "Report on Trip to Greece March 19–May 20, 1951," a 12-page report on her attendance at the ICW meeting there.
186 LAC Long Papers, newspaper clippings 1969–1971, copy of Margaret Aitken column "Between You and Me," n.d.

187 Long Waterloo Papers, Long, "The International Standing Committee on Radio and Television of the International Council of Women," 20.

188 Long's CBC memoir, chapter 6, "National Council of Women." Harris Papers, Box 13, Folder 13-10, 31 October 1946, copy of memo from Long to program director Ada McGeer, outlining the credentials of Christiana H.R. Kalff-Francken, who held a master of law degree and had been a military and government adviser on postwar reparations. She spoke English fluently, organized her own radio series on women in politics, was married to a barrister to the Supreme Court of the Netherlands and had six children. According to a memo from Long, 15 November 1946, one of her daughters died from complications from anaemia, because of lack of protein in her wartime diet; 4 November 1946, Kalff-Francken to Long, and 15 November 1956, copy of condolence letter from Long to Kalff-Francken; 13 September 1946, memo from Long to Ada McGeer, with separate memo to Kalff-Francken, who would be paid $10 per letter. Long wanted the two women to share information and nurture a personal friendship as well. Letter and script to Long from Kalff-Francken, 2 September 1946, and a note from Kalff-Francken to Harris, 7 October 1946, memo from Long to Ada McGeer with a copy to Harris. See also Box 4, Folder 4-4, 24 November 1947, program script #376; Box 5, Folder 5-12, 9 September 1948, program script #534; Box 7, Folder 7-21, c. March–April 1950, no script number given for Harris's meeting with Kalff-Francken in Holland.

189 Long's CBC memoir, chapter 12, "Lorne Green and Visiting Broadcasters."

190 Long Waterloo Papers, File 16, Radio Broadcasts, numerous scripts on many women internationally including Mattie Rotenberg talk on Octavia Hill, London social reformer, 13 February 1950, 2:25–2:26 P.M. This was one of a series called *Fighting Pioneers* broadcast on the Trans-Canada network from Toronto; "Progress of Women," Daisy Bates of Australia, November 1949; "The Maori Tangi," an 11-minute radio talk by Mrs. Sophie McWilliams of New Zealand about her Maori neighbours and their funeral ceremonies, 15 November 1952; File 30, Radio letters by Gwen Wilkins—"Progress of Women"—about Mrs. Pandit, Indian ambassador to the United States and sister of Nehru, 6 May 1949; about Senator Cairine Wilson as delegate to the UN Assembly at Lake Success, 20 September (1949?); Lebanon and the Arab Women's Federation Conference c. 1947 and UN Status of Women conference at Lake Success, April 1950.

191 Jean Hunter Morrison Papers, Vol. 2, File: CBC 25th anniversary 1961, women's programming documents; Rotenberg Papers, Vol. 1, File 1, copy of CBC brochure, "Radio Talks for Women," Winter Programs 1946–1947.

192 McEnaney interview with Bruce; Le Cocq, "Profile," 265; Long's CBC memoirs, chapter 10.

193 Jean Hunter Morrison Papers, Vol. 1, File: "Women's World" 1948, script #6, 5 December 1948; File: "Women's World" 1948–49, dated 31 October 1948, both on working mothers; also script #9, 26 December 1948 on women in politics.

194 Harris Papers, Box 4, Folder 4-17, Elizabeth D. Long to producer Art Sager and Ellen Harris, 27 January 1948, regarding an item from British broadcaster Margaret Cameron; Box 5, Folder 5-27, 17 November 1948, memo from Elizabeth D. Long to her commentators on Christmas in New Zealand.

195 Letter from G. Dickson, head of English Programmes, SABC to Long, 26 February 1954; Long's response to Dickson and a separate memo to Bird, her producer Don Bennett and Pat Boswell, supervisor of Exchange Programs, English section of the CBC's International Service, 11 March 1954.

196 CBC Papers, RG 41, Box 405, File 23-1-6, K.M. Kelly, supervisor of Personnel and Welfare, to Mrs. T.G. Morris, 9 February 1953; letter from Jean I. Hamilton, corresponding secretary of the Canadian Association of Consumers to Alphonse Ouimet, general manager, CBC, with copy and covering letter to A.D. Dunton, chairman, CBC, 3 March 1953.

197 As female staff had to retire at age 60, which, for Long, would have been in 1951, it appears she was kept on as supervisor for another year on contract, which terminated at the end of 1952. She was then made a programming adviser to the new supervisor, Helen James, until 1956. Neil Morrison Papers, Vol. 1, File: Personal Correspondence 1952, Morrison to Long, 12 November 1952, saying her contract would not be renewed. CBC, "Pass the Orchids, Please!" CWPC Winnipeg, Box 6, Scrapbook 1958–1968, clippings of Kay Rex, "Women in Retirement—Keeps Busy with Her Clubs, Writing," *Globe and Mail*, 3 March 1960, 21; Elizabeth Long, "Men Question Value of Women's Groups," *Winnipeg Free Press*, 28 May 1959.

198 Long interview with McEnaney, ISN 248134; Lotta Dempsey, "Private Line," *Toronto Daily Star*, 7 November 1961, 42; McEnaney Papers, Vol. 2, Long, Elizabeth—Letters to M. McEnaney, File 4, Long to McEnaney, 28 January 1961, 21 and 25 November 1961; 13 July, 25 August, 18 September and 19 October 1962; File 3, Long to McEnaney, 26 November and 5 December 1962, 6 and 25 October 1963. File 1, 2 March 1967. Long Waterloo Papers, File 13, Correspondence—Long to (Esther) Michael, 25 January 1968; File 14, Long's form information letter to various members of the Women's International League for Peace and Freedom

199 McEnaney's efforts are documented in McEnaney Papers, Vol. 3, File: Peace Research Institute—correspondence and notes—1961 (1970); File: Peace Research Institute—clippings and circulars 1961–65. McEnaney sheltered American draft dodgers in her home. See McEnaney, "Who Stole the Cakes?" 52–53. On the split between the Institute and VOW, see Candace Loewen, "Making Ourselves Heard: 'Voice of Women' and the Peace Movement in the Early Sixties," in Cook, McLean and O'Rourke, *Framing Our Past*, 248–251.

200 Brett Foley interview with Chisholm.

201 McEnaney Papers, Vol. 2, Long, Elizabeth—Letters to M. McEnaney, File 4, Long to McEnaney, 13 May 1958. Some women accepted the glass ceiling at the time. Cox interview with Bruce.

202 McEnaney Papers, Vol. 2, Long, Elizabeth—Letters to M. McEnaney, File 4, Long to McEnaney, 21 February 1962, her emphasis; Long to McEnaney, 13 October 1965.

203 Bruce, "Women in CBC Radio Talks," 17–18; Taylor, "Window on the World," chapter 5.

204 Long Waterloo Papers, File 5, Bird to Long, 20 October 1967.

205 McEnaney Papers, Vol. 2, Long, Elizabeth—Letters to M. McEnaney, File 1, Long to McEnaney, 13 December 1967, her emphasis; Long to McEnaney, "Sunday," c. November 1967.

206 Her emphases. Long Waterloo Papers, File 5, Long to Bird, 6 November 1967.

207 McEnaney Papers, Vol. 2, Long, Elizabeth—Letters to M. McEnaney, File 1, Long to McEnaney, 2 March 1967.

208 McEnaney Papers, Vol. 2, Long, Elizabeth—Letters to M. McEnaney, File 1, Long to McEnaney, 2 March 1967.

209 Ireton Private Papers, copy of Canadian Women's Press Club Inc., *Triennial Report 1968–1971*, Edith Paterson, report on the Winnipeg CWPC.

210 McEnaney Papers, Vol. 2, Long, Elizabeth—Letters to M. McEnaney, File 1, Long to McEnaney, 2 March 1967; clipping of "Idea Girl Just Likes Libraries," *Winnipeg Free Press*, 13 February 1964.

211 McEnaney Papers, Vol. 2, File: Women—McEnaney correspondence regarding briefs on Royal Commission on the Status of Women, discrimination and rights, 1966–1972, copy of Toronto CWPC brief to the Royal Commission on the Status of Women. She wrote a similar brief to the Special Senate Committee on the Mass Media. McEnaney Papers, Letter of acknowledgment to McEnaney from Nicola Kendall, research director, Special Senate Committee on Mass Media, 2 October 1969, same file. The Senate committee received complaints from other journalists as well. See also CP (Ottawa), "Women Meet Discrimination in the Media," *Montreal Gazette*, 27 April 1970, 14.

212 Freeman, *The Satellite Sex*, chapter 2.
213 McEnaney Papers, Vol. 2, Long, Elizabeth—Letters to M. McEnaney, File 1, Long to McEnaney, 18 May 1968.
214 Freeman, *The Satellite Sex*, chapter 9.
215 Bird interview with Freeman.
216 *Report of the CBC Task Force on the Status of Women* (Toronto: Canadian Broadcasting Corporation, 1975).
217 CBC Papers, RG 41, Box 405, File 23-1-6, Elizabeth Long to William Macdonald, 5 October 1967; McEnaney Papers, Vol. 2, Long, Elizabeth—Letters to M. McEnaney, File 2, Long to McEnaney, File 1, 8 October 1967 and 12 March 1968.
218 Program planners agreed to what appeared to be the first survey of "women's interest" listeners during a *Matinee* planning meeting after Long left the CBC. CBC management was concerned that the otherwise "excellent" program suffered from too many contributions from amateurs with little broadcast training. LAC CBC Papers, RG 41, Vol. 179, File 11-18-2-4, minutes of Trans-Canada *Matinee* Program Meeting, 3 December 1958. On the CBC and audience ratings, which started relatively late, see Ross Eaman, *Channels of Influence: CBC Audience Research and the Canadian Public* (Toronto: University of Toronto Press, 1994).
219 Freeman, *The Satellite Sex*, chapter 2.

Chapter 5

1 Duncan Macpherson cartoon, "Taking Leave of Their Census," *Toronto Daily Star*, 13 May 1970, 6.
2 Ann Thomson, *Winning Choice on Abortion* (Victoria, BC: Trafford, 2004), chapters 5 and 6; Judy Rebick, *Ten Thousand Roses: The Making of a Feminist Revolution* (Toronto: Penguin Canada, 2005), chapter 3; Myrna Kostash, *Long Way from Home: The Story of the Sixties Generation in Canada* (Toronto: James Lorimer, 1980), chapter 11; Frances Jane Wasserlein, "An Arrow Aimed Straight at the Heart: The Vancouver Women's Caucus and the Abortion Campaign 1969–1971," master's thesis, Simon Fraser University, 1990; also Wasserlein, "A Twenty-Five-Year-Old Herstory: Women's Caucus," *Kinesis*, December 1992/January 1993, 18–19, and the reminiscences of Margo Dunn in Cole Dudley, "The Women Are Coming," *Kinesis*, October 1983, 14–16. Media accounts include Karin Wells, "The Women Are Coming," a documentary aired on *Sunday Edition*, CBC Radio One, 11 March 2010.
3 Anne Roberts interview with Barbara Freeman, 2006; Kathryn-Jane Hazel (formerly Keate) interviews with Barbara Freeman, 1995, 2006.
4 If the offending reporters were represented by their union, the Newspaper Guild, they might not be fired but reassigned to other beats where their professional and political conflicts would be minimal. Stuart Keate, *Paper Boy* (Toronto; Vancouver: Clarke, Irwin & Company, 1980), 119; Barbara M. Freeman, *The Satellite Sex: The Media and Women's Issues in English Canada, 1966–1971* (Waterloo, ON: Wilfrid Laurier University Press, 2001), chapter 2; Roberts and Hazel interviews with Freeman. For an assessment of today's journalism standards regarding various degrees of political involvement, see Ken Regan, Scott White and Ivor Shapiro, "Journalists Seeking Public Office: What Are the Ethical Issues?" A panel report for the Canadian Association of Journalists at http://www.caj.ca/?p=1147, 6 April 2011.
5 A small 1970 survey of Canadian Women's Press Club members in Ontario and Quebec testified to the beginnings of the shift in women's page content. "News Change Seen in Women's Pages," *Saskatoon Star-Phoenix*, 30 April 1970, 13. According to Gertrude J. Robinson's calculations for 1975, there were 2450 journalists on daily newspapers in Canada, of which 21 percent were women. Most of them were on small urban dailies and/or dominated the "soft news" beats, like lifestyles, designated for women reporters. The bigger the newspaper, the less chance they had

of covering the "hard news" beats of politics and business, usually designated for male reporters. By that time, some beats, such as local news, were balanced between the two sexes. Gertrude J. Robinson, *Gender, Journalism and Equity: Canadian, U.S. and European Perspectives* (Crestkill, NJ: Hampton Press, 2005), 35–42. The 1967 Canadian Press newsroom guide consistently referred to its employees as males, although Anne Roberts was not the first woman to work for the news agency. CP, "For the Newcomer" (1967), copy in Anne Roberts's personal papers. Women were barely welcome as members in most press clubs at the time. Freeman, *The Satellite Sex,* chapters 2 and 9. See also Simma Holt, *Memoirs of a Loose Cannon* (Hamilton, ON: Seraphim Editions, 2008); Stephen Clarkson, ed., *My Life as a Dame: The Personal and the Political in the Writings of Christina McCall* (Toronto: House of Anansi Press, 2008); Susan Crean, *Newsworthy* (Toronto: Stoddart, 1985). The situation was similar for feminist journalists in the United States. See Patricia Bradley, *Women and the Press: The Struggle for Equality* (Evanston, IL: Northwestern University Press, 2005), especially chapters 2 and 3.

6   By 1971, 39 percent of women aged 15 and over were in the waged workforce, compared with 30 percent in 1961; by 1971, the birthrate dropped to 16.8 per 1000 total population or 1.7 children per family, compared with 1.9 in 1961; and after divorce was liberalized in 1969, the divorce rate almost tripled in one year to 311 per 100,000 people. By 1970, 37 percent of full-time undergraduate and 22 percent of graduate university students were women. Alison Prentice et al., *Canadian Women: A History,* 2nd ed. (Toronto: Harcourt Brace Canada, 1996), 354, 380, 382, 397. About 71 percent of Canadians believed the abortion laws should be liberalized to some degree. In 1968, reader surveys in both the English and French versions of *Chatelaine* magazine showed that 55 percent of the respondents wanted the abortion laws liberalized to include consideration beyond direct danger to the life and health of the mother, such as her financial circumstances. A further 27 percent of the magazines' readers supported abortion on demand. The rest wanted no change in the law. In 1968, just before the birth control laws became liberalized, there were 32,629 live births outside of marriage in Canada, or 8 out of 100. Freeman, *The Satellite Sex,* 176, 179.

7   See, for example, Elaine H. Chalus, "From Friedan to Feminism: Gender and Change at the University of Alberta, 1960–1970," in *Standing on New Ground: Women in Alberta,* ed. Catherine A. Cavanaugh and Randi R. Warne (Edmonton: University of Alberta Press, 1993), 119–145. See also Nancy Adamson, "Feminists, Libbers, Lefties and Radicals: The Emergence of the Women's Liberation Movement," in *A Diversity of Women: Ontario 1945–1980,* ed. Joy Parr (Toronto: University of Toronto Press, 1995), 252–280; Nancy Adamson, Linda Briskin and Margaret McPhail, *Feminists Organizing for Change: The Contemporary Women's Movement in Canada* (Toronto: Oxford University Press, 1988), chapter 2; Francine Descarriers-Belanger and Shirley Roy, "The Women's Movement and Its Currents of Thought," trans. Jennifer Beeman, *The CRIAW Papers,* no. 26 (Ottawa: Canadian Research Institute for the Advancement of Women, 1991); Kostash, *Long Way from Home,* chapter 11.

8   Jacquetta Newman and Linda A. White, *Women, Politics and Public Policy* (Toronto: Oxford University Press, 2006), chapter 4.

9   Adamson, "Feminists, Libbers, Lefties and Radicals," 253; Prentice et al., *Canadian Women,* 420–428; Jane Jensen in Janine Brodie, Shelley A.M. Gavigan and Jane Jensen, *The Politics of Abortion* (Toronto: Oxford University Press, 1992), chapter 2. For a study of the early years of the Trudeau regime in its cultural context, see Paul Litt, "Trudeaumania: Participatory Democracy in the Mass-Mediated Nation," *Canadian Historical Review,* 89:1, March 2008, 27–53.

10 Melissa Haussman, *Abortion Politics in North America* (Boulder, CO; London: Lynne Rienner, 2005), chapter 3. See also Angus McLaren and Arlene Tigar McLaren, *The Bedroom and the State: The Changing Practices and Politics of Contraception*

and Abortion in Canada, 1880–1997, 2nd ed. (Don Mills, ON: Oxford University Press, 1997); and Childbirth by Choice Trust, eds., *No Choice: Canadian Women Tell Their Stories of Illegal Abortions* (Toronto: Childbirth by Choice Trust, 1998). It wasn't until the summer of 1970 that New York State enacted a new law allowing abortions to be performed in medical clinics. As it did not include a residency requirement, Canadian women who could afford to go there did so. Edward Cowan, "Campaign to End Legal Restrictions on Abortions in Canada Begun by Women's Liberation Movement," *New York Times,* 10 May 1970, 29; Jane E. Brody, "'Instant abortions' Urged," *Calgary Herald,* 20 April 1970, 33.

11 Rebick, *Ten Thousand Roses,* 36, 41. Childbirth by Choice Trust, *No Choice,* chapter 4, with illustrations of homemade, illegal abortion devices from the Toronto Police Service Museum Archives, 131–133.

12 Thomson, *Winning Choice on Abortion,* chapter 3; Christabelle Sethna, "The Evolution of the Birth Control Handbook: From Student Peer Education to Feminist Self-Empowerment Text, 1968–1975," *Canadian Bulletin of Medical History/Bulletin canadien d'histoire de la médecine,* 23: 1, 2006, 89–118; Sethna, "The University of Toronto Health Service, Oral Contraception and Student Demand for Birth Control, 1960–1970," *Historical Studies in Education/Revue d'histoire de l'éducation,* 17:2, 265–292; Sethna, "'Chastity Outmoded!' *The Ubyssey,* Sex, and the Single Girl, 1960–70," in *Creating Postwar Canada: Community, Diversity and Dissent, 1945–1975,* ed. Magda Fahrni and Robert Rutherdale (Vancouver: University of British Columbia Press, 2007), 291–314; Sethna, "'WE WANT FACTS, NOT MORALS!' Unwanted Pregnancy, the Toronto Women's Caucus and Sex Education," in *Ontario since Confederation: A Reader,* ed. Edgar-André Montigny and Lori Chambers (Toronto: University of Toronto Press, 2000, 409–428). Unwed mothers who kept their children could be subjected to intrusive government scrutiny. See Lori Chambers, *Misconceptions: Unmarried Motherhood and the Ontario Children of Unmarried Parents Act, 1921 to 1969* (Toronto: Published for the Osgoode Society for Canadian Legal History by University of Toronto Press, 2007).

13 Jensen, *The Politics of Abortion,* 44. The Caravan was inspired by the On-to-Ottawa train trek of unemployed men from British Columbia to Ottawa in 1935, which was not successful because of government and police interference. Jensen, *The Politics of Abortion,* 44. For details, see Victor Howard, "On to Ottawa Trek," *The Canadian Encyclopedia,* at http://www.thecanadianencyclopedia.com, 29 January 2009.

14 Patricia Bradley, *Mass Media and the Shaping of American Feminism 1963–1975* (Jackson: University Press of Mississippi, 2004), especially chapters 2 and 3.

15 Roberts interview with Freeman; Hazel interviews with Freeman, 1995, 2006. Fulford's writers often used the New Journalism technique at *Saturday Night.* Fraser Sutherland, *The Monthly Epic: A History of Canadian Magazines 1789–1989* (Markham, ON: Fitzhenry and Whiteside, 1989), 309–310.

16 Frances Jane Wasserlein, "Women's Caucus," *Kinesis,* December 1992/January 1993, 18–19. For biographies of the women she interviewed who were involved with the Caravan, see Wasserlein, "An Arrow," chapter 2.

17 Kostash, *Long Way from Home,* 181.

18 Thomson, *Winning Choice on Abortion,* chapter 3.

19 Roberts interview with Freeman. On collective feminist groups of the period, see Adamson, "Feminists, Libbers, Lefties and Radicals," 262.

20 Interracial relationships were unusual in Canada at the time; she confirmed the details of hers during a follow-up conversation between Roberts and Freeman, 6 March 2009.

21 Her first few months at CP Edmonton were satisfactory enough to merit a $10 raise to $95 per week. This was in line with CP policy. Roberts private papers, CP General Manager Gillis Purcell to Anne Roberts, 31 July 1969; copy of CP "For the Newcomer: An Introduction to the Canadian Press," 15 July 1967, 4.

22 Simone de Beauvoir, *The Second Sex* (New York: Knopf, 1952); Betty Friedan, *The Feminine Mystique* (New York: Norton, 1963).

23 Hazel interview with Freeman, 1995.

24 Freeman, *The Satellite Sex*, 91–93.

25 Hazel interview with Freeman, 2006.

26 Hazel interview with Freeman, 1995; see also Keate, *Paper Boy*, 166.

27 Hazel interview with Freeman, 1995.

28 Hazel interview with Freeman, 2006.

29 Sethna, "The University of Toronto Health Service," 287.

30 Hazel interview with Freeman, 1995.

31 Hazel interview with Freeman, 2006.

32 On the Abortion Information Service and the B.C. abortion campaign, see Thomson, *Winning Choice on Abortion*, chapters 3–4.

33 Canadian Women's Movement Archives, X10-1, Series 1, Box 125, Vancouver Women's Caucus File, Revised Abortion Caravan schedule.

34 Simon Fraser University Archives, F-162-3-3-0-27, Marge Hollibaugh's Abortion Caravan Scrapbook, "Re: Abortion Strategy" memo addressed to "Dear Sisters," from Vicky Brown, Marge Hollibaugh, Dawn Carrell and Betsy Meadley (a.k.a. Wood), Vancouver Women's Caucus Campaign Coordination Committee, c. December 1969; see also a memo from Marge Hollibaugh and Betsy Meadley, "Re: Abortion Campaign, Federal and Provincial: The Vancouver Women's Caucus Is on the March." Copies of both documents in University of Ottawa, Canadian Women's Movement Archives, X10-1, Series 1, Box 1, Abortion Caravan (May 1970) file. The documents are not numbered. Access to sex education and birth control for high school students later became an ongoing feminist project in Toronto. See Sethna, "WE WANT FACTS," 409–428.

35 Roberts interview with Freeman. The VWC internal debate regarding a single or multiple issue focus was also recalled by Caravanner Marcy Cohen, speaking in a video documentary, who said they did not want it to be a single issue, as they believed suffrage had been. See Nancy Nichol, director, *Struggle for Choice: Part 1. Abortion Caravan*, Horizontal Forest Productions, Toronto, 1986.

36 Wasserlein, "An Arrow," 113–114.

37 Betsy Meadley Wood cited in Rebick, *Ten Thousand Roses*, 39.

38 During that time, *The Pedestal* became a monthly publication. Wasserlein, "An Arrow," 81. Front-page illustration and a copy of the proposal presented to the caucus by Mary Stolk, "Abortion Campaign," *The Pedestal*, Winter 1969, 1; "The Abortion Machine," *The Pedestal*, February 1970, 7. See also Simon Fraser University Archives, Frances Wasserlein Papers, Vancouver Women's Caucus Binder, 1/5, F-162-3-3-0-5, "General Meeting Report: Feb. 1970," *The Pedestal*, c. February 1970, reprint; "Women Declare War," "Hundreds Protest Abortion Laws," and Diana Moore, "Guerrilla Theatre," *The Pedestal*, March 1970, 2, 3; "An Open Letter to Loffman," Bonita Beckman, "Trudeau Passes the Buck," "Women Descend on BC Legislature: 'Strangers in the House,'" "Women Confront Loffman," "Join Cross Canada Abortion Campaign," "Defend Markoff," and "An Open Letter to the Prime Minister," *The Pedestal*, April 1970, 1–3; 7–8; "B.C. Doctors Call Cops on Women," *The Pedestal*, May 1970, 3.

39 Simon Fraser University Archives, F-162-3-3-0-27. Marge Hollibaugh's Abortion Caravan Scrapbook, letter from the Women's Caucus to the Prime Minister and the Ministers of Health and Justice, 19 March 1970. University of Ottawa, Canadian Women's Movement Archives, X10-1, Series 1, Box 1, Abortion Caravan (May 1970) File, "Brief of the Abortion Caravan," May 1970.

40 Ben Tierney, "Abortion Reform 'Not Enough,'" *Calgary Herald*, 18 April 1970, 55, and Tierney, "'Daringly Liberal' Abortion Laws Are Proving Ineffective," *Edmonton Journal*, 21 April 1970, 20.

41   University of Ottawa, Canadian Women's Movement Archives, Box 1, Abortion Caravan and Box 110, Saskatoon Women's Liberation, copies of a letter from Saskatoon Women's Liberation, 8 April 1970, with a copy of their brief to Munro. Simon Fraser University Archives, Frances Wasserlein Fonds, F-165-3-3-0-6, letter from Margaret Mahood in Edmonton to Jean Rands in Vancouver, 17 March 1970. See also "Sask Women Demonstrate for Safe Abortion: Munro Agrees to Talk," *The Pedestal*, May 1970, 2.

42   For the details of the B.C. abortion campaign, see Thomson, *Winning Choice on Abortion*, chapter 4. Wasserlein describes the B.C. campaign in "An Arrow," 79–87. Simon Fraser University Archives, F-162-3-3-0-27. Marge Hollibaugh's Abortion Caravan Scrapbook, document entitled, "Abortion: A Human Right for Women"; letter from caucus members Betsy Meadley (a.k.a. Wood) and Marge Hollibaugh to the provincial attorney-general, Leslie Peterson, and Minister of Health Services and Hospital Insurance, Ralph Loffman, 10 March 1970.

43   "Galleries Invaded," *Vancouver Express*, 26 March 1970; "Women Lose Abortion Bid," "They Want Simple Change in Law: Get Rid of Damned Thing," and "Our View—Freedom to Decide," *Vancouver Express*, 11 April 1970, 1, 3–4. The *Express* was a newspaper put out by the striking staff of Pacific Press, which owned the *Vancouver Sun* and the *Province*. On the strike, see Marc Edge, *Pacific Press: The Unauthorized Story of Vancouver's Newspaper Monopoly* (Vancouver: New Star Books, 2001), chapters 8 and 9. Clement Chapple, "Legislature All Tangled Up in Red Tape," Victoria *Daily Colonist*, 26 March 1970, 1; "Red Streamers Litter Legislature," Victoria *Daily Times*, 26 March 1970, 23; Alan White (CP), "Abortion Reformists Picket PM in BC," Victoria *Daily Times*, 28 March 1970, 1; Douglas Sagi, "Trudeau Attacks the Slopes," *Globe and Mail*, 30 March 1970, 1; Dorothy Wrotnowski, "Caucus Plans Protest on Abortion Practice," Victoria *Daily Colonist*, 25 March 1970, 24. Jeannine Mitchell, "Abortion March a Success," and "Abortion Laws Are Killing People," *Georgia Straight*, 18–25 February 1970, 2, 11; Jeannine Mitchell, "March against Frustration," *Georgia Straight*, 25 March 1970, 1–2; Jeannine Mitchell, "Loffmark: Some Would Be Offended," and Vancouver Women's Caucus, "Trudeau Surprised," appearing under a joint headline, "Trudeau, Loffmark Leave Women Unsatisfied," *Georgia Straight*, 1–8 April 1970, 1–2; Jeannette Mitchell, "Women Ordered from College," *Georgia Straight*, 15–22 April 1970, 3.

44   Roberts interview with Freeman; Anne Roberts, "Legalize Abortions," *The Peak*, 11 February 1970, appearing under the byline Vicki Goodman as "A Valentine's Day Protest for Control of Our Bodies," *The Ubyssey*, 13 February 1970, 2; University of Ottawa, Canadian Women's Movement Archives, Box 125, Vancouver Women's Caucus, 7, "March on Valentine's Day: Protest Inhuman Abortion Laws," c. February 1970. Some of the same language, including a quote from Sanger, was used on the inside of a pamphlet outlining various actions, including the protest in support of Markoff, the appeal to the provincial ministers in Victoria, and the local Mother's Day march in Vancouver. Simon Fraser University Archives, Frances Wasserlein Papers, Vancouver Women's Caucus Binder, 2/5, F-162-3-3-0-6, copy of pamphlet; see also Simon Fraser University Archives, Anne Roberts Fonds, 165, press releases regarding the arrest of Markoff, 17 and 19 March 1970.

45   Roberts was quoted in "Women Demonstrate for Abortion," *The Peak*, 18 February 1970. Clipping in Simon Fraser University Archives, Frances Wasserlein Papers, Vancouver Women's Caucus Binder, 1/5, F-162-3-3-0-5.

46   Simon Fraser University Archives, Anne Roberts Fonds 162, Abortion File, F-166-0-0-0-1, copies of Edmonton Women's Liberation flyers. See also press release about an address from a local doctor on abortion, 29 April 2007.

47   It's unclear when this conversation took place, possibly before the *Sun* staff went on strike in February, but the labour dispute would not have prevented management from interviewing prospective summer staff. This is possibly the same man whom

Simma Holt, a reporter there at the time, remembers as being particularly preju-
diced against women, as were some of her other male colleagues. Holt, *Memoirs
of a Loose Cannon*, chapters 10 and 11.
48 Roberts interview with Freeman; Roberts email to Freeman, 5 April 2009.
49 Untitled drafts in Roberts'private papers. She recalls that the one about the referral service was sent out over the wire, but the one about the doctors likely was not,
apparently because of legal issues. Roberts email to Freeman, 5 April 2009. At CP
Edmonton, she wrote other stories, with bylines, about women's issues, undated
copies of which are also in her personal papers. Anne Roberts (Edmonton CP),
"Why Won't Women Join Unions?" and "Monicas Join Forces to Fight Prejudices,"
about a group of single mothers.
50 CP, "For the Newcomer."
51 Untitled typescript of Abortion Caravan advance story in Roberts's personal papers,
undated, but clearly written before the Caravan left Vancouver. Although she wrote
it in Edmonton, she slugged it CP Vancouver because the story was based in that
city. Upon receiving it, the Vancouver bureau gave it a new lead and edited it, but
still kept a substantial amount of the information she provided, word for word. It
appeared, for example, as (CP-Vancouver), "Abortion Law Protest Planned," *Saint
John Telegraph-Journal*, 28 April 1970, 7; "Coffin on Mother's Day to Protest Abortion Law," *Montreal Star*, 28 April 1970, 19; "Abortion Protest Sets Off," *Toronto Daily
Star*, 28 April 1970, 60; "Abortion Cavalcade Sets Out for Ottawa," *Globe and Mail*,
28 April 13; "Women's Assault on Abortion Law: Coffin Dragged to Ottawa," Victoria *Daily Colonist*, 28 April 1970, 21.
52 Caravan photographs, *The Pedestal*, May 1970; other women who were involved
flew instead, so there were 19 to 20 involved, according to Thomson, *Winning Choice
on Abortion*, 41–44; CP (Vancouver),"Women's Liberation Groups Start Tour across
Canada," Regina *Leader-Post*, 28 April 1970, 15. Wells, "The Women Are Coming,"
erroneously reported the departure date as being in March 1970.
53 Thomson, *Winning Choice on Abortion*, 33–34, n8. Caucus press release, 26 April
1970, in Simon Fraser University Archives, Frances Wasserlein Fonds, Women's
Caucus Binder 3/5, F-162-3307. Marcy Cohen also attributes the death figure to a
local doctor in Nichol, *Struggle for Choice*. Roberts CP typescript in her personal
papers and CP Vancouver's stories with the statistics that were carried across the
country. See, for example (CP Vancouver),"Coffin-Toting Women to March to
Ottawa," *Calgary Herald*, 22 April 1970, 37; "Women's Liberation Groups Start Tour
across Canada," Regina *Leader-Post*, 28 April 1970, 15; "Women Start Full Abortion
Law Attack," Montreal *Gazette*, 28 April 1970, 7. Earlier, Roberts gave the source
as the Bureau of Labour. Roberts, "Legalize Abortions," *The Peak*, 11 February
1970. In Toronto, a *Globe and Mail* reporter said the figure of 1000 deaths came
from a Toronto Women's Liberation projection of local hospital statistics, while the
2000 figure came from the Humanist Association of Canada. Leone Kirkwood,
"Feminists Plan to Haul Coffin to Mark Illegal Abortion Deaths," *Globe and Mail*,
16 April 1970, W10.
54 Cope W. Schwenger, "Abortion as a Public Health Problem and Community Health
Measure," in *Family Planning in Canada: A Source Book*, ed. Benjamin Schlesinger
(Toronto: University of Toronto Press, 1974), 240; Jenson, *The Politics of Abortion*,
51; Sheila Arnopoulos, "More Married Than Single Girls Aborted," *Montreal Star*,
15 February 1969, 67. This article was the second in an eight-part series on reproductive rights.
55 "Brief of the Abortion Caravan, May 1970."
56 Reaction stories included CP (Ottawa), "No Figures," Regina *Leader-Post*, 30 April
1970, 13; "No Count of Illegal Abortions," *Toronto Daily Star*, 30 April 1970, 76;
"235 Legal Abortions Reported in 3 Months," *Toronto Daily Star*, 8 May 1970, 2;
Edward Cowan, "Campaign to End Legal Restrictions on Abortions in Canada

Begun by Women's Liberation Movement," *New York Times*, 10 May 1970, 29; Susan Becker (CP Ottawa), "Abortion Caravan Sits In at 24 Sussex," *Montreal Star*, 11 May 1970 and James Tost, "Women's Cavalcade Hits City to Protest Anti-Abortion Laws," *Ottawa Journal*, 9 May 1970, clippings in Marg Hollibaugh's scrapbook. See also the letter from Olive Heron, "Abortion," *Globe and Mail*, 1 May 1970, 6; Barbara Vedan, "Liberation Group Meets with Toupin, Macking in Abortion Campaign," *Winnipeg Free Press*, 24 April 1970, 20; and Cathy Carlyle-Gordge, "Women's Lib Meeting Ends in Chaos," *Winnipeg Free Press*, 19 June 1970, 17.

57 See, for example, Murray Goldblatt, "Cabinet Ministers Shun Meeting: Abortion Group Holds Hill Rally," *Globe and Mail*, 11 May 1970, 11; CP Ottawa, "Cabinet Rebuffs Protesters," *Calgary Herald*, 8 May 1970, 15; and CP Ottawa, "Angry Women Force Commons to Adjourn," Regina *Leader-Post*, 12 May 1970, 31.

58 University of Ottawa, Canadian Women's Movement Archives, X10-1, Series 1, Box 1, Abortion Caravan (May 1970) File, "Brief of the Abortion Caravan, May 1970" and one-page summary. Box 125, Vancouver Women's Caucus, untitled fact sheet, c. April 1970. SFU Archives, Wasserlein Fonds, F-162-3-3-0-7, Women's Caucus Binder 3/5, press release from the Caravan, including the four demands, 8 May 1970.

59 Roberts interview with Freeman; Margo Dunn cited in Rebick, *Ten Thousand Roses*, 40, also as quoted by Cole Dudley, "The Women Are Coming," *Kinesis*, October 1983, 14; Wasserlein, "An Arrow," 87, 94. See, for example, "Pro-Abortion Women's Group Speaks Here on Way to Ottawa," *Sudbury Star*, 6 May 1970, 19.

60 Roberts interview with Freeman; Thomson, *Winning Choice on Abortion*, 43; Wasserlein recounts the resentment but gives no names. Wasserlein, "An Arrow," 92–94; Sheila McCook, "'Tremendous Pressure' for Abortion Reform—Organizer," *Ottawa Citizen*, 29 April 1970, 43. This article was published after Carrell left Ottawa for Vancouver.

61 Wasserlein, "An Arrow," 90; Lynne Rach, "Abortion Caravan on Move," and "Pregnant Woman's Dilemma Depicted," *Calgary Herald*, 29 April 1970, 77; "Women's Protest Dramatizes Horror of Illegal Abortions," *Edmonton Journal*, 30 April 1970, 18; "Abortion Caravan Visits City," Saskatoon *Star-Phoenix*, 1 May 1970, 3; "Liberation Caravan Visits Regina en Route to Ottawa," Regina *Leader-Post*, 2 May 1970, 9; Pippa Payne, "Women's Liberation Issue Ottawa Ultimatum," Winnipeg *Tribune*, 4 May 1970, 16; Barbara Vedan, "Abortion Campaign Not Whole Story," and "An Open Letter to the Prime Minister," *Winnipeg Free Press*, 4 May 1970, 16. "Pro-Abortion Women's Group Speaks Here on Way to Ottawa," *Sudbury Star*, 6 May 1970, 19; Margaret Weiers, "Feminists Demand No Restrictions on Abortions," *Toronto Daily Star*, 7 May 1970, 77.

62 Lynne Rach, "Abortion Caravan on Move," and "Pregnant Woman's Dilemma Depicted," *Calgary Herald*, 29 April 1970, 77.

63 Roberts interview with Freeman.

64 CP (Edmonton), "Women Protestors Say 'Abortion Is Our Right,'" *Lethbridge Herald*, 30 April 1970, copy in Roberts's private collection. Other coverage, with the anti-abortion woman's photograph, was published as CP (Edmonton), "New Show Arrives: We Are Furious (Women)," *Montreal Star*, 1 May 1970, 30; a shorter version without photos appeared as "Abortion Law Hit at Edmonton Rally," *Ottawa Journal*, 30 April 1970, 23, and "Abortion Law Protest Staged in Edmonton," Saskatoon *Star-Phoenix*, 30 April 1970, 5. A local reporter (no byline) wrote, "Women's Protest Dramatizes Horror of Illegal Abortions," *Edmonton Journal*, 30 April 1970, 18.

65 "Abortion Group Meets Hostility," *Vancouver Express*, 5 May 1970, 21; (CP Saskatoon), "Abortion Group Holds Rally in Saskatoon," *Winnipeg Free Press*, 2 May 1970, 16; "Abortion Caravan Visits City," Saskatoon *Star-Phoenix*, 1 May 1970, 3. "Liberation Caravan Visits Regina en Route to Ottawa," Regina *Leader-Post*, 2 May 1970, 9; CP (Regina), "Abortion Backers in Regina," Saskatoon *Star-Phoenix*, 2 May 1970, 3.

66 Pippa Payne, "Women's Liberation Issue Ottawa Ultimatum," Winnipeg *Tribune*, 4 May 1970, 16.

67 Barbara Vedan, "Abortion Campaign Not Whole Story" and "An Open Letter to the Prime Minister," *Winnipeg Free Press*, 4 May 1970, 16. The *Free Press* had already given it advance publicity, and covered the Manitoba abortion campaign. (CP Vancouver), "Abortion Cavalcade to Cross Country," *Winnipeg Free Press*, 17 April 1970, 21; Judi Gunter, "Women's Liberation Movement Opens Abortion Campaign Here," *Winnipeg Free Press*, 23 April 2007, 19; Barbara Vedan, "Liberation Group Meets with Toupin, Mackling in Abortion Campaign," *Winnipeg Free Press*, 24 April 2007, 20; "Coffin Marks Cavalcade," *Winnipeg Free Press*, 1 May 1970, 23.

68 "Abortion Caravan Due Here," *Fort William Daily Times-Journal*, 30 April 1970, 2; "Local Women Protest: Abortion Caravan Meets Resistance," *Fort William Daily Times-Journal*, 4 May 1970, 1, 2; another story corrected the information that all the protesters were from a local Catholic church. They preferred to refer to themselves as "concerned citizens." "Women Protest," *Fort William Daily Times-Journal*, 5 May 1970, 1. The rival newspaper ran only a photo with caption, "Abortion Caravan Wins Support Here," *Port Arthur News Chronicle*, 4 May 1970, 2.

69 Wasserlein, "An Arrow," 92–93. Simon Fraser University Archives, Frances Wasserlein Fonds, Women's Caucus Binder 3/5, F-162-3-3-0-7, press release, 8 May 1970.

70 Christabelle Sethna and Steve Hewitt, "Clandestine Operations: The Vancouver Women's Caucus, the Abortion Caravan and the RCMP," *Canadian Historical Review*, 90:3, September 2009, 463–495.

71 Thomson, *Winning Choice on Abortion*, 47. Kay MacIntyre, "Cavalcade Was Surprisingly Young....There's Nobody Home in Ottawa?" and CP (Ottawa), "Caucus Calls PM Irresponsible," *The Sault Daily Star*, 5 May 1970, 15.

72 "Pro-Abortion Women's Group Speaks Here on Way to Ottawa," *Sudbury Star*, 6 May 1970, 19. The article copies the same phrasing used at different points in Anne Roberts, "Legalize Abortions," *The Peak*, 11 February 1970, 2, and in one of the Vancouver Caucus/Edmonton Women's Liberation pamphlets in her personal papers.

73 Roberts interview with Freeman.

74 University of Ottawa, Canadian Women's Movement Archives, X10-1, Series 1, Box 1, Abortion Caravan (May 1970) File, document 0092, Melodie Mayson and Peggy Morton for Toronto Women's Liberation, "Abortion Caravan Proposals," c. February 1970. See also edited draft of a pamphlet issued in Toronto, "Abortion Is Our Right. Women's Liberation Movement." They also challenged provincial politicians. Sally Barnes, "Feminists Confront Wells on Issue of Easier Abortions," *Toronto Daily Star*, 28 April 1970, 80.

75 Bonnie Kreps was a founder. See Kreps, "Radical Feminism 1," in *Women Unite!* (Toronto: Women's Educational Press, 1972), 71–75. There were several articles about them, including Jean Sharp (CP Women's Bureau), "New Feminists Are Revolutionary," Saskatoon *Star-Phoenix*, 14 April 1970, 7.

76 Thomson, *Winning Choice on Abortion*, chapter 5; Wasserlein, "An Arrow," 95–96. The dispute was aired later in Mary Trew, "How We Differ," Gwen Hauser, "Free Abortion on Demand—Parliament Forced to Listen," and "These Women Understand the Democratic Procedure," *The Pedestal*, June 1970, 1, 7–6, 8–9.

77 Simon Fraser University Archives, Frances Wasserlein Fonds, Women's Caucus Binder 3/5, F-162-3307, undated letter to MPs from Mary Matheson and Dodie Weppler, Vancouver Women's Caucus, c. April–May 1970. CP (Ottawa), "Ottawa Men Disappoint Lib Group," *Winnipeg Free Press*, 8 May 1970, 31.

78 CP (Ottawa), "Ottawa Men Disappoint Lib Group," *Winnipeg Free Press*, 8 May 1970, 31; also Victor Mackie, "Protesters Force House to Adjourn—Women Carry 'Abortion War' into Commons Galleries," *Winnipeg Free Press*, 12 May 1970, 1, 4.

79 Margaret Weiers, "Feminists Demand No Restrictions on Abortions," *Toronto Daily Star*, 7 May 1970, 77; see also "300 Expected to Join Abortion March in Ottawa,"

Toronto *Telegram*, 7 May 1970, 7, and "Abortion Cavalcaders Will Attend Meeting—Will PM?" clipping attributed to the *Globe and Mail*, 7 May 1970 in Hollibaugh scrapbook; CP, "Abortion, Birth Control Controversy World-Wide—Women Will Fight Ottawa for 'Dying Sisters,'" *Montreal Star*, 6 May 1970, 88; "Cabinet Rebuffs Protestors," *Calgary Herald*, 8 May 1970, 15; Mary Jukes, "Pregnant Women Attend, Parents Bring Children—500 in Pro-Abortion Demonstration Orderly, Attentive," *Globe and Mail*, 8 May 1970, 10; Edward Cowan, "Campaign to End Legal Restrictions on Abortions in Canada Begun by Women's Liberation Movement," *New York Times*, 10 May 1970, 29.

80 Wasserlein, "An Arrow," 96. CBC Radio Archives, Accession #700-512-05/00, "Assignment," 12 May 1970, report by Mary Lawson.

81 Recollection of Jackie Larkin, a member of an Ottawa Women's Liberation Movement group, in Nichol, *Struggle for Choice*. Their demonstration during the medical association meeting was reported in CP (Ottawa), "Women Urge Doctors to Back Legal Abortions," *Toronto Daily Star*, 8 May 1970, 42. Larkin, one of the Waffle women, explained that it was their group that helped organize the political activities when the Caravan arrived in Ottawa. Wells, "The Women Are Coming."

82 Hazel interviews with Freeman, 1995, 2006.

83 Hazel interview with Freeman, 2006.

84 Simon Fraser University Archives, Frances Wasserlein Fonds, Women's Caucus Binder 3/5, F-162-3-3-0-7, press release, 8 May 1970.

85 James Tost, "Women's Cavalcade Hits City to Protest Anti-Abortion Laws," *Ottawa Journal*, 9 May 1970, clipping in Hollibaugh's scrapbook.

86 "FLF Won't Be Along, but Backs English," *Montreal Star*, 8 May 1970, 23; Berl Francis, "Local Women Join Pro-Abortion March," Montreal *Gazette*, 8 May 1970, 26, and "Abortion Backers Parade," Montreal *Gazette*, 11 May 1970. "In Ottawa and Montreal—Women's Lib Plan Abortion Law Protest," *Montreal Star*, 7 May 1970, 22. Wasserlein, "An Arrow," 101, n77.

87 Zoe Bieler, "Abortion: Operation Simple but Aftereffects Traumatic," "Liberalized Canadian Criminal Code Doesn't Help Women Get Abortions," and "'Butcher' or Baby," *Montreal Star*, 9 May 1970, 65–66; see also Sandra Dolan, "Women Seek Abortion Rights on Mother's Day," and "Pressure Abortion Boards, Doctor Tells Women's Group," *Montreal Star*, 11 May 1970, 11; CP (Montreal), "100 Women Protest Canada's Abortion Laws," Fredericton *Daily Gleaner*, 11 May 1970, 2, and "Montreal Rally," *Globe and Mail*, 11 May 1970, 11. Other features on abortion that appeared in the press around the same time included Lisa Hobbs, "Figure May Be Hundreds a Week—Abortions a Large Part of Toronto's Everyday Life: Doctors," *Globe and Mail*, 18 May 1970, 1, 10. See also Marion K. Sanders, "Abortion Laws Tough Because Sex Bothers People," republished from *Harper's* magazine; Mike Royko, "But Where Is the Man Who Will Lead Them?" reprinted from the *Chicago Daily News*; and Patricia Maginnis and Lana Clark Phelan, "Why Not a Poll on Cancer?" reprinted from the *Abortion Handbook*, all in the *Vancouver Sun*, 16 May 1970, 5.

88 See, for example, Ann Barling, "In Unladylike Language—Abortion Laws Disputed Here," *Vancouver Sun*, 15 May 1970, 43; "Abortion Reformers Invade Hospital," *Calgary Herald*, 11 May 1970, 30; "Marchers Urge Special Clinics for Abortions," *Edmonton Journal*, 11 May 1970, 22; Susan Janz, "Coffin Carried to Protest Abortion Deaths," Winnipeg *Tribune*, 11 May 1970, 8.

89 Haussman, *Abortion Politics*, chapter 3. See also Catherine Dunphy, *Morgentaler: A Difficult Hero; A Biography* (Toronto: Random House Canada, 1996).

90 The Just Society was an ironic reference to promises made by Prime Minister Pierre Trudeau. On the JSM, see Margaret Hillyard Little, "Militant Mothers Fight Poverty: The Just Society Movement, 1968–1971," *Labour/Le Travail*, 59, Spring 2007, 179–197.

91 Thomson, 53–54. None of the newspapers mentioned the crowd's reaction to Morgentaler. Wasserlein, "An Arrow," 99; University of Ottawa, Canadian Women's

Movement Archives, Box 1, Abortion Caravan and Box 46, Just Society Movement, copies of Power's statement to Abortion Caravan, 1970. The same CP story ran in several newspapers. The full list of demands and the photograph of Gail Nystrom were included in Susan Becker (CP Ottawa), "Crowd Favoring Abortion Invade PM's Residence," *Sudbury Star*, 11 May 1970, 37. Some details of the rally, a photo of the demonstrators and comments from Doris Power and an anti-abortion spokeswoman were included in "Abortion Caravan Protests PM's Absence with Sit-In," *Montreal Star*, 11 May 1970, 12. Shorter versions included "Caravan Reaches Ottawa," Saskatoon *Star-Phoenix*, 11 May 1970, 20; "Group Protests Abortion Laws," Regina *Leader-Post*, 11 May 1970, 16; "Abortion Caravan Groups Critical of PM Trudeau," Fort *William Times-Journal*, 11 May 1970, 3; "Peaceful Sit-In Climaxes End of Abortion Campaign," *Port Arthur News Chronicle*, 11 May 1970, 5, with Nystrom's photo on page 8. *The Sault Daily Star* ran the photo with an explanatory caption, 11 May 1970, 2. See also Sheila McCook, "Pleas for Abortion Greeted By Silence"; "List for PM —Brief Outlines Feminists Demands " and "Ladies Talking Tough to Make Their Points," *Ottawa Citizen*, 11 May 1970, 25; "Angry Feminists Cry Out for 'Free Abortion' Laws," "Easy Abortion Termed Cancer of Women's Rights," and Pledge War against Gov't on Abortion," *Ottawa Journal*, 11 May 1970, 1, 3.

92   Murray Goldblatt, "Abortion Group Holds Hill Rally," *Globe and Mail*, 11 May 1970, 11.

93   The march to 24 Sussex Drive was Doris Power's idea, according to Marcy Cohen, speaking in Nichol, *The Struggle for Choice*.

94   Susan Becker (CP Ottawa), "Crowd Favoring Abortion Invade PM's Residence," *Sudbury Star*, 11 May 1970, 37; Grace Rajnovich, "Cavalcade Waited by PM's Door," *The Sault Daily Star*, 11 May 1970, 15; "Abortion Caravan Protests PM's Absence with Sit-In," *Montreal Star*, 11 May 1970, 12; "Caravan Reaches Ottawa," Saskatoon *Star-Phoenix*, 11 May 1970, 20; "Group Protests Abortion Laws," Regina *Leader-Post*, 11 May 1970, 16; "Abortion Law Repealers Leave Coffin at PM's," Halifax *Chronicle-Herald*, 11 May 1970, 3. See also "Angry Feminists Cry Out for 'Free Abortion' Laws," and "Pledge War against Gov't on Abortion," *Ottawa Journal*, 11 May 1970, 1, 3. Sheila McCook, "Pleas for Abortion Greeted by Silence"; "List for PM: Brief Outlines Feminists Demands," *Ottawa Citizen*, 11 May 1970, 25; Maggie Siggins, "Ottawa Demonstration: Abortion Law Protesters Take Coffin to PM's House," Toronto *Telegram*, clipping in Hollibaugh scrapbook.

95   Kathryn Keate, "Out from Under, Women Unite! Life Inside Women's Liberation," *Saturday Night*, July 1970, 15–20.

96   Margo Dunn cited by Cole Dudley, "The Women Are Coming," *Kinesis*, October 1983, 15 and by Wasserlein, "An Arrow," 99. Dunn later said the crowd laughed off the fact that the police had guns. Thomson, *Winning Choice on Abortion*, 55. A recent CBC documentary with several of the women who took part in the Caravan reported that the police did pull out guns, and that it was an RCMP supervisor who persuaded Trudeau that the women should not be arrested. Wells, "The Women Are Coming."

97   Keate, "Out from Under," 16; Hazel interviews with Freeman, 1995, 2006.

98   Margo Dunn cited in Rebick, *Ten Thousand Roses*, 40.

99   Keate, "Out from Under."

100 Wasserlein, "An Arrow," 105.

101 Hazel interview with Freeman, 2006.

102 Hazel interview with Freeman, 1995.

103 Hazel interview with Freeman, 2006.

104 Gerald McDuff, "Abortion Law Protesters Break Up House Sitting," *Toronto Daily Star*, 12 May 1970, 1, 8. Margo Dunn remembers a guard checking her purse before Saturday's rally and allowing her inside the building with it. Apparently, he did not notice that she was carrying implements for performing an illegal abortion. Dunn cited in Rebick, *Ten Thousand Roses*, 40.

105 Thomson, *Winning Choice on Abortion*, 57.

106 Keate, "Out from Under."

107 Hazel interview with Freeman, 2006. Other members of the Caravan recall that they obtained blank guest passes from some MPs' offices and just filled them in. Wells, "The Women Are Coming."

108 Hazel interview with Freeman, 1995.

109 Victor Mackie, "Protesters Force House to Adjourn—Women Carry 'Abortion War' into Commons Galleries," *Winnipeg Free Press*, 12 May 1970, 1, 4.

110 CP accounts include Gerard McNeil, CP Ottawa, "Abortion Backers Upset Commons," *The Sault Daily Star*, 12 May 1970, 1; McNeil, "Free Abortion on Demand—25 Women Demonstrators Ejected from Commons," *Fort William Times-Journal*, 12 May 1970, 3; "'... Worse Than the Farmers'—Women Disrupt Commons," *Port Arthur News Chronicle*, 12 May 1970, 1; "Abortion Advocates Stall Commons," Saskatoon *Star-Phoenix*, 12 May 1970, 12; "Angry Women Force Commons to Adjourn," Regina *Leader-Post*, 12 May 1970, 31; "Women Chant Demands—Abortion Supporters Halt House," *Montreal Star*, 11 May 1970, 1; "Women Chain Themselves to Seats—Pro-Abortionists Close House—Parliament Rings with Shouting," Victoria *Daily Times*, 11 May 1970, 1; "Demonstrators Hold Up House Business," Halifax *Chronicle-Herald*, 12 May 1970, 1–2; Abortion Demonstration Forces House Recess," Saint John *Telegraph-Journal*, 12 May 1970, 1; "Angry Women Force Commons to Adjourn," Regina *Leader-Post*, 12 May 1970, 31.

111 *Hansard, House of Commons Debates*, 11 May 1970, 6793–6796.

112 For example, Clyde Sanger, "Angry, Shouting Women Disrupt House Sitting," *Globe and Mail*, 12 May 1970, 1–2. See also Gordon Pape, "Women Yelling for Abortion Halt Commons," Montreal *Gazette*, 12 May 1970, 1–2; Greg Connolley, "Pro-Abortion Protest—House Screams to a Halt," and "Parliament Aborted—NDP Blamed for Women in the House," *Ottawa Citizen*, 12 May 1970, 1, 33; "Abortion Row Halts Parliament," *Vancouver Express*, 12 May 1970, 1; Province Ottawa Bureau, "These Are the Weeks That Were—Ottawa Diary," Vancouver *Province*, 15 May 1970, 13; Richard Jackson, "Chanting Women Close House," Victoria *Daily Colonist*, 12 May 1970, 1, 21; Richard Jackson, "Some Chained to Seats—Screaming Women Halt the Commons," and Marjorie Nichols, "Won't Submit to 'Blackmail'—Turner Refused Women's Ultimatum," *Ottawa Journal*, 12 May 1970, 1, 12; Richard Jackson, "Chant for Free Abortions—Screaming Tumult of Women Activists Closes Down the House of Commons," *Sudbury Star*, 12 May 1970, 1; Ben Tierney and Peter Calamai, "'Free Abortionists' Bring House to Halt—Gallery Uproar Jolts Commons," *Calgary Herald*, 11 May 1970, 1; Gerald McDuff, "Abortion Law Protesters Break Up House Sitting," *Toronto Daily Star*, 12 May 1970, 1, 8. The surviving RCMP record of the protest has been heavily censored, according to Wells, "The Women Are Coming."

113 Keate, "Out from Under," 19–20.

114 Library and Archives Canada, CJOH-TV Ottawa collection, demonstrations footage, ISNs #183711, a clip of the sit-in at 24 Sussex Drive and #183712, a clip of the demonstration around the Eternal Flame. CBC Radio had clips of the women chanting outside, used in Wells, "The Women Are Coming."

115 Marjorie Nichols, "Abortion Paraders Pledge 'Total War,'" Victoria *Daily Colonist*, 12 May 1970, 2; Victor Mackie, "Protesters Force House to Adjourn—Women Carry 'Abortion War' into Commons Galleries," *Winnipeg Free Press*, 12 May 1970, 1, 4; Arthur Blakely, "'Nor Hell a Fury,' as MPs Found Out," Montreal *Gazette*, 14 May 1970, 7.

116 None of the Caravanners discuss this charge in any written source I have found, including Thomson, *Winning Choice on Abortion*, chapter 6 and Rebick, *Ten Thousand Roses*, chapter 3. Wasserlein mentions only that they made the "necessary arrangements" to get passes. Wasserlein, "An Arrow," 102–103. *Hansard, House of Commons Debates*, 12 May 1970, 6843–6844. Clyde Sanger, "MPs Say Names Forged

on Protesters' Passes," *Globe and Mail*, 13 May 1970, 2; Greg Connolley, "RCMP Probing Case of the Forged Passes," *Ottawa Citizen*, 13 May 1970, 1; Gerald McDuff, "Abortion Law Protesters Used Forged Passes, MPs Say," *Toronto Daily Star*, 12 May 1970, 60; Wayne MacDonald, "After Women's Invasion—Protective Shield Urged for MPs," *Vancouver Sun*, 15 May 1970, 23; Brian McKenna, "MPs Study Ways to Curb Disruptions," and "MP's Charge Signature Forged," *Montreal Star*, 12 May 1970, 1–2; Brian McKenna, "House Intrigued by Forged Passes," *Montreal Star*, 13 May 1970, 68; CP (Ottawa), "MP Signatures Claimed Forged by Protesters," Saskatoon *Star-Phoenix*, 13 May 1970, 12; "MPs' Names Reported Forged by Protestors," Regina *Leader-Post*, 13 May 1970, 25; "Commons Abortion Demonstration May Cause Access Restrictions," Victoria *Daily Times*, 12 May 1970, 21; Ben Tierney, "Tight Security in the House Likely," Winnipeg *Tribune*, 12 May 1970, 2; and Tierney, "Committee to Investigate Commons Security Rules," Winnipeg *Tribune*, 13 May 1970, 1.

117 Editorial, "Suffragettes," *Montreal Star*, 12 May 1970, 8; "Abortion: The State's Choice or Woman's?" *Toronto Daily Star*, 12 May 1970, 6; "Open the Abortion Debate," *Globe and Mail*, 19 May 1970, 6; Douglas Fisher, "This Noise of Women Gags Voice of Reason," *Vancouver Sun*, 19 May 1970, 4; "Disorderly Conduct," *Ottawa Journal*, 12 May 1970, 6; "Threat to Democracy," *Calgary Herald*, 12 May 1970, 4; "Contempt for Law," *Winnipeg Free Press*, 12 May 1970, 2; "How to Lose a Cause," *Ottawa Citizen*, 13 May 1970, 6. Columnist Pat Wallace, "What People Are Doing," Vancouver *Province*, 15 May 1970, 34; see also Zita Cameron, "Mother's Day Marchers Want to Stop Coffin," Halifax *Chronicle-Herald*, 7 May 1970, 7.

118 Marjorie Sheard Carter, "Abortion," *Globe and Mail*, 20 May 1970, 6; other examples include a letter from Penny Kondaks, "How Can Doctors See the Results of Butchery and Still Refuse to Help?" *Montreal Star*, 13 May 1970, 10, also published under the caption "Legalized Abortion or Self-Surgery," Montreal *Gazette*, 15 May 1970, 6.

119 Errol Young, photograph, *Toronto Daily Star*, 11 May 1970, 1, and *Saturday Night*, July 1970, front cover; the other photos appeared in the same issue of the magazine, pages 15–20.

120 See, for example, letter to the editor from Mrs. Venetia Staffe under the heading, "A Reader's Blushes," *Saturday Night*, October 1970, 4; letter to the editor from Sydney J. Cook under the heading "'Out from Under,'" *Saturday Night*, November 1970, 9.

121 Hazel interviews with Freeman, 1995, 2006.

122 Hazel interview with Freeman, 1995. On the magazine's money problems during that period, see Robert Fulford, *Best Seat in the House: Memoirs of a Lucky Man* (Toronto: Collins, 1988), chapter 11.

123 Hazel interview with Freeman, 2006.

124 Hazel interview with Freeman, 1995.

125 Immediately afterwards, there were follow-up stories. See, for example, CP (Ottawa), "No Change on Abortions," *Vancouver Sun*, 21 May 1970, 23; Stan McDowell, "B.C. Feminists Call Trudeau a 'Murderer,'" *Toronto Daily Star*, 30 May 1970, 4; Douglas Sagi and John Burns, "Women Protest against Abortion Law—Trudeau Returns, Faces Screams of Anger," *Globe and Mail*, 30 May 1970, 1; CP (Vancouver), "PM Defends Abortion Laws," *Globe and Mail*, 16 June 1970, 10. Ann Barling, "Wary of Criminal Code—Doctors Have Fear of Present Abortion Law," *Vancouver Sun*, 23 May 1970, 40; CP (Hamilton, Ontario), "Girl Died in Friend's Arms after Abortion," *Toronto Daily Star*, 30 May 1970, 72.

126 Keate, "Out from Under," 20.

127 There was no specific rule against conflict of interest in the 1967 CP newcomer's guide in Roberts's papers.

128 Roberts interview with Freeman.

129 CBC *Take 30*, ISN 1970-10-6, aired 6 October 1970, after the Abortion Caravan.
130 Mainstream journalists were often skeptical of, and frustrated with, left-wing feminists who gave them a hard time in return. Dawn MacDonald, "Women's Liberation—Year 2," *Chatelaine*, November 1970, 25, 52, 54–56; Hilda Kearns, "Local Women's Liberation: Membership Growing Fast, Demonstrations Begin," and "Reporter Refused, Woman Welcome," *Montreal Star*, 9 May 1970, 65–66. Some, like Maggie Siggins of the Toronto *Telegram*, were attracted to their ideas but tried to follow newsroom procedures. Barbara M. Freeman, "'The Day of the Strong-Minded Frump Has Passed': Journalists and News of Feminism in Canada," in *Framing Our Past: Canadian Women's History in the Twentieth Century*, ed. Sharon Anne Cook, Lorna R. McLean and Kate O'Rourke (Montreal; Kingston: McGill-Queen's University Press, 2001), 385–391.
131 Quotes from Hazel interview with Freeman, 1995. Further information is from her 2006 interview with Freeman, her resumé, and follow-up emails.
132 See, for example, Bradley, *Mass Media and the Shaping of American Feminism*; Maryann Barakso and Brian F. Schaffner, "News Media Portrayals of the Women's Movement, 1969–2004," *Press/Politics*, 11:4, 2006, 22–44; Julie D'Acci, "Leading Up to Rowe v. Wade: Television Documentaries in the Abortion Debate," in Haralovich and Lauren Rabinovitz, eds., *Television, History and American Culture: Feminist Critical Essays* (Durham, NC; London: Duke University Press, 1999, 120–143; Maggie Jones Patterson and Megan Williams Hall, "Abortion, Moral Maturity and Civic Journalism," *Critical Studies in Mass Communication*, 15, 1998, 91–115.
133 Freeman, *The Satellite Sex*.
134 Barakso and Schaffner, "News Media Portrayals," 26–27.
135 Wasserlein, "An Arrow," 6.
136 Dustin Harp, "Newspapers' Transition from Women's to Style Pages: What Were They Thinking?" *Journalism*, 7:2, 2006, 197–216; Freeman, *The Satellite Sex*, chapters 2 and 9.
137 Jensen argues that the Court decision gave women equal access to a medical procedure under the Charter of Rights and Freedoms, but did not give a ruling on whether women's rights trumped fetal rights, the issue that still divides pro-choice and anti-abortion activists. Jensen, *The Politics of Abortion*, 16–20.
138 Lianne McTavish, "Virtual Activism and the Pro-Choice Movement in Canada," *Canadian Woman Studies*, 25:3/4, Summer 2006, 121–127. Catherine Dunphy, "We're the New Faces of the Abortion Debate," *Chatelaine*, April 2009, 206–210.

Chapter 6

1 Cover photo by Lori J. Meserve; Debbie Mathers and Megan Ardyche, "Why Does 'That Word' Have So Much Power?" *Pandora*, December 1987, 4.
2 Nancy Adamson, "Feminists, Libbers, Lefties and Radicals: The Emergence of the Women's Liberation Movement," in *A Diversity of Women: Ontario 1945–1980*, ed. Joy Parr (Toronto: University of Toronto Press, 1995), 252–280; Becki L. Ross, *The House That Jill Built: A Lesbian Nation in Formation* (Toronto: University of Toronto Press, 1995); Miriam Smith, *Lesbian and Gay Rights in Canada: Social Movements and Equality Seeking, 1971–1995* (Toronto: University of Toronto Press, 1999); Sharon Dale Stone, ed., *Lesbians in Canada* (Toronto: Between the Lines Press, 1990); L. Pauline Rankin, "Sexualities and National Identities: Re-Imagining Queer Nationalism," *Journal of Canadian Studies/Revue d'études canadiennes*, 35:2, Summer 2000, 176–196.
3 Barbara M. Freeman, *The Satellite Sex: The Media and Women's Issues in English Canada, 1966–1971* (Waterloo, ON: Wilfrid Laurier University Press, 2001); Freeman, "From No Go to No Logo: Lesbian Lives and Rights in *Chatelaine*," *Canadian Journal of Communication*, 31:4, 2006, 815–841; Valerie J. Korinek, *Roughing It in the Sub-*

urbs: Reading Chatelaine *Magazine in the Fifties and Sixties* (Toronto: University of Toronto Press, 2000); Korinek, "'Don't Let Your Girlfriend Ruin Your Marriage': Lesbian Imagery in *Chatelaine* Magazine, 1950–1969," *Journal of Canadian Studies*, 33:3, Fall 1998, 83–109.

4 Barbara Godard, "Feminist Periodicals and the Production of Cultural Value: The Canadian Context," *Women's Studies International Forum*, 25:2, 2002, 209–223; Barbara L. Marshall, "Communication as Politics: Feminist Print Media in English Canada," *Women's Studies International Forum*, 18:4, 1995, 463–474; Philinda Masters, "Women, Culture and Communications," in Ruth Roach Pierson et al., *Canadian Women's Issues: Twenty-five Years of Women's Activism in English Canada, Vol. I: Strong Voices* (Toronto: James Lorimer and Company, 1993), 394–417; Michèle Martin, "Changing the Picture: Women and the Media in Québec," in *Changing Patterns: Women in Canada*, 2nd ed., ed. Sandra Burt, Lorraine Code and Lindsay Dorney (Toronto: McClelland and Stewart, 1993), 177–211.

5 Smith, *Lesbian and Gay Rights in Canada*; Tom Warner, *Never Going Back: A History of Queer Activism in Canada* (Toronto: University of Toronto Press, 2002).

6 Godard, "Feminist Periodicals"; Marshall, "Communication as Politics"; Philinda Masters, "Feminist Press: Front Page Challenge, *Broadside*, June 1983, 8–9; Philinda Masters, "A Word from the Press: A Brief Survey of Feminist Publishing," *Resources for Feminist Research/ Documentation sur la recherche féministe*, 20:1 and 2, Spring/Summer 1991, 27–35; Mary Anne Coffey, "Feminist Print Media in Canada," a synopsis of Eleanor Wachtel, *Feminist Print Media* (Ottawa: Government of Canada, Secretary of State, 1982) and Wachtel, *Update on Feminist Periodicals* (Ottawa: Government of Canada, Secretary of State, 1985), in *Resources for Feminist Research/ Documentation sur la recherche féministe*, 20:1 and 2, Spring/Summer 1991, 25–26; Canadian Women's Movement Archives (hereafter CWMA), X10-1, Box 124, Vancouver Status of Women Papers (hereafter VSW), File 1, Jo Lazenby, Editor and VSW Vice-President, "*Kinesis* Report," *Vancouver Status of Women Annual Report*, June 1, 1975–May 31, 1976; "*Broadside* Wants to Be Read Outside the Movement," *Kinesis*, August 1979, 16. On *Pandora*, see Ingrid MacDonald, "Publishing Priorities," *Broadside*, June 1986, 7. Philinda Masters interview with Barbara Freeman, 2008, and Esther Shannon interview with Freeman, 2008.

7 Becki L. Ross, "Tracking Lesbian Speech: The Social Organization of Lesbian Periodical Publishing in English Canada, 1973–1988," in *Women's Writing and the Literary Institution*, ed. Claudine Potvin and Janice Williamson (Edmonton: Research Institute for Comparative Literature, University of Alberta, 1992), 173–185; "Index of Can. Lesbian mags," *Kinesis*, September 1991, 2. In the United States, there were a few lesbian publications, and gay male magazines and interests tended to dominate there as well. Rodger Streitmatter, *Unspeakable: The Rise of the Gay and Lesbian Press in America* (Boston; London: Faber and Faber, 1995).

8 Freeman, "From No Go to No Logo." In some areas of the country, including Saskatoon, the men and women integrated better than they did in large cities. Valerie J. Korinek, "'The most openly gay person for at least a thousand miles': Doug Wilson and the Politicization of a Province," *Canadian Historical Review*, 4:4, December 2003, 517–550. On the feminist collective, see Adamson, "Feminists, Libbers, Lefties and Radicals."

9 The number of women on each collective varied, but usually numbered between five and a dozen. Emma Kivisild interview with Barbara Freeman, 8 and 13 March 2009, which will be treated as the same interview; Shannon interview with Freeman; Nancy Pollak interview with Freeman, 2008; Fatima Jaffer interview with Freeman, 2008; Masters interview with Freeman, 2008; Bethan (formerly Betty-Ann) Lloyd interview with Freeman, 2008; Debbie Mathers interview with Freeman, 2008.

10 Some Vancouver Status of Women and *Kinesis* documents for 1971–1978 can be found in Special Collections at the University of British Columbia Library, and in

the Canadian Women's Movement Archives at the University of Ottawa (CWMA), X10-1. Further records are in Nancy Pollak's private collection, *Kinesis* records 1988–1992. CWMA holds a few documents regarding *Broadside*, X10-66, but there appears to be no archive for *Pandora*. The publications themselves can be found in various libraries and archives.

11 Nancy Fraser and other feminist scholars countered Habermas's historical construct of the role of communication in public debate, arguing that his original conception of an 18th-century "public sphere" involving an informed citizenship was too narrowly confined to bourgeois white men, and that other constituents, including women, formed a "counter-public" or "subaltern" sphere. Marshall, "Communication as Politics." On *Chatelaine*, see Freeman, *The Satellite Sex* and "From No Go to No Logo;" Korinek, *Roughing It in the Suburbs* and "Don't Let Your Girlfriend Ruin Your Marriage." A *Broadside* writer criticized *Chatelaine* for giving short shrift to women's achievements, especially in nontraditional areas such as sport. See Helen Lenskyj, "Myth Making Spoils Sports," *Broadside*, June 1984, 4. Cynthia Low, "New Women of Colour Magazine: Zine but Not Herd," *Kinesis*, February 1993, 4, 6; Nicole Redman, Tonia Bryan and Sherece Taffe, interviewed by E. Centime Sleek, "Talking with De Poonani Posse: Flowing with Da Juice," and "Da Juice" call for submissions, *Kinesis*, June 1995, 15, 23; Sur Mehat, "Review: *Sami Yoni: A Journal for Asian Lesbians.* 'The Power Is Now Mine,'" *Kinesis*, May 1993, 17.

12 Marshall, "Communication as Politics," and Godard, "Feminist Periodicals."

13 Letter from L. Zeldowicz, M.D., *Kinesis*, July 1977, 2; letter from Susan Crowley, *Kinesis*, August 1977, 22. Editorial, "More than a Fringe Phenomenon," *Broadside*, June 1984, 2. Some complainers bought a subscription, nonetheless. Letter from Helga Hoffman, *Pandora*, 1 December 1985, 5. On the issue of the appropriateness of lesbian visibility in professional advertisements, see letter from Jeanne Morouney, "Ad Maddens Every Time," *Kinesis*, December 1991/January 1992, 24, and response from Delyse Ledgard, "A Matter of Invisibility," *Kinesis*, February 1992, 19.

14 Joanne K. Jefferson, "Abortion, Lesbian, Growth Issues Not to Be Funded by SecState," *Pandora*, September–December 1987, 18.

15 Philinda Masters, "Feminist Press: Front Page Challenge"; Masters, "*Broadside* and Beyond," *Broadside*, August/September, 1989, 3; and Masters, "A Word from the Press." Ingrid MacDonald, "Publishing Priorities," *Broadside*, June 1986, 7. Karen Dubinsky, "Forces of Opposition," *Broadside*, April 1987, 5–6; editorial, "Standing Firm," *Broadside*, August/September 1987, 2. Noreen Shanahan, "Bye Bye *Broadside*," *Kinesis*, April 1989, 7. Emma Kivisild, "Feminist Periodical Conference a First" and "Media Under Attack," *Kinesis*, July/August 1985, 1, 4. "Target—*Kinesis*," *Kinesis*, March 1986, 6. "As *Kinesis* Goes to Press," and Nancy Pollak, "SecState Funding Cuts: Death of a Thousand Cuts," *Kinesis*, March 1993, 2, 3.

16 CWMA, X-10-1, Box 46, *Kinesis* Papers, copy of Reader Survey 1984. "Readers Survey," *Kinesis*, October 1984, 2, 34; Allisa McDonald, "*Kinesis* Survey Results Now In," *Kinesis*, October 1988, 3–4; "The Survey: What You Think of Us," *Kinesis*, February 1994, 15.

17 Eve Zaremba, "Movement Comment—Periodical Process," *Broadside*, February 1986, 7; Jaffer interview with Freeman.

18 Susan De Rosa, "Our Feminist Presses Deserve Our Support," *Pandora*, June 1988, 4. "*Kinesis* Editorial and Advertising Policy," *Kinesis*, July/August 1985, 2, and City of Vancouver Archives, PAM 1990-83, "*Kinesis* Writer's Guidelines," 1990. In *Pandora*, for example, St. Mary's University sponsored an ad for Women's Employment Outreach, according to a thank-you letter from Diann Graham, *Pandora*, 1 June 1986, 6. Other examples of typical ads appeared in *Pandora*, 1 September 1985, 10 and 28.

19 Pollak, Masters and Mathers interviews with Freeman.

20 In the early 1990s, for example, *Kinesis* was available at about 20 outlets in Vancouver, most of them alternative bookstores. Distribution list, *Kinesis*, April 1994, 2.

21 A typical rate in the early 1980s was $34 for a small ad, or 25 cents a word. Classifieds form, *Broadside*, February 1983, 14. In 1986, *Kinesis* increased its annual subscription rate from $15 to $17.50 and the newsstand price by 50 cents to $1.75 a copy. "*Kinesis* Price to Go Up to $1.75," *Kinesis*, February 1986, 2.

22 Examples of lesbian rights coverage include "Church May Ordain Lesbians," *Kinesis*, June 1984, 5; Helen Lenskyj, "From Prejudice to Policy," *Broadside*, April 1987, 4; S.V., "Custody Battle Reflects Classic Power Struggle," *Pandora*, March 1990, 13. *Kinesis* extensively covered the Gay Games in Vancouver, *Broadside* covered gay and lesbian theatre plays, and they all reviewed books. See, for example, "Can You Believe the Roar of the Crowd?" *Kinesis*, July/August 1990, 12–16; Amanda Hale, "Final Say," *Broadside*, February 1987, 13; Darl Wood, "Lesbian Novel Has New Positive Image," *Pandora*, Spring 1986, 15.

23 My research assistants and I came up with these totals, based on page space, and examined the themes of each article. Debbie Mathers did a count of overall lesbian content in *Pandora* during its tenure and also came up with about 8 percent of the total. Mathers interview with Freeman. Regarding the issue of lesbian content in francophone feminist publications, see Suzanne de Rosa and Jeanne Maranda, "La presse féministe est différente!" *Canadian Woman Studies/les cahiers de la femme*, 8:1, 33–34.

24 The same welcoming atmosphere for lesbians existed at *Kinesis* and *Broadside*. Kivisild, Shannon, Pollak and Jaffer interviews with Freeman; *Broadside* Papers, Box 6, "Correspondence 1979–1989," letter from Eve Zaremba to Pauline Belanger, 6 April 1983.

25 Kivisild interview with Freeman.

26 Shannon interview with Freeman. The article was "Women Who Rape," *Kinesis*, November 1985, 15–16.

27 Pollak interview with Freeman.

28 Between 1984 and 1988, under Kivisild and Shannon, lesbian content in *Kinesis* averaged five pages per edition; between 1988 and 1992 under Pollak, it dipped to two pages, and then went back up to four pages, perhaps because Jaffer (1992–1994) made it a point to include articles about women of colour who were also lesbians. During these years, most issues of *Kinesis* were between 24 and 28 pages.

29 Nancy Pollak's *Kinesis* documents, welcome to new editor, Fatima Jaffer, collective meeting minutes of 9 March 1992. Jaffer interview with Freeman. Fatima Jaffer, "Lesbians of Colour: Speaking from the Heart," a review of Makeda Silvera, ed., *Piece of My Heart: A Lesbian of Colour Anthology* (Toronto: Sister Vision Press, 1991), in *Kinesis*, March 1992, 17. See also "Interview with Makeda Silvera: Out in the Village," as told to Fatima Jaffer, *Kinesis*, February 1994, 19.

30 "Socreds Dump VSW," *Kinesis*, May 1984, 1, 3; "Update on *Kinesis* and VSW," *Kinesis*, September 1984, 1.

31 The newspaper's annual budget was $65,000 in 1990. Pollak Papers, "*Kinesis* at a Glance," an information kit for volunteers issued by *Kinesis* in September 1990.

32 Pollak, "Inside *Kinesis*," *Kinesis*, September 1989, 2. Pollak Private Collection, memo from Esther (Shannon) to the editorial board, 15 May 1989, and Pollak memo to the editorial board, 28 June 1989.

33 Pollak, "Inside *Kinesis*," *Kinesis*, July/August 1989, 2; see also Pollak, "Services in Peril," *Kinesis*, June 1989, 3.

34 Pollak, "No Centres, No Staff, No Service," *Kinesis*, March 1990, 3; "Inside *Kinesis*," *Kinesis*, July/August 1990, 2; "Let's Tie Up Parliament," *Kinesis*, September 1990, 2.

35 "Inside *Kinesis*," *Kinesis*, April 1991, 2; "Inside *Kinesis*," *Kinesis*, May 1991, 2; "Inside *Kinesis*," *Kinesis*, October 1991, 2; "Inside *Kinesis*," *Kinesis*, November 1991, 2; Pollak Papers, *Kinesis* editorial board meeting minutes, 11 October 1989; 10 January,

13 March, 9 May and 12 September 1990; 13 March 1991; 10 February 1992. Pollak has no clear memory of how her position was funded over the next year or so, but she believes it was from these financial efforts. Esther Shannon, who was a VSW administrator at the time, explains that SecState would not have directly funded the editor's position, but VSW would have found room for it in its own budget. Nancy Pollak email to Barbara Freeman, 12 March 2010; Esther Shannon email to Barbara Freeman, 13 March 2010. Pollak covered the feminist fight to have funds restored to women's services in *Kinesis*. See Pollak, "Playing Football with Our Funds," *Kinesis*, April 1990, 3–4; Pollak, "Feminists in Spirited Resistance across the Country," *Kinesis*, May 1990, 10–11; Pollak, "A Little Money Now Less Money Later," *Kinesis*, June 1990, 3; Pollak, "Where Have All the Funders Gone?" *Kinesis*, October 1990, 3; Pollak, "Girls Just Want to Have Funds," *Kinesis*, February 1991, 3; Pollak, "We Got the Blue Budget Blues," *Kinesis*, March 1991, 3.

36 Jaffer interview with Freeman. For example, the regional SecState office did help fund and distribute a 25th anniversary issue of *Kinesis*. See *Kinesis*, Special 25th Anniversary Supplement, December–January, 1999–2000, 9. The editor's salary was about $23,800 in 1992, but under negotiation, when it was still being advertised as such. Pollak papers, *Kinesis* employment ad, c. February 1992. On the 1993 budget cuts, see "As *Kinesis* Goes to Press," February 1993, 2; Pollack, "SecState Funding Cuts: Death of a Thousand Cuts," *Kinesis*, March 1993, 3.

37 Michele Valiquette, "Triple Whammy for Feminists," *Kinesis*, November 1989, 19. "Inside *Kinesis*," *Kinesis*, March 1998, 2. See also Mary Vipond, *The Mass Media in Canada*, 3rd ed. (Toronto: Lorimer, 2000), 59.

38 Masters interview with Freeman; Masters, "*Broadside* and Beyond."

39 Masters made about $14,000 a year, while the newspaper's annual budget was about $30,000. Masters interview with Freeman; *Broadside* masthead, March 1986, 2.

40 Noreen Shanahan, "Bye-bye *Broadside*," *Kinesis*, April 1989, 7. Masters, "*Broadside* and Beyond," and "A Word from the Press." CWMA, *Broadside* Papers, 18 April 1989, letter to subscribers; letter from Susan G. Cole to former contributors, circa spring 1989, asking them to donate $100, if possible.

41 Masters, "*Broadside* and Beyond."

42 Lloyd interview with Freeman; see also Betty-Ann Lloyd, "We Just Couldn't Keep the Lid on *Pandora!*" *Pandora*, 1 September 1985, 4.

43 Lloyd email to Freeman 22 January 2011 and Lloyd interview with Freeman.

44 Betty-Ann Lloyd, "Hearing Women into Speech: The Feminist Press and the Women's Community," *Canadian Woman Studies/les cahiers de la femme*, 1:1, Spring 1987, 29–32; Lloyd interview with Freeman.

45 "Lesbian, Abortion Rights Activists Question Their Deliberate Exclusion," *Pandora*, Spring 1986, 13; Dianne Duggan, "Lesbian Visibility Draws Attack from Right," *Pandora*, June 1986, 7. For an overview of women's groups in Nova Scotia, see Naomi Black, "Feminism in Nova Scotia: Women's Groups, 1990–2004," *Atlantis*, 31:1, 2006, 64–75.

46 Betty-Ann Lloyd, "Editorial Response: Let's Consider Context," to letter from Helga Hoffman, "Question Sexual Perspectives: Wide Range of Contributors Positive," *Pandora*, December 1985, 5. The stories Hoffman complained about were both written by Darl Wood, "Centre Welcomes Lesbians," and "International Gay Association Conference: Reserve Me a Space Next Year, Please!" *Pandora*, September 1985, 6, 22.

47 Mathers interview with Freeman.

48 "Conference Calls for Heterosexism Dialogue," *Pandora*, September 1986, 19.

49 Nor, for the same reason, could they persuade Mount St. Vincent University, a traditionally Roman Catholic institution, to provide the meeting venue. Lloyd interview with Freeman.

50 *"Pandora's* Letter Policy," *Pandora*, March 1990, 5.
51 Amani Wassef, *"Pandora* Challenges Sex Discrimination Complaint," *Pandora*, June 1991, 4; A member of the *Pandora* collective, "Victory for *Pandora* ... and All of Us," *The Womanist*, Spring 1992, 32. Faith Jones, "Feminist Publishing in Canada: *Pandora* Folds," *Kinesis*, July/August 1994, 3. Lloyd and Mathers interviews with Freeman.
52 Lloyd and Mathers interviews with Freeman.
53 *Pandora* Collective, "An Open Letter to *Pandora* Supporters" and *"Pandora* Women Have a Dream," *Pandora*, March 1994, insert and back page. Lloyd recalls that most women of colour were, up to that point, more involved with their own community groups rather than with feminism. Lloyd interview with Freeman.
54 On lesbian sensibility and the culture it promoted, see Heather Murray, "Free for All Lesbians: Lesbian Cultural Production and Consumption in the United States during the 1970s," *Journal of the History of Sexuality*, 16:2, May 2007, 251–275. Nonfiction, fiction and music by lesbians for lesbians were easily accessible only to women who lived in cities with independent alternative bookstores. Margaret Nicholls, "Lesbianism ... Then and Now," *Kinesis*, August 1975, 18. Susan Levin, "The Women's Bookstore," *Kinesis*, March 1975, 18; Connie Smith, "Ruby Music," *Kinesis*, November 1984, 20, and December 1984, 34–35. On portrayal of lesbians in the media, see Lynn Day, "Lesbian Issues: From Invisible to Sensational," Media Committee of Lesbian Feminist Liberation, "How to Portray Lesbians in the Media," and "Selective Reporting Devalues Feminist Challenge to Status Quo," *Pandora*, March 1992, 13.
55 "From Us to You," *Kinesis*, January 1979, 30.
56 Jean Wilson, "Nicole Brossard: Fictions and Realities," *Broadside*, June 1981, 11, 18. This article was republished in *Broadside*, May 1982, 20–23. See also Lise Moisan, "Nicole Brossard and Adrienne Rich: Literature and the Lesbian Conscience" (trans.), *La vie en rose*, 3, September 1981, 50–51. Brossard had been influenced by the writing of Simone de Beauvoir and Kate Millet, among others. She started a monthly feminist newspaper in Quebec called *Les Têtes de pioche* (pick-axe heads), published from 1976 until 1979, predating *La vie en rose* (1980–1987). Her lyric, erotic poem "Sous La Langue/Under Tongue" was later co-published by two feminist companies, L'Essentielle of Montreal and gynergy of Charlottetown. Betsy Nuse, "Essential Energies," *Broadside*, July 1987, 12.
57 For example, Genevieve Côtrés, "To My Similar (Partner)" (trans.), *La vie en rose*, 33, February 1986, 25, 32.
58 Michaela Johnson, "Nurturing Long-Term Relationships," Sara Diamond, "From Our Past—A Lesbian Politic Emerges," Lorna Zaback, "Facts about Lesbian Health," Betty Baxter, "Lesbians and Sport: The Dilemma of Coming Out," and Rosalie Hawrylko, Joyce Penner and Joan Woodward, "Bisexuality and Women," *Kinesis*, July/August 1983, 15–20.
59 "Are You Politically Correct?" *Pandora*, 1 September 1985, 6.
60 Lloyd interview with Freeman. According to the article, these were discussion points at an International Women's Day workshop on heterosexism in 1987, but the participants were not identified. "Being Lesbian Is Not about Sex: Workshop Explores Cultural Differences." See also two accompanying articles: "Heterosexist World Enforces Invisibility," and "She Loved Her Jockey Underwear: Her Mother Wonders What She Did Wrong ..." *Pandora*, June 1987, 6.
61 Eve Zaremba, "Movement Comment—Voicing the Unspeakable," *Broadside*, July 1981, 19. She referred her readers to Adrienne Rich, *On Lies, Secrets and Silence: Selected Prose 1966–1978* (New York: Norton, 1979).
62 Alex Keir, "Is There Sex after Feminism? Solidarity, Sisterhood and Lots of Talk," *Pandora*, 1 December 1985, 20; Ross, *The House That Jill Built*.
63 Lillith Finkler, "Lesbians Who Sleep with Men," *Broadside*, November 1983, 4.

64 "Lesbian Conference: Whereas ... Be It Resolved That ..." *Kinesis*, September/October 1981, 19–21. See also the letter from Bran Way, "Bisexuality a Valid Choice Too," *Kinesis*, May 1982, 19. Maureen Fitzgerald and Daphne Morrison, "Lesbian Conference: Agony and Audacity," *Broadside*, July 1981, 4.

65 Joanne K. Jefferson, "Politics of Bisexuality," *Pandora*, September 1986, 18.

66 Taggart Oneil (pseudonym), "Psychiatric Report: A Fictionalized Account of One Woman's Experience," *Pandora*, December 1988, 18; Winnie, "A Love Story," *Pandora*, June 1988, 23.

67 Anonymous, "Dear Daughter" and "Dear Mom," *Pandora*, September 1986, 10; Jeanne, "It's Tuesday Night—Women's Night at Rumours and This Time I'm Going!!!" *Pandora*, December 1986, 20.

68 Lloyd interview with Freeman. Paige Prichard Kennedy, "Womb-Like Pavilion Symbolizes Shelter, Support from Homophobic Reality," *Pandora*, March 1992, 18.

69 Maureen Fitzgerald and Daphne Morrison, "Lesbian Conference: Agony and Audacity," *Broadside*, July 1981, 4.

70 "Lesbian Conference: Whereas ... Be It Resolved That ..." *Kinesis*, September/October 1981, 19–21.

71 Judy Leifschultz, "What Is This Thing Called Love?" *Broadside*, April 1982, 7.

72 Mariana Valverde, "Movement Matters—Lesbian Sexuality Conference: Coming On Strong," *Broadside*, July 1984, 5, 10.

73 Editorials, "Feminism's Psychic Imperative," *Broadside*, August/September 1985, 2, and "Second Thoughts," *Broadside*, March 1986, 2.

74 Darl Wood, "International Gay Association Conference: Reserve Me a Space Next Year, Please!" *Pandora*, 1 September 1985, 22. A letter to *Pandora* congratulated Wood for her openness to examining her own prejudices as a lesbian feminist and, although Wood did not mention it in her article, her public support of six lesbians who had earlier been ejected from the military at Shelburne, Nova Scotia. The two publishers of a San Francisco publication, *Lesbian Inciter*, also congratulated *Pandora*. Letters from Liz Archibald Calder, and Mariel Rae and Kate Anne of *Lesbian Inciter*, *Pandora*, 1 December 1985, 5 and 6.

75 See, for example, Joan Nestle, *A Restricted Country* (Ithica, NY: Firebrand Books, 1987); Lillian Faderman, *Odd Girls and Twilight Lovers: Lesbianism in Twentieth Century America* (New York: Columbia University Press, 1991); Elizabeth Lapovsky Kennedy and Madeline D. Davis, *Boots of Leather, Slippers of Gold: The History of a Lesbian Community* (New York: Routledge, 1993); Cameron Duder, *Awfully Devoted Women: Lesbians in Canada, 1900–1965* (Vancouver: University of British Columbia Press, 2010).

76 Susan G. Cole, "Broadsides—Cruising Windows," *Broadside*, March 1980, 6. Cythea Sand, "*Personal Best* Ruined by Superficiality, Compromise," *Kinesis*, April 1982, 18. Catherine Kerr, "*By Design* Distorts Lesbians," *Kinesis*, April 1983, 23, 26.

77 Jeannie Lockrie, "Lesbian Film Fest—Memory, Sexual Desire on the Screen," and a different opinion on other films she reviewed from Lorna Boschman, "Another View—A Feast for Intensity Addicts," *Kinesis*, December 1988/January 1989, 20.

78 Kathleen Oliver, "Vancouver International Film Festival: A Forbidden Love No More," a review of *Forbidden Love*, directed by Aerlyn Weissman and Lynne Fernie, National Film Board, 1992, in *Kinesis*, November 1992, cover and 15. On other films about lesbians, see Cori Howard, "Review: *From Lesbian to Queer*," *Kinesis*, May 1995, 15; Donna Gollan, review of *Desert Hearts*, *Broadside*, April 1986, 10; Nancy Pollak, "A Visual Evidence Video: Lesbians Playing with Fire," *Kinesis*, September 1987, 16; Susan G. Cole, "Vera Goes Nuts," *Broadside*, March 1988, 12. Sandra McPherson objected to what she considered a racialized story line in "Reviewing the Viewing of *When Night Is Falling*: When Dykes Are Stalking," *Kinesis*, July/August 1995, 20. A reader agreed with her. Letter from Nora Fras, *Kinesis*, Sep-

tember 1995, 16. Fatima Jaffer, "Lesbians on Screen at theVancouver International Film Festival: *Fire Leaves Myths in Ashes*," *Kinesis*, November 1996, 15, 20.

79 Jaffer interview with Freeman; *Kinesis*, November 1992, cover.

80 Tulchinsky was also a member of the ILW Committee. Karen X.Tulchinsky, "International Lesbian Week: Big, Bigger, BiggerYet." The Butch/Femme Panel was in the ILW listings she compiled, "One Helluva Week," *Kinesis*, February 1993, 14. Brookes later tried to organize a reunion of women who went through coming-out support groups over the years. Letter from Mary Brookes, "CallingVancouver Lesbians," *Kinesis*, April 1994, 20.

81 Lisa Walker, *Looking like What You Are: Sexual Style, Race and Lesbian Identity* (NewYork: NewYork University Press, 2001).

82 Freeman, "From No Go to No Logo"; Becki L. Ross, "A Lesbian Politics of Erotic Decolonization," in *Painting the Maple: Essays on Race, Gender and the Construction of Canada*, ed.Veronica Strong-Boag, Joan Anderson, Sherrill E. Grace and Avigail Eisenberg (Vancouver: UBC Press 1998), 187–214; Ross, *The House That Jill Built*; and Stone, *Lesbians in Canada*.

83 Book review of *Loving Ourselves: A Lesbian Sex Manual*, by "Win," *Kinesis*, September 1976, 13; excerpts from the *Hite Report* about same-sex desire among American women, in "Sexism, Not Sexuality, Is Pornographic," *Kinesis*, May 1977, 15; and a critical commentary about sexual frankness in the writing of American feminist Kate Millett. Helen Potrebenko, "TheWitch's Cat," *Kinesis*, July 1977, 11–14. She was referring to Millett's memoir, *Flying* (NewYork: Ballantine Books, 1974).

84 For an overview of these debates at the time, see Mariana Valverde, *Sex, Power and Pleasure* (Toronto: Women's Press, 1985).

85 JEB (Joan E. Biren), "Lesbian Images in Photography, 1850–1980." She had earlier published her photographs in *Eye to Eye: Portraits of Lesbians* (Washington, DC: Glad Hag Books, distributed by Naiad Press, 1979). Emphasis in the original by Anonymous, "Lesbian Photography: Neck and Neck," *Broadside*, April 1981, 15. See also Martha Keaner, "Focus on Focus," *Broadside*, June 1981, 15; Cy-Thea Sand, "Lust Is a Four Letter Word," *Kinesis*, October 1986, 18–19. Tee A. Corinne photograph "Yantra #30," from her series, *Yantras of Womanlove*, at http://rcswww.urz .tu-dresden.de/~english1/photo/photo/photo_new_women_corinne.htm, 26 March 2008.

86 Pollak interview with Freeman.

87 Masters interview with Freeman; editorial, "Sudden Death," *Broadside*, February 1987, 2; Ingrid MacDonald, "Customary Bias," *Broadside*, July 1987, 4; Nancy Pollak andYvonne Van Ruskenveld, "The Election Issues: As We See Them," *Kinesis*, November 1988, 12–13.

88 Susan G. Cole, "Millett on Sexuality: Describing Arcs of Our Own," *Broadside*, May 1984, 8–9.

89 Susan G. Cole, "Electromagnetics," *Broadside*, July 1984, 5.

90 Ingrid MacDonald, "Women's Sexuality Conference—So Few Words: So Many Metaphors," *Broadside*, November 1985, 3.

91 Editorial, "No Unanimity Here," *Broadside*, April 1985, 2; Susan G. Cole, "Sexuality and Its Discontents," *Broadside*, April 1985, 8–9.

92 Masters interview with Freeman.

93 Mariana Valverde, "Movement Matters—Lesbian Sexuality Conference: Coming On Strong," *Broadside*, July 1984, 5, 10.

94 Ingrid MacDonald, "Women's Sexuality Conference—So Few Words: So Many Metaphors," *Broadside*, November 1985, 3, and MacDonald, "Bongos and Barbies," *Broadside*, December 1986/January 1987, 11.

95 Lorraine Chisholm, "JoAnn Loulan: Lesbian Dolphins and Sex and Laughter," *Kinesis*, December 1988/January 1989, 8. See also Ingrid MacDonald, "Women's Sexuality Conference—So Few Words: So Many Metaphors," *Broadside*, November

1985, 3. JoAnn Loulan, *Lesbian Sex* (San Francisco, CA: Spinsters Ink Books, 1984); Loulan, *Lesbian Passion: Loving Ourselves and Each Other* (Duluth, MN: Spinster's Ink Books, 1987). Ten years later, Loulan fell in love with a man, contributing to a media discussion about the fluidity of sexual orientation. See, for example, Ted Gideonse, "The Sexual Blur," *The Advocate*, June 1997, at http://gideonse.com/articles/sexual_blur.htm, 12 May 2008.

96   Cy-Thea Sand, "Lust Is a Four Letter Word," *Kinesis*, October 1986, 18–19.

97   JoAnn P., " Commentary—Dyke Disillusioned with Community," *Kinesis*, March 1989, 24. There were strip shows earlier at another gay venue, but they did not last. Mary Woo Simms, "Lucy's Strives to Be No-Attitude Bar," *Kinesis*, October 1982, 8; "Update on Lucy's," *Kinesis*, December/January 1983, 2. Going to striptease shows was not confined to Vancouver. In Edmonton, 40 percent of the lesbians asked approved of strippers at their dances. When Pauline Belanger wrote to Eve Zaremba in Toronto, asking her to vet her draft essay criticizing the practice, Zaremba encouraged her to make her reservations public as "we need not be silent when something which we think will harm women takes place. I think you are doing the right thing but don't expect much thanks or understanding. You will be called a prude, I guarantee." CWMA, *Broadside* Papers, Box 6, "Correspondence 1979–1989," letter with draft essay from Pauline Belanger to Eve Zaremba, 10 March 1983, and response from Zaremba to Belanger, 6 April 1983.

98   The article was also published in the periodical *Diversity* at the same time. Pollak Papers, editorial board minutes, 14 February 1989 and 15 March 1989. Letter from Bonnie Waterstone, "More on Stripping," *Kinesis*, April 1989, 21.

99   Karen X. Tulchinsky, "Int'l Lesbian Week," *Kinesis*, February 1992, 19. See also Hazel Beech, "Int'l Lesbian Week Rolls Around," *Kinesis*, February 1991, 14; "International Lesbian Week," *Kinesis*, February 1994, 18.

100   Karen X. Tulchinsky, "International Lesbian Week: Big, Bigger, Bigger Yet," and the ILW listings she compiled, "One Helluva Week," *Kinesis*, February 1993, 14.

101   Pat Feindel, "On the Wall—A Delicious Display of Lesbian Sex," *Kinesis*, September 1988, 17. On other artists who created similar material, see Randi Spires, "Our Bodies, Our Art," *Broadside*, August/September 1989, 18.

102   Kivisild interview with Freeman. The Kiss & Tell collective consisted of photographer Susan Stewart and models Persimmon Blackbridge and "Lizard Jones" (Kivisild). The exhibit was later presented in a video and as a postcard book, Kiss & Tell, *Drawing the Line: Lesbian Sexual Politics on the Wall* (Vancouver: Press Gang, 1991). The exhibit did not reach Halifax but the book was reviewed by Töne Meeg, "Provocative Lesbian Images Challenge Censorship Issues," *Pandora*, March 1992, 18.

103   Pat Feindel, "On the Wall—A Delicious Display of Lesbian Sex," *Kinesis*, September 1988, 17.

104   She was reviewing Samois, ed., *Coming to Power: Writing and Graphics on Lesbian S./M.* (Berkeley, CA: Samois, 1981). Mariana Valverde, "Coming to Power—Bottoms Out," *Broadside*, September 1982, 4.

105   Lorna Weir and Eve Zaremba, "Boys and Girls Together," and "Lesbians and Feminism," *Broadside*, October 1982, 6–7, 9.

106   Freeman interviews with Kivisild and Shannon.

107   Susan White, "Lesbian SM—Anti-feminist or a Valid Choice?" *Kinesis*, July/August 1982, 22.

108   Suzanne Gerard, "Porn Is Winning," *Kinesis*, September 1982, 19, 22. Another letter shared her sentiments. Annette Clough, "S&M Sex Perpetrates Patriarchal Attitudes," *Kinesis*, September 1982, 20–21.

109   Kivisild interview with Freeman.

110   Pollak interview with Freeman.

111   Jaffer interview with Freeman.

112 Shannon interview with Freeman.

113 Carolyn Jones, "Lesbian Conference," and Nym Hughes, "Connecting Province-Wide," *Kinesis*, July/August 1983, 13–14; Pauline Rankin, "Lesbians, Gays Build Bridges," *Kinesis*, June 1988, 5. Bet Cecil, "Lesbian Feminist Conference—So Many Workshops, So Little Time," *Kinesis* November 1989, 9. Mariana Valverde, "Movement Matters—Lesbian Sexuality Conference: Coming On Strong," *Broadside*, July 1984, 5, 10.

114 Nora D. Randall, "A Night in the Streets," *Kinesis*, May 1988, 10. Letters from POWER and Dykes for Dykedom, "S/M, Leather Dykes Respond," and Randall's reply, *Kinesis*, June 1988, 20.

115 Shannon e. Ash, "Review: Unleashing Feminism: Resisting the 'Culture of Violence,'" a review of Irene Reti, ed., *Unleashing Feminism: Critiquing Lesbian Sadomasochism in the Gay Nineties* (Santa Cruz, CA: HerBooks, 1993), *Kinesis*, March 1995, 20–21. Even more criticism came from Helen Story, "Review: *The Lesbian Heresy*," *Kinesis*, May 1995, 13. Story was praising a book by Sheila Jeffreys, another lesbian feminist who opposed S&M. See Jeffreys, *The Lesbian Heresy* (Melbourne, Australia: Spinifex, 1993).

116 Bet Cecil, Susan Stewart, Shaira Holman, Patrice Leung and Nora D. Randall, "Sexploitations," *Kinesis*, June 1991, 10–14. Transcribed by Terry Thomson. Readers' responses, pro and con, to this feature included letters from Olive Johnson, "Since Lesbianism and Feminism Are Not Synonymous ..." and Carol Perz, "Homophobia in Scarborough, Ont.," *Kinesis*, July/August 1991, 20; from Anne Miles, "Heterosexual Reader Appreciates 'Sexploitations,'" Allison Bond, "Silencing Lesbians Affects All Women's Struggles," Sima Elizabeth Shefrin, "Lesbianism a Core Issue for All Feminists," Cathryn Craik, "Differentiating between Sex and Sexuality," and Aleson Kase, "Since When Is 10 Percent a General Slant?" *Kinesis*, September 1991, 18–19.

117 Judy Leifschultz, "Movement Comment—High Standards for Low Life," *Broadside*, February 1982, 9.

118 Pixie Woods, "Man Crazy Dyke?" Vicky B. Goode, "I Dream of Performing ... in Public," and Micki Prude, "My Nipples Retreat ... My Shame Grows," *Kinesis*, October 1986, 27.

119 Photo taken in 1993 by Shannon e. Ash; graphic for 1994 ILW by Susan Gray, "International Lesbian Week," *Kinesis*, February 1994, 18.

120 "Dear Crabby: Straight Advice from the Heart" and "Quest" from "The Chosen Family" comic strip, *Pandora*, November 1991, 11; Lois, "Untitled," *Pandora*, September 1992, 14; LMSSL, "Untitled," *Pandora*, March 1993, 7; Shannon Gowans, "What It Means to Be a Sensual Feminist" and Lois Schroeder Lowen, "... and a Canuck Dyke," *Pandora*, July 1993, 6.

121 Brenda Beagan, "42 Days, 10,801 km, Wonderful Food and Remarkably Little Bickering Later: March on Washington Focus of Dykes across America Trip," *Pandora*, July 1993, 8–9.

122 Pollak, Jaffer, Masters and Lloyd interviews with Freeman; see also Masters, "A Word from the Press"; Bet Cecil, Susan Stewart, Shaira Holman, Patrice Leung and Nora D. Randall, "Sexploitations," *Kinesis*, June 1991, 10–14. Transcribed by Terry Thomson.

Chapter 7

1 Alanis Obomsawin, director, *Mother of Many Children*, National Film Board of Canada, 1977.

2 Alanis Obomsawin, director, *Richard Cardinal: Cry from the Diary of a Métis Child*, National Film Board of Canada, 1986; Alanis Obomsawin, director, *Spudwrench*, National Film Board of Canada, 1997.

3   Gail Guthrie Valaskakis, *Indian Country: Essays on Contemporary Native Culture* (Waterloo, ON: Wilfrid Laurier University Press, 2005), introduction.

4   Valaskakis included "clan mothers" here, but that designation is not automatic. Obomsawin points out that in the Mohawk tradition, for example, one must be chosen as a clan mother by one's people. Valaskakis, *Indian Country*, 143; Alanis Obomsawin telephone phone conversation with Barbara Freeman, 28 July 2009.

5   Alanis Obomsawin interview with Barbara Freeman, 22 July 2009.

6   Obomsawin interview with Freeman.

7   Nancy Baele, "Obomsawin's Acclaimed Film Is Too Strong for the CBC," *Ottawa Citizen*, final edition, 14 October 1993, D1.

8   Randolph Lewis, *Alanis Obomsawin: The Vision of a Native Filmmaker* (Lincoln: University of Nebraska Press, 2006), 81; see, for example, Christopher E. Gittings, *Canadian National Cinema: Ideology, Difference and Representation* (London; New York: Routledge, 2008), 217–225; Zuzana Pick, "'This Land Is Ours'" and "Storytelling and Resistance," in *Gendering the Nation: Canadian Women's Cinema*, ed. Kay Armatage, Kass Banning, Brenda Longfellow and Janine Marchessault (Toronto: University of Toronto Press, 1999), 76–93; also Pick, "'This Land Is Ours'—Storytelling and History in Kanehsatake: 270 Years of Resistance" in *Candid Eye: Essays on Canadian Documentaries*, ed. Jim Leach and Jeannette Sloniowski (Toronto: University of Toronto Press, 2003), 181–196; Jerry White, "Alanis Obomsawin, Documentary Form and the Canadian Nation(s)," in *North of Everything: English-Canadian Cinema since 1980*, ed. William Beard and Jerry White (Edmonton: University of Alberta Press, 2002), 364–375; and Anthony Adah, "On the Field of Battle: First Nations Women Documentary Filmmakers," in *The Gendered Screen: Canadian Women Filmmakers*, ed. Brenda Austin-Smith and George Melnyk (Waterloo, ON: Wilfrid Laurier University Press, 2010), 165–183. For a listing of the many honours Obomsawin has received, see http://films.nfb.ca/alanis-obomsawin/bio.php.

9   Obomsawin interview with Freeman; Sarah Hampson, "The Hampson Interview: Alanis Obomsawin," *Globe and Mail*, 21 October 2006, R3.

10 · Alanis Obomsawin, director, *Is the Crown at War with Us?* National Film Board of Canada, 2002; and Alanis Obomsawin, director, *Our Nationhood*, National Film Board of Canada, 2003.

11   Obomsawin interview with Freeman.

12   Maurie Alioff and Susan Schouten Levine, "The Long Walk of Alanis Abomsawin," *Cinema Canada*, June 1987, 14.

13   Shannon Avison and Michael Meadows, "Speaking and Hearing: Aboriginal Newspapers and the Public Sphere in Canada and Australia," *Canadian Journal of Communication*, 25:3, 2000, 347–366; Pick, "'This Land Is Ours,'" and "Storytelling and Resistance"; Gail Guthrie Valaskakis, Guest Editor's Introduction, "Parallel Voices: Indians and Others: Narratives of Cultural Struggle," *Canadian Journal of Communication*, 18:3, 1993, at http://www.cjc-online.ca/index.php/journal/article/view/756/662, 13 December 2010.

14   Lewis, *Alanis Obomsawin*, 75; Alioff and Levine, "The Long Walk of Alanis Abomsawin," 13.

15   Adrian Harewood, "Alanis Obomsawin: A Portrait of a First Nation's Filmmaker," *Take One*, 1 June 2003, at http://www.thefreelibrary.com, 11 May 2009.

16   She also feels that she is "spending public money" as an NFB filmmaker and should not, therefore, be dwelling on infighting, but emphasizing the broader issues. Obomsawin interview with Freeman.

17   Obomsawin interviewed in Katerina Cizek, *Alanis Obomsawin: Dream Magic*, National Film Board of Canada, 2008, at http://www.nfb.ca/explore-by/director/cizek-katerina; bell hooks, *Feminist Theory from Margin to Center* (Boston: South End Press, 1989); Gittings, *Canadian National Cinema*, 217.

18 Obomsawin explained that her parents were both Abenaki from Odanak, but her mother was working in the United States when she was born; her father was working in the bush. They lost four of their five children to illness, and Obomsawin almost died herself as a small child from an unknown ailment while she was living in Odanak. Another aunt, who was a healer, took over her care for several months while she recovered. Obomsawin telephone conversation with Freeman, 17 August 2009; also her interview with Eleanor Wachtel, *Wachtel on the Arts in the Summer*, CBC Radio, 4 September 2009.

19 Harewood, "Alanis Obomsawin."

20 Lewis, *Alanis Obomsawin*; Obomsawin interview with Wachtel.

21 Gary Evans, *In the National Interest: A Chronicle of the National Film Board of Canada from 1949 to 1989* (Toronto: University of Toronto Press, 1991), 3–7.

22 Zoe Druick, *Projecting Canada: Government Policy and Documentary Film at the National Film Board of Canada* (Montreal: McGill-Queen's University Press, 2007), 165.

23 Obomsawin interview with Freeman.

24 White, "Alanis Obomsawin"; NFB producer Bob Verrin interviewed in Cizek, "Alanis Obomsawin: Dream Magic," chapter 1.

25 Gail Vanstone, *D Is for Daring: The Women behind the Films of Studio D* (Toronto: Sumach Press, 2007), 135, 140; Rina Franticelli, "'Would I Ever Like to Work'": The 'Working Mothers' Films and the Construction of Community," in *Challenge for Change: Activist Documentary at the National Film Board of Canada*, ed. Thomas Waugh, Michael Brendan Baker and Ezra Winton, with a foreword by Naomi Klein (Montreal; Kingston: McGill-Queen's University Press, 2010), 311. On the IFC program, see Michelle Stewart, "The Indian Film Crews of Challenge for Change: Representation and the State," *Canadian Journal of Film Studies*, 16:2, Fall 2007, 37. Obomsawin's *Amisk* and her *Mother of Many Children* are not listed in Waugh et al.'s *Challenge for Change* filmography, pages 453–512, which corrects Stewart's erroneous inclusion of them in the series. Stewart, 66–67, 76 n44.

26 Alioff and Levine, "The Long Walk of Alanis Obomsawin," 10–11; Obomsawin in *Our Dear Sisters*, National Film Board of Canada, 1976.

27 Druick, *Projecting Canada*, 165.

28 Evans, *In the National Interest*, 210–212.

29 Vanstone, *D Is for Daring*, chapter 4.

30 Lewis, *Alanis Obomsawin*, 1; Alioff and Levine, "The Long Walk of Alanis Obomsawin," 10–15; Maurie Alioff, "Alanis Obomsawin after Oka," *Matrix*, 33, Spring 1991, 5–9; Alanis Obomsawin, director, *Waban-Aki: People from Where the Sun Rises*, National Film Board of Canada, 2007; liner notes for Alanis Obomsawin, director, *Kanehsatake: 270 Years of Resistance*, National Film Board of Canada, 1993; Vanstone, *D Is for Daring*, 16, 55–56.

31 Obomsawin in an interview with Lewis, *Alanis Obomsawin*, 72.

32 Obomsawin interview with Freeman.

33 Joyce Green, "Taking Account of Aboriginal Feminism," and Verna St. Denis, "Feminism Is for Everybody: Aboriginal Women, Feminism and Diversity," in Green, ed., *Making Space for Indigenous Feminism* (Winnipeg, MB: Fernwood, 2007), 14–32, 33–52.

34 Obomsawin interview with Freeman.

35 Lewis, *Alanis Obomsawin*, chapter 3.

36 Obomsawin interview with Freeman.

37 Pick, "Storytelling and Resistance," 77. See also Judy Rebick, "Indian Rights for Indian Women: Changing the Indian Act," in *Ten Thousand Roses: The Making of a Feminist Revolution* (Toronto: Penguin Canada, 2005), 107–115.

38 Lewis, *Alanis Obomsawin*, 81–82.

39 The other Aboriginal filmmakers include Christine Welsh, whose *Keepers of the Fire* (NFB and Omni Film Productions, 1994) focuses more directly on the roles

Aboriginal women have taken in their communities, including during the Oka crisis. For critiques of Aboriginal media stereotypes, see Frances Henry and Carol Tator, *Discourses of Domination: Racial Bias in the Canadian English-Language Press* (Toronto: University of Toronto Press, 2002), chapter 10, case study #1, 2002. Marilyn Burgess and Gail Guthrie Valaskakis, *Indian Princesses and Cowgirls: Stereotypes from the Frontier* (Montreal: OBORO, 1992). Debbie Wise Harris, "Colonizing Mohawk Women: Representations of Women in Mainstream Media," *Resources for Feminist Research/Documentation sur la recherche féministe*, 20:1, 2, 1991, 15–20; Lorna Roth, "Cultural and Racial Diversity in Canadian Broadcast Journalism, " in *Deadlines and Diversity: Journalism Ethics in a Changing World*, ed. Valerie Alia, Brian Brennan and Barry Hoffmaster (Halifax, NS: Fernwood, 1996), 72–85; Gail Guthrie Valaskakis, "Rights and Warriors: First Nations, Media and Identity," in *The Mass Media and Canadian Diversity*, ed. Stephen E. Nancoo and Robert S. Nancoo (Mississauga, ON: Canadian Educators Press, 1997), 110–123; Valaskakis, *Indian Country*, chapter 2; Mary Ann Weston, *Native Americans in the News: Images of Indians in the Twentieth Century Press* (Westport, CT: Greenwood Press, 1996); Avison and Meadows, "Speaking and Hearing."

40   Adah, for example, analyzes Obomsawin's film *Kanehsatake*, but does not explore the ways she depicted female Aboriginal leaders during the standoff. Adah, "On the Field of Battle," 166–172. See also Gittings, *Canadian National Cinema*, 223; Marc Grenier, "Native Indians in the English-Canadian Press: The Case of the 'Oka Crisis,'" *Media, Culture and Society*, 6:2, 1994, 313–336; Warren H. Skea, "The Canadian Newspaper Industry's Portrayal of the Oka Crisis, *Native Studies Review*, 9, Spring, 1993–94, 15–31.

41   Valaskakis, "Parallel Voices: Indians and Others."

42   Valaskakis "Parallel Voices: Indians and Others" and *Indian Country*, chapter 5.

43   Alanis Obomsawin, "Report on Native Production," 3 October 1975, NFB Archives. Cited in Stewart, "The Indian Film Crews," 79, n77; Lewis, *Alanis Obomsawin*, 77.

44   Valaskakis, *Indian Country*, 226–230.

45   Valaskakis, *Indian Country*, chapter 8; Barbara M. Freeman, *The Satellite Sex: The Media and Women's Issues in English Canada, 1966–1971* (Waterloo, ON: Wilfrid Laurier University Press, 2001), chapter 8.

46   Obomsawin in Nancy Baele, "Obomsawin's Acclaimed Film Is Too Strong for the CBC," *Ottawa Citizen*, final edition, 14 October 1993, D1.

47   Obomsawin telephone conversation with Freeman, 24 July 2009.

48   Obomsawin interview with Wachtel.

49   Obomsawin, "Of the Earth and Of the Sea," in Obomsawin, director, *Mother of Many Children*, National Film Board of Canada, 1977, cited in Alioff, "Alanis Obomsawin after Oka," *Maxtrix*, 33, Spring 1991, 7.

50   Obomsawin interview with Freeman and follow-up phone conversation, 24 July 2009.

51   Alioff and Levine, "The Long Walk of Alanis Obomsawin," 14–15.

52   Lavallee in Obomsawin, *Mother of Many Children*.

53   Freeman, *The Satellite Sex*, chapter 8.

54   Jeannette Corbière Lavell speaking in person at Library and Archives Canada, 8 March 2007, at the Ottawa premiere of *Waban-Aki*, directed by Alanis Obomsawin, National Film Board of Canada, 2006.

55   Obomsawin, speaking at the premiere of *Waban-Aki*, Library and Archives Canada, Ottawa, 8 March 2007; reiterated in Obomsawin interview with Freeman.

56   Pick, "'This Land Is Ours,'" 193.

57   Alioff and Levine, "The Long Walk of Alanis Obomsawin," 15.

58   The numerous challenges to the NFB's documentary film agendas from the 1960s onward have been discussed by several scholars, including Waugh et al., *Challenge for Change*; Gittings, *Canadian National Cinema*; Evans, *In the National Interest*; Druick, *Projecting Canada*; Vanstone, *D Is for Daring*.

59 Alioff and Levine, "The Long Walk of Alanis Obomsawin," 14–15; Alanis Obomsawin, director, *Incident at Restigouche*, National Film Board of Canada, 1984.
60 Druick, *Projecting Canada*, chapter 7.
61 See Waugh et al., *Challenge for Change*; Gittings, *Canadian National Cinema*; Evans, *In the National Interest*; Druick, *Projecting Canada*; Vanstone, *D Is for Daring*.
62 Obomsawin interview with Wachtel; Gittings, *Canadian National Cinema*, 217–218; Alanis Obomsawin, director, *Incident at Restigouche*, National Film Board of Canada, 1984. One of her earlier films documented a concert featuring herself and other entertainers to support the James Bay Cree, who were being displaced by a massive hydroelectric project. Alanis Obomsawin, *Amisk*, National Film Board of Canada, 1977.
63 Alioff and Levine, "The Long Walk of Alanis Obomsawin," 14–15.
64 Alioff and Levine, "The Long Walk of Alanis Obomsawin," 10–15.
65 Obomsawin, *Waban-Aki*.
66 Obomsawin, speaking at the premiere of *Waban-Aki*, Library and Archives Canada, Ottawa, 8 March 2007.
67 Obomsawin, *Waban-Aki*.
68 Valaskakis, *Indian Country*, 228.
69 Obomsawin, *Waban-Aki*; Obomsawin, speaking at the premiere of *Waban-Aki*, Library and Archives Canada, Ottawa, 8 March 2007.
70 Obomsawin interview with Freeman.
71 Obomsawin, *Waban-Aki*; Obomsawin speaking at the premiere of *Waban-Aki*, Library and Archives Canada, Ottawa, 8 March 2007. For an explanation of the various Section 6 categories, see Michelle M. Mann, *Indian Registration: Unrecognized and Unstated Paternity* (Ottawa: Status of Women Canada, 2005).
72 Shelagh Day and Joyce Green, "Sharon McIvor's Fight for Equality," *Herizons*, Summer 2010, 6–7. Gloria Galloway, "Status Debate Mounts as Bill Offers Benefits to Another 45,000 Natives," *Globe and Mail*, 12 March 2010, 1; "New Law to Extend Benefits to Thousands," *CBC News*, at http://www.cbc.ca/news/canada/north/story/2010/03/11/status-indian.html, 11 March 2010; "B.C. Court Tells Ottawa to Amend the Indian Act," *CBC News*, at http://www.cbc.ca/news/canada/story/2009/04/08/indian-act-bc008.html, 8 April 2009; "Indian Rights for Indian Women—Take 2," a fundraising brochure outlining her case, and Shirley McIvor, speaking at the Ottawa premiere of *Waban-Aki*, 8 March 2007. See also Shirley D. McIvor, "Aboriginal Women's Rights as 'Existing Rights' (Canada)," *Canadian Women's Studies*, 15:2/3, Spring/Summer 1995, 34–38. McIvor describes herself as an Aboriginal feminist in McIvor with Rauna Kuokkanen, "Sharon McIvor: Woman of Action," in *Making Space for Indigenous Feminism*, ed. Joyce Green (Winnipeg, MB: Fernwood, 2007), 241–254.
73 Obomsawin, *Waban-Aki*.
74 Pick, "'This Land Is Ours,'" and "Storytelling and Resistance"; White, "Alanis Obomsawin"; Lewis, *Alanis Obomsawin*.
75 Valaskakis, "Rights and Warriors"; Valaskakis, *Indian Country*, chapter 2.
76 Valaskakis, *Indian Country*, chapter 2.
77 Lewis, *Alanis Obomsawin*, 110.
78 Video liner notes for Obomsawin, director, *My Name Is Kahentiiosta*, National Film Board of Canada, 1995.
79 Obomsawin in Lorna Roth, Beverley Nelson and Kassennahawi Marie David, "Three Women, a Mouse, a Microphone and a Telephone: Information (Mis)Management during the Mohawk/Canadian Governments' Conflict of 1990," in *Feminism, Multiculturalism and the Media: Global Diversities*, ed. Angharad N. Valdivia (Thousand Oaks, CA: Sage, 1995), 50–51; Obomsawin as writer and narrator, *Rocks at Whiskey Trench*, National Film Board of Canada, 2000.
80 Alioff, "Alanis Obomsawin after Oka," 6.

81 Obomsawin interview with Freeman.
82 Alioff, "Alanis Obomsawin after Oka," 6; Obomsawin interviewed in Cizek, "Alanis Obomsawin: Dream Magic," chapter 4. Obomsawin spoke of her fear in her interview with Wachtel.
83 Footage from *My Name Is Kahentiiosta.*
84 Kahentiiosta in *My Name Is Kahentiiosta.*
85 Gabriel in *Kanehsatake.*
86 "Wizard," the women, and Gabriel in *Kanehsatake.*
87 Garrow in *Kanehsatake.*
88 Etienne in *Kanehsatake.*
89 Delisle in *Rocks at Whiskey Trench.*
90 Obomsawin, *Rocks at Whiskey Trench.* On Obomsawin's unsuccessful attempts to get the police and other people who attacked the motorcade to speak with her, see Matthew Hays, "Oka Crisis: Worst Moment Revisited," *Globe and Mail*, 21 June 2000, R3.
91 Jacobs in *Rocks at Whiskey Trench.*
92 Gabriel in *Kanehsatake.*
93 Chicky in *Kanehsatake.*
94 Footage from *Kanehsatake.*
95 Alioff, "Alanis Obomsawin after Oka," 6.
96 Footage from *Kanehsatake.*
97 Obomsawin, *My Name Is Kahentiiosta.*
98 Footage from *Kanehsatake.*
99 Lewis, *Alanis Obomsawin*, 96.
100 Nelson in Roth, Nelson and David, "Three Women," 61–71.
101 David in Roth, Nelson and David, "Three Women," 54–57; Valaskakis, *Indian Country*, chapter 2.
102 Cizek, "Alanis Obomsawin: Dream Magic," chapter 4.
103 Alioff and Levine, "The Long Walk of Alanis Obomsawin," 15. Favourable press coverage of her work included Sid Adilman, "Film about Oka Crisis Tells Two Tales of Courage," *Toronto Star*, 25 September 1993, H4; Barry Came, "Kanehsatake: 270 Years of Resistance," *Maclean's*, 31 January 1994, 58–60.
104 Obomsawin, quoted in Hays, "Oka Crisis." See also Nancy Baele, "Obomsawin's Acclaimed Film Is Too Strong for the CBC," *Ottawa Citizen*, final edition, 14 October 1993, D1; Tony Atherton, "CBC Aims to Revive Documentary," *Ottawa Citizen*, 1 November 1993, F3.
105 Druick, *Projecting Canada*, 168.
106 Vanstone, *D Is for Daring*, 181; National Film Board at www.nfb.ca.
107 Vanstone, *D Is for Daring*, chapter 4. On Tracey Deer, see "Six Filmmakers," at Landsights, an Aboriginal film festival organization, of which Obomsawin is president, http://www.nativelynx.qc.ca/en/cineastes/deer.html, 8 November 2010.
108 Valaskakis, *Indian Country*, 144.
109 Alioff and Levine, "The Long Walk of Alanis Obomsawin," 14.

Conclusion

1 Early in her career, Coleman playfully told readers who accused her of being a man that Kit could be short for either Christopher or Kathleen. Her enduring public persona, particularly her motherly advice to her "shadow children" readers, accurately reflected her real sex. Barbara M. Freeman, *Kit's Kingdom: The Journalism of Kathleen Blake Coleman* (Ottawa: Carleton University Press, Women's Experience Series, No. 1, 1989), chapter 1.
2 Jessica Bennett, Jesse Ellison and Sarah Ball, "Are We There Yet?" *Newsweek*, 19 March 2010, at http://www.newsweek.com, 22 March 2010. My thanks to Sandra Gabriele for bringing this article to my attention.

3 Minelle Mahtani, "Mapping the Meanings of 'Racism' and 'Feminism' among Women Television Broadcast Journalists in Canada," in *Feminism and Antiracism: International Struggles for Justice*, ed. Frances Winddance Twine and Katherine M. Blee (New York: New York University Press, 2001), 349–367.

4 Carrie Best, *That Lonesome Road* (Halifax, NS: Clarion, 1977); *All In A Day*, an interview about Carrie Best, CBC Radio, Ottawa, 11 February 2011, at http://www.cbc .ca/allinaday/2011/02/11/a-stamp-for-carrie-best/.

5 Library and Archives Canada, Marjorie McEnaney Papers, R2389-09-E, Vol. 2, Long, Elizabeth—Letters to M. McEnaney, File 4, Long to McEnaney, 17 February 1962.

6 Kanchana Fernando, "'Television For and About Women': The Story of WTN," *Atlantis*, 29:3, Fall 2005, 41–51.

BIBLIOGRAPHY

Adah, Anthony. "On the Field of Battle: First Nations Women Documentary Film-makers." In *The Gendered Screen: Canadian Women Filmmakers*, edited by Brenda Austin-Smith and George Melnyk, 165–183.

Adamson, Nancy. "Feminists, Libbers, Lefties and Radicals: The Emergence of the Women's Liberation Movement." In *A Diversity of Women: Ontario 1945–1980*, edited by Joy Parr, 252–280. Toronto: University of Toronto Press, 1995.

Adamson, Nancy, Linda Briskin and Margaret McPhail. *Feminists Organizing for Change: The Contemporary Women's Movement in Canada.* Toronto: Oxford University Press, 1988.

Adilman, Sid. "Film about Oka Crisis Tells Two Tales of Courage." *Toronto Star,* 25 September 1993, H4.

Alia, Valerie, Brian Brennan and Barry Hoffmaster, eds. *Deadlines and Diversity: Journalism Ethics in a Changing World.* Halifax, NS: Fernwood, 1996.

Alioff, Maurie. "Dream Magic: Alanis Obomsawin after Oka." *Matrix* (Quebec) 33, Spring 1991, 5–9.

Alioff, Maurie and Susan Sohouten Levine. "The Long Walk of Alanis Obomsawin." *Cinema Canada,* June 1987, 10–15.

Allen, Gene. "News across the Border." *Journalism History,* 31:4, 2006, 206–216.

Ardzrooni, Leon, ed. *Essays in Our Changing Order.* New York: Viking Press, 1945.

Armatage, Kay, Kass Banning, Brenda Longfellow and Janine Marchessault, eds. *Gendering the Nation: Canadian Women's Cinema.* Toronto: University of Toronto Press, 1999.

Aronson, Amy. *Taking Liberties: Early American Women's Magazines and Their Readers.* Westport, CT: Praeger, 2002.

Artibise, Allan F.J. "Divided City: The Immigrant in Winnipeg Society, 1874–1921." In *The Canadian City: Essays in Urban and Social History,* edited by Gilbert A. Stetler and Allan F.J. Artibise, 300–336.

Ash, Juliet and Elizabeth Wilson, eds. *Chic Thrills: A Fashion Reader.* Berkeley and Los Angeles: University of California Press, 1993.

Atherton, Tony. "CBC Aims to Revive Documentary." *Ottawa Citizen,* 1 November 1993, F3.

Austin-Smith, Brenda and George Melnyk, eds. *The Gendered Screen: Canadian Women Filmmakers.* Waterloo, ON: Wilfrid Laurier University Press, 2010.

Avery, Donald. "Ethnic and Class Relations in Western Canada during the First World War: A Case Study of European Immigrants and Anglo-Canadian Nativism." In *Canada and the First World War: Essays in Honour of Robert Craig Brown,* edited by David MacKenzie, 272–299.

Avison, Shannon and Michael Meadows. "Speaking and Hearing: Aboriginal Newspapers and the Public Sphere in Canada and Australia." *Canadian Journal of Communication,* 25:3, 2000, 347–366.

Backhouse, Constance. *Petticoats and Prejudice: Women and Law in Nineteenth-Century Canada.* Toronto: Osgoode Society/Women's Press, 1991.

Nancy Baele, "Obomsawin's Acclaimed Film Is Too Strong for the CBC." *Ottawa Citizen,* 14 October 1993, D1.

Banner, Lois W. *American Beauty.* New York: Alfred A. Knopf, 1983.

Barakso, Maryann and Brian F. Schaffner. "News Media Portrayals of the Women's Movement, 1969–2004," *Press/Politics,* 11:4, 2006, 22–44.

Barber, Marilyn. "Below Stairs: The Domestic Servant." *Material History Bulletin,* 19, Spring 1984.

Barber, Marilyn. "The Women Ontario Welcomed: Immigrant Domestics in Ontario Homes, 1870–1930. In *The Neglected Majority,* Vol. II, edited by Alison M. Prentice and Susan Mann Trofimenkoff, 102–121.

Barbour, Noel. *Those Amazing People: The Story of the Canadian Magazine Industry, 1778–1967.* Toronto: Crucible Press, 1982.

Bates, Christina. "Shop and Factory: The Ontario Millinery Trade in Transition, 1870–1930." In *Fashion,* edited by Alexandra Palmer, 113–138.

Beard, William and Jerry White, eds. *North of Everything: English-Canadian Cinema since 1980.* Edmonton: University of Alberta Press, 2002.

Beasley, Maurine. "Recent Directions for the Study of Women's History in American Journalism." *Journalism Studies,* 2:2, 2001, 207–220.

Beauvoir, Simone de. *The Second Sex.* New York: Knopf, 1952.

Beauvoir, Simone de. *All Said and Done.* New York: Putman, 1974.

Bennett, Jessica, Jesse Ellison and Sarah Ball. "Are We There Yet?" *Newsweek,* http://www.newsweek.com, 19 March 2010.

Berger, Carl and Ramsay Cook, eds. *The West and the Nation: Essays in Honour of W. L. Morton.* Toronto: McClelland and Stewart, 1976.

Best, Carrie. *That Lonesome Road.* Halifax, NS: Clarion, 1977.

Beynon, Francis Marion. *Aleta Dey.* London, C.W. Daniel, 1919.

Bird, Florence. *Anne Francis: An Autobiography.* Toronto: Clark, Irwin, 1974.

Black, Naomi. "Feminism in Nova Scotia: Women's Groups, 1990–2004." *Atlantis,* 31:1, 2006, 64–75.

Boutilier, Beverly. "Helpers or Heroines? The National Council of Women, Nursing and 'Women's Work' in Late Victorian Canada." In *Caring and Curing: Historical Perspectives on Women and Healing in Canada,* edited by Dianne Dodd and Deborah Gorham, 17–47.

Boutilier, Beverly. "Women's Rights and Duties: Sarah Anne Curzon and the Politics of Canadian History." In *Creating Historical Memory*, edited by Beverly Boutilier and Alison Prentice, 53–57.

Boutilier, Beverly and Alison Prentice, eds. *Creating Historical Memory: English-Canadian Women and the Work of History.* Vancouver: University of British Columbia Press, 1997.

Bradley, Patricia. *Mass Media and the Shaping of American Feminism, 1963–1975.* Jackson: University Press of Mississippi, 2003.

Bradley, Patricia. *Women and the Press: The Struggle for Equality.* Evanston, IL: Northwestern University Press, 2005.

Brake, Laurel, Bill Bell and David Finkelstein, eds. *Nineteenth-Century Media and the Construction of Identities.* Basingstoke, Hampshire: Palgrave, 2000.

Brennen, Bonnie and Hanno Hardt, eds. *Picturing the Past: Media, History and Photography.* Chicago: University of Illinois Press, 1999.

Brodie, Janine, Shelley A.M. Gavigan and Jane Jensen. *The Politics of Abortion.* Toronto: Oxford University Press, 1992.

Brouwer, Ruth Compton. "The 'Between-Age' Christianity of Agnes Machar." *Canadian Historical Review,* 65:3, September 1984, 347–370.

Brouwer, Ruth Compton. "Moral Nationalism in Victorian Canada: The Case of Agnes Machar." *Journal of Canadian Studies/Revue d'études canadiennes,* 20:1, 1985, 90–108.

Brouwer, Ruth Compton. "Transcending the 'Unacknowledged Quarantine': Putting Religion into English-Canadian Women's History." *Journal of Canadian Studies/Revue d'études canadiennes,* 27:3, Autumn 1993, 47–61.

Bruce, Jean. "Women in CBC Radio Talks and Current Affairs." *Canadian Oral History Association Journal,* 5:1, 1981–82, 7–18.

Brun, Josette, ed. *Interrelations femmes-médias dans Amériques française.* Laval, QC: Presses Université Laval, 2009.

Brun, Josette et Barbara M. Freeman, "L'après-8 mars au Canada anglais et au Québec: Une célébration contrastée." *Sciences de la Société journal,* Presses Universitaires du Mirail, Toulouse, France, 2007, 149–163.

Buckner, Philip and R. Douglas Francis, eds. *Canada and the British World: Culture, Migration and Identity.* Vancouver: University of British Columbia Press, 2006.

Burgess, Marilyn and Gail Guthrie Valaskakis. *Indian Princesses and Cowgirls: Stereotypes from the Frontier.* Montreal: OBORO, 1992.

Burke, Sara Z. "New Women and Old Romans: Co-education at the University of Toronto, 1884–95," *Canadian Historical Review,* 80:2, June 1999, 219–241.

Burr, Christina. "Gender, Sexuality and Nationalism in J.W. Bengough's Verses and Political Cartoons." *Canadian Historical Review,* 83:5, December 2002, 505–554.

Burr, Christina. *Spreading the Light: Work and Labour Reform in Late-Nineteenth-Century Canada.* Toronto: University of Toronto Press, 1999.

Burt, Sandra, Lorraine Code and Lindsay Dorney, eds. *Changing Patterns: Women in Canada,* 2nd ed. Toronto: McClelland and Stewart, 1993.

Buss, Helen and Marlene Kadar, eds. *Working in Women's Archives: Researching Women's Private Literature and Archival Documents.* Waterloo, ON: Wilfrid Laurier University Press, 2001.

Buxton, William J. and Catherine McKercher. "Newspapers, Magazines and Journalism in Canada: Towards a Critical Historiography." *Acadiensis*, 28:1, Autumn 1998, 103–126.

Calhoun, Craig, ed. *Habermas and the Public Sphere*. Cambridge, MA: MIT Press, 1992.

Came, Barry. "Kanehsatake: 270 Years of Resistance." *Maclean's*, 31 January 1994, 58–60.

Canadian Broadcasting Corporation, "Pass the Orchids, Please!" *CBC Radio Magazine*, 12:3, April 1956, 6–7.

Capaldi, Nicholas. *John Stuart Mill: A Biography*. Cambridge; New York: Cambridge University Press, 2004.

Careless, J.M.S. *Brown of the* Globe, 2 vols. Toronto: Macmillan, 1959, 1963.

Cataudella, Julia. "When Women Came to Queen's." *Canadian Medical Association Journal*, 161:5, 7 September 1999, http://www.cmaj.ca/.

Caton, Susan Turnbull. "Fashion and War in Canada, 1939–1945." In *Fashion*, edited by Alexandra Palmer, 249–269.

Cavanaugh, Catherine A. and Randi R. Warne, eds. *Standing on New Ground: Women in Alberta*. Edmonton: University of Alberta Press, 1993.

Cavell, Richard. "Introduction: The Cultural Production of Canada's Cold War." *In Love, Hate and Fear in Canada's Cold War*, edited by Richard Cavell, 3–32.

Cavell, Richard, ed. *Love, Hate and Fear in Canada's Cold War*. Toronto: University of Toronto Press, 2004.

Chalus, Elaine H. "From Friedan to Feminism: Gender and Change at the University of Alberta, 1960–1970." In *Standing on New Ground*, edited by Catherine A. Cavanaugh and Randi R. Warne, 119–145.

Chamberlain, Mary. "Narrative Theory." In *Thinking about Oral History: Theories and Applications*, edited by Thomas L. Charlton, Lois E. Myers and Rebecca Sharpless, 142–165.

Chambers, Deborah, Linda Steiner and Carole Fleming. *Women and Journalism*. London; New York: Routledge, 2004.

Chambers, Lori. *Misconceptions: Unmarried Motherhood and the Ontario Children of Unmarried Parents Act, 1921 to 1969*. Toronto: Published for the Osgoode Society for Canadian Legal History by University of Toronto Press, 2007.

Charlton, Thomas L., Lois E. Myers and Rebecca Sharpless, eds. *Thinking about Oral History: Theories and Applications*. New York; Toronto: Altamira Press, 2008.

Chenier, Elise. "Reading Class in Lesbian Bar Culture: Living 'The Gay Life' in Toronto, 1955–1965," *Left History* 9:2, Spring/Summer 2004, 85–118.

Chenier, Nancy. "Agnes Maule Machar: Her Life, Her Social Concerns and a Preliminary Bibliography of Her Writing," Master of Arts thesis, Carleton University, 1977.

Childbirth by Choice Trust, eds. *No Choice: Canadian Women Tell Their Stories of Illegal Abortions*. Toronto: Childbirth by Choice Trust, 1998.

Clarke, Brian. "The Parish and the Hearth: Women's Confraternities and the Devotional Revolution among the Irish Catholics of Toronto, 1850–1885." In *Age of Transition: Readings in Canadian Social History, 1800–1900*, edited by Norman Knowles, 357–370.

Clarkson, Stephen, ed. *My Life as a Dame: The Personal and the Political in the Writings of Christina McCall*. Toronto: House of Anansi Press, 2008.

Coffey, Mary Anne. "Feminist Print Media in Canada," a synopsis of Eleanor Wachtel, *Feminist Print Media*. Ottawa: Government of Canada, Secretary of State, 1982, and Wachtel, *Update on Feminist Periodicals*. Ottawa: Government of Canada, Secretary of State, 1985. *Resources for Feminist Research/Documentation sur la recherche féministe*, 20:1/2, Spring/Summer 1991, 25–26.

Cook, Cynthia. "Dressing Up: A Consuming Passion." In *Fashion*, edited by Alexandra Palmer, 41–67.

Cook, Ramsay. "Francis Marion Beynon and the Crisis of Christian Reformism." In *The West and the Nation*, edited by Carl Berger and Ramsay Cook, 187–208.

Cook, Ramsay. *The Politics of J.W. Dafoe and the Free Press*. Toronto: University of Toronto Press, 1963.

Cook, Ramsay. *The Regenerators: Social Criticism in Late Victorian English Canada*. Toronto: University of Toronto Press, 1985.

Cook, Ramsay and Wendy Mitchinson, eds. *The Proper Sphere: Woman's Place in Canadian Society*. Toronto: Oxford University Press, 1976.

Cook, Sharon Anne. *Through Sunshine and Shadow: The Woman's Christian Temperance Union, Evangelicalism and Reform in Ontario, 1974–1930*. Montreal; Kingston: McGill-Queen's University Press, 1995.

Cook, Sharon Anne, Lorna R. McLean and Kate O'Rourke, eds. *Framing Our Past: Canadian Women's History in the Twentieth Century*. Montreal; Kingston: McGill-Queen's University Press, 2001.

Copps, Terry. "The Military Effort, 1914–1918." In *Canada and the First World War*, edited by David MacKenzie, 35–61.

Crean, Susan. *Newsworthy*. Toronto: Stoddart, 1985.

Creedon, Pamela J., ed. *Women in Mass Communication: Challenging Gender Values*, 2nd ed. Newbury Park, CA: Sage, 1993.

Cumming, Carman. *Secret Craft: The Journalism of Edward Farrer*. Toronto: University of Toronto Press, 1992.

Cumming, Carman. *Sketches from a Young Country: The Images of Grip Magazine*. Toronto: University of Toronto Press, 1997.

Cunningham, Patricia A. and Susan Voso Lab, eds. *Dress and Popular Culture*. Bowling Green, OH: Bowling Green State University Popular Press, 1991.

Curran, James. "Media and the Making of British Society, c. 1700–2000." *Media History*, 8:2, 2002, 135–154.

D'Acci, Julie. "Leading Up to Rowe v. Wade: Television Documentaries in the Abortion Debate." *Television, History and American Culture*, edited by Mary Beth Haralovich and Lauren Rabinovitz, 120–143.

Dagg, Ann. "Canadian Voices of Authority: Non-Fiction and Early Women Writers." *Journal of Canadian Studies/Revue d'études canadiennes*, 7:2, Summer 1992, 107–122.

Damon-Moore, Helen. *Magazines for the Millions: Gender and Commerce in the Ladies' Home Journal and the Saturday Evening Post, 1890–1910*. New York: State University of New York, 1994.

Daumier, Honoré. *Intellectuelles (Bas Bleus) et Femmes Socialistes*. Paris: Editions Vilo-Paris, 1974.

Dean, Misao. *A Different Point of View: Sara Jeannette Duncan.* Montreal: McGill-Queen's University Press, 1991.

Desbarats, Peter. *Guide to Canadian News Media.* Toronto: Harcourt Brace Jovanovich Canada, 1990.

Descarriers-Belanger, Francine and Shirley Roy. "The Women's Movement and Its Currents of Thought." Translated by Jennifer Beeman. *The CRIAW Papers,* No. 26. Ottawa, ON: Canadian Research Institute for the Advancement of Women, 1991.

Dicenzo, Maria. "Feminist Media and History: A Response to James Curran." *Media History,* 10:1, 2004, 43–49.

Dodd, Dianne and Deborah Gorham, eds. *Caring and Curing: Historical Perspectives on Women and Healing in Canada.* Ottawa: University of Ottawa Press, 1994.

Donnelly, Murray. *Dafoe of the Free Press.* Toronto: Macmillan of Canada, 1968.

Downie, Jill. *A Passionate Pen: The Life and Times of Faith Fenton.* Toronto: HarperCollins, 1996.

Druick, Zoe. *Projecting Canada: Government Policy and Documentary Film at the National Film Board of Canada.* Montreal: McGill-Queen's University Press, 2007.

Duder, Cameron. *Awfully Devoted Women: Lesbians in Canada, 1900–1965.* Vancouver: University of British Columbia Press, 2010.

Dunphy, Catherine. *Morgentaler: A Difficult Hero; A Biography.* Toronto: Random House Canada, 1996.

Dunphy, Catherine. "We're the New Faces of the Abortion Debate." *Chatelaine,* April 2009, 206–210.

Dyhouse, Carol. *Girls Growing Up in Late Victorian and Edwardian England.* London: Routledge and Kegan Paul, 1981.

Eaman, Ross. "Canadian Broadcasting Corporation," revised by Sasha Yusufali, *Canadian Encyclopedia,* http://www.thecanadianencyclopedia.com.

Eaman, Ross. *Channels of Influence: CBC Audience Research and the Canadian Public.* Toronto. University of Toronto Press, 1994.

Eaman, Ross. *Historical Dictionary of Journalism.* Latham, MD: Scarecrow Press, 2009.

Easley, Alexis. "Authorship, Gender and Power in Victorian Culture: Harriet Martineau and the Periodical Press." In *Nineteenth-Century Media and the Construction of Identities,* edited by Laurel Brake, Bill Bell and David Finkelstein, 154–164.

Edge, Marc. *Asper Nation: Canada's Most Dangerous Media Company.* Vancouver: New Star Books, 2007.

Edge, Marc. *Pacific Press: The Unauthorized Story of Vancouver's Newspaper Monopoly.* Vancouver: New Star Books, 2001.

Ehrenreich, Barbara and Deirdre English. *For Her Own Good: 150 Years of the Experts' Advice to Women.* New York: Doubleday, 1978.

Elliott, Jayne, Meryn Stuart and Cynthia Toman, eds. *Place and Practice in Canadian Nursing History.* Vancouver: University of British Columbia Press, 2008.

Epp, Marlene, Franca Iacovetta and Frances Swyripa, eds. *Sisters or Strangers? Immigrant, Ethnic and Racialized Women in Canadian History.* Toronto: University of Toronto Press, 2004.

Errington, Elizabeth Jane. "Ladies and School Mistresses: Educating Women in Early Nineteenth-Century Upper Canada." In *Age of Transition*, edited by Norman Knowles, 121–140.

Errington, Elizabeth Jane. *Wives and Mothers, School Mistresses and Scullery Maids: Working Women in Upper Canada, 1790–1840*. Montreal; Kingston: McGill-Queen's University Press, 1995.

Evans, Gary. *In the National Interest: A Chronicle of the National Film Board of Canada from 1949 to 1989*. Toronto: University of Toronto Press, 1991.

Faderman, Lillian. *Odd Girls and Twilight Lovers: Lesbianism in Twentieth Century America*. New York: Columbia University Press, 1991.

Fahrni, Magda. "'Ruffled' Mistresses and 'Discontented' Maids: Respectability and the Case of Domestic Service, 1880–1914." *Labour/Le Travail*, 39, Spring 1997, 69–97.

Fahrni, Magda and Robert Rutherdale, eds. *Creating Postwar Canada: Community, Diversity and Dissent, 1945–1975*. Vancouver: University of British Columbia Press, 2007.

Fahrni, Magda Suzanne Morton and Joan Sangster. "Feminism and the Making of Canada: Historical Reflections/Le féminisme et le façonnement du Canada: Réflexions sur l'histoire." *Atlantis*, 30:1, 2005, 3–6.

Farney, James and Bohdan S. Kordan. "The Predicament of Belonging: The Status of Enemy Aliens in Canada." *Journal of Canadian Studies/Revue d'études canadiennes*, 39:1, Winter 2005, 74–89.

Fernando, Kanchana. "'Television For and About Women': The Story of WTN." *Atlantis*, 29:3, Fall 2005, 41–51.

Fiamengo, Janice. "'Abundantly Worthy of Its Past': Agnes Maule Machar and Early Canadian Historical Fiction." *Studies in Canadian Literature*, 27:1, 2002, 15–31.

Fiamengo, Janice. "'Even in This Canada of Ours': Suffering, Sympathy and Social Justice in Late-Victorian Social Reform Discourse." PhD. dissertation, University of British Columbia, 1996.

Fiamengo, Janice. "A Legacy of Ambivalence: Responses to Nellie McClung." *Journal of Canadian Studies/Revue d'études canadiennes*, 34:4, Winter 1999/2000, 70–87.

Fiamengo, Janice. "Rediscovering Our Foremothers Again: Racial Ideas of Canada's Early Feminists, 1880–1945." In *Rethinking Canada: The Promise of Women's History*, 5th ed., edited by Mona Gleason and Adele Perry, 150–153.

Fiamengo, Janice. *The Woman's Page: Journalism and Rhetoric in Early Canada*. Toronto: University of Toronto Press, 2008.

Finkelstein, David. "'Long and Intimate Connections': Constructing a Scottish Identity for *Blackwood's* Magazine." In *Nineteenth-Century Media and the Construction of Identities*, edited by Laurel Brake, Bill Bell and David Finkelstein, 326–338.

Flitton, Marilyn G. *An Index to the Canadian Monthly and National Review and to Rose-Belford's Canadian Monthly and National Review, 1872–1882*. Toronto: Bibliography Society of Canada/University of Toronto Press, 1976.

Forestell, Nancy. "Mrs. Canada Goes Global: Canadian First Wave Feminism Revisited." *Atlantis*, 30:1, 2005, 7–20.

Francis, Anne (Florence Bird). "The Rights of Women," *Behind the Headlines Series*, 10:4, Canadian Association for Adult Education and the Canadian Institute of International Affairs, 1950.

Franticelli, Rina. "'Would I Ever Like to Work': The 'Working Mothers' Films and the Construction of Community." In *Challenge for Change*, edited by Thomas Waugh, Michael Brendan Baker and Ezra Winton, with a foreword with Naomi Klein, 303–313.

Franzen, Monika and Nancy Ethiel. *Make Way! 200 Years of American Women in Cartoons*. Chicago: Chicago Review Press, 1988.

Fraser, Nancy. "Rethinking the Public Sphere: A Contribution to the Critique of Actually Existing Democracy." In *Habermas and the Public Sphere*, edited by Craig Calhoun, 109–142.

Fraser, Nancy. *Unruly Practices: Power, Discourse and Gender in Contemporary Social Theory*. Minneapolis: University of Minnesota Press, 1989.

Freeman, Barbara M. "The Day of the Strong-Minded Frump Has Passed: Journalists and News of Feminism in Canada." In *Framing Our Past*, edited by Sharon Anne Cook, Lorna R. McLean and Kate O'Rourke, 385–391.

Freeman, Barbara M. "From No Go to No Logo: Lesbian Rights in *Chatelaine* Magazine, 1966–2004." *Canadian Journal of Communication*, 4:31, Fall 2006, 815–841.

Freeman, Barbara M. *Kit's Kingdom: The Journalism of Kathleen Blake Coleman*. Women's Experience Series, No. 1. Ottawa: Carleton University Press, 1989.

Freeman, Barbara M. "Laced In and Let Down: Women's Fashion Features in the Toronto Daily Press, 1890–1900." In *Fashion*, edited by Alexandra Palmer, 291–314.

Freeman, Barbara M. "Mother and Son: Gender, Class and War Propaganda in Canada, 1939–1945." *American Journalism*, Special Issue on World War II, 12:3, Summer 1995, 260–275.

Freeman, Barbara M. *The Satellite Sex: The Media and Women's Issues in English Canada, 1966–1971*. Waterloo, ON: Wilfrid Laurier University Press, 2001.

Friedan, Betty. *The Feminine Mystique*. New York: Norton, 1963.

Fry, John J. *The Farm Press, Reform and Rural Change, 1895–1920*. New York; London: Routledge, 2005.

Fulford, Robert. *Best Seat in the House: Memoirs of a Lucky Man*. Toronto: Collins, 1988.

Furniss, Elizabeth. "Aboriginal Justice, the Media, and the Symbiotic Management of Aboriginal/Euro-Canadian Relations." *American Indian Culture and Research Journal*, 25:2, 2001, 1–36.

Gabriele, Sandra. "Gendered Mobility, the Nation and the Women's Page." *Journalism: Theory, Practice and Criticism*, 7, 2006, 174–196.

Galloway, Gloria. "Status Debate Mounts as Bill Offers Benefits to Another 45,000 Natives." *Globe and Mail*, 12 March 2010, A1.

Garvey, Ellen Gruber. *The Adman in the Parlour: Magazines and the Gendering of Consumer Culture, 1880s–1910s*. New York: Oxford University Press, 1996.

Gerson, Carole. "Locating Female Subjects in the Archives." In *Working in Women's Archives*, edited by Helen M. Buss and Marlene Kadar, 12–13.

Gerson, Carole. "Three Writers of Victorian Canada." In *Canadian Writers and Their Works*, edited by Robert Lecker, Jack David and Ellen Quigley, 197–218.

Gideonese, Ted. "The Sexual Blur," *The Advocate*, June 1997, http://gideonse.com/articles/sexual_blur.htm.

Gittings, Christopher E. *Canadian National Cinema: Ideology, Difference and Representation.* London; New York: Routledge, 2008.

Gleason, Mona and Adele Perry, eds. *Rethinking Canada: The Promise of Women's History,* 5th ed. Don Mills, ON: Oxford University Press, 2006.

Gluck, Sherna Berger. "Women's Oral History: Is It So Special?" In *Thinking about Oral History,* edited by Thomas L. Charlton, Lois E. Myers and Rebecca Sharpless, 115–141.

Godard, Barbara. "Feminist Periodicals and the Production of Cultural Value: The Canadian Context." *Women's Studies International Forum,* 25:2, 2002, 209–223.

Goody, Alex. "Consider Your Grandmothers: Modernism, Gender and the New York Press." *Media History,* 7:1, 2001, 47–56.

Gordon, Lady Ishbel of Aberdeen and Temair. "The National Council of Women of Canada: What It Means and What It Does." S.I. unknown, 1900.

Gosselin, Cheryl. "Remaking Waves: The Québec Women's Movement in the 1950s and 1960s." *Canadian Women's Studies/les cahiers de la femme,* 25:3/4, Summer 2006, 34–39.

Granatstein, J.L. "Conscription in the Great War." In *Canada and the First World War,* edited by David MacKenzie, 62–75.

Green, Joyce, ed. *Making Space for Indigenous Feminism.* Winnipeg, MB: Fernwood, 2007.

Green, Joyce. "Taking Account of Aboriginal Feminism." In *Making Space for Indigenous Feminism,* edited by Joyce Green, 14–32.

Grenier, Marc. "Native Indians in the English-Canadian Press: The Case of the 'Oka Crisis.'" *Media, Culture and Society,* 6:2, 1994, 313–336.

Griffiths, N.E.S. *The Splendid Vision: Centennial History of the National Council of Women of Canada.* Ottawa: Carleton University Press, 1993.

Guard, Julie. "Canadian Citizens or Dangerous Foreign Women? Canada's Radical Consumer Movement, 1947–1950." In *Sisters or Strangers?* edited by Marlene Epp, Franca Iacovetta and Frances Swyripa, 161–189.

Gwyn, Sandra. *The Private Capital.* Toronto: McClelland and Stewart, 1984.

Haig, Kennethe M. *Brave Harvest: The Life Story of E. Cora Hind.* Toronto: Thomas Allen, 1945.

Haller, John S. and Robin M. *The Physician and Sexuality in Victorian America.* Urbana: University of Illinois Press, 1974.

Hallett, Mary and Marilyn Davis. *Firing the Heather: The Life and Times of Nellie McClung.* Saskatoon, SK: Fifth House, 1993.

Hallman, Dianne. "Agnes Maule Machar on the Higher Education of Women." *Historical Studies in Education/Revue d'histoire de l'éducation,* 13:2 (2001), 165–182.

Hallman, Dianne. "Cultivating a Love of Canada through History: Agnes Maule Machar, 1837–1927." In *Creating Historical Memory,* edited by Beverly Boutilier and Alison Prentice, 25–50.

Hallman, Dianne. "Religion and Gender in the Writing and Work of Agnes Maule Machar, 1837–1927," Ph.D. dissertation, University of Toronto, 1994.

Hallman, Dianne. "Rights, Justice, Power: Gendered Perspectives on Prohibition in Late Nineteenth- Century Canada." *History of Intellectual Culture,* 1:2, 2002, 1–14, http://www.ucalgary.ca/hic.

Hampson, Sarah. "The Hampson Interview: Alanis Obomsawin," *Globe and Mail*, 21 October 2006, R3.

Hansard, House of Commons Debates, 11 May 1970, 6793–6796; 12 May 1970, 6843–6844.

Haralovich, Mary Beth and Lauren Rabinovitz, eds. *Television, History and American Culture: Feminist Critical Essays*. Durham, NC; London: Duke University Press, 1999.

Hardt, Hanno. "Without the Rank and File: Journalism History, Media Workers and Problems of Representation." In *News Workers*, edited by Hanno Hardt and Bonnie Brennen, 1–29.

Hardt, Hanno and Bonnie Brennen, eds. *News Workers: Toward a History of the Rank and File*. Minneapolis: University of Minnesota Press, 1995.

Harewood, Adrian. "Alanis Obomsawin: A Portrait of a First Nation's Film Maker." *Take One*, 1 June 2003, http://www.thefreelibrary.com.

Harkness, Ross. *J.E. Atkinson of the Star*. Toronto: University of Toronto Press, 1963.

Harp, Dustin. "Newspapers' Transition from Women's to Style Pages: What Were They Thinking?" *Journalism: Theory, Practice and Criticism*, 7:2, 2006, 197–216.

Harris, Debbie Wise. "Colonizing Mohawk Women: Representations of Women in Mainstream Media." *Resources for Feminist Research/Documentation sur la recherche féministe*, 20:1, 2, 1991, 15–20.

Haussman, Melissa. *Abortion Politics in North America*. Boulder, CO; London: Lynne Rienner, 2005.

Hays, Matthew. "Oka Crisis: Worst Moment Revisited." *Globe and Mail*, 21 June 2000, R3.

Henry, Frances and Carol Tator. *Discourses of Domination: Racial Bias in the Canadian English-Language Press*. Toronto: University of Toronto Press, 2002.

Henry, Susan. "Changing Media History through Women's History." In *Women in Mass Communication*, edited by Pamela J. Creedon, 341–362.

Hicks, Anne. "Francis Beynon and the *Guide*." In *First Days, Fighting Days: Women in Manitoba History*, edited by Mary Kinnear, 41–52.

Hicks, Anne. Introduction to Francis Marion Beynon, *Aleta Dey*. London: Virago Modern Classics, 1988, v–xv.

Hilmes, Michele. "Desired and Feared: Women's Voices in Radio History." In *Television, History and American Culture*, edited by Mary Beth Haralovich and Lauren Rabinovitz, 17–35.

Hilmes, Michele and Jason Loviglio, eds. *Radio Reader: Essays in the Cultural History of Radio*. New York: Routledge, 2002.

Hollander, Anne. *Seeing through Clothes*. New York: Viking Press, 1978.

Holt, Simma. *Memoirs of a Loose Cannon*. Hamilton, ON: Seraphim Editions, 2008.

Houston, Susan E. and Alison Prentice. *Schooling and Scholars in Nineteenth Century Ontario*. Toronto: University of Toronto Press, 1988.

Howard, Victor. "On to Ottawa Trek." *Canadian Encyclopedia*, http://www.thecanadianencyclopedia.com.

Iacovetta, Franca. "Gendering Trans/National Historiographies: Feminists Rewriting Canadian History." *Journal of Women's History*, 19:1, 2007, 206–213.

Iacovetta, Franca and Mariana Valverde, eds. *Gender Conflicts: New Essays in Women's History.* Toronto: University of Toronto Press, 1992.

Jackel, Susan. "First Days, Fighting Days: Prairie Presswomen and Suffrage Activism." In *First Days, Fighting Days,* edited by Mary Kinnear, 53–75.

Jagger, Gill. *Judith Butler: Sexual Politics, Social Change and the Power of the Performative.* London; New York: Routledge, 2008.

JEB (Joan E. Biren). *Eye to Eye: Portraits of Lesbians.* Washington, DC: Glad Hag Books, 1979.

Johnston, Russell. *Selling Themselves: The Emergence of Canadian Advertising.* Toronto: University of Toronto Press, 2001.

Kay, Linda. *The Reading List.* Crestkill, NJ; Lanham, MD: Hamilton Books, 2005.

Kealey, Linda, ed. *A Not Unreasonable Claim: Women and Reform in Canada, 1880s–1920s.* Toronto: Women's Educational Press, 1979.

Kealey Linda and Joan Sangster, eds. *Beyond the Vote: Canadian Women and Politics.* Toronto: University of Toronto Press, 1989.

Keate, Kathryn. "Out from Under, Women Unite! Life Inside Women's Liberation." *Saturday Night,* July 1970, 15–20.

Keate, Stuart. *Paper Boy.* Toronto; Vancouver: Clarke, Irwin and Company, 1980.

Kelcey, Barbara E. "Dress Reform in Nineteenth Century Canada." In *Fashion,* edited by Alexandra Palmer, 229–248.

Kelcey, Barbara E. and Angela E. Davis, eds. *A Great Movement Underway: Women and the* Grain Growers' Guide, *1908–1928.* Winnipeg: Manitoba Record Society Publications, Vol. 12, 1997.

Kennedy, Elizabeth Lapovsky. "Telling Tales: Oral History and the Construction of Pre-Stonewall Lesbian History." In *The Oral History Reader,* edited by Robert Perks and Alistair Thomson, 344–355.

Kennedy, Elizabeth Lapovsky and Madeline D. Davis. *Boots of Leather, Slippers of Gold: The History of a Lesbian Community.* New York: Routledge, 1993.

Keshen, Jeffrey. *Propaganda and Censorship during Canada's Great War.* Edmonton: University of Alberta Press, 1996.

Kessler-Harris, Alice. *A Woman's Wage: Historical Meanings and Social Consequences.* Lexington: University Press of Kentucky, Blazer Lecture Series, 1990.

Kinahan, Anne-Marie. "Commodifying Women's Citizenship: Gender, Consumption and *Everywoman's World.*" A paper presented at the annual meeting of the Canadian Communication Association, Ottawa, 2009.

Kinahan, Anne-Marie. "Creating the Citizen/Consumer: Early 20th Century Canadian Women's Magazines and the Female Audience." A paper presented at the annual meeting of the Canadian Communication Association, Vancouver, 2008.

Kinahan, Anne-Marie. "Cultivating the Taste of the Nation: The National Council of Women of Canada and the Campaign against 'Pernicious' Literature at the Turn of the Twentieth Century." *Canadian Journal of Communication,* 32:2, 2007, 161–179.

Kinahan, Anne-Marie. "Finding the Political in the Domestic: Feminist Media History and Canadian Women's Magazines." A paper presented at the biannual meeting of the Canadian Association of Cultural Studies, Montreal, 2009.

Kinahan, Anne-Marie. "'A Splendid Army of Organized Womanhood': Gender, Communication and the National Council of Women of Canada, 1893–1918." Ph.D. dissertation, Carleton University, 2005.

Kinnear, Mary. *A Female Economy: Women's Work in the Prairie Provinces, 1870–1970.* Montreal; Kingston: McGill-Queen's University Press, 1998.

Kinnear, Mary, ed. *First Days, Fighting Days: Women in Manitoba History.* Regina: Canadian Plains Research Center, University of Regina, 1987.

Kiss & Tell Collective. *Drawing the Line: Lesbian Sexual Politics on the Wall.* Vancouver: Press Gang, 1991.

Kitch, Carolyn. "Changing Theoretical Perspectives on Women's Media Images: The Emergence of Patterns in a New Area of Historical Scholarship." *J&MC Quarterly,* 74:3, 1997, 477–489.

Kitch, Carolyn. *The Girl on the Magazine Cover: The Origins of Visual Stereotypes in American Mass Media.* Chapel Hill: North Carolina Press, 2001.

Knowles, Norman, ed. *Age of Transition: Readings in Canadian Social History, 1800–1900.* Toronto: Harcourt Brace Canada, 1998.

Korinek, Valerie. "'Don't Let Your Girlfriend Ruin Your Marriage': Lesbian Imagery in *Chatelaine* Magazine, 1950–1969." *Journal of Canadian Studies/Revue d'études canadiennes,* 33:3, Fall 1998, 83–109.

Korinek, Valerie J. "'The Most Openly Gay Person for at Least a Thousand Miles': Doug Wilson and the Politicization of a Province." *Canadian Historical Review,* 4:4, December 2003, 517–550.

Korinek, Valerie J. *Roughing It in the Suburbs: Reading* Chatelaine *Magazine in the Fifties and Sixties.* Toronto: University of Toronto Press, 2000.

Kostash, Myrna. *Long Way from Home: The Story of the Sixties Generation in Canada.* Toronto: James Lorimer, 1980.

Kreps, Bonnie. "Radical Feminism1." In *Women Unite! An Anthology of the Canadian Women's Movement.* Toronto: Women's Educational Press, 1972, 71–75.

Kuffert, L.B. *A Great Duty: Canadian Responses to Modern Life and Mass Culture, 1939–1967.* Montreal; Kingston: McGill-Queen's University Press, 2003.

Kuffert, L.B. "What Do You Expect of This Friend? Canadian Radio and the Intimacy of Broadcasting." *Media History,* 15:3, 2009, 303–319.

Kulba, Tracy and Victoria Lamont. "The Periodical Press and Western Woman's Suffrage Movements in Canada and the United States." *Women's Studies International Forum,* 29, 2006, 265–278.

Lang, Marjory. *Women Who Made the News: Female Journalists in Canada, 1880–1945.* Montreal; Kingston: McGill-Queen's University Press, 1999.

Langham, Josephine. "Tuning In—Canadian Radio Resources." *Archivaria,* 9, Winter 1979–1980, 105–124.

Laver, James. "Taste and Fashion since the French Revolution." In *Fashion Marketing,* edited by Gordon Willis and David Midgley, 380–381.

Leach, Jim and Jeannette Sloniowski, eds. *Candid Eyes: Essays on Canadian Documentaries.* Toronto: University of Toronto Press, 2003.

Lecker, Robert, Jack David and Ellen Quigley, eds. *Canadian Writers and Their Works.* Downsview, ON: ECW Press, 1983.

Le Cocq, Thelma. "Profile: Elizabeth Long." *Food for Thought,* March 1958, 262–266.

Lewis, Randolph. *Alanis Obomsawin: The Vision of a Native Filmmaker*. Lincoln: University of Nebraska Press, 2006.

Litt, Paul. "Trudeaumania: Participatory Democracy in the Mass-Mediated Nation." *Canadian Historical Review*, 89:1, March 2008, 27–53.

Little, Margaret Hillyard. "Militant Mothers Fight Poverty: The Just Society Movement, 1968–1971." *Labour/Le Travail*, 59, Spring 2007, 179–197.

Lloyd, Betty-Ann. "Hearing Women into Speech: The Feminist Press and the Women's Community." *Canadian Woman Studies/Les cahiers de la femme*, 1:1, Spring 1987, 29–32.

Loewen, Candace. "Making Ourselves Heard: 'Voice of Women' and the Peace Movement in the Early Sixties." In *Framing Our Past*, edited by Sharon Cook, Lorna R. McLean and Kate O'Rourke, 248–251.

Long, Elizabeth. "A Welcome Guest in Every Home." *CBC Times*, 2, July 1950.

Loulan, JoAnn. *Lesbian Passion: Loving Ourselves and Each Other*. Duluth, MN: Spinster's Ink Books, 1987.

Loulan, JoAnn. *Lesbian Sex*. San Francisco, CA: Spinster's Ink Books, 1984.

Luck, Kate. "Trouble in Eden, Trouble with Eve: Women, Trousers and Utopian Socialism in Nineteenth-Century America." In *Chic Thrills*, edited by Juliet Ash and Elizabeth Wilson, 200–212.

MacDonald, Dawn. "Women's Liberation—Year 2." *Chatelaine*, November 1970, 25.

Machar, Agnes Maule. "The Citizenship of Women." *Woman's Century*, 3, March 1916, 9.

MacKenzie, David, ed. *Canada and the First World War: Essays in Honour of Robert Craig Brown*. Toronto: University of Toronto Press, 2005, 272–299.

MacLellan, Anne F. "Women, Radio Broadcasting and the Depression: A 'Captive' Audience from Household Hints to Story Time and Serials." *Women's Studies*, 37:6, 2008, 616–633.

Mahtani, Minelle. "Mapping the Meanings of 'Racism' and 'Feminism' among Women Television Broadcast Journalists in Canada." In *Feminism and Antiracism*, edited by Frances Winddance Twine and Katherine M. Blee, 349–367.

Mann, Michelle M. *Indian Registration: Unrecognized and Unstated Paternity*. Ottawa: Status of Women Canada, 2005.

Marks, Lynne. "'A Fragment of Heaven on Earth'? Religion, Gender, and the Family in Turn-of-the Century Canadian Church Periodicals." *Journal of Family History*, 26:2, April 2001, 252.

Marshall, Barbara L. "Communication as Politics: Feminist Print Media in English Canada." *Women's Studies International Forum*, 18:4, 1995, 463–474.

Marshall, David. "'Death Abolished: Changing Attitudes to Death and the Afterlife in Nineteenth-Century Canadian Protestantism." In *Age of Transition*, edited by Norman Knowles, 370–387.

Martin, Michéle. "Changing the Picture: Women and the Media in Québec." In *Changing Patterns*, edited by Sandra Burt, Lorraine Code and Lindsay Dorney, 177–211.

Martin, Michéle. *Images at War: Illustrated Periodicals and Constructed Nations*. Toronto: University of Toronto Press, 2006.

Martin, Peggy. *Lily Lewis: Sketches of a Canadian Journalist; A Bio-critical Study*. Calgary: University of Calgary Press, 2006.

Masters, Philinda. "Women, Culture and Communications." In Ruth Road Pierson et al., *Canadian Women's Issues,* Vol. 1, 394–417.

Masters, Philinda. "A Word from the Press: A Brief Survey of Feminist Publishing." In *Resources for Feminist Research/Documentation sur la recherche féministe*, Spring/Summer 1991, 20:1/2, 27–35.

McClung, Nellie L. *In Times like These*. Toronto, McLeod and Allen, 1915.

McClung, Nellie L. *The Stream Runs Fast*. Toronto: Thomas Allen, 1945.

McEnaney, Marjorie. *Who Stole the Cakes? A Memoir by Marjorie Winspear McEnaney*. Erin, ON: Boston Mills Press, 1981.

McIntosh, Brian. "Sweated Labour: Female Needleworkers in Industrializing Canada." In *Age of Transition*, edited by Norman Knowles, 179–191.

McIvor, Shirley D. "Aboriginal Women's Rights as 'Existing Rights.'" *Canadian Women's Studies/Les cahiers de la femme*, 15:2/3, Spring/Summer 1995, 34–38.

McIvor, Sharon with Rauna Kuokkanen. "Sharon McIvor: Woman of Action." In *Making Space for Indigenous Feminism*, edited by Joyce Green, 241–254.

McKay, Ian. "The Liberal Order Framework: A Prospect for the Reconnaissance of Canadian History." *Canadian Historical Review*, 81:4, 2000, 617–645.

McKay, Ian. *Reasoning Otherwise: Leftists and the People's Enlightenment in Canada, 1890–1920*. Toronto: Between the Lines Press, 2008.

McKercher, Catherine. *Newsworkers Unite: Labor, Convergence, and North American Newspapers*. Lanham MD: Rowan and Littlefield, 2002.

McKie, Craig and Benjamin Singer, eds. *Communications in Canadian Society*, 6th ed. Toronto: Thompson Books, 2001.

McKillop, A.B. *Pierre Berton: A Biography*. Toronto: McClelland and Stewart, 2008.

McLaren, Angus and Arlene Tigar McLaren. *The Bedroom and the State: The Changing Practices and Politics of Contraception and Abortion in Canada, 1880–1997*, 2nd ed. Don Mills, ON: Oxford University Press, 1997.

McLean, Lorna R. and Marilyn Barber. "In Search of Comfort and Independence: Irish Immigrant Domestic Servants Encounter the Courts, Jails and Asylums in Nineteenth Century Ontario." In *Sisters or Strangers*, edited by Marlene Epp, Franca Iacovetta and Frances Swyripa, 133–160.

McTavish, Lianne. "Virtual Activism and the Pro-Choice Movement in Canada." *Canadian Woman Studies/Les cahiers de la femme*, 25:3/4, Summer 2006, 121–127.

A Member of the Pandora Collective. "Victory for Pandora ... and All of Us." *The Womanist*, Spring 1992, 32.

Millett, Kate. *Flying*. New York: Ballantine Books, 1974.

Mitchinson, Wendy. *The Nature of Their Bodies: Women and Their Doctors in Victorian Canada*. Toronto: University of Toronto Press, 1991.

Montigny, Edgar-André and Lori Chambers, eds. *Ontario since Confederation: A Reader*. Toronto: University of Toronto Press, 2000.

Morgan, Cecilia. *Public Men and Virtuous Women: The Gendered Languages of Religion and Politics in Upper Canada, 1791–1850*. Toronto: University of Toronto Press, 1996.

Morgan, Henry. *Canadian Men and Women of the Time*. Toronto: William Briggs, 1912.

Morgan, Nicole. *The Equality Game: Women in the Federal Public Service, 1908–1987*. Ottawa: Canadian Advisory Council on the Status of Women, 1988.

Morton, Desmond. "Supporting Soldiers' Families: Separation Allowance, Assigned Pay, and the Unexpected." In *Canada and the First World War*, edited by David MacKenzie, 194–229.

Murray, Heather. "Free for All Lesbians: Lesbian Cultural Production and Consumption in the United States during the 1970s." *Journal of the History of Sexuality*, 16:2, May 2007, 251–275.

Murray, Heather. "Great Works and Good Works: The Toronto Women's Literary Club, 1877–1883." *Historical Studies in Education/Revue d'histoire de l'éducation*, 11:2, Fall/ 1999, 1–15, http://www.edu.uwo.HSE/99murray/html.

Nancoo, Stephen E. and Robert S. Nancoo, eds. *The Mass Media and Canadian Diversity*. Mississauga, ON: Canadian Educators Press, 1997.

National Council of Women of Canada. *Annual Yearbook of the National Council of Women of Canada, 1894*. Ottawa: NCWC, c. 1894.

National Council of Women of Canada. *Women of Canada: Their Life and Work*. Compiled by the National Council of Women of Canada at the Request of the Hon. Sydney Fisher for distribution at the Paris International Exhibition, 1900.

Nestle, Joan. *A Restricted Country*. Ithaca, NY: Firebrand Books, 1987.

Newman, Jacquetta and Linda A. White. *Women, Politics and Public Policy.* Toronto: Oxford University Press, 2006.

Newman, Kathy M. "Poisons, Potions, and Profits: Radio Rebels and the Origins of the Consumer Movement." In *Radio Reader*, edited by Michele Hilmes and Jason Loviglio, 157–181.

Newton, Stella Mary. *Health, Art and Reason: Dress Reformers of the 19th Century*. London: John Murray, 1974.

Osborne, Brian S. *The Rock and the Sword*. Kingston, ON: Heinrich Heine Press at Grass Creek, 2004.

Osborne, Brian S. "The World of Agnes Maule Machar: Social Reform, Nation, Empire, Nature." Kingston Historical Society at http://www.heritage.kingston.org/wok/machar.html.

Palmer, Alexandra, ed. *Fashion: A Canadian Perspective.* Toronto: University of Toronto Press, 2004.

Park, David W. and Jefferson Pooley, eds. *The History of Media and Communication Research: Contested Memories.* New York: Peter Lang, 2008.

Parr, Joy and Gunilla Ekberg. "Mrs. Consumer and Mrs. Keynes in Postwar Canada and Sweden." *Gender and History*, 8:2, August 1996, 212–230.

Partington, Angela. "Popular Fashion and Working-Class Affluence." In *Chic Thrills*, edited by Juliet Ash and Elizabeth Wilson, 145–146.

Patterson, Maggie Jones and Megan Williams Hall. "Abortion, Moral Maturity and Civic Journalism." *Critical Studies in Mass Communication*, 15, 1998, 91–115.

Peiss, Kathy. *Cheap Amusements: Working Women and Leisure in Turn-of-the-Century New York*. Philadelphia: Temple University Press, 1986.

Peiss, Kathy. *Hope in a Jar: The Making of America's Beauty Culture*. New York: Metropolitan Books, Henry Holt and Company, 1998.

Perks, Robert and Alistair Thomson, eds. *The Oral History Reader*. London; New York: Routledge, 1998.

Phelps, Minnie. "Unequal Pay for Equal Work, 1890." In *The Proper Sphere*, edited by Ramsay Cook and Wendy Mitchinson, 182.

Phillips, Paul T. *The Controversialist: An Intellectual Life of Goldwin Smith*. Westport, CT: Praeger, 2002.

Pick, Zuzana. "Storytelling and Resistance: The Documentary Practice of Alanis Obomsawin." In *Gendering the Nation*, edited by Kay Armatage et al., 76–93.

Pick, Zuzana. "'This Land Is Ours': Storytelling and History in *Kanehsatake: 270 Years of Resistance*." In *Candid Eyes*, edited by Jim Leach and Jeannette Sloniowski, 181–196.

Pierson, Ruth Roach, Marjorie Griffin Cohen, Paula Bourne and Philinda Masters. *Canadian Women's Issues: Twenty-five Years of Women's Activism in English Canada. Vol. I: Strong Voices*. Toronto: James Lorimer and Company, 1993.

Potvin, Claudine and Janice Williamson, eds. *Women's Writing and the Literary Institution*. Edmonton: Research Institute for Comparative Literature, University of Alberta, 1992.

Prentice, Alison. "Bluestockings, Feminists, or Women Workers? A Preliminary Look at Women's Early Employment at the University of Toronto." *Journal of the Canadian Historical Association*, New Series, 2, 1991, 231–261.

Prentice, Alison, Paula Bourne, Gail Cuthbert Brandt, Beth Light, Wendy Mitchinson and Naomi Black. *Canadian Women: A History*, 2nd ed. Toronto: Harcourt Brace Canada, 1996.

Prentice, Alison and Marjorie Theobald. *Women Who Taught: Perspectives on the History of Women and Teaching*. Toronto: University of Toronto Press, 1991.

Rakow, Lana. "Feminist Historiography and the Field: Writing New Histories." In *The History of Media and Communication Research*, edited by David W. Park and Jefferson Pooley, 113–139. New York: Peter Lang, 2008.

Rankin, L. Pauline. "Sexualities and National Identities: Re-Imagining Queer Nationalism." *Journal of Canadian Studies/Revue d'études canadiennes*, 35:2, Summer 2000, 176–196.

Rapoport, Nessa. "Recollections of Mattie Levi Rotenberg." Jewish Women's Archive, http://jwa.org/discover/recollections/rotenberg.htm.

Rebick, Judy. "Indian Rights for Indian Women: Changing the Indian Act." In Judy Rebick, *Ten Thousand Roses*, 107–115.

Rebick, Judy. *Ten Thousand Roses: The Making of a Feminist Revolution*. Toronto: Penguin Canada, 2005.

Regan, Ken, Scott White and Ivor Shapiro. "Journalists Seeking Public Office: What Are the Ethical Issues?" A panel report for the Canadian Association of Journalists at http://www.caj.ca/?p=1147, 6 April 2011.

Report of the CBC Task Force on the Status of Women. Toronto: Canadian Broadcasting Corporation, 1975.

Rex, Kay. *No Daughter of Mine: The Women and History of the Canadian Women's Press Club, 1904–1971*. Toronto: Cedar Cave Books, 1995.

Rhodes, Jane. *Mary Ann Shadd Cary: The Black Press and Protest in the Nineteenth Century*. Bloomington: University of Indiana Press, 1998.

Rich, Adrienne. *On Lies, Secrets and Silence: Selected Prose 1966–1978*. New York: Norton, 1979.

Roach, Mary Ellen and Kathleen Ehle Musa. *New Perspectives on the History of Western Dress.* New York: NutriGuides, 1980.

Roberts, Barbara. *A Reconstructed World: A Feminist Biography of Gertrude Richardson.* Kingston; Montreal: McGill-Queen's University Press, 1996.

Roberts, Barbara. "Women against War." In *Up and Doing,* edited by Janice Williamson and Deborah Gorham, 48–65.

Roberts, Barbara. "Women's Peace Activism in Canada." In *Beyond the Vote,* edited by Linda Kealey and Joan Sangster, 276–308.

Roberts, Wayne. "Rocking the Cradle for the World: The New Woman and Maternal Feminism, Toronto 1977–1914." In *A Not Unreasonable Claim,* edited by Linda Kealey, 15–45.

Robinson, Gertrude J. *Gender, Journalism and Equity: Canadian, U.S. and European Perspectives.* Crestkill, NJ: Hampton Press, 2005.

Robson, Ann P. and John M. Robson, eds. *Sexual Equality: Writings by John Stuart Mill, Harriet Taylor Mill, and Helen Taylor.* Toronto: University of Toronto Press, 1994.

Rooke, P.T. and R.L. Schnell. *No Bleeding Heart: Charlotte Whitton: A Feminist on the Right.* Vancouver: University of British Columbia Press, 1987.

Rosa, Suzanne de and Jeanne Marand. "La Presse Féministe est Différente!" *Canadian Woman Studies/Les cahiers de la femme,* 8:1, 33–34.

Rosner, Cecil. *Behind the Headlines: A History of Investigative Journalism.* Don Mills, ON: Oxford University Press, 2008.

Ross, Becki L. *The House That Jill Built: A Lesbian Nation in Formation.* Toronto: University of Toronto Press, 1995.

Ross, Becki L. "A Lesbian Politics of Erotic Decolonization." In *Painting the Maple,* edited by Veronica Strong-Boag et al., 187–214.

Ross, Becki L. "Tracking Lesbian Speech: The Social Organization of Lesbian Periodical Publishing in English Canada, 1973–1988." In *Women's Writing and the Literary Institution,* edited by Claudine Potvin and Janice Williamson, 173–185.

Rotenberg, Lori. "The Wayward Worker: Toronto's Prostitute at the Turn of the Century." In *Women at Work,* edited by Janice Acton, Penny Goldsmith and Bonnie Shepard, 48–49.

Roth, Lorna. "Cultural and Racial Diversity in Canadian Broadcast Journalism." In *Deadlines and Diversity,* edited by Valerie Alia, Brian Brennan and Barry Hoffmaster, 72–85.

Roth, Lorna, Beverley Nelson and Kassennahawi Marie David. "Three Women, a Mouse, a Microphone and a Telephone: Information (Mis)Management during the Mohawk/Canadian Governments' Conflict of 1990." In *Feminism, Multiculturalism and the Media,* edited by Angharad N. Valdivia, 48–81.

Rutherford, Paul. *A Victorian Authority: The Victorian Press in Late Nineteenth Century Canada.* Toronto: University of Toronto Press, 1982.

Sager, Eric. "Women Teachers in Canada, 1981–1901." *Canadian Historical Review,* 88:2, June 2007, 201–236.

Samois, ed. *Coming to Power: Writing and Graphics on Lesbian S/M.,* 3rd ed. New York: Alyson Books, 1983.

Sangster, Joan. "Consuming Issues: Women on the Left, Political Protest and the Organization of Homemakers, 1920–1960." In *Framing Our Past*, edited by Sharon Cook, Lorna R. McLean and Kate O'Rourke, 246–247.

Sangster, Joan. "Introduction, Part 4: Women's Activism and the State." In *Framing Our Past*, edited by Sharon Cook, Lorna R. McLean and Kate O'Rourke, 201–211.

Sangster, Joan. "Mobilizing Women for War." In *Canada and the First World War*, edited by David MacKenzie, 157–193.

Sangster, Joan. "Telling Our Stories: Feminist Debates and the Use of Oral History." *Women's History Review*, 3:1, 1994, 5–28.

Sangster, Joan. *Transforming Labour: Women and Work in Post-war Canada.* Toronto: University of Toronto Press, 2010.

Sangster, Margaret E. "A Sermon to Girls: To Those Who Desire to Write for the Papers." *New Dominion Monthly*, November 1876, 435–437.

Sauvageau, Florian et David Hemmings Pritchard. *Les journalistes canadiens: un portrait de fin de siècle.* Sainte-Foy, QC: Presses de l'Université Laval, 1999.

Scanlon, Jennifer. *Inarticulate Longings: The* Ladies' Home Journal, *Gender, and the Promise of Consumer Culture.* New York: Routledge, 1995.

Schlesinger, Benjamin, ed. *Family Planning in Canada: A Source Book.* Toronto: University of Toronto Press, 1974.

Schlesinger, Benjamin, ed. *Sexual Behaviour in Canada: Patterns and Problems.* Toronto: University of Toronto Press, 1977.

Schwenger, Cope W. "Abortion as a Public Health Problem and Community Health Measure." In *Family Planning in Canada*, edited by Benjamin Schlesinger. 238–244.

Scott, Jean Thomson. "The Conditions of Female Labour in Ontario." In *Toronto University Studies in Political Science*, First Series, No. 3, edited by W.J. Ashley. Toronto: University of Toronto Press, 1889, 18–25. Republished in *The Proper Sphere*, edited by Ramsay Cook and Wendy Mitchinson, 172–182.

Sethna, Christabelle. "'Chastity Outmoded!' The *Ubyssey*, Sex, and the Single Girl, 1960–70." In *Creating Postwar Canada*, edited by Magda Fahrni and Robert Rutherdale, 291–314.

Sethna, Christabelle. "The Evolution of the Birth Control Handbook: From Student Peer Education to Feminist Self-Empowerment Text, 1968–1975." *Canadian Bulletin of Medical History/Bulletin canadien d'histoire de la médecine*, 23:1, 2006, 89–118.

Sethna, Christabelle. "The University of Toronto Health Service, Oral Contraception and Student Demand for Birth Control, 1960–1970." *Historical Studies in Education/Revue d'histoire de l'éducation*, 17:2, 265–292.

Sethna, Christabelle. "'WE WANT FACTS, NOT MORALS!' Unwanted Pregnancy, the Toronto Women's Caucus and Sex Education." In *Ontario since Confederation*, edited by Edgar-André Montigny and Lori Chambers, 409–428.

Sifton, Elizabeth. "Montreal's Fashion Mile: St. Catherine Street, 1890–1930." In *Fashion*, edited by Alexandra Palmer, 203–226.

Silvera, Makeda, ed. *Piece of My Heart: A Lesbian of Colour Anthology.* Toronto: Sister Vision Press, 1991.

Sims, Sally. "The Bicycle, the Bloomer and Dress Reform in the 1890s." In *Dress and Popular Culture*, edited by Patricia A. Cunningham and Susan Voso Lab, 125–145.

Skea, Warren H. "The Canadian Newspaper Industry's Portrayal of the Oka Crisis." *Native Studies Review*, 9, Spring 1993–94, 15–31.

Smith, Miriam. *Lesbian and Gay Rights in Canada: Social Movements and Equality Seeking, 1971–1995*. Toronto: University of Toronto Press, 1999.

Socknat, Thomas. *Witness against War: Pacifism in Canada, 1900–1945*. Toronto: University of Toronto Press, 1987.

Sotiron, Minko. *From Politics to Profit: The Commercialization of Canadian Daily Newspapers, 1890–1920*. Montreal; Kingston: McGill-Queen's University Press, 1997.

Spencer, David. "The 'Art' of Politics: Victorian Canadian Political Cartoonists Look at Canada–U.S. Relations," http://facstaff.elon.edu/dcopeland/mhm/mhmjour 6-1.pdf.

Spencer, David. "Bringing Down Giants: Thomas Nast, John Wilson Bengough and the Maturing of Political Cartooning." In *Communications in Canadian Society*, edited by Craig McKie and Benjamin Singer, 67–80.

Spencer, David. "Double Vision: The Victorian Bi-Cultural World of Henri Julien." *International Journal of Comic Art*, 2:2, Fall 2000, 1–32.

Spencer, David. "Fact or Fantasy: Pictorial Visions of War in the French and English Press, in Canada 1914–1917." In *Picturing The Past*, edited by Bonnie Brennen and Hanno Hardt, 182–205.

St. Denis, Verna. "Feminism Is for Everybody: Aboriginal Women, Feminism and Diversity." In *Making Space for Indigenous Feminism*, edited by Joyce Green, 33–52.

Steele, Valerie. *Fashion and Eroticism: Ideals of Feminine Beauty from the Victorian Age to the Jazz Age*. New York; Oxford: Oxford University Press, 1985.

Steele, Valerie. *Fetish: Fashion, Sex and Power*. New York; Oxford: Oxford University Press, 1996.

Stetler, Gilbert A. and Allan F.J. Artibise, eds. *The Canadian City: Essays in Urban and Social History*. Ottawa: Carleton University Press, 1984.

Stewart, Bill. *A Picture by Christmas: Early CBC Television in Nova Scotia*. Halifax, NS: Nimbus Books, 2002.

Stewart, Michelle. "The Indian Film Crews of Challenge for Change: Representation and the State." *Canadian Journal of Film Studies*, 16:2, Fall 2007, 49–81.

Stone, Sharon Dale, ed. *Lesbians in Canada*. Toronto: Between the Lines Press, 1990.

Streitmatter, Rodger. *Unspeakable: The Rise of the Gay and Lesbian Press in America*. Boston; London: Faber and Faber, 1995.

Strong-Boag, Veronica. "Canada's Wage-Earning Wives and the Construction of the Middle-Class, 1945–1960." *Journal of Canadian Studies/Revue d'études canadiennes*, 29:3, Autumn 1994, 5–25.

Strong-Boag, Veronica. "Canada's Women Doctors: Feminism Constrained." In *A Not Unreasonable Claim*, edited by Linda Kealey, 109–129.

Strong-Boag, Veronica. *Parliament of Women: The National Council of Women of Canada*. Ottawa: National Museums of Canada, 1976.

Strong-Boag, Veronica, Joan Anderson, Sherrill E. Grace and Avigail Eisenberg, eds. *Painting the Maple: Essays on Race, Gender and the Construction of Canada.* Vancouver: University of British Columbia Press, 1998.

Sutherland, Fraser. *The Monthly Epic: A History of Canadian Magazines, 1789–1989.* Markham, ON: Fitzhenry and Whiteside, 1989.

Tauskey, Thomas E. *Sara Jeannette Duncan: Novelist of Empire.* Port Credit, ON: P.D. Meany, 1980.

Tausky, Thomas E., ed. *Selected Journalism: Sara Jeannette Duncan.* Ottawa: Tecumseh Press, 1978.

Taylor, Alison. "Window on the World: A History of Women in CBC Radio Talks and Public Affairs, 1936–1966." Master of Arts thesis, Carleton University, 1985.

Taylor, Georgina M. "'Ground for Common Action.' Violet McNaughton's Agrarian Feminism and the Origins of the Farm Women's Movement in Canada." Ph.D. dissertation, Carleton University, 1997.

Taylor, Jeffery. *Fashioning Farmers: Ideology, Agricultural Knowledge and the Manitoba Farm Movement, 1890–1925.* Regina, SK: Canadian Plains Research Center, 1994.

Taylor, Kate. "My First Battle—It's Always Education." *Globe and Mail,* 8 May 2009, R3.

Thomson, Ann. *Winning Choice on Abortion.* Victoria, BC: Trafford, 2004.

Trofimenkoff, Susan. "One Hundred and Two Muffled Voices: Canada's Industrial Women in the 1880's." *Atlantis,* 3:1, Fall 1977, 69–80.

Tusan, Michelle Elizabeth. *Women Making News: Gender and Journalism in Modern Britain.* Champagne: University of Illinois Press, 2005.

Twine, Frances Winddance and Katherine M. Blee, eds. *Feminism and Antiracism: International Struggles for Justice.* New York: New York University Press, 2001.

Valaskakis, Gail Guthrie. Guest Editor's Introduction, "Parallel Voices: Indians and Others: Narratives of Cultural Struggle." *Canadian Journal of Communication,* 18:3, 1993. http://www.cjc-online.ca/index.php/journal/article/view/756/662.

Valaskakis, Gail Guthrie. *Indian Country: Essays on Contemporary Native Culture.* Waterloo, ON: Wilfrid Laurier University Press, 2005.

Valaskakis, Gail Guthrie. "Rights and Warriors: First Nations, Media and Identity." In *The Mass Media and Canadian Diversity,* edited by Stephen E. Nancoo and Robert S. Nancoo, 110–123.

Valdivia, Angharad N., ed. *Feminism, Multiculturalism and the Media: Global Diversities.* Thousand Oaks, CA: Sage, 1995.

Valverde, Mariana. *Sex, Power and Pleasure.* Toronto: Women's Press, 1985.

Vanstone, Gail. *D Is for Daring: The Women behind the Films of Studio D.* Toronto: Sumach Press, 2007.

Van Zoonen, Liesbet. *Feminist Media Studies.* Thousand Oaks, CA: Sage, 1994.

Veblen, Thorstein. "The Economic Theory of Woman's Dress." In *Essays in Our Changing Order,* edited by Leon Ardzrooni, 67–74.

Veblen, Thorstein. *Theory of the Leisure Class.* New York: Macmillan, 1912.

Vickery, Amanda. "Golden Age to Separate Spheres? A Review of the Categories and Chronology of English Women's History." *The Historical Journal,* 36:2, 1993, 383–414.

Vipond, Mary. "Blessed Are the Peacemakers: The Labour Question in Canadian Social Gospel Fiction." *Journal of Canadian Studies/Revue d'études canadiennes*, 10:3, 1975, 32–43.

Vipond, Mary. "The Canadian Broadcasting Commission in the 1930s: How Canada's First Public Broadcaster Negotiated 'Britishness.'" In *Canada and the British World*, edited by Phillip Buckner and R. Douglas Francis, 270–287.

Vipond, Mary. "Censorship in a Liberal State: Regulating Talk on Canadian Radio in the Early 1930s." *Historical Journal of Film, Radio and Television*, 30:1, March 2010, 75–94.

Vipond, Mary. "Comrades in Arms: War Work at the CBC." A paper presented at the annual conference of the Canadian Communication Association, Vancouver, 2008.

Vipond, Mary. "Going Their Own Way: The Relationship between the Canadian Radio Broadcasting Commission and the BBC, 1933–1936." *Media History*, 15:1, 2009, 71–83.

Vipond, Mary. *Listening In: The First Decade of Canadian Broadcasting, 1922–1932*. Montreal; Kingston: McGill-Queen's University Press, 1992.

Vipond, Mary. *The Mass Media in Canada*, 3rd ed. Toronto: Lorimer, 2000.

Walker, Lisa. *Looking like What You Are: Sexual Style, Race and Lesbian Identity*. New York: New York University Press, 2001.

Wallin, Pamela. *Since You Asked*. Toronto: Random House of Canada, 1998.

Ware, Susan. *It's One o'Clock and Here Is Mary Margaret McBride: A Radio Biography*. New York: New York University Press, 2005.

Warne, R.R. "Nellie McClung and Peace." In *Up and Doing*, edited by Janice Williamson and Deborah Gorham, 35–47.

Warner, Tom. *Never Going Back: A History of Queer Activism in Canada*. Toronto: University of Toronto Press, 2002.

Warren, Lynne. "'Women in Conference': Reading the Correspondence Columns in *Woman*, 1890–1910." In *Nineteenth-Century Media and the Construction of Identities*, edited by Laurel Brake, Bill Bell and David Finkelstein, 122–134.

Wasserlein, Frances Jane. "An Arrow Aimed Straight at the Heart: The Vancouver Women's Caucus and the Abortion Campaign 1969–1971." Master of Arts thesis, Simon Fraser University, 1990.

Waugh, Thomas, Michael Brendan Baker and Ezra Winton, eds. *Challenge for Change: Activist Documentary at the National Film Board of Canada*, with a foreword with Naomi Klein. Montreal; Kingston: McGill-Queen's University Press, 2010.

Westell, Anthony. *The Inside Story: A Life in Journalism*. Toronto: Dundurn Press, 2002.

Weston, Mary Ann. *Native Americans in the News: Images of Indians in the Twentieth Century Press*. Westport, CT: Greenwood Press, 1996.

Whitaker, Reg and Gary Marcus. *Cold War Canada: The Making of a National Insecurity State, 1945–1957*. Toronto: University of Toronto Press, 1994.

White, Jerry. "Alanis Obomsawin, Documentary Form and the Canadian Nation(s)." In *North of Everything*, edited by William Beard and Jerry White, 364–375.

Whitt, Jan. *Women in American Journalism: A New History*. Champagne: University of Illinois Press, 2008.

Williamson, Janice and Deborah Gorham, eds. *Up and Doing: Canadian Women and Peace.* Toronto: The Women's Press, 1989.

Willis, Gordon and David Midgley, eds. *Fashion Marketing.* London: George Allen and Unwin, 1973.

Wilson, Elizabeth. "Fashion and the Postmodern Body." In *Chic Thrills*, edited by Juliet Ash and Elizabeth Wilson, 3–16.

Winseck, Dwayne R. *Communication and Empire: Media, Markets and Globalization, 1860–1930.* Durham, NC: Duke University Press, 2007.

Wright, Cynthia. "'Feminine Trifles of Vast Importance': Writing Gender into the History of Consumption." In *Gender Conflicts*, edited by Franca Iacovetta and Mariana Valverde, 229–259.

Yow, Valerie Raleigh. "Biography and Oral History." In *Thinking about Oral History*, edited by Thomas L. Charlton, Lois E. Myers and Rebecca Sharpless, 183–222.

Zelizer, Barbie, ed. *Explorations in Communication and History.* New York: Routledge, 2009.

Zelizer, Barbie. *Taking Journalism Seriously: News and the Academy.* Thousand Oaks, CA: Sage, 2004.

Zukerman, Mary Ellen. *A History of Popular Women's Magazines in the United States.* Westport, CT: Greenwood Press, 1998.

Archival Material

Archives of Manitoba, Lillian Beynon Thomas Papers, MG9 A53; Quill Club, MG 10; Political Equality League of Manitoba, P192, 1912–1924; Canadian Women's Press Club Papers, Winnipeg Branch, MG 10 A1, M612 and M13; Hudson's Bay Company Archives, United Farmers of Manitoba Papers, MG 10 E1.

Archives of the University of Manitoba, United Grain Growers' Ltd. Fonds (UGG) and Public Press, Limited, MSS 76.

Library and Archives Canada, Kate Aitken Papers, R4490-0-0-E; Florence Bayard Bird Papers, R4801-0-0-E; Jean Bruce Fonds, R5638-0-8; Canadian Broadcasting Corporation, RG 41; Elspeth Chisholm Fonds, R4875-0-7-E and R4875-1-9-E; Ernest Bushnell Papers, R6602-0-X-E; Rene Landry Papers, R6202-6-4-F; Elizabeth Long Papers, R2179-0-2-E; Marjorie McEnaney Papers, R2389-09-E; Media Club of Canada (Canadian Women's Press Club) Papers, R2800-0-3-E including C.W.P.C. Newspacket, 1939–1945; Hugh Morrison Papers, R2207-0-X-E; Jean Hunter Morrison Papers, R1859-0-X-E; Neil Morrison Papers, R2551-0-4-E; Mattie Rotenberg Papers, R4878-0-9-E; E. Austin Weir Fonds, R2327-0-5-E, Biography/Administrative History; J.S. Woodsworth Papers, R5904-0-1-E, Volumes 2, 15.

Queen's University Archives, George F. Chipman Fonds, Location 2141 and T.A. Crerar Fonds, Location 2117.

Saskatchewan Archives Board, Violet McNaughton Papers, A1.

Simon Fraser University Archives, F-162-3-3-0-27, Marge Hollibaugh's Abortion Caravan Scrapbook; Anne Roberts Fonds; Frances Wasserlein Papers, Vancouver Women's Caucus Binder.

University of British Columbia Library, Special Collections, Ellen Harris Papers.

University of Ottawa, Canadian Women's Movement Archives, X10-1, Series 1, Box 1, Abortion Caravan (May 1970) File; Box 6, Broadside; Box 110, Saska-

toon Women's Liberation; Box 124, Vancouver Status of Women Papers; Box 125, Vancouver Women's Caucus File.
University of Waterloo Library, Doris Lewis Rare Books Room, Elizabeth Long Papers, WA14; Claire Wallace Papers, WA16.

Private Papers

Julie Ireton
Nancy Pollak
Anne Roberts

Alternative and Feminist Periodicals

Broadside, 1979–1989.
Georgia Straight, 1970.
Herizons, 2010.
Kinesis, 1974–2001.
La vie en rose, 1980–1987.
Pandora, 1985–1994.
The Peak, 1970.
The Pedestal, 1970.
The Ubyssey, 1970.
The Voice, 1917–1918.
The Womanist, 1992–1994.

General Circulation Periodicals

Canadian Illustrated News, 1869–1883.
Canadian Monthly and National Review, 1872–1878.
Grip, 1873–1894.
Rose-Belford's Canadian Monthly and National Review, 1878–1882.
The Week, 1883–1896.

Daily Newspapers

The Calgary Herald, AB, 1970.
Chronicle-Herald, Halifax, NS, 1970.
Daily Colonist, Victoria, BC, 1970.
Daily Gleaner, Fredericton, NB, 1970.
Daily Mail, Toronto, ON, 1890–1900.
The Edmonton Journal, AB, 1970.
The Empire, Toronto, ON, 1890–1895.
Fort William Daily Times-Journal, ON, 1970.
The Gazette, Montreal, QC, 1970.
The Globe, Toronto, ON, 1890–1900.
The Globe and Mail, Toronto, ON, 1970.
The Leader-Post, Regina, SK, 1970.
Lethbridge Herald, AB, 1970.
Mail and Empire, Toronto, ON, 1895–1900.

Manitoba Free Press, MB, 1914–1918.
Montreal Herald, QC, 1899–1900.
The Montreal Star, QC, 1970.
The New York Times, NY, 1970.
The Ottawa Citizen, ON, 1970.
The Ottawa Journal, ON, 1970.
Port Arthur News Chronicle, ON, 1970.
The Province, Vancouver BC, 1969–1970.
The Sault Daily Star, ON, 1970.
The Star-Phoenix, Saskatoon, SK, 1970.
The Sudbury Star, ON, 1970.
The Telegram, Toronto, ON, 1970.
Telegraph-Journal, Saint John, NB, 1970.
Toronto Daily Star, ON, 1892–1900, 1961, 1969–1994.
The Tribune, Winnipeg, MB,.1970, 1978.
Vancouver Daily World, BC, 1895.
The Vancouver Express, BC, 1970.
The Vancouver Sun, BC, 1969–1970.
Victoria Daily Times, BC, 1970.
Winnipeg Free Press, MB, 1970, 1978.

Weekly Periodicals

The Free Press and Prairie Farmer
The Grain Growers' Guide, 1912–1920.

Sound Recordings: Radio

Julie Ireton, "One Woman, Two Names," *Sunday Morning*, CBC Radio, July 2004. Copy in Ireton Private Collection.
Eleanor Wachtel, *Wachtel on the Arts in the Summer*, CBC Radio, 4 September 2009.
Karin Wells, "The Women Are Coming," *Sunday Edition*, CBC Radio One, 11 March 2010.

Barbara M. Freeman Interviews (Private Collection)

Florence Bird, Ottawa, 18 November 1992.
Kathryn-Jane Hazel (formerly Keate), London, ON, 27 July 1995; Nanaimo, BC, 1 April 2006.
Fatima Jaffer, Vancouver, 3 June 2008.
Emma Kivisild, Vancouver, 8 and 13 March 2009.
Bethan (formerly Betty-Ann) Lloyd, Vancouver, 6 June 2008.
Philinda Masters, Toronto, 8 November 2008.
Debbie Mathers, Halifax, NS, 5 July 2008.
Nancy Pollak, Vancouver, 5 June 2008.
Anne Roberts, Vancouver, 24 May 2006.
Esther Shannon, Vancouver, 4 June 2008.

Library and Archives Canada: Sound and Moving Images

Canadian Broadcasting Corporation Programs

CBC *All In A Day*, an interview about Carrie Best, CBC Radio, Ottawa, 11 February 2011, at http://www.cbc.ca/allinaday/2011/02/11/a-stamp-for-carrie-best/

CBC *Take 30*, 6 October 1970, ISN 1970-10-6.

Trans-Canada Matinee, ISN 267606, 13 July 1954, Shirley Brett interview with Elizabeth Long.

Trans-Canada Matinee, ISN 38963, 30 May 1958, Shirley Brett's farewell broadcast.

CJOH-TV Ottawa Collection

Abortion Carvavan demonstration news footage, ISN 183711, 9 and 11 May 1970.

LAC Jean Bruce Interviews

Florence Bird, October 1980, LAC ISN 304761.

Elspeth Chisholm, July 1981, LAC ISN 304786.

Margaret Colpitts ("Joan Marshall"), November 1980, LAC ISBN 304762.

Dorothea Cox, September 1980, LAC ISN 304753.

Margaret Howes, October 1980, LAC ISN 304774, and 10 March 1981, LAC ISN 04776.

Helen James, October 1980, LAC ISN 304767.

Dolores MacFarlane, February 1981, LAC ISN 304772.

Marjorie McEnaney, March 1981, LAC ISN 304779.

Neil Morrison, November 1980, LAC ISN 304763.

Mattie Rotenberg, March 1981, LAC ISN 304778.

LAC Elspeth Chisholm Interview

Shirley Brett Foley, 4 August 1983, ISN 9504.

Marjory McEnaney Interview

Elizabeth Long, c. 1962, ISN 248134 and ISN 248152.

LAC Alison Taylor Interview

Canadian Broadcasting Corporation Head Office Collection, R1190-3-X-E, Neil Morrison, 27 September 1983, ISN 265660.

Documentaries: Visual

Cizek, Katerina. *Alanis Obomsawin: Dream Magic*, National Film Board of Canada, 2008, at http://www.nfb.ca/explore-by/director/cizek-katerina

Nichol, Nancy, director, *Struggle for Choice, Part 1: Abortion Caravan*, Horizontal Forest Productions, Toronto, 1986.

National Film Board

Directed by Alanis Obomsawin:

Amisk (1977)

Mother of Many Children (1977)

Incident at Restigouche (1984)

Richard Cardinal: Cry from the Diary of a Métis Child (1986)

Kanehsatake: 270 Years of Resistance (1993)

My Name Is Kahentiiosta (1995)
Spudwrench (1997)
Rocks at Whiskey Trench (2000)
Is the Crown at War with Us? (2002)
Our Nationhood (2003)
Waban-Aki: People from Where the Sun Rises (2006)

Directed by Kathleen Shannon:
Our Dear Sisters (1976)

Directed by Aerlyn Weissman and Lynne Fernie:
Forbidden Love (1992)

Directed by Christine Welsh:
Keepers of the Fire (1994)

INDEX

abortion, decriminalization of, 123, 124, 126; limited access to legal abortions, 126; backstreet abortions, 126; rights, 7, 10, 124. *See also* Abortion Caravan; therapeutic abortion committee (TAC)

Abortion Caravan, 10, 12, 123, 125, 215; goals, 133; planning of, 127, 133; media placement of stories, 155–56; national publicity plan, 136; rhetoric in press dealings, 154

Abortion Caravan and the press, 138; even-handed coverage, 141, 145; mixed media messages, 139; *Saturday Night* article, 150–51; strong reaction to House of Commons protest, 149, 150; use of rhetoric, 154

Abortion Caravan media strategies, 124; advance publicity, 138; balance of voices in stories, 153; careful preparation, 137; demands in media, 134; disruption of House of Commons, 147–49; media activists, 133

Abortion Caravan stops: Calgary, 139; Edmonton, 139; Ottawa, 144; Saskatoon, 139; Regina, 140; Sault Ste. Marie, 140; Sudbury, 141; Thunder Bay, 140; Toronto, 142; Vancouver, 137; Winnipeg, 140

Adam, Graeme Mercer, 27

advice columns, 52

advocacy journalism, 161

Aitken, Kate, 99

Allen, Gene, 3

Allen, Jane. *See* Elizabeth Long

Anderson, Doris, 7

Anti-Conscription League, 87

Ash, Shannon E., 183

Atkinson, Ella S. *See* Elmina Elliott Atkinson

Atkinson, Elmina Elliott ("Madge Merton," "Ella S. Atkinson"), 8, 46, 53, 54, 56–58, 62, 64, 65; biography, 48–49

Atkinson, Joseph E., 48

Banner, Lois, 59, 60

Beasley, Maurine, 3

Beauvoir, Simone de, 103

Bengough, John Wilson, 21, 22, 30, 39

Berton, Pierre, 3

Beynon, Francis Marion, 9, 67, 68, 75, 79, 89, 214; against racism and disenfranchisement of non-Canadians, 79; background, 70–71; conflict with George Chipman, 69; complex outlook, 91; on conscription, 90; continued activism, 87; "Country Homemakers" column, 9, 71, 74, 77, 79, 85; criticism of conscription, 83, 90; departure from *Guide*, 90–92; disagreement with McClung, 69, 70, 79, 80; discouraged, 84; editorial autonomy, 74; editorial line, 91; editorial

Books in the Film+Media Studies Series
Published by Wilfrid Laurier University Press

The Young, the Restless, and the Dead: Interviews with Canadian Filmmakers / George Melnyk, editor / 2008 / xiv + 134 pp. / photos / ISBN 978-1-55458-036-1

Programming Reality: Perspectives on English-Canadian Television / Zoë Druick and Aspa Kotsopoulos, editors / 2008 / x + 344 pp. / photos / ISBN 978-1-55458-010-1

Harmony and Dissent: Film and Avant-garde Art Movements in the Early Twentieth Century / R. Bruce Elder / 2008 / xxxiv + 482 pp. / ISBN 978-1-55458-028-6

He Was Some Kind of a Man: Masculinities in the B Western / Roderick McGillis / 2009 / xii + 210 pp. / photos / ISBN 978-1-55458-059-0

The Radio Eye: Cinema in the North Atlantic, 1958–1988 / Jerry White / 2009 / xvi + 284 pp. / photos / ISBN 978-1-55458-178-8

The Gendered Screen: Canadian Women Filmmakers / Brenda Austin-Smith and George Melnyk, editors / 2010 / x + 272 pp. / ISBN 978-1-55458-179-5

Feeling Canadian: Nationalism, Affect, and Television / Marusya Bociurkiw/ 2011 / viii + 184 pp. / ISBN 978-1-55458-268-6

Beyond Bylines: Media Workers and Women's Rights in Canada / Barbara M. Freeman / xii + 330 pp. / ISBN 978-1-55458-269-3